BARRON'S

GED

WRITING WORKBOOK

3RD EDITION

Katherine S. Hogan, M.A.T.
President
Write Away, Inc.

BARRON'S

®GED is a registered trademark of the GED Testing Service of the American Council on Education, which was not involved in the production of, and does not endorse, this product.

ACKNOWLEDGMENTS
To my family, especially Joe

All inquiries should be addressed to:
Barron's Educational Series, Inc.
250 Wireless Boulevard
Hauppauge, New York 11788
www.barronseduc.com

Library of Congress Catalog No. 2009928382

ISBN-13: 978-0-7641-4205-5
ISBN-10: 0-7641-4205-4

PRINTED IN THE UNITED STATES OF AMERICA
9 8 7 6 5 4 3 2 1

BARRON'S

GED

WRITING WORKBOOK

Contents

Tips for the Student

The GED Test

WHAT IS THE GED TEST, AND WHY SHOULD I TAKE IT?

The GED, the Tests of General Educational Development, is a key that opens doors. The GED examines the same material that students learn in high school. It has five exams that cover writing skills, literature and the arts, social studies, sciences, and mathematics. Some states require an additional test on the U.S. Constitution or state government. The GED test, which is offered by the American Council of Education (ACE), is designed for adults who do not have a high school degree. A GED certificate is viewed by employers, colleges, and technical schools as comparable to a high school diploma.

The GED certificate creates opportunities. Students who earn GED certificates have the chance to pursue various careers and educational options. Many employers, technical schools, and vocational programs require a high school diploma or the equivalent. Likewise, colleges and universities will only enroll students who have a high school diploma or the equivalent.

The GED is offered in English, Spanish, French, and Braille. It is also available on audiocassette and in large print.

WHERE AND WHEN CAN I TAKE THE TEST?

The GED test is offered throughout the year at many different sites in the United States, Canada, and some territories. To find the test location nearest you, call the GED Hot Line at 1-800-MY-GED (1-800-626-9433), or visit the ACE web site at www.acenet.edu.

WHAT SCORES DO I NEED TO PASS THE TEST?

The American Council on Education (ACE) requires a minimum score on each test and a minimum average score for all five tests. In the United States, the ACE calls for a minimum score of 410 points on each test and a minimum average score of 450 points for all five tests. Canada and some regions of the United States have additional requirements. To get the most recent information for your area, contact your local GED center; call 1-800-MY-GED (1-800-626-9433), or visit the ACE web site at www.acenet.edu.

Students who want to improve their scores may retake the tests. However, the rules for retaking tests vary from one area to another. Before retaking a test, contact your local adult education center and check the GED testing regulations for your area.

Test Preparation

WHAT WILL BE ON THE TESTS?

The GED tests material that is taught in high school. Note the test descriptions in the box.

OVERVIEW OF THE GED TESTS

Test	Topics	Length of Test (minutes)	Number of Questions
Language Arts, Writing, Part I	Sentence Structure Grammar and Usage Mechanics Organization	75	50
Language Arts, Writing, Part II	Essay	45	1 essay
Social Studies	Geography U.S. History (Canadian History for GED in Canada) World History Economics Civics and Government	70	50
Science	Life Science Earth and Space Science Physical Science	80	50
Language Arts, Reading	Fiction Nonfiction Poetry Drama	65	40
Mathematics	Number Operations and Number Sense Data Analysis, Statistics, Probability Algebra Functions and Patterns Measurement and Geometry	90	50

WHAT IS ON THE LANGUAGE ARTS, WRITING TEST?

LANGUAGE ARTS, WRITING TEST, PART I

The GED Language Arts, Writing Test has a multiple-choice section and an essay. Part I, the multiple-choice section, tests sentence structure, mechanics, usage, and organization. It contains several passages, which are followed by questions. Each question focuses on one or two sentences from the preceding passage. For Part I of the test, you will have 75 minutes to answer 50 questions.

The test questions for Part I are divided into four categories: sentence structure, mechanics, usage, and organization.

LANGUAGE ARTS, WRITING TEST, PART I: CONTENT	
Content	**Description**
Sentence Structure	These questions focus on writing complete sentences that are punctuated correctly. You may need to rewrite sentences, combine sentences, or correct sentences.
Mechanics	These questions focus on correct punctuation, capitalization, and some spelling (homonyms, possessives, and contractions only).
Usage	These questions focus on using the right word for a particular job. They may ask you to choose the correct pronoun, verb, or verb tense. These items also may include work on possession, homonyms, and contractions.
Organization	These questions focus on organizing a paragraph. You may need to move sentences within a paragraph or create new paragraphs.

There are three different types of questions for Part I. Note the descriptions in the following box.

LANGUAGE ARTS, WRITING, PART I: TYPES OF QUESTIONS	
Type	**Description**
Sentence Correction	These questions will focus on one sentence from the passage. The sentence may have one error, or it may be correct. You will need to find the error—if there is one—and correct the sentence. The sentence may require replacing a word, correcting punctuation, or moving a phrase.
Sentence Revision	These questions will have one or two sentences with underlined sections. You will need to decide the best way to write the underlined section. You may choose the original version, or you may change the wording or punctuation.
Rewriting, Combining, or Moving Sentences	These questions will focus on one or two sentences. You will need to write new, correct sentences that have the same meaning as the original sentences. For some items, you will be required to rewrite one sentence using a different word order. Other questions will ask you to combine two sentences into one clear, correct sentence. Additional questions will require you to move a sentence to a new location in the passage.

LANGUAGE ARTS, WRITING, PART II

Part II of the Language Arts, Writing Test is an essay. You will be given a topic, and you will have 45 minutes to write one essay on the assigned topic. The essay topics are designed to be interesting and thought provoking; you do not need any specific content knowledge to write the essay. The essay topics encourage writers to draw upon their own personal experiences, knowledge, and observations. The completed essay will receive a holistic score based on content, organization, clarity, and use of standard English.

HOW CAN I PREPARE FOR THE LANGUAGE ARTS, WRITING TEST?

Start with this book, which will help you study effectively. After you take the Pretest, work through the whole book and focus on areas that are challenging for you. Make sure that you complete the exercises carefully and practice writing essays. When you feel confident about the material, complete the Posttest and review sections as needed.

In addition to completing this book, you may want to enroll in a test preparation class. GED study programs are offered at adult education centers, libraries, community colleges, and religious institutions. These preparation classes provide individualized instruction in a comfortable setting. To find a GED program in your area, contact your local library, call 1-800-MY-GED (1-800-626-9433), or visit the ACE web site at www.acenet.edu or www.gedtest.org.

STUDY SKILLS

The following skills can make a big difference:

- GET ORGANIZED. Set up a schedule so that you can study regularly, either every day or a few days a week. Use a separate notebook or folder for each subject, and keep all of your materials in one place.
- FIND A GOOD PLACE TO STUDY. You will need a quiet, comfortable place with no distractions. If you do not have space in your home, try your local library or an open classroom at a nearby school.
- READ AND WRITE OFTEN. Like other skills, reading and writing improve with practice. Read newspapers, magazines, and books. Write shopping lists, notes, letters, and journals. Read and write things that are part of your everyday life or items that simply interest you. As your skills improve, focus on materials that are more challenging.
- IMMEDIATELY USE WHAT YOU HAVE LEARNED. For example, after you learn to spell words correctly, write them in a letter. Likewise, once you have mastered pronouns, say them correctly to family or friends. Make correct grammar a natural part of your daily life.
- PRACTICE SPEAKING CORRECTLY. When you speak correctly, you are more likely to write correctly. As you work through this book, read aloud the examples and the correct answers.
- KEEP TRACK OF YOUR PROGRESS. Make a list of the topics that are hard for you, and spend extra time in these areas. Once you have mastered a difficult topic, check it off of your list and reward yourself.

Test-Taking Strategies

THE DAY BEFORE THE TEST

- VISIT THE TEST CENTER. Make sure that you know which route to take, how long you will need to get there, where to park, and which door to enter.
- ORGANIZE YOURSELF. Gather everything that you will need for the test including: your admissions ticket (if necessary), identification, two or more ballpoint pens, three or more sharpened No. 2 pencils, erasers, a watch, and food.
- RELAX! Eat a good meal and get to bed early. If you prepared well for the test, your work is done. Cramming now will not help you.

TEST DAY

- EAT WELL AND DRESS COMFORTABLY. A good meal will give you energy and help you think. On the other hand, uncomfortable clothing will be distracting.
- PACK FOOD. If you will be testing all day, bring a lunch. Otherwise, a snack may be enough.
- ARRIVE EARLY. Be at the test center twenty minutes before the test is scheduled to begin. Find the room where you will take the test, the nearest bathroom, and a water fountain (if necessary).

STRATEGIES FOR THE LANGUAGE ARTS, WRITING TEST

- READ THE DIRECTIONS CAREFULLY. If the directions are unclear, ask the test administrator for help. (Remember, it may be inappropriate for the test administrator to answer some questions.)
- BE AWARE OF THE TIME LIMIT. Part I is 75 minutes long, and Part II is 45 minutes long. Write down the finish time for the test and check your progress.
- READ THE PASSAGE FIRST. If you notice obvious errors while reading the passage, circle them. Then answer the questions. Refer to the sentence in the passage before you choose an answer—especially if the question focuses on verb tense.
- ANSWER EVERY QUESTION. If you are not sure of the answer, cross out answers that you know are wrong and make an educated guess. (Students who repeatedly read answers that they know are incorrect often get confused.)
- CHOOSE THE BEST ANSWER. Read every option and cross out answers that you know are wrong.
- BUDGET YOUR TIME. Do not spend too much time on any one question. If a question is particularly hard for you, go back to it later. (If you skip a question, carefully check the numbers on your answer sheet to make sure that answers are correctly marked.)
- FILL IN YOUR ANSWER SHEET CLEARLY AND CAREFULLY. Mark only one answer for each item and erase mistakes completely. When you are done, make sure that you have answered every question on the answer sheet. (Double-check items that you skipped.)
- RELAX! If you have prepared for this test, you should feel confident.

How to Use This Book

Regardless of your writing skills, this book can help you. All students should complete the Pretest and the Pretest Skills Chart before starting the units. After you have identified the skills that are hard for you, work through the book. Depending on your skill level, you may choose to focus on specific sections or complete the whole book.

Note the following useful features:

- The Pretest and Pretest Skills Chart will help you identify your strengths and weaknesses.
- Chapter previews will highlight the information that you need to learn.
- Each chapter is divided into sections that are easy to master.
- Exercises will help you test yourself on each section and chapter.
- A step-by-step guide to essay writing will walk you through the writing process.
- The clear, complete answer key will help you learn from your mistakes.
- After you have completed the book, the Posttest and Posttest Skills Chart will help you decide whether or not you are ready to take the actual GED test.
- A glossary and an index will help you locate information quickly.

After you have finished the units, take the Posttest and complete the Posttest Skills Chart. The Posttest will help you decide if you need more review.

Good luck!

Language Arts Writing, Part I

DIRECTIONS

1. This test has paragraphs with numbered sentences. The sentences may have errors, or they may be correct as written. First read the paragraphs. Then answer the related questions. Choose the best answer for each question. The best answer should be consistent with the point of view and verb tense that is used throughout the passage.

2. Answer every question. If you are not sure of the answer, make a logical guess.

3. Allow yourself 75 minutes to answer the 50 questions. When time is up, underline the last item that you completed. Then finish the test. This will help you monitor your time for the actual GED test.

4. Write your answers to the questions on the answer grid. For each question, mark the number that matches the answer you chose.

5. After you have finished the test, check your answers and complete the Pretest Skills Chart to see which sections are difficult for you.

EXAMPLE

Sentence 1: **Parents need to give there children a lot of attention.**

What correction should be made to this sentence?

(1) replace *Parents* with *Parents'*

(2) change *there* to *their*

(3) replace *need* with *needed*

(4) insert a comma after *children*

(5) no correction necessary

1. ① ● ③ ④ ⑤

In this sentence, *their* is the correct word to use.

Answer Sheet

PRETEST

1. ① ② ③ ④ ⑤
2. ① ② ③ ④ ⑤
3. ① ② ③ ④ ⑤
4. ① ② ③ ④ ⑤
5. ① ② ③ ④ ⑤
6. ① ② ③ ④ ⑤
7. ① ② ③ ④ ⑤
8. ① ② ③ ④ ⑤
9. ① ② ③ ④ ⑤
10. ① ② ③ ④ ⑤
11. ① ② ③ ④ ⑤
12. ① ② ③ ④ ⑤
13. ① ② ③ ④ ⑤
14. ① ② ③ ④ ⑤
15. ① ② ③ ④ ⑤
16. ① ② ③ ④ ⑤
17. ① ② ③ ④ ⑤
18. ① ② ③ ④ ⑤
19. ① ② ③ ④ ⑤
20. ① ② ③ ④ ⑤
21. ① ② ③ ④ ⑤
22. ① ② ③ ④ ⑤
23. ① ② ③ ④ ⑤
24. ① ② ③ ④ ⑤
25. ① ② ③ ④ ⑤

26. ① ② ③ ④ ⑤
27. ① ② ③ ④ ⑤
28. ① ② ③ ④ ⑤
29. ① ② ③ ④ ⑤
30. ① ② ③ ④ ⑤
31. ① ② ③ ④ ⑤
32. ① ② ③ ④ ⑤
33. ① ② ③ ④ ⑤
34. ① ② ③ ④ ⑤
35. ① ② ③ ④ ⑤
36. ① ② ③ ④ ⑤
37. ① ② ③ ④ ⑤
38. ① ② ③ ④ ⑤
39. ① ② ③ ④ ⑤
40. ① ② ③ ④ ⑤
41. ① ② ③ ④ ⑤
42. ① ② ③ ④ ⑤
43. ① ② ③ ④ ⑤
44. ① ② ③ ④ ⑤
45. ① ② ③ ④ ⑤
46. ① ② ③ ④ ⑤
47. ① ② ③ ④ ⑤
48. ① ② ③ ④ ⑤
49. ① ② ③ ④ ⑤
50. ① ② ③ ④ ⑤

Directions: Choose the best answer for each question.

Questions 1 through 8 refer to the following paragraphs.

(A)

(1) The United States of America have long been known as a nation of immigrants. (2) People have come to America from many different countries and for a variety of reasons. (3) War, poverty, famine, and persecution have driven people away from their homelands and to America the land of opportunity. (4) Likewise, many people have come to the United States for educational opportunities, financial gain, and the hope of a better life.

(B)

(5) From 1880 to 1920, more than 23 million immigrants came to the United States. (6) These immigrants were mostly from southern and eastern Europe. (7) In recent years, American immigration has changed in many ways. (8) In the beginning, many of these immigrants suffered from discrimination and language barriers. (9) Over time, however, most of them were able to build successful lives for themselves and their families.

(C)

(10) Today, most immigrants come to the United States from Asia and Latin America. (11) In addition, various laws have restricted whom may enter the country legally. (12) Nonetheless, 15 million new immigrants entered the United States in the 1990s. (13) In the new century, the Immigration and Naturalization Service (INS) expects legal immigration to continue at that rate. (14) In addition, millions of individuals are expected to illegally cross the borders and settle permanently in the United States. (15) Although some people debate the pros and cons of immigration for America's future, the United States remains the land of opportunity for people from around the world.

1. Sentence 1: **The United States of America have long been known as a nation of immigrants.**

   What correction should be made to this sentence?

   (1) change <u>have</u> to <u>has</u>
   (2) change <u>United States of America</u> to <u>united states of America</u>
   (3) insert a comma after <u>nation</u>
   (4) change <u>United States of America</u> to <u>United States of america</u>
   (5) no correction necessary

2. Sentence 3: **War, poverty, famine, and persecution have driven people away from their homelands and to America the land of opportunity.**

   What correction should be made to this sentence?

   (1) change <u>their</u> to <u>they're</u>
   (2) insert a comma after <u>America</u>
   (3) remove the comma after <u>famine</u>
   (4) change <u>America</u> to <u>america</u>
   (5) no correction necessary

3. Sentences 5 and 6: **From 1880 to 1920, more than 23 million immigrants came to the United States. These immigrants were mostly from southern and eastern Europe.**

   The most effective combination of sentences 3 and 4 would include which of the following words?

   (1) who were
   (2) because they
   (3) which was
   (4) that were
   (5) since they

4. Sentence 7: **In recent years, American immigration has changed in many ways.**

   Which revision should be made to the placement of sentence 7?

   (1) move sentence 7 to the beginning of paragraph A
   (2) move sentence 7 to follow sentence 11
   (3) move sentence 7 to follow sentence 4
   (4) move sentence 7 to the beginning of paragraph C
   (5) move sentence 7 to follow sentence 2

5. Sentence 11: **In addition, various laws have restricted whom may enter the country legally.**

   What correction should be made to this sentence?

   (1) remove the comma after <u>addition</u>
   (2) change <u>have</u> to <u>has</u>
   (3) insert a comma after <u>restricted</u>
   (4) replace <u>whom</u> with <u>who</u>
   (5) no correction necessary

6. Sentence 12: **Nonetheless, 15 million new immigrants entered the United States in the 1990s.**

   What correction should be made to this sentence?

   (1) remove the comma after <u>Nonetheless</u>
   (2) change <u>million</u> to <u>Million</u>
   (3) replace <u>entered</u> with <u>enter</u>
   (4) insert a comma after <u>United States</u>
   (5) no correction necessary

7. Sentence 14: **In addition, millions of individuals are expected to illegally cross the borders and settle permanently in the United States.**

   What correction should be made to this sentence?

   (1) insert a comma after <u>borders</u>
   (2) replace <u>are</u> with <u>is</u>
   (3) remove the comma after <u>addition</u>
   (4) move <u>illegally</u> after <u>borders</u>
   (5) no correction necessary

8. Sentence 15: **Although some people debate the pros and cons of immigration for America's future, the United States remains the land of opportunity for people from around the world.**

   If you rewrote this sentence beginning with

   <u>Some people debate the pros and cons of immigration</u>

   the next words should be

   (1) for America's future; however, the United States
   (2) for America's future. But the United States
   (3) for America's future; therefore, the United States
   (4) for America's future. Because the United States
   (5) for America's future, and the United States

Questions 9 through 17 refer to the following document.

How to Interview for a Job

(A)

(1) Job interviews can be difficult for some people. (2) Sometimes, individuals who is quite talented workers struggle to get through the interview process. (3) However, with a little research planning, and practice, job interviews can be great experiences that lead to new opportunities.

(B)

(4) Before an interview, it is important to choose an appropriate outfit to wear. (5) One should also gather information about the company. (6) For most jobs one should wear nice, conservative business clothes. (7) A job interview is not the place to try out a flashy new look, wear bright nail polish, or overload on jewelry. (8) Learning about the company and its needs will help you demonstrate how you can help the organization. (9) For the actual interview it is important to be on time, prepared, and enthusiastic. (10) Plan on arriving at least ten minutes before the interview starts, so you can collect your thoughts and shows that you are responsible. (11) Likewise, you should bring a folder with an extra copy of your resume as well as a list of questions that you may want to ask at the end of the interview. (12) Your body language will show your enthusiasm. (13) A firm handshake, good eye contact, and careful listening will show that you are a confident, eager candidate. (14) Likewise, answering the interview questions clearly will demonstrate your abilities. (15) In your answers, be sure to include specific examples that show your strengths.

(C)

(16) After the interview, write a letter to the interviewer that not only thanks him or her for the interview, but also highlight how your skills can help the company. (17) The follow-up letter is a good way to leave a great impression. (18) A great impression could help you get the job.

9. Sentence 2: **Sometimes, individuals who is quite talented workers struggle to get through the interview process.**

What correction should be made to sentence 2?

(1) replace <u>is</u> with <u>are</u>
(2) insert a comma after <u>workers</u>
(3) replace <u>who</u> with <u>whom</u>
(4) remove the comma after <u>Sometimes</u>
(5) no correction necessary

10. Sentence 3: **However, with a little research planning, and practice, job interviews can be great experiences that lead to new opportunities.**

What correction should be made to sentence 3?

(1) remove the comma after <u>However</u>
(2) replace <u>can be</u> with <u>were</u>
(3) replace <u>that</u> with <u>which</u>
(4) insert a comma after <u>research</u>
(5) no correction necessary

11. Sentences 4 and 5: **Before an interview, it is important to choose an appropriate outfit to wear. One should also gather information about the company.**

Which shows the best combination of sentences 4 and 5?

(1) Before an interview, it is important not only to choose an appropriate outfit to wear, but also to gather information about the company.
(2) It is important to choose an appropriate outfit to wear; one should also gather information about the company before an interview.
(3) Before an interview, it is important to choose an appropriate outfit to wear; however, one should also gather information about the company.
(4) Before an interview, it is important to choose an appropriate outfit to wear while gathering information about the company.
(5) Before an interview, it is important to choose an appropriate outfit to wear, besides gathering information about the company.

12. Which change would improve the organization of the document?

    Begin a new paragraph with

    (1) sentence 5
    (2) sentence 9
    (3) sentence 10
    (4) sentence 14
    (5) sentence 15

13. Sentence 10: **Plan on arriving at least ten minutes before the interview starts, so you can collect your thoughts and shows that you are responsible.**

    What correction should be made to sentence 10?

    (1) remove the comma after <u>starts</u>
    (2) change <u>your</u> to <u>you're</u>
    (3) replace <u>are</u> with <u>is</u>
    (4) replace <u>shows</u> with <u>show</u>
    (5) no correction necessary

14. Sentence 11: **Likewise, you should bring a folder with an extra copy of your resume as well as a list of questions that you may want to ask at the end of the interview.**

    What correction should be made to sentence 11?

    (1) remove the comma after <u>Likewise</u>
    (2) replace <u>should bring</u> with <u>should have brought</u>
    (3) insert a comma after <u>resume</u>
    (4) replace <u>to ask</u> with <u>asked</u>
    (5) no correction necessary

15. Sentences 12 and 13: **Your body language will show your enthusiasm. A firm handshake, good eye contact, and careful listening will show that you are a confident, eager candidate.**

    The best combination of sentences 12 and 13 would include which group of words?

    (1) your enthusiasm; a firm handshake
    (2) your enthusiasm, yet a firm handshake
    (3) your enthusiasm; nonetheless, a firm handshake
    (4) your enthusiasm unless a firm handshake
    (5) your enthusiasm, but also a firm handshake

16. Sentence 16: **After the interview, write a letter to the interviewer that not only thanks him or her for the interview, but also highlight how your skills can help the company.**

    What correction should be made to sentence 16?

    (1) replace <u>your</u> with <u>you're</u>
    (2) replace <u>highlight</u> with <u>highlights</u>
    (3) insert a comma after <u>interviewer</u>
    (4) replace <u>but also</u> with <u>and</u>
    (5) no correction necessary

17. Sentences 17 and 18: **The follow-up letter is a good way to leave a great impression. A great impression could help you get the job.**

    The best combination of sentences 17 and 18 would include which group of words?

    (1) a great impression: however, a great impression could help you
    (2) a great impression, which could help you
    (3) a great impression; therefore, a great impression could help you.
    (4) a great impression before you get the job.
    (5) a great impression; on the other hand, a great impression could help you

Questions 18 through 27 refer to the following paragraphs.

(A)

(1) Better health care is something that millions of Americans need. (2) In 2003, Americans' spent more than $900 billion on health care. (3) Yet, people often did not receive the medical treatment that they needed. (4) Many people are covered by Medicaid which insures low-income Americans, or Medicare, which insures older Americans. (5) Others are covered by private insurance companies, who generally work through employers. (6) Generally, the uninsured either pay for they're medical expenses out-of-pocket or do without treatment. (7) As a result, they often do not have access to preventive medicine, which could significantly improve their health. (8) The remaining individuals, more than 25 million Americans, have no insurance at all. (9) Some political leaders and private citizens want a National insurance plan, which would insure every American citizen. (10) Under this system, tax dollars would be used by the government to pay for all medical expenses.

(B)

(11) Although the plan for every citizen would guarantee health coverage, it would also have drawbacks. (12) Critics of the plan argues that many Americans would not have the high-quality health care that they currently enjoy. (13) Some people fear that a national plan would limit which doctors they could see. (14) Others are concerned that they may be denied treatments that are expensive or unproven. (15) Americans believe that health care is a problem for our country, but few can agree on a possible solution.

18. Sentence 1: **Better health care is something that millions of Americans need.**

    If you rewrote this sentence beginning with

    Millions of Americans need

    the next word would be

    (1) something
    (2) better
    (3) health
    (4) is
    (5) care

19. Sentence 2: **In 2003, Americans' spent more than $900 billion on health care.**

    What correction should be made to this sentence?

    (1) remove the comma after 2003
    (2) replace than with then
    (3) change Americans' to Americans
    (4) move on health care after 2003
    (5) no correction necessary

20. Sentence 4: **Many people are covered by Medicaid which insures low-income Americans, or Medicare, which insures older Americans.**

    What correction should be made to this sentence?

    (1) replace are with is
    (2) insert a comma after low-income
    (3) change Medicare to medicare
    (4) insert a comma after Medicaid
    (5) no correction necessary

21. Sentence 5: **Others are covered by private insurance companies, who generally work through employers.**

    What correction should be made to this sentence?

    (1) replace <u>who</u> with <u>which</u>
    (2) change <u>companies</u> to <u>Companies</u>
    (3) change <u>Others</u> to <u>Others'</u>
    (4) remove the comma after <u>companies</u>
    (5) no correction necessary

22. Sentence 8: **The remaining individuals, more than 25 million Americans, have no insurance at all.**

    What change should be made to the placement of sentence 8?

    (1) move sentence 8 to the beginning of paragraph B
    (2) move sentence 8 to follow sentence 5
    (3) move sentence 8 to the end of paragraph B
    (4) move sentence 8 to follow sentence 10
    (5) move sentence 8 to follow sentence 3

23. Sentence 6: **Generally, these people either pay for they're medical expenses out-of-pocket or do without treatment.**

    What correction should be made to this sentence?

    (1) remove the comma after <u>generally</u>
    (2) replace <u>or</u> with <u>nor</u>
    (3) change <u>they're</u> to <u>their</u>
    (4) insert a comma after <u>expenses</u>
    (5) no correction necessary

24. Sentence 9: **Some political leaders and private citizens want a National insurance plan, which would insure every American citizen.**

    What correction should be made to this sentence?

    (1) insert a comma after <u>leaders</u>
    (2) change <u>National</u> to <u>national</u>
    (3) remove the comma after <u>plan</u>
    (4) replace <u>American</u> with <u>american</u>
    (5) no correction necessary

25. Sentence 10: **Under this system, <u>tax dollars would be used by the federal government</u> to pay for all medical expenses.**

    What is the best way to write the underlined portion of the sentence? If you think the original is best, choose option (1).

    (1) tax dollars would be used by the federal government
    (2) the federal government would use tax dollars
    (3) tax dollars were used by the federal government
    (4) the Federal Government may have used tax dollars
    (5) the federal government and tax dollars were used

26. Sentence 11: **Although the plan for every citizen would guarantee health coverage, it would also have drawbacks.**

    What correction should be made to this sentence?

    (1) remove the comma after <u>coverage</u>
    (2) move <u>for every citizen</u> after <u>coverage</u>
    (3) replace <u>it</u> with <u>they</u>
    (4) change <u>would</u> to <u>wood</u>
    (5) no correction necessary

27. Sentence 12: **Critics of the plan argues that many Americans would not have the high-quality health care that they currently enjoy.**

What correction should be made to this sentence?

(1) insert a comma after <u>care</u>
(2) change <u>Americans</u> to <u>americans</u>
(3) change <u>Critics</u> to <u>Critic's</u>
(4) replace <u>argues</u> with <u>argue</u>
(5) no correction necessary

<u>Questions 28 through 36</u> refer to the following letter.

Advanced Vocational Institute

Ms. Madeline Hamm
45 Lakeshore Dr.
Huntsville, AL 33340

Dear Ms. Hamm:

(A)

(1) Across America skilled electricians, plumbers, and carpenters are in high demand. (2) Throughout the country, the construction industry is booming. (3) At the same time, many professionals in this field are retiring. (4) As a result, there is a tremendous need for skilled craftsmen in the construction industry.

(B)

(5) Unfortunately, young people often do not here about the rewards that the construction industry can offer. (6) These high-paying careers offer excellent benefits, job training, and advancement for careers. (7) With specialized training from Advanced Vocational Institute you can be a part of this growing field.

(C)

(8) The Advanced Vocational Institute will send you strait to the top of your field. (9) Through hands-on experiences and on-the-job training you will learn about all aspects of your trade. (10) You will have solid technical skills. (11) You also will have the business sense you need to run projects effectively. (12) Our graduates go on to advanced construction projects throughout the nation.

(D)

(13) If you are interested in one of these exciting careers, complete the enclosed application. (14) When classes begin in September you will be on your way to a promising new future.

Sincerely,
Miguel Lopez
Admissions Director

28. Sentences 2 and 3: **Throughout the country, the construction industry is booming. At the same time, many professionals in this field are retiring.**

Which is the best way to combine sentences 2 and 3?

(1) Throughout the country, the construction industry is booming before many professionals in this field are retiring.
(2) Throughout the country, the construction industry is booming while many professionals in this field are retiring.
(3) Throughout the country, the construction industry is booming; therefore, many professionals in this field are retiring.
(4) Throughout the country, the construction industry is booming: many professionals in this field are retiring.
(5) Throughout the country, the construction industry is booming because many professionals in this field are retiring.

29. Sentence 4: **As a result, there is a tremendous need for skilled crafts-men in the construction industry.**

    What correction should be made to sentence 2?

    (1) remove the comma after <u>result</u>
    (2) replace <u>is</u> with <u>are</u>
    (3) replace <u>there</u> with <u>their</u>
    (4) insert a comma after <u>craftsmen</u>
    (5) no correction necessary

30. Sentence 5: **Unfortunately, young people often do not here about the rewards that the construction indus-try can offer.**

    What correction should be made to sentence 5?

    (1) remove the comma after <u>unfortu-nately</u>
    (2) replace <u>here</u> with <u>hear</u>
    (3) insert a comma after <u>rewards</u>
    (4) replace <u>can offer</u> with <u>can offers</u>
    (5) no correction necessary

31. Sentence 6: **These high-paying careers offer excellent benefits, job training, and advancement for careers.**

    What correction should be made to this sentence?

    (1) replace <u>high</u> with <u>hi</u>
    (2) remove the comma after <u>training</u>
    (3) replace <u>advancement for careers</u> with <u>career advancement</u>
    (4) replace <u>offer</u> with <u>offers</u>
    (5) no correction necessary

32. Sentence 7: **With specialized training from Advanced Vocational Institute you can be a part of this growing field.**

    What correction should be made to this sentence?

    (1) insert a comma after <u>Institute</u>
    (2) replace <u>can be</u> with <u>were</u>
    (3) replace <u>Advanced Vocational Institute</u> with <u>advanced vocational institute</u>
    (4) insert a comma after <u>growing</u>
    (5) no correction necessary

33. Sentence 8: **The Advanced Vocational Institute will send you strait to the top of your field.**

    What correction should be made to this sentence?

    (1) replace <u>Advanced Vocational Insti-tute</u> with <u>advanced vocational institute</u>
    (2) insert a comma after <u>you</u>
    (3) replace <u>will send</u> with <u>sends</u>
    (4) replace <u>strait</u> with <u>straight</u>
    (5) no correction necessary

34. Sentence 9: **Through hands-on expe-riences and on-the-job training you will learn about all aspects of your trade.**

    What correction should be made to this sentence?

    (1) insert a comma after <u>training</u>
    (2) replace <u>your</u> with <u>you're</u>
    (3) insert a comma after <u>experiences</u>
    (4) replace <u>learn</u> with <u>teach</u>
    (5) no correction necessary

35. Sentences 10 and 11: **You will have solid technical skills. You also will have the business sense you need to run projects effectively.**

    What is the best way to combine sentences 10 and 11?

    (1) You will have solid technical skills, but also the business sense you need to run projects effectively.
    (2) You will have solid technical skills; the business sense you need to run projects effectively.
    (3) You will have solid technical skills. However, you will also have the business sense you need to run projects effectively.
    (4) Before you have solid technical skills, you will have the business sense you need to run projects effectively.
    (5) You will have solid technical skills and the business sense you need to run projects effectively.

36. Sentence 14: **When classes begin in September you will be on your way to a promising new future.**

    What correction should be made to this sentence?

    (1) replace your with you're
    (2) insert a comma after begin
    (3) replace September with september
    (4) insert a comma after September
    (5) replace will be with were

Questions 37 through 45 refer to the following paragraphs.

(A)

(1) The foods we eat provide nutrients that help our bodies grow and stay healthy. (2) Carbohydrates, proteins, and lipids, for example, give our bodies energy. (3) Vitamins, which are used in small amounts, help our bodies perform necessary chemical reactions. (4) Likewise, minerals, such as calcium and iron, is used to perform chemical reactions and to maintain specific body parts, particularly teeth and bones.

(B)

(5) The digestive system breaks food down so that our bodies can absorb the nutrients that it needs. (6) As soon as food enters the mouth, digestion begins. (7) In the mouth, teeth break the food into smaller pieces saliva makes the food easier to swallow. (8) When food is swallowed, it moves into the esophagus, a long, muscular tube that connect the mouth to the stomach. (9) In the stomach, it is combined with chemicals that break the pieces down even more. (10) The stomach pushes the partially digested food into the small intestine. (11) The small intestine absorbs important nutrients through the villi. (12) Material that cannot be digested then moves to the large intestine, which prepared the waste that will leave the body.

37. Sentence 1: **The foods we eat provide nutrients that help our bodies grow and stay healthy.**

    What correction should be made to this sentence?

    (1) insert a comma after grow
    (2) replace help with helps
    (3) change nutrients to nutrients'
    (4) replace that with which
    (5) no correction necessary

38. Sentence 4: **Likewise, minerals, such as calcium and iron, is used to perform chemical reactions and to maintain specific body parts, particularly teeth and bones.**

    What correction should be made to this sentence?

    (1) replace Likewise with However
    (2) replace is with are
    (3) remove the comma after parts
    (4) insert a comma after teeth
    (5) no correction necessary

39. Sentence 5: **The digestive system breaks food down so that our bodies can absorb the nutrients that it needs.**

    What correction should be made to this sentence?

    (1) replace it needs with they need
    (2) replace breaks with broke
    (3) replace digestive system with Digestive System
    (4) replace nutrients with nutrients'
    (5) no correction necessary

40. Sentence 6: **As soon as food enters the mouth, digestion begins.**

    What is the best way to write the underlined portion of the sentence? If you think that the original is best, choose option (1).

    (1) mouth, digestion
    (2) mouth: digestion
    (3) mouth. Digestion
    (4) mouth; digestion
    (5) mouth, but digestion

41. Sentence 7: **In the mouth, teeth break the food into smaller pieces saliva makes the food easier to swallow.**

    What is the best way to write the underlined portion of the sentence? If you think that the original is best, choose option (1).

    (1) pieces saliva
    (2) pieces: and saliva
    (3) pieces, and saliva
    (4) pieces; therefore, saliva
    (5) pieces because saliva

42. Sentence 8: **When food is swallowed, it moves into the esophagus, a long, muscular tube that connect the mouth to the stomach.**

    What correction should be made to this sentence?

    (1) remove the comma after swallowed
    (2) change moves to moved
    (3) replace connect with connects
    (4) change esophagus to Esophagus
    (5) no correction necessary

43. Sentence 9: **In the stomach, it is combined with chemicals that break the pieces down even more.**

    What correction should be made to this sentence?

    (1) remove the comma after stomach
    (2) replace it with the food
    (3) replace that with which
    (4) replace is with are
    (5) no correction necessary

44. Sentences 10 and 11: **The stomach pushes the partially digested food into the_small intestine. The small intestine absorbs** important nutrients through the villi.

What is the best way to write the underlined section of these sentences? If you think that the original is best, choose option (1).

(1) small intestine. The small intestine absorbs
(2) small intestine, because the small intestine absorbs
(3) small intestine, the small intestine absorbs
(4) small intestine, yet absorbs
(5) small intestine, which absorbs

45. Sentence 12: **Material that cannot be digested then moves to the large intestine, which prepared the waste that will leave the body.**

What is the best way to write the underlined portion of the sentence? If you think that the original is best, choose option (1).

(1) intestine, which prepared
(2) intestine, that prepared
(3) intestine, which prepares
(4) intestine; that prepares
(5) intestine, which did prepare

<u>Questions 46 through 50</u> refer to the following letter.

Ms. Alexa Mamat
Software Solutions Online
5699 International Drive
Herndon, VA 03380

Dear Ms. Mamat:

(A)

(1) On December 4, I ordered a Creative Minds software program through your web site, Software Solutions Online. (2) It was clearly stated by the order form that the product would ship within one to two days and it would arrive by December 14—well in time for the holidays. (3) On December 22, the product still had not arrived, but you're company charged my credit card account for the program.

(B)

(4) On December 23, I called Creative Minds several times, but no one answered my calls. (5) I even left an e-mail on the Creative Minds web site, but the customer service department never responded. (6) When I called your customer service department on December 22, Cheryl told me that I needed to contact Creative Minds directly.

(C)

(7) On January 8, the software program arrived. (8) Obviously, I am no longer interested in the Creative Minds program. (9) Yet, the holidays are over, and the program will be outdated soon. (10) I have bought many products through Software Solutions Online, but I will have stopped shopping at your web site if this situation is not handled properly.

(D)

(11) I expect Software Solutions Online to reimburse me $30.00 for this product. (12) I also want your company to pay for shipping, so I can send the program back to Creative Minds. (13) If you need additional information to process my refund, please contact me.
(14) Thank you for your assistance.

Sincerely,
Brianna Sayre

46. Sentence 2: **It was clearly stated by the order form that the product would ship within one to two days and it would arrive by December 14—well in time for the holidays.**

    What is the best way to write the underlined section? If you think that the original is best, choose option (1).

    (1) It was clearly stated by the order form
    (2) The order form clearly stated
    (3) On the order form, it was clearly stated
    (4) On the clear order form, it was stated
    (5) It has been clearly stated on the order form

47. Sentence 3: **On December 22, the product still had not arrived, but you're company charged my credit card account for the program.**

    Which correction should be made to sentence 3?

    (1) remove the comma after December 22
    (2) replace charged with charges
    (3) remove the comma after arrived
    (4) replace you're with your
    (5) no change is necessary

48. Sentence 6: **When I called your customer service department on December 22, Cheryl told me that I needed to contact Creative Minds directly.**

    What change should be made to the placement of sentence 6?

    (1) move sentence 6 to the beginning of paragraph B
    (2) move sentence 6 to follow sentence 2
    (3) move sentence 6 to the beginning of paragraph D
    (4) move sentence 6 to follow sentence 4
    (5) move sentence 6 to the end of paragraph C

49. Sentence 8: **Obviously, I am no longer interested in the Creative Minds program. Yet, the holidays are over and the program will be outdated soon.**

    What is the best way to write the underlined section? If you think that the original is the best, choose option (1).

    (1) Minds program. Yet, the
    (2) Minds program. Nonetheless, the
    (3) Minds program, and the
    (4) Minds program, but the
    (5) Minds program; the

50. Sentence 10: **I have bought many products through Software Solutions Online, but I will have stopped shopping at your web site if this situation is not handled properly.**

    What change should be made to sentence 10?

    (1) replace I will have stopped with I will stop
    (2) remove the comma after Online
    (3) change Software Solutions Online to software solutions online
    (4) replace your with you're
    (5) no correction is necessary

Answers to Pretest

1. **1 change <u>have</u> to <u>has</u>** *The United States of America* is one country. Therefore, *has,* which is the singular form of the verb, should be used.

2. **2 insert a comma after <u>America</u>** (See Chapter 6—Punctuation) *The land of opportunity* is an appositive that renames *America.* Nonrestrictive phrases should be set apart with commas. Option (1) is wrong because *their* shows possession. Option (3) is wrong because the items in the series should be separated with commas. Option (4) is wrong because *America* should be capitalized.

3. **1 who were** (See Chapter 9—Writing Clear Sentences: Combining Sentences) *Who were mostly from southern and western Europe* is an adjective clause that describes *immigrants.* The other options do not show the correct relationship between the sentences. *From 1880 to 1920, more than 23 million immigrants, who were mostly from southern and eastern Europe, came to the United States.*

4. **4 move sentence 7 to the beginning of paragraph C** *In recent years, immigration has changed in many ways* shows a change in time. Paragraph B refers to immigration from 1880 to 1920. Paragraph C, on the other hand, focuses on immigration today. Placing this sentence at the beginning of paragraph C provides direction.

5. **4 replace <u>whom</u> with <u>who</u>** (See Chapter 5—Pronouns: Who and Whom) In this sentence, various laws have restricted *who may enter the country legally.* The entire clause receives the action, and *who* is the subject of the clause.

6. **5 no correction necessary** Option (1) is wrong because *Nonetheless* is an introductory word, which should be set apart with a comma. Option (2) is wrong because *million* should not be capitalized. Option (3) is wrong because *entered* correctly reflects the past tense. Option (4) is wrong because there is no reason to place a comma after *United States.*

7. **4 move <u>illegally</u> after <u>borders</u>** (See Chapter 1—Parts of Speech: Verbs) *To cross* is an infinitive, which never should be divided. *In addition, millions of individuals are expected to cross the borders illegally and settle permanently in the United States.* Option (1) is wrong because there is no reason to place a comma after *borders.* Option (2) is wrong because *are* agrees with *millions.* Option (3) is wrong because *in addition* is an introduction, which should be set apart with a comma.

8. **1 for America's future; however, the United States** (See Chapter 9—Writing Clear Sentences: Rewriting Sentences) *Although* and *however* show a contrast between the two clauses. Options (2), (3), (4), and (5) do not show the correct relationship between the two clauses. *Some people debate the pros and cons of immigration for America's future; however, the United States remains the land of opportunity for people from around the world.*

9. **1 replace <u>is</u> with <u>are</u>** *Individuals* is plural, so the plural form of the verb should be used.

10. **4 insert a comma after <u>research</u>** *Research, planning, and practice* form a series. A comma should separate each item in the series.

11. **1 Before an interview, it is important not only to choose an appropriate outfit to wear, but also to gather information about the company.** Both of the original sentences focus on things that should be done before an interview. However, the

two actions are quite different. Only option (1) shows the correct relationship between both sentences.

12. **2 sentence 9** This passage is organized according to time—before the interview, during the interview, and after the interview. Sentence 9 provides a good overview for what should happen during the interview. Therefore, a new paragraph should begin with sentence 9.

13. **4 replace <u>shows</u> with <u>show</u>** In this sentence, *collect* and *show* form a compound verb for the subject, *you*, which is singular.

14. **3 insert a comma after <u>resume</u>** In this sentence, insert a comma after *resume* to add clarity.

15. **1 your enthusiasm; a firm handshake** Sentence 13 further explains the information in sentence 12. In the new sentence, the semicolon is used instead of a conjunction to join two independent clauses. *Your body language will show your enthusiasm; a firm handshake, good eye contact, and careful listening will show that you are a confident, eager candidate.* The other options suggest that there is a contrast between the two sentences. Therefore, they do not show the correct relationship between the two independent clauses.

16. **2 replace <u>highlight</u> with <u>highlights</u>** In this sentence, *letter* is the subject of *thanks* as well as *highlights*. Both verbs need to be in the singular form. Option (1) is incorrect because *your* shows possession. Whose skills are they? Option (3) is wrong because there is no need for a comma after *interviewer*. Option (4) is wrong because *not only* and *but also* work together as a team. *And* would be incorrect in this situation.

17. **2 a great impression, which could help you** Sentence 18 provides additional information about *a great impression. The follow-up letter is a good way to leave a great impression, which could help you get the job.*

18. **2 better** In the new sentence, *millions* is the subject. *Millions of Americans need better health care.*

19. **3 change <u>Americans'</u> to <u>Americans</u>** *Americans* is the subject of this sentence. It is not possessive, so there is no need for an apostrophe.

20. **4 insert a comma after *Medicaid*** (See Chapter 6—End Marks and Commas: Nonrestrictive Words, Phrases, and Clauses) *Which insures low-income Americans* is an adjective clause that describes *Medicaid*. It is a nonrestrictive clause, which should be set apart with commas. Option (1) is wrong because *are* must agree with *people*. Option (2) is wrong because there is no reason to place a comma after *low-income*. Option (3) is wrong because *Medicare* is a proper noun.

21. **1 replace *who* with *which*** (See Chapter 9—Clauses: Who, Which, and That) Use *who* for people. Use *which* and *that* for animals and things. Option (2) is wrong because *companies* is a common noun, which should not be capitalized. Option (3) is wrong because *others* is the subject of the sentence, and it is not possessive. Option (4) is wrong because *who generally work through employers* is a nonrestrictive clause, which should be set apart with a comma.

22. **2 move sentence 8 to follow sentence 5** Sentences 4 and 5 describe different forms of insurance coverage. Sentences 6 and 8 describe people who do not have insurance. Sentence 6 gives additional information about sentence 8. Therefore, sentence 8 should precede sentence 6.

23. **3 change *they're* to *their*** (See Chapter 8—Word Choice: Commonly Confused Words) Whose medical expenses? Use *their* to show possession, and use *they're* as a contraction for *they are*. Option (1) is wrong because *generally* is an introductory word, which should be set apart with a comma. Option (2) is wrong because *or* is used with *either*. Option (4) is wrong because there is no reason to insert a comma after *expenses*.

24. **2 change *National* to *national*** (See Chapter 7—Capitalization) *National* is an adjective that describes *insurance plan*. It should not be capitalized. Option (1) is wrong because there is no reason to place a comma after *leaders*. Option (3) is wrong because *which would insure every American citizen* is a nonrestrictive clause, which should be set apart with a comma. Option (4) is wrong because *American* should be capitalized.

25. **2 the federal government would use tax dollars** Ideas should be expressed clearly. In this sentence, because the federal government performs the action, it should be the subject of the sentence. Rewording the sentence makes the information flow more smoothly. *Under this system, the federal government would use tax dollars to pay for all medical expenses.* Options (3), (4), and (5) use different verb tenses, which do not agree with the rest of the paragraph.

26. **2 move *for every citizen* after *coverage*** (See Chapter 9—Writing Clear Sentences: Misplaced Modifiers) *For every citizen* modifies *health coverage*, not *plan*. The original sentence implies that there is a separate plan for every citizen. Option (1) is wrong because the comma sets apart an introductory clause. Option (3) is wrong because *it* refers to *the plan*. Option (4) is wrong because *would* is spelled correctly. *Wood* comes from a tree.

27. **4 replace *argues* with *argue*** (See Chapter 4—Subject-Verb Agreement: Difficult Subjects) *Argue* must agree with *critics*. Option (1) is wrong because *that they currently enjoy* is a restrictive clause. Option (2) is wrong because *Americans* should be capitalized. Option (3) is wrong because *Critics* is the subject of the sentence; it should not be possessive.

28. **2 Throughout the country, the construction industry is booming while many professionals in this field are retiring.** *At the same time*

clearly shows the relationship between the two sentences. In option (2), *while* expresses the same relationship. In options (1), (3), and (5) *before, therefore,* and *because* show a different relationship between the clauses. Option 4 uses a colon, which doesn't explain the relationship at all.

29. **5 no correction necessary** This sentence is written correctly.

30. **2 replace <u>here</u> with <u>hear</u>** (See Chapter 8—Word Choice) Remember, *hear* is what we do with our ears.

31. **3 replace <u>advancement for careers</u> with <u>career advancement</u>** *Excellent benefits, job training, and advancement for careers* form a series. Each item in the series should be in the same form and separated by commas. *These high-paying careers offer excellent benefits, job training, and career advancement.* Option (1) is wrong because *high* is used correctly. Option (2) is wrong because it removes a necessary comma from a series. Option (4) is wrong because *offer* must agree with *careers*, which is plural.

32. **1 insert a comma after <u>Institute</u>** *With specialized training from Advanced Vocational Institute* is an introductory phrase, which should be set apart with a comma.

33. **4 replace <u>strait</u> with <u>straight</u>** (See Chapter 8—Word Choice) Remember, *strait* is generally used as a noun to mean a narrow space or waterway. *Straight*, on the other hand, means "not bent or curved." In this sentence, *straight* means without changing direction.

34. **1 insert a comma after <u>training</u>** *Through hands-on experiences and on-the-job training* is an introductory phrase, which should be set apart with a comma.

35. **5 You will have solid technical skills and the business sense you need to run projects effectively.** Sentences 10 and 11 describe equally important skills that *you* will acquire at the same time. The

new sentence must show the same relationship between the skills. Option 1 is wrong because *but also* should work as a team with *not only*. Option 2 is wrong because it implies that the skills are the same. Option 3 is wrong because *however* suggests a contrast that does not exist. Option 4 is wrong because *before* suggests that the skills are not developed at the same time.

36. **4 insert a comma after <u>September</u>** *When classes begin in September* is an introductory clause, which should be set apart with a comma.

37. **5 no correction necessary** Option (1) is wrong because there is no reason to place a comma after *grow*. Option (2) is wrong because *help* agrees with *nutrients*. Option (3) is wrong because *nutrients* is the plural form of *nutrient*. There is no reason to use the possessive form. Option (4) is wrong because *that* is used for restrictive clauses, which are not set apart with commas.

38. **2 replace *is* with *are*** (See Chapter 4—Subject-Verb Agreement: Difficult Subjects) *Are* agrees with *minerals*, the subject of the sentence. Option (1) is wrong because *however* signals a contrast. This sentence adds information. Option (3) is wrong because a comma should separate *parts* from *particularly teeth and bones*. Option (4) is wrong because there is no reason to place a comma after *teeth*.

39. **1 replace *it needs* with *they need*** (See Chapter 9—Writing Clear Sentences: Consistent Pronouns) *They need* agrees with *bodies*, the subject of the clause. Option (2) is wrong because the sentence is in the present tense. Option (3) is wrong because *digestive system* is a common noun, which should not be capitalized. Option (4) is wrong because *nutrients* is the plural form of *nutrient*. There is no reason to use the possessive form.

40. **1 mouth, digestion** (See Chapter 6—Punctuation and Chapter 9—Writing Clear Sentences) *As soon as food enters the mouth* is an introductory clause that works as an adverb. It should be set apart with a comma. Options (2), (3), and (4) are wrong because the punctuation is incorrect. Option (5) is wrong because *but* changes the relationship between the clauses.

41. **3 pieces, and saliva** (See Chapter 9—Writing Clear Sentences) Both clauses are related. They show what happens in the mouth. Option (1) is incorrect because it leaves out the necessary punctuation to separate the clauses. Option (2) is wrong because there is no reason to use a colon. Options (4) and (5) are wrong because they do not show the correct relationship between the two clauses.

42. **3 replace <u>connect</u> with <u>connects</u>** *Connects* agrees with *esophagus*. Option (1) is wrong because *when food is swallowed* is an introductory clause. Option (2) is wrong because *moves* agrees with *it*. Option (3) is wrong because *esophagus* is a common noun, which should not be capitalized.

43. **2 replace <u>it</u> with <u>the food</u>** (See Chapter 9—Writing Clear Sentences: Consistent Pronouns) The original sentence is unclear. The reader does not know whether *it* refers to the stomach, the food, or even the esophagus. Replacing *it* with *the food* clarifies the sentence. Option (1) is wrong because the comma after *stomach* follows an introductory phrase. Option (3) is wrong because *that break down the pieces even more* is a restrictive clause. Option (4) is wrong because *is* agrees with *it*, which is singular.

44. **5 small intestine, which absorbs** Sentence 11 provides additional information about the small intestine. When the two sentences are combined, the second sentence becomes an adjective clause. *The stomach pushes the partially digested food into the small intestine, which absorbs important nutrients through the villi.* Options (2) and (4) do not show the correct relationship between the two

clauses. Option (3) is repetitive, and it is punctuated incorrectly.

45. **3 intestine, which prepares** The verb *prepares* should be in the same tense as *moves*. Options (1), (2), and (3) are incorrect because *prepared* and *did prepare* are the wrong tense. Option (4) is wrong because *which* should be used for nonrestrictive clauses.

46. **2 The order form clearly stated** The original sentence is too wordy. In the new sentence, the subject and verb are clear, and the message is direct. *The order form clearly stated that the product would ship within one to two days and it would arrive by December 14—well in time for the holidays.* The other options simply rearrange the words. They do not improve the sentence.

47. **4 replace you're with your** Whose company is it? *Your* shows possession. *You're* is the contraction for *you are.*

48. **1 move sentence 6 to the beginning of paragraph B** Paragraph B is about the writer's attempt to contact Creative Minds directly. Sentence 6 provides a good transition from the shipping problems in paragraph A to the communication problems in paragraph B.

49. **5 Minds program; the** *Obviously, I am no longer interested in the Creative Minds program; the holidays are over, and the program will be outdated soon.* Clearly the second sentence explains why the writer is no longer interested in the program. *Yet* is not a good transitional word in this sentence because it does not show the correct relationship between the clauses. *Nonetheless, and,* and *but* do not show the correct relationship either. The semicolon, on the other hand, provides a good link between the statement and the explanation.

50. **1 replace I will have stopped with I will stop** *I will have stopped* is in the future perfect tense, which means that the action will stop at a particular time in the future. The original sentence does not provide a specific time. *I have bought many products through Software Solutions Online, but I will stop shopping at your web site if this situation is not handled properly.*

Pretest Skills Chart

DIRECTIONS

Check your answers to the Pretest and circle the items that you got wrong. While studying for the actual GED, focus particularly on the topics that are difficult for you.

TOPICS	QUESTION NUMBERS
Sentence Structure	
Combining Sentences	3, 11, 15, 17, 28, 35, 44, 49
Rewriting Sentences	8, 18, 25, 40, 41, 43, 49
Active Voice	25, 46
Misplaced Modifier	26
Parallel Structure	31
Grammar and Usage	
Subject-Verb Agreement	1, 9, 13, 16, 27, 38, 39, 42, 45
Who, Whom, Which, That	5, 21
Word Choice	23, 30, 33, 47
Split Infinitive	7
Verb Tense	50
Organization	
Sentence Placement	4, 22, 48
Paragraph Organization	12
Mechanics	
Commas	2, 5, 10, 14, 19, 20, 32, 34, 36
Apostrophes	19
Capitalization	24
No Correction	6, 29, 37

UNIT 1

FUNDAMENTALS

Parts of Speech

CHAPTER 1

IN THIS CHAPTER YOU WILL LEARN:

- How to identify the subject and the predicate (page 31)
- How to use nouns (page 33)
- How to use verbs (page 35)
- How to use adjectives (page 39)
- How to use adverbs (page 41)
- How to use prepositions (page 43)

As a writer, you are the boss, and the words are your workers. Each word in a sentence has a job to do. This chapter will help you understand how words are used in sentences so that you can use the right word for any job.

Subjects and Predicates

All sentences have a subject and a predicate. The subject is someone or something. The predicate describes the subject or shows the subject in action.

EXAMPLES	
Subject	**Predicate**
Charities	are important.
They	help people reach their goals.
Individuals and companies	give money to charities.

PARTS OF SPEECH

Part of Speech	Description	Examples
Noun	Names persons, places, things, or ideas.	Abraham Lincoln, Virginia, car, anger
Pronoun	Substitutes for nouns and works as nouns.	I, you, he, she, it, they, we, this, that, who, whom, which, everybody, myself
Verb	Connects related words or shows action.	is, are, smell, talk, create, run
Adjective	Tells the size, shape, number, owner, or appearance of a noun or pronoun.	large, round, some, tall, his
Adverb	Gives information about verbs, adjectives, or other adverbs.	carefully, very, today, soon, quickly
Preposition	Links words or groups of words.	above, behind, at, between, with, for, until

Remember, the function of a word determines its part of speech.

The subjects name people and things such as *charities, they, individuals,* and *companies.* The predicates describe the subject or show actions. For example, *are important* describes *charities.* The words *help people reach their goals* show the action that *they* take. Likewise, the words *give money to charities* show the action of *individuals and companies.*

NOTE

Certain words such as *a, an,* and *the* often come before nouns. They are called **articles,** and they work as adjectives. When an article appears, a noun soon follows.

EXERCISE 1

Draw a line between the subject and the predicate in each of the following sentences.

SAMPLE: Many parents / need day care for their children.

1. The girl ate a donut.
2. Some people cannot afford health care.
3. Lions, tigers, elephants, and horses perform tricks at the circus.
4. Mr. Po read the poem to the class.
5. The flu strikes many people in the winter.
6. Some workers have to develop their skills.
7. Cal caught the ball, ran to second base, and tagged the runner.
8. Juan dreams of playing in the pros.
9. Parents want decent jobs, safe streets, and good schools.
10. Some people come to America to start a new life.

Answers are on page 311.

Nouns

Everything that has a name is a noun. Nouns name persons, places, things, or ideas.

Examples

Mrs. Durkin is a great teacher.

Mrs. Durkin and *teacher* name a person.

Washington, D.C. and New York City are large cities.

Washington, D.C., New York City, and *cities* are places.

The tall tree is bending in the wind.

Tree and *wind* are things.

Most workers want success and happiness.

Workers are persons. *Success* and *happiness* are ideas.

Nouns can be found easily. Articles such as *a, an,* and *the* come before nouns. Likewise, adjectives—words that describe the size, shape, number, owner, or appearance of nouns—often precede nouns.

Examples

1. The dedicated athlete won an award.
   Athlete and *award* are nouns. *The* and *an* are articles that come before *athlete* and *award.*
2. The fancy, red car sped through the intersection.
   Car and *intersection* are nouns. *Fancy* and *red* are adjectives that describe the *car. The* is an article that comes before both *car* and *intersection.*

Most nouns can be made plural by adding *-s* or *-es.*

Examples

1. All five tests were on the same day.
   Test was made plural by adding an *-s* to form *tests.*
2. Several boxes fell to the ground.
   Box was made plural by adding *-es* to form *boxes.*

> **REMEMBER**
>
> Remember these facts about nouns:
> - Nouns name persons, places, things, or ideas.
> - Most nouns can be made plural by adding *-s* or *-es.*
> - Articles are soon followed by a noun.
> - Nouns often follow adjectives, which are words that describe the size, shape, number, owner, or appearance of nouns.

EXERCISE 2

Underline the nouns in the following sentences.

1. The manager ran through the store.
2. The coach gave Saul a gold medal.
3. A judge ordered Chris to pay for the car.
4. The coffee destroyed my notebook.

5. The fire raced through our house.

6. Sean typed three letters on the new computer.

7. Lynn needs a sitter for the baby.

8. Ty wants a job with decent hours and good pay.

9. Paul did not fix the leaks in the ceiling.

10. Students want to have success in school.

Answers are on page 311.

Pronouns

Generally pronouns substitute for nouns and work as nouns do in a sentence. Note the pronouns that are listed in the box.

PRONOUNS			
I	it	them	who
everybody	me	themselves	whoever
he	myself	they	whom
her	she	this	whomever
herself	some	us	you
him	such	we	
himself	that	which	

Example

Kathy is a doctor. <u>She</u> works with patients from all over the city. <u>They</u> come to <u>her</u> with many different health problems. <u>She</u> helps people <u>who</u> cannot afford other medical services.

(*She* substitutes for Kathy. *They* substitutes for patients. *Her* substitutes for Kathy. *She* substitutes for Kathy, and *who* substitutes for people.)

Personal pronouns (*I, you, he, she, it, we, they, me, him, her, us, them*) substitute for a specific person or persons. Personal pronouns and the pronoun *who* change form in different sentences. (See more on pronouns in Chapter 5.)

> **REMEMBER**
>
> Remember, pronouns substitute for nouns and work as nouns do in a sentence.

EXERCISE 3

Underline the pronouns in the following sentences.

1. Leigh picked up the wallet and returned it.

2. The FBI wanted to question whomever they saw.

3. Who will volunteer to organize the bake sale?

4. After Nate cut himself, he rushed to the hospital.

5. Everybody wanted to win the prize.

6. They hurt themselves on the field.

7. I do not want this.

8. You need to fill out the forms before you see the doctor.

9. It is the only way to get her to take care of herself.

10. Which is the right way?

Answers are on page 312.

Verbs

There are two types of verbs, linking verbs and action verbs. Linking verbs connect related words, and action verbs show action.

Examples

1. Sean and James <u>are</u> wrestlers.
   Are is a linking verb that connects *Sean and James* to *wrestlers.* *Wrestlers* renames *James* and *Sean.*
2. Suzanne <u>plays</u> the violin in the orchestra.
   Plays is an action verb. It shows *Suzanne's* action.

LINKING VERBS

Linking verbs form connections. They link the subject to words that rename or describe the subject. Think of a linking verb as an arrow (↔) that links related words.

LINKING VERBS		
Forms of *Be*	**Verbs of the Senses**	**Unusual Linking Verbs**
be	look	become
am	smell	appear
is	taste	grow
are	sound	remain
was	feel	stay
were		seem
been		
being		

Remember to test the verbs of the senses and the unusual linking verbs using a form of be or an arrow (↔).

Examples

1. Einstein was brilliant.
   Einstein ↔ brilliant
2. The cake tastes great.
   The cake ↔ great
3. Her date seemed nervous.
   Her date ↔ nervous

Memorizing the list of linking verbs will help you find them more easily. However, the verbs that are listed do not always work as linking verbs. If you are not sure, substitute a form of *be* and an arrow (↔) for the verb. If the sentence still makes sense, the verb is a linking verb.

Examples

1. Brianna <u>looks</u> beautiful.
   Brianna ↔ beautiful
   Brianna is beautiful makes sense.
   Looks is a linking verb.
2. She <u>felt</u> the cold weather.
   She ↔ cold weather
   She is the cold weather does not make sense. *Felt* is an action verb.
3. The cookies <u>smelled</u> great.
   The cookies ↔ great
   The cookies were great makes sense. *Smelled* is a linking verb.
4. She <u>smelled</u> the cake baking.
   She ↔ the cake baking
   She is the cake baking does not make sense. In this case *smelled* is an action verb.
5. Her grandfather <u>remained</u> sick.
   Her grandfather ↔ sick
   Her grandfather was sick makes sense. *Remained* is a linking verb.

Note: Make sure you use the correct form of *be*.

Forms of *Be*		
Past	**Present**	**Future**
I **was**	I **am**	I **will be**
He **was**	He **is**	He **will be**
She **was**	She **is**	She **will be**
It **was**	It **is**	It **will be**
We **were**	We **are**	We **will be**
You **were**	You **are**	You **will be**

For more information on verb usage, see Chapter 3.

ACTION VERBS

Action verbs simply show action. Most verbs are action verbs. The subject of the sentence either does the action or receives it.

Examples

1. The batter <u>hit</u> the ball far.
   The subject, *the batter*, performed the action.

2. The batter <u>was hit</u> by the ball.
   The subject, *the batter*, received the action.

EXERCISE 4

Underline the verb in the following sentences.

1. That band seems awful.
2. Juan stayed in the hospital for days.
3. Ahmed felt the hot sun on his back.
4. My soup tastes salty.
5. She smells the flowers on the table.
6. Carl grew three inches last year.
7. Taste the cheesecake.
8. After the lawsuit, Ray remained angry for months.
9. Kaila appeared sick after lunch.
10. We grew tired of his empty promises.

Answers are on page 312.

> **NOTE**
>
> *Infinitive = to + verb*
>
> Always keep *to* and the verb together.
>
> *Wrong:* He wanted <u>to</u> really <u>run</u>.
>
> *Right:* He really wanted <u>to run</u>.

EXERCISE 5

Decide if each of the following sentences has a split infinitive. If you find one, rewrite the sentence correctly.

1. Jenna wanted to really study hard for her exam.

   _____

2. Max needed to rest before he played the game.

   _____

3. Mirabel tried to quickly bake a cake before her guests arrived.

   _____

4. At Gettysburg, Abraham Lincoln spoke to the hearts of many Americans.

_____

5. While doing medical research, scientists try to carefully monitor their experiments.

_____

Answers are on page 312.

HELPING VERBS

Sometimes verbs need help to show action. Helping verbs support the main verb in a sentence. The helping verb(s) and the main verb work like a team. Together they form a verb phrase. The last verb in the phrase is the main verb.

HELPING VERBS			
am	could	have	was
are	did	is	were
be	do	may	will
been	does	might	would
being	had	shall	
can	has	should	

Example

She <u>should have been studying</u> for the test.
HELPING VERB(S) + MAIN VERB = VERB PHRASE
should, have, been + studying = should have been studying
Some verbs can work alone or as helping verbs.

Examples

1. Ruth and Russ <u>are</u> at the movies.
   Are is the main verb. It is a linking verb.
2. Ruth and Russ <u>are eating</u> popcorn.
   Are is a helping verb. *Eating* is the main verb. It is the last verb in the verb phrase.
3. Ruth and Russ <u>should have seen</u> a different movie.
   Should and *have* are both helping verbs. *Seen* is the main verb. It is the last verb in the verb phrase.

EXERCISE 6

Underline the verbs and verb phrases in the following sentences.

1. Jim and Alice are at the beach.

2. The two lawyers were arguing about the case.

3. Mike and Joe could have eaten better food.

4. Khan should have thought about his future.

5. In two weeks, we will be going on a vacation.

6. Who is the best worker?

7. Pam has been working from home.

8. Keith's mom will watch the two children.

9. Jan moved to a new home.

10. The judge could have asked the jury.

Answers are on page 312.

Adjectives

Adjectives give information. They tell the size, shape, number, owner, or appearance of nouns or pronouns. Adjectives often appear in front of the nouns they describe and after linking verbs.

To identify adjectives, you must first find the nouns in the sentence. Then ask yourself the following questions about the nouns: How many? How much? Which one? What type? Whose?

Examples

1. John threw <u>three</u> stones into the <u>cold</u> water.
   Three tells how many stones. *Cold* tells what type of water.
2. <u>Tricia's</u> fabric was sewn into a <u>beautiful</u> quilt.
   Tricia's tells whose fabric. *Beautiful* tells what type of quilt.
3. The book is <u>large</u> and <u>red</u>.
   Large and *red* tell which book. These adjectives follow a linking verb.

EXERCISE 7

Underline the adjectives in the following sentences.

1. Rhea applied to three companies before she found her new job.

2. My small paycheck does not cover the monthly bills.

3. Kind friends helped our poor family.

4. The old, brick building was destroyed in the violent earthquake.

5. English is a hard language.

6. The best team will go to the final round.

7. David broke his right elbow when he fell on the hard ground.

8. Good child care remains expensive.

9. Many parents want more time with their children.

10. High-paying jobs often require a good education.

Answers are on page 313.

USING ADJECTIVES TO MAKE COMPARISONS

Adjectives can compare nouns. There are three different forms of adjectives that are used for specific comparisons. Note how adjectives are used in the box below.

Examples

1. Laura is a <u>fast</u> runner.
   Laura is the only person mentioned. The basic form is used.
2. However, Jennifer is fast<u>er</u> than Laura.
   Two people, Jennifer and Laura, are compared. The *-er* form is used.
3. Ellen is the fast<u>est</u> runner of the three.
   Three people are compared. The *-est* form is used.

Not all adjectives follow this pattern. For example, some adjectives change form completely; other adjectives use *more* and *most* to make comparisons.

COMPARISONS WITH ADJECTIVES		
One Person, Place, Thing, or Idea (basic form)	**Two Persons, Places, Things, or Ideas (*-er* form)**	**Three or More Persons, Places, Things, or Ideas (*-est* form)**
tall	taller	tallest
good	better	best
bad	worse	worst
beautiful	more beautiful	most beautiful
frightening	more frightening	most frightening
	Generally, use *more* for adjectives with two or more syllables.	Generally, use *most* for adjectives with two or more syllables.

EXERCISE 8

Underline the correct adjective for the following sentences.

1. Susan is a (brave, bravest) girl.

2. Mark is the (better, best) player on the whole football team.

3. Our new phone needs to be (more, most) reliable than the old one.

4. I want the (more, most) careful person on staff for this job.

5. For some, Spanish is an (easier, easiest) language than French.

6. Wayne is a (more, most) talented dentist than his partner.

7. If you want to be the (better, best) salesperson in your company, you will need to work hard.

8. Chris is the (shorter, shortest) person in the sophomore class.

9. This is the (worse, worst) movie I have ever seen.

10. If you want to earn a raise, you will have to be a (better, best) waiter than Ken.

Answers are on page 313.

Adverbs

Adverbs give information about verbs, adjectives, and other adverbs. They also can give information about whole groups of words. Adverbs often end in *-ly*, but not always. Look at a word's job in the sentence to decide if it's an adverb.

To find adverbs, ask the following questions about verbs, adjectives, or other adverbs: How? Where? When? Why? How often? How much? Some adverbs will answer more than one question.

> **NOTE**
>
> *Not* and *never* are adverbs. They answer the question *how often*. Likewise, *too* is an adverb. It answers the question *how*.

Examples

1. He <u>quickly</u> ran <u>home</u>.
   Quickly tells how he ran. *Home* tells where he ran.
2. <u>Yesterday</u> we <u>carefully</u> painted the sign.
   Yesterday tells when the sign was painted. *Carefully* tells how the sign was painted.
3. Bob <u>completely</u> understands the new lesson.
   Completely tells how much Bob understands.
4. Mrs. Mallett is <u>very</u> happy <u>today</u>.
   Very tells to what extent Mrs. Mallett is happy. *Today* tells when Mrs. Mallet is happy.

REMEMBER

Remember these <u>facts about adverbs</u>:

• Adverbs give information about verbs, adjectives, and other adverbs.

• To find adverbs, ask the following questions about verbs, adjectives, or other adverbs: How? Where? When? Why? How often? How much?

• Adverbs often end in *-ly*, but not always. Look at a word's job in the sentence to decide if it's an adverb.

• *Not, never,* and *too* are adverbs.

• Adverbs use *-er* and *-est* endings or the words *more* and *most* to make comparisons.

EXERCISE 9

Underline the adverbs in the following sentences.

1. The whole crew worked very hard.

2. We often pay our bills late.

3. Today the chorus sang beautifully.

4. We never told anyone about the good news.

5. Steve is quite talented.

6. The friendly dog quickly ate his food.

7. Jay really wants a raise soon.

8. The plumber truly fixed the problem with my sink.

9. The cat ran away yesterday.

10. Edith promptly walked straight home.

11. Because Maciah arrived too late for the job interview, he never met with the personnel manager.

12. Rashael said that she would not leave the store without a refund.

Answers are on page 313.

USING ADVERBS TO MAKE COMPARISONS

Adverbs compare verbs, adjectives, and other adverbs. Adverbs also use the *-er* and *-est* endings in addition to *more* and *most.*

COMPARISONS WITH ADVERBS		
One item (basic form)	**Two items (*-er* form)**	**Three or more items (*-est* form)**
fast soft careful	faster softer more careful	fastest softest most careful
	Generally, use *more* for adjectives with two or more syllables.	Generally, use *most* for adjectives with two or more syllables.

Examples

1. The alarm rang <u>late</u>.
   Late is the basic form.

   The alarm rang lat<u>er</u> today than it did yesterday.
   The sentence requires the *-er* form because the alarm rang twice, today and yesterday.

   Of all six days that the alarm rang, it rang lat<u>est</u> on Friday.
   The alarm rang six times. The sentence needs the *-est* form.

2. She <u>carefully</u> explained the information.

   She explained the information <u>more</u> carefully today than yesterday.
   She explained the information twice, today and yesterday. *More* is used because carefully has more than one syllable.

   Of all five instructors, she explained the information <u>most</u> carefully.
   The information was explained five times. *Most* is used because careful has more than one syllable.

EXERCISE 10

Underline the correct form for each of the following adverbs.

1. The hiker entered the cave (faster, fastest) this afternoon than this morning.

2. The team played (harder, hardest) today than yesterday.

3. Of all six speakers, Colin spoke (more, most) forcefully.

4. She is the (better, best) dressed woman in Hollywood.

5. Eve ran (more, most) quickly today than on Friday.

6. This shirt is the (more, most) colorful one in the store.

7. Ted yelled (louder, loudest) at his secretary than at me.

8. When Guy speaks, he rambles (worse, worst) than you do.

9. This building was destroyed (more, most) abruptly than that one.

10. Unsolicited phone calls during the day are (less, least) annoying than calls during dinner.

Answers are on page 314.

Prepositions

Prepositions link words or groups of words. Many prepositions are easy to find because they are used often. If prepositions are hard for you to find, think of a preposition as an arrow (>) that points to related words. Use the following scenario to help you.

Note how prepositions are used in the following paragraph:

When I was driving **to** work yesterday, two deer ran **across** the road and **into** oncoming cars. One driver swerved **toward** me to avoid the deer. Another driver drove **off** the road and **into** a drainage ditch. I had to slip **between** two cars and eventually stopped **beside** a row of trees. **Until** yesterday, I had never seen deer **around** that area—except **during** mating season. Now when I drive **down** that road, I will watch **for** deer more carefully.

When I was driving → work yesterday, two deer ran → the road and → oncoming cars. One driver swerved → me to avoid the deer. Another driver drove → the road and → a drainage ditch. I had to slip → two cars and eventually stopped → a row of trees. → yesterday, I had never seen deer → that area— → mating season. Now when I drive → that road, I will watch → deer more carefully.

An arrow → cannot substitute for every preposition. Nonetheless, this exercise may help you.

COMMON PREPOSITIONS

about	past	beside(s)	with
like	around	under	during
above	since	between	within
near	at	underneath	except
across	through	beyond	without
of	before	unlike	for
after	throughout	but	as far as
off	behind	until	from
against	till	by	in spite of
on	below	up	in
along	to	concerning	because of
over	beneath	upon	into
among	toward	down	

EXERCISE 11

Choose prepositions from the box and write them on the appropriate lines. When you are finished, make sure the paragraph makes sense. The first two lines have been completed for you. Remember, there may be more than one correct answer for each blank.

Last night, a bird flew **about** our house. We chased the bird **around** the kitchen and _____ the living room. Everyone was helping— _____the dog. Her barking scared the bird so much, it wouldn't fly _____ the open windows. Eventually, the dog followed the bird _____ our garage and forced it _____ the car right _____ the front wheel. The bird stayed _____ the car _____ the night. Finally _____ the morning _____ I went _____ work, the bird flew _____ the garage door.

Answers are on page 314.

OBJECT OF THE PREPOSITION

Prepositions connect nouns or pronouns to other words in the sentence. The noun or pronoun is called the object of the preposition. In other words, the arrow (❯) points to the object of the preposition. To find the object of the preposition, ask yourself *whom?* or *what?* after the preposition.

Examples

1. Jamie ran <u>behind his brother</u>.
   Jamie ran *behind* whom? ❯ *his brother*
2. He leaned <u>against the fence</u>.
   He leaned *against* what? ❯ *the fence*
3. The police officer saved the pedestrian <u>from the speeding car</u>.
   The police officer saved the pedestrian *from* what? ❯ *the speeding car*

Preposition	Object of the Preposition
behind	his brother
against	the fence
from	the speeding car

Usually the object follows the preposition, but in speech and informal writing the preposition may follow the object. (What is the story *about?*)

PREPOSITIONAL PHRASES

The preposition, its object, and any modifiers form a prepositional phrase. The prepositional phrase can work like an adjective, an adverb, and sometimes even a noun.

Examples

1. The actor <u>with the great voice</u> has the lead role <u>in the play</u>.
   With the great voice is a prepositional phrase that describes *actor. In the play* is a prepositional phrase that describes *role.* Both prepositional phrases work like adjectives in the sentence.
2. The cat ran <u>up the tree during the storm</u>.
   Up the tree is a prepositional phrase that describes where the cat ran. *During the storm* is a prepositional phrase that tells when the cat ran. Both prepositional phrases work like adverbs.
3. <u>Behind the door</u> is a great place to hide.
   Behind the door is a prepositional phrase that works as the subject of the sentence. Prepositional phrases rarely are used this way.

> **REMEMBER**
>
> Remember these <u>facts about prepositions</u> :
>
> - Prepositions connect nouns or pronouns to other words in the sentence.
> - The preposition, its object, and any modifiers form a prepositional phrase.
> - Prepositions usually come before their objects.
> - To find the object of the preposition, ask yourself *whom?* or *what?* after the preposition.
> - Prepositional phrases usually work as adverbs and adjectives. Sometimes a prepositional phrase works as a noun.

PREPOSITIONAL PHRASES

Preposition	a word that connects nouns or pronouns to another word in the sentence	He ran <u>up</u> the stairs.
Object of the Preposition	a word or group of words that is connected to the sentence by a preposition	He ran up <u>the stairs</u>.
Prepositional Phrase	the preposition, its object, and any modifiers	He ran <u>up the wooden stairs</u>.

EXERCISE 12

Underline the prepositional phrases in the following sentences.

1. The student with the red hat is running to her class.
2. The rainbow appeared after the storm and stretched across the sky.
3. In spite of her broken arm, Jane rode the horse into town.
4. During spring break, she went to Florida with her friends.
5. Before noon, the president will tell the press something about his new staff.
6. Jong climbed up the steps and sat behind me.
7. Because of the cramp in her leg, she will only run as far as that tree.
8. The two parties differ on many issues besides crime.
9. You will find the box below the shelf in the basement.
10. Because of her hard work, Rose earned more vacation days with pay.

Answers are on page 314.

IN THIS CHAPTER YOU HAVE LEARNED:

- How to identify the subject and the predicate (page 31)
- How to use nouns (page 33)
- How to use pronouns (page 34)
- How to use verbs (page 35)
- How to use adjectives (page 39)
- How to use adverbs (page 41)
- How to use prepositions (page 43)

Review sections that are difficult for you.

Chapter Review

EXERCISE 1

Choose the best answer for each question. Questions 1 through 6 refer to the following passage.

Ms. Kaila Marie
Innovative Solutions
23 Tech Boulevard
Reston, VA 21980

Dear Ms. Marie:
(1) Thank you for your proposal to improve the computer systems at Magic Mirrors, Inc. (2) Two of the plans we received were promising. (3) However, after careful review, I decided that your proposal is more better than the other plan we were considering. (4) Your hardware is more dependable, and your software programs are most flexible. (5) As long as you am committed to the project, we can do business together. (6) We do need to discuss how we will pay the work and when it will be completed, so I contact you next week to review the contract terms.

Thank you again.
Sincerely,
Jenna Colleen
President, Magic Mirrors, Inc.

1. Sentence 2: **Two of the plans we received <u>were promising</u>.**

    What is another way to write the underlined portion of the sentence?
    (1) be promising
    (2) is promising
    (3) am promising
    (4) looked promising
    (5) being promising

2. Sentence 3: **However, after careful review, I decided that your proposal is <u>more better</u> than the other plan we were considering.**

    What is the best way to write the underlined portion of this sentence?
    (1) more better
    (2) most better
    (3) better
    (4) best
    (5) bestest

3. Sentence 4: **Your hardware is more dependable, and your software programs are <u>most flexible</u>.**

    What is the best way to write the underlined portion of this sentence?
    (1) most flexible
    (2) more flexible
    (3) flexibler
    (4) flexiblest
    (5) none of the above

4. Sentence 5: **As long as you <u>am</u> committed to the project, we can do business together.**

    What is the best way to write the underlined portion of this sentence?
    (1) am
    (2) be
    (3) are
    (4) is
    (5) was

5. Sentence 6: **We do need to discuss how we will <u>pay the work</u> and when it will be completed, so I contact you next week to review the contract terms.**

    What is the best way to write the underlined portion of this sentence?
    (1) pay the work
    (2) pay work
    (3) pay for the work
    (4) pay works
    (5) pay about the work

6. Sentence 6: **We do need to discuss how we will pay the work and when it will be completed, so I <u>contact</u> you next week to review the contract terms.**

    What correction should be made to this sentence?
    (1) will contact
    (2) were contacting
    (3) is contacting
    (4) are contacting
    (5) no correction necessary

Answers are on page 315.

Parts of a Sentence

CHAPTER 2

IN THIS CHAPTER YOU WILL LEARN:

- How to write a complete sentence (page 49)
- How to identify objects of a verb (page 52)
- How to identify subject complements (page 56)

The parts of a sentence are like the parts of a car. Alone, each part is useless. However, when the parts work together, the sentence runs well. This chapter will help you find the main parts of a sentence so that you can learn to write complete sentences and use words correctly.

Complete Subjects and Predicates

Every sentence must have a subject and a predicate. It also must express a complete thought. A group of words that does not meet these requirements is called a fragment.

Beware! Some sentences don't seem to have subjects when they actually do. These sentences are called commands because one person tells someone else what to do.

The verb is stated, but the subject is not. For example, in the sentence *Beware!* you know the sentence is about you, the reader. When you see a command, the subject is *you.*

> **NOTE**
>
> Commands have implied subjects.
>
> 1. Pay attention!
> 2. Eat your dinner.
>
> One person tells someone else what to do. The implied subject is *you.*

COMPLETE SENTENCES

A complete sentence must have a
1. subject
2. predicate
3. complete thought

EXAMPLES OF COMPLETE SENTENCES

Subject	Predicate
1. The big pile of leaves	blew away in the wind.
2. Jane and her friends	ran to the store.
3. (You)	Beware of wet paint!

Examples of Fragments

1. The big pile of leaves.
   What about the leaves?
2. Ran to the store.
   Who ran to the store?
3. Wet paint!
   What about the wet paint?

There are two easy ways to correct a fragment—either reword it or add words so that you have a subject and a predicate.

EXERCISE 1

Read each group of words. If it is a complete sentence, write a *C* in the space. If it is a fragment, write an *F* in the space, and write a complete sentence using the group of words.

1. The women with the pink shirt. ____

   _____

2. The tall man in the red hat asked me for directions. ____

   _____

3. Watch your step. ____

   _____

4. The coaches, the teams, and the officials. ____

   _____

5. Before the drop in the stock market and the accounting scandals. ____

   _____

6. Take off your shoes before you go into the house. ____

   _____

7. After water skiing at the lake house, Katherine, Russell, and Andrew. ____

   _____

8. Notice how many people volunteered for this event.

   _____

9. The man in charge of payroll.

   _____

10. Try to save money on your taxes.

   _____

Answers are on page 315.

Complete Thoughts

In the last chapter, you learned about two types of verbs—linking verbs and action verbs. Remember, linking verbs link the subject to words that rename or describe it (be, am, is, are). Action verbs (drive, talk, run) show the subject doing something.

There are two types of action verbs. Some action verbs can be used just with a subject to make a complete sentence.

Examples

Subject	Verb
1. The leaves	fell.
2. Time	flies.

These sentences make sense even though they only have a subject and a verb.

Some sentences need a noun after the verb to make a complete sentence.

Examples

Subject	Verb	Noun
1. The blizzard	closed	the schools.
2. The actor	wanted	a new TV show.

If these sentences did not have a noun after the verb, the sentences would not give a complete thought. You would want to know what the blizzard closed and what the actor wanted.

EXERCISE 2

Read the following paragraph. In the space provided, write a *C* for complete sentences and an *F* for fragments.

1. This past winter was terrible. _____ 2. The snow buried _____ 3. Schools were closed for several days, and many people could not get to work. _____ 4. Pipes froze. _____ 5. Some roofs collapsed. _____ 6. Luckily, no one was _____ 7. Next winter may be even worse. _____ 8. Watch out! _____

Answers are on page 316.

COMPOUND SUBJECTS AND VERBS

Keep in mind, a sentence can have more than one subject or verb. Some sentences use conjunctions (*and, but, or, nor*) to combine two or more parts that are equally important.

Examples

Compound Subject
1. Exercise and a balanced diet are important.
2. Juan and I will be working on a new project in June.

Compound Verb
3. Olympic athletes train hard and eat nutritious meals.
4. He not only worked hard to improve children's lives but also was a role model for many.

Subject	Verb
exercise diet	are important
Juan I	will be working
athletes	train eat
He	worked was

Objects of the Verb

Some action verbs need nouns to make a complete sentence. These nouns, which are called objects, receive the action in the sentence. To find the object of the verb in a sentence, say the subject, the verb, and then whom or what. Reading this section aloud may help.

Examples

Subject + verb + whom or what?

1. Kyle sent a gift for Jackie's birthday?
   Kyle sent *what*? **A gift**

2. The student body elected Juan.
   The student body elected *whom*? **Juan**

3. The fast, new player has been scoring many goals.
   The fast, new player has been scoring *what*? **Goals**

4. Thomas Jefferson wrote the Declaration of Independence.
   Thomas Jefferson wrote *what*? **The Declaration of Independence**

Subject	Verb	Object
Kyle	sent	a gift
The student body	elected	Juan
The fast, new player	has been scoring	many goals
Thomas Jefferson	wrote	the Declaration of Independence

EXERCISE 3

Decide if the following sentences have objects. If a sentence has an object, write it in the space provided. If a sentence does not have an object, write an *X* in the space.

1. Jasmine bathed her baby last night.

   _____

2. The thunder rolled across the sky.

   _____

3. Abdul passed his math test.

   _____

4. Deena didn't win, but she tried hard.

   _____

5. Before we left, I saw the sunrise.

   _____

6. Before riding, Amal straps a helmet on his head.

   _____

7. Brian, Steven, and Patrick raced around the bend and over the hill.

   _____

8. When the stock market fell, many people lost their college savings.

   _____

9. After an intense investigation, the prosecutor charged the defendant with a felony.

   _____

10. Megan and Andy bought a new house near their relatives and close to work.

   _____

Answers are on page 316.

Some sentences have more than one object.

Examples

Subject	Verb	Object	Object
1. The coach	handed	Brian	the game ball.
2. The company	gave	the schools	free software.

The verb affects both objects in the sentence. *Brian* was handed *the game ball,* and *the schools* were given *free software.* To find the second object, say the subject, the verb, and to or for whom or what.

Examples

Subject + verb + to or for whom or what?

1. The food store gave the shelter free meals.
   The food store gave *to what?* **The shelter**
2. Don bought Bobby a birthday cake.
   Don bought *for whom?* **Bobby**
3. Banks charge people interest.
   Banks charge *to whom?* **People**
4. Politicians send voters information about the election.
   Politicians send *to whom?* **Voters**

Examples

Subject	Verb	Object	Object
The food store	gave	the shelter	free meals
Don	bought	Bobby	a birthday cake
Banks	charge	people	interest
Politicians	send	voters	information

EXERCISE 4

Each of the following sentences has at least one object that receives action. Write the object(s) in the spaces provided.

1. Doyle offered me free tickets.

   _____

2. We mailed the check yesterday.

   _____

3. The post office sent us the mail.

   _____

4. The coach gave Mansi an award.

   _____

5. Kim baked the cookies Friday.

   _____

6. While he was racing down the field, Ian gave Brianna a great lead pass.

   _____

7. Kaila and Logan wrote their teachers thank-you notes for their patience and hard work.

   _____

8. When the armed men entered, the bank teller gave the manager a worried look.

   _____

9. After a long wait in line at the job fair, Colin and Luke submitted their resumes to several companies.

   _____

10. As soon as she arrived on the scene, Jenna extinguished the blazing fire.

    _____

Answers are on page 316.

COMPOUND OBJECTS OF THE VERB

Some sentences use conjunctions to form compound objects of the verb.

Examples

1. Anita's mother bought Katerina clothes and a new bike for her birthday.
2. Nga gave both her secretary and me nice bonuses for the holidays.
3. The store owner sent me discount coupons and a gift card.
4. The instructor offered Taylor and me new equipment and better supplies.

Subject	Verb	Object	Object
Anita's mother	bought	Katerina	clothes bike
Nga	gave	her secretary me	bonuses
owner	sent	me	coupons gift card
instructor	offered	Taylor me	equipment supplies

Subject Complements

Subject complements, which can be nouns or adjectives, follow linking verbs. Nouns rename the subject, and adjectives describe the subject. If you can recognize linking verbs, subject complements are easy to find. (See linking verbs on page 35.)

Examples

Subject	Linking Verb	Subject Complement
1. Many of the players	are	my friends. (noun)
2. Jill	will become	a doctor. (noun)
3. The haunted house	was	scary. (adjective)
4. The carrot cake	smelled	delicious. (adjective)

Remember, you can think of a linking verb as an arrow (↔) that links related words. This may help you find subject complements.

Examples

SUBJECT ↔ SUBJECT COMPLEMENT
1. Many of the players ↔ my friends. (noun)
2. Jill ↔ a doctor. (noun)
3. The haunted house ↔ scary. (adjective)
4. The carrot cake ↔ delicious. (adjective)

PARTS OF A SENTENCE

Part of a Sentence	Job	Example
Subject	does the action in the sentence	<u>Alice</u> gave Jen a gift.
Verb	shows action or connects the subject to words that rename or describe the subject.	Alice <u>gave</u> Jen a gift. Susan <u>is</u> a great cook.
Object of the Verb	receives the action.	Alice gave <u>Jen</u> a <u>gift</u>. (Both *Jen* and *gift* are objects of the verb.)
Subject Complement	follows a linking verb and describes or renames the subject of the sentence.	The cookies were <u>delicious</u>. Joe is an <u>engineer</u>.

EXERCISE 5

Underline the verb and double underline the subject complement in each sentence.

1. Those flowers are lilacs.

   _____

2. The cars seem costly.

   _____

3. The water appears deep.

   _____

4. He will remain a lawyer.

   _____

5. Megan will be thrilled.

   _____

6. Courtney looks sad.

   _____

REMEMBER

Remember these facts about subject complements:

- Subject complements are used with linking verbs.
- Nouns that follow linking verbs rename the subject, and adjectives that follow linking verbs describe the subject.

7. Gas prices are high.

_____

8. The milk smells sour.

_____

9. My ride for work is late.

_____

10. Groceries are more expensive.

_____

Answers are on page 317.

IN THIS CHAPTER YOU HAVE LEARNED:

- How to write a complete sentence (page 49)
- How to identify objects of a verb (page 52)
- How to identify subject complements (page 56)

Review sections that are difficult for you.

Chapter Review

EXERCISE 1

Choose the best answer for each question. Questions 1 through 7 refer to the following passage.

(1) Hurricane season remains. A difficult time for families who live along the Gulf Coast. (2) Before the season begins, organizations educate hurricane preparations. (3) Families stock food, and they gather. (4) When a hurricane is about to strike, leaders often urge residents. (5) Evacuations are challenging, and many people do not want to leave their homes. (6) After a hurricane strikes, relief workers and government agencies assess the damage and provide (7) Sometimes, families simply need food and basic supplies. (8) In other situations, people need help relocating and rebuilding. (9) After some hurricanes, it takes years for a community to rebuild.

1. Sentence 1: **Hurricane season <u>remains. A difficult time</u> for families who live along the Gulf Coast.**

   What is the best way to write the underlined portion? If you think that the original is best, choose option (1).
   (1) remains. A difficult time
   (2) sounds difficult. Time
   (3) remains a difficult time
   (4) remains difficult. Time

2. Sentence 2: **Before the season begins, <u>organizations educate hurricane preparations</u>.**

   What is the best way to write the underlined portion of the sentence? If you think that the original is best, choose option (1).
   (1) organizations educate hurricane preparations
   (2) organizations educate people about hurricane preparations
   (3) organizations will educate hurricane preparations
   (4) organizations educate. Hurricane preparations

3. Sentence 3: **Families stock food, and they gather.**

   What change would improve this sentence?
   (1) insert <u>and</u> before <u>food</u>
   (2) replace <u>stock</u> with <u>taste</u>
   (3) insert <u>supplies</u> after <u>gather</u>
   (4) no correction necessary

4. Sentence 4: **When a hurricane is about to strike, leaders often urge residents.**

   What change would improve this sentence?
   (1) insert <u>and help</u> after <u>urge</u>
   (2) add <u>or tornado</u> after <u>hurricane</u>
   (3) insert <u>to evacuate</u> after <u>residents</u>
   (4) no improvement necessary

5. Sentence 5: **Evacuations are challenging, and many people do not want to leave their homes.**

   What change would improve this sentence?
   (1) insert <u>difficult</u> after <u>are</u>
   (2) remove <u>challenging</u>
   (3) remove <u>want to leave</u>
   (4) no correction necessary

6. Sentence 6: **After a hurricane strikes, relief workers and government agencies assess the damage and provide.**

   What change would improve this sentence?
   (1) insert <u>assistance</u> after <u>provide</u>
   (2) replace <u>and</u> with <u>but</u>
   (3) remove <u>relief workers and government agencies</u>
   (4) no correction necessary

7. Sentence 7: **Sometimes, families simply need food and basic supplies.**

   What change would improve this sentence?
   (1) remove <u>food and basic supplies</u>
   (2) remove <u>families</u>
   (3) insert a period (.) after <u>food</u>
   (4) no correction necessary

Answers are on page 317.

UNIT 2

USAGE

Verb Usage

The subject in a sentence is like the main character in a film. Subjects make things happen. The verb, on the other hand, is the action; it shows what the subject is doing. This chapter will teach you about different verbs. You will learn about verb tenses, irregular verbs, and verbs that are troublesome.

Verb Tense

Verb tense tells when an action takes place. There are different types of verb tenses, and they each have a specific job to do. You need to know about the different verb tenses so you can use verbs correctly and explain your thoughts clearly.

THE SIMPLE TENSES: PRESENT, PAST, AND FUTURE

First we will focus on the simple tenses, which are the ones you already know best. The simple tenses are the present tense, the past tense, and the future tense.

PRESENT TENSE

The present tense is used for actions that are happening now, actions that occur repeatedly, and general truths, which are statements that are always true.

HINT

As you go through this chapter, read the examples and correct answers aloud many times. If you practice saying the verbs correctly, you will be more likely to write them correctly.

Examples

1. Beth and Phil <u>study</u> hard in school. (happening now)
2. Debby <u>balances</u> her checkbook each month. (happens repeatedly)
3. Newborns <u>cry</u>. (general truth)

PAST TENSE

The past tense simply shows that an action happened in the past. To form the past tense, add *-ed* to the plain form of regular verbs.

NOTE

Regular verbs follow a pattern to form different tenses. Irregular verbs do not follow the same pattern. See more on irregular verbs on page 69.

Examples

1. Judy campaig<u>ned</u> in the last election.
2. Scott wash<u>ed</u> the car yesterday.

FUTURE TENSE

The future tense shows that an action will happen in the future. To form the future tense, use the helping verb *will* and the plain form of the verb.

Examples

1. She <u>will finish</u> her work tomorrow.
2. They <u>will walk</u> ten miles to raise money for charity.

SIMPLE TENSES		
Past	**Present**	**Future**
walked	walk(s)	will walk
helped	help(s)	will help
washed	wash(es)	will wash

HINTS ABOUT TIME

A sentence often has words that show when the action happened. Look for words that signal a specific time (see the box that follows) and for other verbs that may give a clue.

Examples

1. <u>Yesterday</u>, I weeded the garden and planted flowers.
2. <u>Now</u> we need new tires for the car.
3. We will be in New York <u>soon</u>.

SIGNAL WORDS FOR SIMPLE TENSES			
yesterday	today	tomorrow	many times
last year	now	next week	often
last week	soon	every day	usually

EXERCISE 1

Underline the correct verb for each of the following sentences. Check your work, and read the correct answers aloud.

1. Kerry (baked, bakes, will bake) cookies every Monday.

2. Last week, I (helped, help, will help) my mom in the yard and (played, play, will play) ball with my friends.

3. Nate (received, receive, will receive) his last paycheck next Monday.

4. He (started, starts, will start) school next fall.

5. Yesterday, Blake (ripped, rips, will rip) a hole in his jacket while working on the car.

6. Tomorrow night, the news (showed, shows, will show) the new bear cub at the zoo.

7. Flowers (bloomed, bloom, will bloom) in the spring.

8. My dad (exploded, explode, will explode) with anger when he noticed the dent in the car.

9. She often (rowed, rows, will row) the boat all the way to the island.

10. Last night at the party, Rita (raved, raves, will rave) about the dessert.

Answers are on page 317.

PERFECT TENSES

The perfect tenses show an action finished before a certain time or another action. Keep in mind, perfect means "completed." Thus, the perfect tenses show when something was or will be completed.

Past Perfect	Present Perfect	Future Perfect
an action completed before another action in the past	an action that started in the past and continues to the present *or* an action that just finished	an action that will be finished by a specific time in the future
had played	has played have played	will have played
had helped	has helped have helped	will have helped

PRESENT PERFECT TENSE

The present perfect tense shows actions that started in the past and continue into the present. It also shows actions that have just finished. We form the present perfect tense by using *have* or *has* and the *-ed* form (past participle) of the verb.

Examples

1. I <u>have lived</u> in Maine for three years.
   This action started in the past and continues into the present.
2. Jeff <u>has answered</u> every letter.
   This action just finished.

PAST PERFECT TENSE

The past perfect tense shows that an action was finished before a specific time in the past. It also shows that one action was completed before another action. This tense is formed by using *had* with the *-ed* form (past participle) of the verb.

Examples

1. He <u>had trained</u> in America before the 2010 Olympics.
   This action was finished before a specific time in the past.
2. We <u>had climbed</u> down the mountain before the snow fell.
   This action was finished before another action in the past.

THE FUTURE PERFECT TENSE

The future perfect tense shows an action that will be finished by a specific time in the future. It also shows that an action will be completed before another action. It is formed by using *will have* and the *-ed* form (past participle) of the verb.

Examples

1. We <u>will have finished</u> the report by next Friday.
   The action will be completed by a specific time in the future.
2. Before they move to New York, he <u>will have retired</u> from the company.
   The action will be completed before another action.

HINTS ABOUT TIME

Some words signal the perfect tenses. Keep in mind, the perfect tenses are used to show that an action was or will be completed before a specific time or action. Look for words that signal a specific time. See the examples in the box.

SIGNAL WORDS FOR PERFECT TENSES

already	by	just	next
before	for	last	since

Examples

1. I have *just* learned about the storm.
2. He has made plans *already.*
3. *Before* she finished the book, she had heard about the ending.
4. *Since last* year, we have saved money.
5. *For* the past month, I have worked late.
6. *By next* week, he will have cleaned his room.

EXERCISE 2

Circle words that tell you when the action happened in each sentence. Then underline the correct verb tense. Check your work, and read the correct answers aloud.

1. Before running for office last year, Joel (considered, has considered, had considered) all of his options.

2. By tomorrow, Pam (has completed, completed, will have completed) the contract.

3. Since last week, Mark (is jogging, has jogged, will jog) every day.

4. Hien (will study, studies, has studied) already for the test.

5. Kerry, Jack, and Joseph (finish, are finishing, will have finished) their swim lessons by next spring.

6. John and Tricia already (have painted, paint, will paint) their new house.

7. Before July 4, 1776, few people in the New World (dream, have dreamed, had dreamed) of creating a new nation.

8. By 2050, people (travel, are traveling, will have traveled) to new planets.

9. Before they built the new building last year, Pete's company (destroys, had destroyed, will have destroyed) the old complex.

10. By next fall, Sue (applies, has applied, will have applied) to four colleges.

Answers are on page 318.

REMEMBER
Remember these <u>facts about perfect tenses</u>:
• Perfect means "completed." The perfect tenses show that an action was or will be completed before a specific time or action.
• The present perfect tense shows actions that started in the past and continue into the present and actions that have just finished (have worked).
• The past perfect tense shows that an action was finished before a specific time or another action in the past (had worked).
• The future perfect tense shows an action that will be finished by a specific time or another action in the future (will have worked).
• Signal words will help you decide when the different tenses should be used.

CONTINUING TENSES

The continuing tenses are also called the progressive tenses because they show an action in progress.

PRESENT CONTINUING TENSE

The present continuing tense shows an action that is going on now.

Examples

1. He <u>is running</u> away from me.
2. I <u>am watching</u> them play in the water.
3. We <u>are writing</u> letters to our friends.

As you can see, we form the present continuing tense by using the *-ing* form of the verb and *am, is,* or *are* as helping verbs.

PAST CONTINUING TENSE

The past continuing tense shows an action that was going on for some time in the past.

Examples

1. They <u>were planning</u> to go on a trip to Mexico.
2. Bob and Colleen <u>were working</u> towards retirement.
3. She <u>was thinking</u> about buying a new bike.

We form the past continuing tense by using the *-ing* verb form and *was* or *were* as helping verbs.

FUTURE CONTINUING TENSE

The future continuing tense shows action that will be going on in the future.

Examples

1. After this game, the team <u>will be training</u> for the World Cup.
2. He <u>will be playing</u> his new songs on tour.
3. I <u>will be asking</u> many questions during the meeting.

As you can see, the future continuing tense is formed by using the *-ing* verb form and the helping verbs *will be.*

Past Continuing Tense	Present Continuing Tense	Future Continuing Tense
an action that was going on for some time in the past	an action that is going on now	an action that will be going on in the future
was working were working	am working is working are working	will be working
was running were running	am running is running are running	will be running

EXERCISE 3

For each sentence, circle words that show when the action occurs and underline the correct verb tense. Check your work, and read the correct answers aloud.

1. Right now I (was working, am working, will be working) on my rough draft.

2. Yesterday, we (were watching, are watching, will be watching) the football game on TV.

3. Next year, they (were living, are living, will be living) in Colorado.

4. We (were shoveling, are shoveling, will be shoveling) snow all day last Friday.

5. Next fall, Nga and Van (were playing, are playing, will be playing) on a different soccer team.

6. This morning, the dogs (were barking, are barking, will be barking) so loudly they woke up the whole family.

7. Next spring, he still (was studying, is studying, will be studying) to get his degree.

8. James (was trying, is trying, will be trying) to calm the baby all morning yesterday.

9. In the spring next year, you (were struggling, are struggling, will be struggling) to save money.

10. At present, they (were putting, are putting, will be putting) new shingles on the roof.

Answers are on page 318.

Answers are on page 318.

REMEMBER

REMEMBER

Remember these facts about continuing tenses:

- The continuing tenses show action in progress.

- The present continuing tense shows an action that is going on now (is working).

- The past continuing tense shows an action that was going on for some time in the past (was working).

- The future continuing tense shows action that will be going on in the future (will be working).

Irregular Verbs

Most verbs follow a pattern when they change tenses. They are called regular verbs.

REGULAR VERBS		
Verb	**Past Tense**	**Past Participle**
want	wanted	wanted
live	lived	lived

The past participle, or -ed form, is used for the perfect tenses. (I <u>have wanted</u>. She <u>had lived</u>.)

Verbs that do not follow this pattern are called irregular verbs. You already know many irregular verbs.

Examples

Note the irregular verbs in the following paragraph.

Yesterday, Ken <u>ran</u> out of the house on the way to work and <u>forgot</u> his wallet. Luckily, he <u>found</u> money in his coat pocket to pay the tolls. His boss <u>paid</u> for a cup of coffee, and his friends <u>bought</u> him lunch. By the afternoon, Ken had <u>gotten</u> help from everyone in the office.

The good news is that you already know many irregular verbs; the bad news is that you will have to learn the ones you do not know. Focus on the plain form, the past tense, and the past participle, which is used for the perfect tenses.

FORMS OF *BE*

You must learn these!

Present	Past	Past Participle
am, is, are	was, were	been

EXERCISE 4

Cover the box on Forms of *Be* and complete the following chart. After you have tried the verbs, check your work. Practice saying the correct answer aloud.

SAMPLE: *be* Last week I <u>was</u>.
This week I <u>am</u>.

be Last week she <u>was</u>.
This week she has <u>been</u>.

1. *be* Last week she _____.
   This week she _____.

2. *be* Last week they _____.
   This week they _____.

3. *be* Last week it _____.
   This week it _____.

4. *be* Last week I _____.
   This week I _____.

5. *be* Last week he _____.
   This week he has _____.

6. *be* Last week they _____.
   This week they have _____.

7. *be* Last week I _____.
   This week I have _____.

8. *be* Last week Tim _____.
   This week Tim has _____.

Answers are on page 319.

EXERCISE 5

For each sentence, underline the correct verb form. Check your work and read the correct answers aloud.

1. For the past week, Karim has (are, were, been) late for work.

2. This year Colin (is, was, am) ready for kindergarten.

3. The presidential candidates have (are, were, been) running attack ads for months.

4. Our math teacher (was, is, been) making the work harder now.

5. I (am, is, were) exhausted today.

6. We have (are, were, been) working on this project for two weeks.

7. The mayor (is, be, been) in trouble for tax evasion.

8. Food allergies (are, was, been) a bigger problem than they used to be.

9. Yesterday, Jackson (was, be, been) injured during the football game.

10. Kit has (is, are, been) hospitalized many times.

Answers are on page 319.

**COMMON IRREGULAR VERBS
YOU MUST LEARN THESE!**

Verb	Past	Past Participle
bring, brings	brought	brought
buy, buys	bought	bought
come, comes	came	come
do, does	did	done
go, goes	went	gone
has, have	had	had
run, runs	ran	run
see, sees	saw	seen

The past participle is used for the perfect tenses. (I <u>have brought</u>. She <u>had seen</u>.)

EXERCISE 6

Cover the box on irregular verbs with a piece of paper and complete the following chart. After you have tried all of the verbs, check your work. Practice reading the correct answers aloud.

SAMPLE: *see* Last week I <u>saw</u>
This week I have <u>seen</u>

1. *bring* Last week I _____.
This week I have _____.

2. *buy* Last week I _____.
This week I have _____.

3. *come* Last week I _____.
This week I have _____.

4. *do* Last week I _____.
This week I have _____.

5. *go* Last week I _____.
This week I have _____.

6. *have* Last week I _____.
This week I have _____.

7. *run* Last week I _____.
This week I have _____.

8. *see* Last week I _____.
This week I have _____.

Answers are on page 319.

EXERCISE 7

For each sentence, underline the correct verb form. Check your work, and read the correct answers aloud.

1. I have (see, saw, seen) many people try to jump over that fence.

2. Yesterday, Russ (go, went, gone) for a walk to clear his mind.

3. Chris and Tom have (runs, ran, run) almost ten miles.

4. Have you (comes, came, come) here to ask me a question?

5. He has (do, did, done) many great things for the community.

6. Have you (buy, buys, bought) presents for everyone?

7. We have (have, has, had) a great vacation!

8. Who (bring, brings, brought) the donuts to the office last Friday?

9. For the past two days, she has (go, went, gone) to the store to buy milk.

10. The gusty winds and heavy rain (come, comes, came) quickly last night.

Answers are on page 319.

ONE LETTER CHANGES

Some irregular verbs change form by simply changing one letter. Look at the examples in the box.

ONE LETTER CHANGES		
Present	**Past**	**Past Participle**
begin, begins	began	begun
drink, drinks	drank	drunk
win, wins	won	won

The past participle is used for the perfect tenses.
(I <u>have begun</u>. She <u>had won</u>.)

EXERCISE 8

Cover the box on irregular verbs with a piece of paper and complete the following chart. After you have tried all of the verbs, check your work. Practice reading the correct answers aloud.

SAMPLE: *win* Last week I <u>won</u>.
This week I have <u>won</u>.

1. *begin* Last week I _____.
   This week I have _____.

2. *drink* Last week I _____.
   This week I have _____.

3. *win* Last week I _____.
   This week I have _____.

Answers are on page 320.

EXERCISE 9

For each sentence, underline the correct verb form. Check your work, and read the correct answers aloud.

1. By nine o'clock tomorrow, we will have (begin, began, begun) the new project.

2. Have you ever (win, won) a close game?

3. Chau had (drink, drank, drunk) two glasses of water before the race.

4. Yesterday, Hoa finally (begins, began, begun) the book she bought for her trip.

5. Fakrah has (wins, win, won) every match that she has entered.

Answers are on page 320.

ENDINGS WITH *N* OR *EN*

Many irregular verbs have *n* or *en* endings in their past participle form. Look at the examples in the box.

ENDINGS WITH *N* OR *EN*		
Present	**Past**	**Past Participle**
choose, chooses	chose	chosen
eat, eats	ate	eaten
forget, forgets	forgot	forgotten
get, gets	got	gotten
give, gives	gave	given
know, knows	knew	known
write, writes	wrote	written

The past participle is used for the perfect tenses.
(I have written. She had forgotten.)

EXERCISE 10

Cover the box on irregular verbs with a piece of paper and complete the following chart. After you have tried all of the verbs, check your work. Practice reading the correct answers aloud.

SAMPLE: *write* Last week I <u>wrote</u>
This week I have <u>written</u>

1. *choose* Last week I _____.
This week I have _____.

2. *eat* Last week I _____.
This week I have _____.

3. *get* Last week I _____.
This week I have _____.

4. *give* Last week I _____.
This week I have _____.

5. *know* Last week I _____.
This week I have _____.

6. *write* Last week I _____.
This week I have _____.

Answers are on pages 320.

EXERCISE 11

For each sentence, underline the correct verb form. Check your work and read the correct answers aloud.

1. By nine o'clock last night, the coach had (choose, chose, chosen) the starting lineup for the game.

2. We all (eat, ate, eaten) pumpkin pie at Thanksgiving last year.

3. Have you (give, gave, given) Beth a gift for her birthday?

4. I have just (write, wrote, written) Mom a letter.

5. Jane (know, knew, known) all of the answers on the test yesterday.

6. He has (got, get, gotten) frostbite on his fingers from the harsh living conditions.

Answers are on page 320.

Troublesome Verbs

Lie-lay and *rise-raise* are irregular verbs that often cause trouble. The words have different meanings, but their tenses often look and sound alike. Nonetheless, these verbs have different jobs, and they are used for a specific reason.

Present Tense	Past Tense	Past Participle
lie (to recline)	lay	lain
lay (to place)	laid	laid

Examples

For this section, we will focus on the most common uses of these verbs. Read these examples aloud.

1. Faith <u>lies</u> down to take a nap every afternoon. *(present tense)*

2. When Haley was sick, she lay in bed for hours. *(past tense)*

3. Luke laid his books on the table. *(past tense)*

4. The workers had laid the foundation before the storm hit. *(past participle)*

Present Tense	Past Tense	Past Participle
rise (to stand)	rose	risen
raise (to grow, to lift, or to increase)	raised	raised

Examples

For this section, we will focus on the most common uses of these verbs. Read these examples aloud.

1. The jury must <u>rise</u> when the judge enters the courtroom. (present tense)

2. Last week, Megan <u>rose</u> every morning at sunrise. (past tense)

3. Andy had <u>risen</u> before the angry crowd arrived. (past participle)

4. Farmer Rick <u>raised</u> sheep for many years. (past tense)

REMEMBER

Remember these facts about troublesome verbs:

• *Lie-lay* and *rise-raise* have different jobs.

EXERCISE 12

Underline the correct verb to complete each sentence. Check your work, and read the correct answers aloud.

1. Jong (rises, raises) early every morning and jogs before work.

2. Rose (lay, laid) her notes on your desk before she left the office.

3. Madge has (raised, risen) flowers for years.

4. Yesterday, I (lay, laid) down for just a few minutes.

5. Last Friday, José (rose, raised) quickly and left the meeting when he heard the news.

6. The workers will have (lain, laid) the new roof on the house by noon on Tuesday.

Answers are on page 320.

IN THIS CHAPTER YOU HAVE LEARNED:

• How to form the present, past, and future tenses (page 63)
• How to form the perfect tenses (page 65)
• How to form the continuing tenses (page 67)
• How to form the tenses for irregular verbs (page 69)
• How to form the tenses for troublesome verbs (page 75)

Review sections that are difficult for you.

Chapter Review

EXERCISE 1

Read the paragraph. Then underline the correct verb tense for each sentence. Pay attention to the different time clues.

Yesterday I (decided, decide, will decide) to change my study habits. I (wanted, want, will want) to be more successful in school. I always (worked, work, will work) hard, but my hard work does not pay off. I (studied, study, will study) differently from now on. Tomorrow, I will go to my teacher, and I (asked, ask, will ask) her for advice. Then I (listed, list, will list) all of the changes that I will make. I will put that list on my desk, and I (looked, look, will look) at it at night when I study. The list (frustrated, frustrate, will frustrate) me sometimes, but I know it will help me in the long run. If I (improved, improve, will improve) my skills now, I (studied, study, will study) better in the future.

Answers are on page 321.

EXERCISE 2

Read the paragraph. For each sentence, underline the correct verb form.

Brie has (go, went, gone) through a major change. Last year, she (is, are, was) in terrible shape. She could not run a mile, and she (has, have, had) bad eating habits. Recently Brie has (is, was, been) training for a triathlon. For the past six months, she has (go, went, gone) to the gym every day. In February, she (see, sees, saw) a great bike in a store window, and she (buy, buys, bought) it. Now she rides her bike and (ran, runs, run) as often as she can. I (see, sees, saw) her last week, and I (do, did, done) not even know her. She (is, was, been) so different now. She (came, come, comes) up to me and introduced herself. This new lifestyle has (is, was, been) good for her.

Answers are on page 321.

EXERCISE 3

Choose the best answer for each question. <u>Questions 1 through 10</u> refer to the following passage.

(1) Now that television has become a major part of most American households, researchers have founding that our TV viewing habits affect our lives in more ways than we could imagine. (2) Certainly, some television programs are educational, and others were simply fun to watch. (3) However, the negative effects of excessive television are hard to ignore. (4) According to some studies, American children spend more time watching television than they spend in school each year. (5) By 18 years old, the average American child had saw over 200,000 acts of violence on television—including 16,000 murders. (6) Researchers had blamed excessive

television for everything from obesity and poor school performance to aggressive behavior and sleeping disorders. (7) Even though the statistics are alarming, there are solutions.

(8) Parents can take several steps to make sure their children have positive viewing habits. (9) For instance, parents have needed to know what programs their children are watching and how much time their children are spending in front of the television. (10) Caregivers should avoid using the television as a babysitter. (11) Instead, try to get the children interested in books, crafts, or other engaging activities. (12) Parents should view programs with their children and discussing what the children are watching. (13) Turn the TV off during mealtime. (14) Watching TV during meals can created bad eating habits and poor communication skills. (15) When the TV was on, people tend to eat more and talk less. (16) With a few simple changes, parents can control the negative effects of excess television.

1. Sentence 1: **Now that television has become a major part of most American households, researchers <u>have founding</u> that our TV viewing habits affect our lives in more ways than we could imagine.**

   What is the best way to write the underlined part of the sentence?
   (1) have founding
   (2) have found
   (3) will be founding
   (4) founded

2. Sentence 2: **Certainly, some television programs are educational, and others were simply fun to watch.**

   What correction should be made to this sentence?
   (1) replace <u>were</u> with <u>are</u>
   (2) replace <u>are</u> with <u>will have been</u>
   (3) replace <u>were</u> with <u>was</u>
   (4) no correction necessary

3. Sentence 3: **However, the negative effects of excessive television are hard to ignore.**

   What correction should be made to this sentence?
   (1) insert <u>have</u> before <u>are</u>
   (2) replace <u>are</u> with <u>had been</u>
   (3) replace <u>are</u> with <u>be</u>
   (4) no correction necessary

4. Sentence 5: **By 18 years old, the average American child <u>had saw</u> over 200,000 acts of violence on television—including 16,000 murders.**

   What is the best way to write the underlined part of the sentence?
   (1) had saw
   (2) has seen
   (3) saw
   (4) will have been seeing

5. Sentence 6: **Researchers <u>had blamed</u> excessive television for every-thing from obesity and poor school performance to aggressive behavior and sleeping disorders.**

   What is the best way to write the underlined portion of the sentence?
   (1) had blamed
   (2) are blaming
   (3) will be blaming
   (4) will blame

6. Sentence 9: **For instance, parents <u>have needed</u> to know what pro-grams their children are watching and how much time their chil-dren are spending in front of the television.**

   What is the best way to write the underlined part of the sentence?
   (1) have needed
   (2) will have needed
   (3) need
   (4) are needing

7. Sentence 10: **Caregivers <u>should avoid</u> using the television as a babysitter.**

   What is the best way to write the underlined part of the sentence?
   (1) have avoided
   (2) will be avoiding
   (3) should avoiding
   (4) no correction necessary

8. Sentence 12: **Parents should view programs with their children and discussing what the children are watching.**

   What correction should be made to this sentence?
   (1) replace <u>should view</u> with <u>should have viewed</u>
   (2) replace <u>discussing</u> with <u>discuss</u>
   (3) insert <u>are</u> before <u>discussing</u>
   (4) no correction necessary

9. Sentence 14: **Watching TV during meals <u>can created</u> bad eating habits and poor communication skills.**

   What is the best way to write the underlined part of the sentence?
   (1) can create
   (2) had created
   (3) will be creating
   (4) had been creating

10. Sentence 15: **When the TV was on, people tend to eat more and talk less.**

    What correction should be made to this sentence?
    (1) insert <u>going</u> after <u>was</u>
    (2) replace <u>tend</u> with <u>will be tending</u>
    (3) replace <u>was</u> with <u>is</u>
    (4) no correction necessary

Answers are on page 321.

CHAPTER 4

Subject-Verb Agreement

IN THIS CHAPTER YOU WILL LEARN:

- How to form singular and plural verbs (page 81)
- How to create the singular and plural forms of *be* and *have* (page 82)
- How to work with difficult subjects (page 83)
- How to work with a different word order (page 84)
- How to work with indefinite pronouns (page 85)
- How to work with compound subjects (page 87)
- How to work with linking verbs (page 87)

You write to get a message to the reader. Therefore, you need to make sure that the subject and the verb in each sentence send the same message. This is called subject-verb agreement.

Guidelines

Present tense verbs can be singular or plural. Make most verbs singular by adding *-s* or *-es.*

Plural (more than one)	wait catch	The workers <u>wait</u> for their paychecks. Infielders <u>catch</u> the ball.
Singular (one)	wait<u>s</u> catch<u>es</u>	The cashier <u>waits</u> for her paycheck. The shortstop <u>catches</u> the ball.

PRONOUNS

The pronouns *I* and *you* do not follow this pattern. When the subject of the sentence is *I* or *you,* the verb does not have an *-s* or *-es.*

PRONOUNS AND VERBS		
Subject	**Verb**	**Example**
We, They, I, You	want wash	I <u>want</u> my friend. They <u>wash</u> the dishes.
He, She, It	want<u>s</u> wash<u>es</u>	She <u>wants</u> his friend. He <u>washes</u> the dishes.

EXERCISE 1

Underline the verb form that agrees with the subject.

1. Her dry skin (itch, itches) in the morning.

2. You (read, reads) to your children every night.

3. I (look, looks) out the window often to check on the weather.

4. The players (practice, practices) hard to win more games.

5. They (think, thinks) about selling the land.

6. Ted (want, wants) to find a new job.

7. The children (open, opens) many gifts during the holidays.

8. The peaches (fall, falls) to the ground when they are too ripe.

9. Kay (wear, wears) some of her mother's earrings.

10. The girls (dress, dresses) their dolls with old baby clothes.

Answers are on page 321.

Special Situations

BE AND *HAVE*

Be and *have* are irregular verbs. Nonetheless, the basic rules for verbs still work. The singular forms do end in *-s,* and the plural forms do not end in *-s.*

BE		
Subject	**Verb**	**Example**
Plural Subjects and *We, They, You*	are were	The players <u>are</u> ready now. We <u>are</u> ready now. Yesterday, you <u>were</u> tired. Yesterday, they <u>were</u> tired.
Singular Subjects and *I, He, She, It*	is am was	The goalie <u>is</u> ready now. I <u>am</u> ready now. He <u>is</u> ready now. Yesterday, she <u>was</u> tired.

HAVE		
Subject	**Verb**	**Example**
Plural Subjects and *We, They, You, I*	have	The players <u>have</u> the ball. We <u>have</u> the ball. I <u>have</u> the ball.
Singular Subjects and *He, She, It*	has	The goalie <u>has</u> the ball. He <u>has</u> the ball.

EXERCISE 2

For each of the following sentences, underline the correct verb form. Check your work, and read the correct answers aloud.

1. Yesterday, we (was, were) in the store when we heard the fire alarms.

2. Megan (has, have) more money now that she is working.

3. The children (has, have) new toys.

4. They (is, are) the best cookies that I have ever had.

5. He (is, am) the new mayor in town.

6. (Are, Is) you sure that the movie starts at 7 o'clock?

7. Last week, the boys (were, was) playing in the mud down by the river.

8. I (has, have) enough money for the train and a cup of coffee.

9. Steve (is, am) a foot taller than his younger brother.

10. (Is, Are) the last flight to New York about to leave?

Answers are on page 322.

REMEMBER

Remember these facts about <u>subject-verb agreement</u>:

- Make most verbs singular by adding an *–s* or *–es*. (He walk<u>s</u>. Abby watch<u>es</u>.)

- *Be* and *have* are irregular verbs. You must learn their singular and plural forms.

DIFFICULT SUBJECTS

Some subjects are harder to find than others. For example, sometimes prepositional phrases separate the subject and the verb. Crossing out the prepositional phrases will help you find the subjects more easily.

Examples

Read these examples aloud.

1. The student ~~with the big backpack and heavy books~~ earns very good grades.
2. The boxes ~~under the lodge near the door~~ are full.
3. Marie, ~~along with her sisters~~, went to the play last night.

Sometimes other words that describe the subject are located between the subject and the verb. These words usually are set off by commas, *that*, or *which*. They do not change the relationship between the subject and the verb. Cross out these descriptive words so you can focus on the subject and the verb.

Examples

Read these examples aloud.

1. The <u>bleachers</u>, ~~freshly painted and ready for the big game~~, <u>were</u> full of people.

2. The <u>trees</u> ~~that are full of color~~ <u>are</u> my neighbor's.

3. My <u>bike</u>, ~~which needs new tires~~, <u>is</u> in the shop.

HOW TO FIND DIFFICULT SUBJECTS

1. Cross out prepositional phrases and descriptive words set off by commas, *that*, or *which*.

2. Find the subject.

3. Select the verb that agrees with the subject.

EXERCISE 3

Underline the correct verb for each sentence. Make sure that you focus on the subject and the verb, not the words in between. Check your work, and read the correct answers aloud.

1. The horse that jumped over four fences (is, are) in the lead.

2. The crate of apples (sit, sits) next to the pears.

3. Juan, together with his brothers, (work, works) at the paper mill.

4. The fence in the backyard by the barn (need, needs) a repair.

5. Rose, along with her children, (was, were) at the mall today.

6. The desk that has two chairs (is, are) mine.

7. The plants on the shelf over by the window (has, have) died.

8. The workers with long trips home (like, likes) to leave early on Fridays.

9. Nga's salary, as well as her benefits, (increase, increases) every fall.

10. The haunted house, full of rats and bats, (scare, scares) many people at night.

Answers are on page 322.

REMEMBER

Remember these facts about difficult subjects:

- Focus only on the subject and the verb.

- Cross out prepositional phrases and words that are set off by commas, *that*, or *which*.

DIFFERENT WORD ORDER

Sometimes the subject is difficult to find because it follows the verb. Questions and sentences that begin with *here* or *there* often have the verb before the subject. To find the subject more easily, rephrase the sentence. Rewrite questions as statements and reword sentences that begin with *here* or *there*.

Examples

Original Sentence	New Sentence
Here are the <u>tickets</u> for the show.	The <u>tickets</u> for the show are here.
Do <u>you</u> build roads and bridges?	<u>You</u> do build roads and bridges.
There are many <u>reasons</u>.	Many <u>reasons</u> are there.

Once you find the subject, you can make sure that the subject and the verb agree.

EXERCISE 4

For each of the following sentences, underline the correct verb. Check your work, and read the correct answers aloud.

1. Where (is, are) my shoes?

2. There (is, are) two reasons for your success.

3. Do you (want, wants) more sugar for your coffee?

4. There (go, goes) Khan.

5. Where (is, are) Joe going on his trip?

6. What (is, are) you doing with my new coat?

7. Here (is, are) the horse from the stables across the road.

8. (Do, Does) your mother still drive to the store every day?

9. How (do, does) you win every time you play chess?

10. (Do, Does) Chad believe in ghosts?

Answers are on page 322.

> **REMEMBER**
>
> Remember, rephrase sentences that have a different word order. Rewrite questions as statements and reword sentences that begin with *here* or *there*.

INDEFINITE PRONOUNS

Indefinite pronouns make vague references. They do not refer to specific persons, places, or things. Some indefinite pronouns are always singular. Other indefinite pronouns are always plural. A few pronouns can be singular or plural depending on the sentence. See the chart on the next page.

Always Singular (usually end with *one*, *body*, or *thing*)			Always Plural	Singular or Plural
one	no one	anyone	several	some
each (one)	nobody	anybody	few	all
either (one)	nothing	anything	both	any
neither (one)	someone	everyone	many	most
	somebody	everybody		none
	something	everything		part
				half
				(Use the prepositional phrase that follows.)

Examples

Read these examples aloud.

1. <u>Everyone</u> in the office <u>thinks</u> the air is too cold.

2. <u>Nothing</u> <u>beats</u> coming home after a hard day at work.

3. <u>Several</u> of the boys <u>need</u> new books.

4. <u>Most</u> of the <u>money</u> was stolen. (*Most* refers to *money*, which is singular. The verb must be singular.)

5. <u>Some</u> of the <u>cars</u> were damaged. (*Some* refers to *cars*, which is plural. The verb must be plural.)

REMEMBER

Remember these facts about indefinite pronouns:

- Pronouns that end in *-one*, *-body*, or *-thing* are always singular (someone, somebody, something, no one, nobody, nothing).

- Some pronouns are always plural (several, few, both, many).

- A few pronouns can be singular or plural depending on the sentence (some, all, any, most, none). You must look at the prepositional phrase that follows to choose the correct verb.

EXERCISE 5

Underline the correct verb form. Check your work, and read the correct answers aloud.

1. Nobody (want, wants) to go to the movies with me.

2. (Does, Do) anyone need a ride to work?

3. Neither (likes, like) the new color of the house.

4. (Has, Have) everybody found a partner for the dance?

5. Each (knit, knits) a new sweater in the fall.

6. No one (care, cares) enough about morals today.

7. Either (is, are) a great plan for the old building on Main Street.

8. Somebody (cut, cuts) a hole in my newspaper every day.

9. (Does, Do) anybody know who broke Mom's vase?

10. Something (needs, need) to be done about the broken glass in the playground.

11. Some of my friends (is, are) going out to dinner.

12. Several of my peers (want, wants) to change how they live their lives.

13. All of my change (falls, fall) out of my wallet when I open my purse.

14. None of my siblings (is, are) going to work in my dad's company.

15. Both of the coaches (think, thinks) that they will win the big game tonight.

Answers are on page 323.

COMPOUND SUBJECTS

Some sentences use conjunctions (and, or, nor) to combine two or more subjects that are equally important. These combinations are called compound subjects. For compound subjects joined by *and,* use the plural form of the verb. For compound subjects joined by *or* or *nor,* use the verb that agrees with the closest subject. To follow this rule easily, underline the subject that is closest to the verb.

Conjunction	Verb	Examples
and	plural	Bob <u>and</u> Sheri <u>are</u> good students. Braden <u>and</u> Keegan <u>think</u> the price is too high.
or, nor	agrees with the closest subject	Either the cats <u>or</u> the dog <u>wants</u> food. The coach <u>or</u> the players <u>need</u> a break. Neither Allison <u>nor</u> Courtney <u>is</u> working.

EXERCISE 6

For each of the following sentences, underline the correct verb. Check your work, and read the correct answers aloud.

1. The tiger or the bear (growl, growls) at me every time I go to the zoo.

2. The chef and the waiters (work, works) hard all week.

3. Neither the coach nor his players (know, knows) how tough this game will be.

4. Red, blue, and yellow (is, are) primary colors.

5. The doctor and the nurses (think, thinks) that the boy will be just fine.

6. Carl or his sisters (join, joins) the family for dinner each Sunday.

7. The cats or the dog (knock, knocks) my plants over when I leave the house.

8. The cold air, snow, and high winds (make, makes) this a harsh winter.

9. Neither the flowers nor the tree (flourish, flourishes) in this bad weather.

10. The teacher or the students (erase, erases) the wrong answers and write the correct ones.

Answers are on page 323.

> **REMEMBER**
>
> Remember these facts about compound subjects:
>
> - For compound subjects joined by *and,* use the plural form of the verb.
> - For compound subjects joined by *or* or *nor,* use the verb that agrees with the closest subject.

LINKING VERBS

Linking verbs connect the subject to subject complements, words that rename or describe the subject. Do not let subject complements confuse you. When you write, make sure the verb agrees with the subject of the sentence.

Examples

Read these examples aloud.

1. <u>Hard work</u> and <u>discipline</u> <u>are</u> the key to success. *Hard work* and *discipline* are the subjects. The verb must be plural.
2. The <u>key</u> to success <u>is</u> hard work and discipline. *The key* is the subject. The verb must be singular.

EXERCISE 7

Underline the correct verb form for each sentence.

1. A great athlete (is, are) focused and dedicated.

2. Cars (was, were) a passion for Nate.

3. His main interest (is, are) sports.

4. A lovely sight in the fall (is, are) the trees with their leaves changing color.

5. The trees with their leaves changing color (is, are) a lovely sight in the fall.

6. His main concern when he goes to work (is, are) crazy drivers.

7. Nga's best idea for the store (is, are) more shelves.

8. A bigger backstop and more bleachers (was, were) Khan's idea.

9. A nicer sign or more ads (was, were) Beth's plan for a better image.

10. More voter turnout and better polls (was, were) the key for the campaign.

Answers are on page 323.

> **REMEMBER**
>
> Remember, make sure that the verb agrees with the <u>subject</u> of the sentence.

IN THIS CHAPTER YOU HAVE LEARNED:

- How to form singular and plural verbs (page 81)
- How to create the singular and plural forms of *be* and *have* (page 82)
- How to work with difficult subjects (page 83)
- How to work with a different word order (page 84)
- How to work with indefinite pronouns (page 85)
- How to work with compound subjects (page 87)
- How to work with linking verbs (page 88)

Review sections that are difficult for you.

Chapter Review

EXERCISE 1

<u>Questions 1 through 10</u> refer to the following passage.

(1) Health care is a tough issue for many people these days. (2) Everybody want to have the best care at the lowest cost. (3) Yet, poor people and ill people lack the health care that they need. (4) The problem are high costs and scanty coverage. (5) Neither medicine nor doctors are affordable for many people. (6) Every year politicians, looking for votes and full of hot air, promises to improve health care, but nothing seems to change.

(7) Even the thought of choosing a health plan is hard for some. (8) In our office alone, there is five different health plans. (9) My boss, along with some others, belong to an HMO. (10) Many of the other employees see private doctors. (11) Yet, no one is happy. (12) The forms that we all complete seems endless. (13) Few of the doctors is available when we need them, and the cost keeps rising. (14) Better health plans is a great idea, but who knows how to improve them? (15) Somebody is going to find a solution to this problem someday, but it will not be soon enough.

1. Sentence 2: **Everybody want to have the best care at the lowest cost.**

    What correction should be made to this sentence?
    (1) replace <u>want</u> with <u>wants</u>
    (2) insert <u>had</u> before <u>want</u>
    (3) replace <u>want</u> with <u>is wanting</u>
    (4) no correction necessary

2. Sentence 3: **Yet, poor people and ill people lack the health care that they need.**

    What correction should be made to this sentence?
    (1) insert <u>will</u> before <u>lack</u>
    (2) replace <u>lack</u> with <u>lacks</u>
    (3) replace <u>lack</u> with <u>lacking</u>
    (4) no correction necessary

3. Sentence 4: **The problem are high costs and scanty coverage.**

    What correction should be made to this sentence?
    (1) replace <u>are</u> with <u>is</u>
    (2) replace <u>are</u> with <u>will be</u>
    (3) insert <u>having</u> after <u>are</u>
    (4) no correction necessary

4. Sentence 6: **Every year politicians, looking for votes and full of hot air, promises to improve health care, but nothing seems to change.**

   What correction should be made to this sentence?
   (1) replace <u>promises</u> with <u>will be promising</u>
   (2) insert <u>had</u> before <u>promises</u>
   (3) replace <u>promises</u> with <u>promise</u>
   (4) no correction necessary

5. Sentence 8: **In our office alone, there is five different health plans.**

   What correction should be made to this sentence?
   (1) replace <u>is</u> with <u>are</u>
   (2) insert <u>being</u> after <u>is</u>
   (3) replace <u>is</u> with <u>be</u>
   (4) no correction necessary

6. Sentence 9: **My boss, along with some others, belong to an HMO.**

   What correction should be made to this sentence?
   (1) replace <u>belong</u> with <u>belonging</u>
   (2) insert <u>have</u> before <u>belong</u>
   (3) replace <u>belong</u> with <u>belongs</u>
   (4) no correction necessary

7. Sentence 10: **Many of the other employees see private doctors.**

   What correction should be made to this sentence?
   (1) insert <u>have</u> before <u>see</u>
   (2) replace <u>see</u> with <u>sees</u>
   (3) replace <u>see</u> with <u>seeing</u>
   (4) no correction necessary

8. Sentence 12: **The forms that we all complete seems endless.**

   What correction should be made to this sentence?
   (1) replace <u>seems</u> with <u>seem</u>
   (2) insert <u>have</u> before <u>seems</u>
   (3) replace <u>seems</u> with <u>seeming</u>
   (4) no correction necessary

9. Sentence 13: **Few of the doctors is available when we need them, and the cost keeps rising.**

   What correction should be made to this sentence?
   (1) replace <u>keeps</u> with <u>keep</u>
   (2) replace <u>is</u> with <u>were</u>
   (3) replace <u>is</u> with <u>are</u>
   (4) no correction necessary

10. Sentence 14: **Better health plans is a great idea, but who knows how to improve them?**

    What correction should be made to this sentence?
    (1) replace <u>knows</u> with <u>know</u>
    (2) replace <u>is</u> with <u>are</u>
    (3) replace <u>is</u> with <u>be</u>
    (4) no correction necessary

Answers are on page 324.

Pronouns

CHAPTER 5

IN THIS CHAPTER YOU WILL LEARN:

- How to use subject pronouns (page 91)
- How to use object pronouns (page 93)
- How to use possessive pronouns (page 94)
- How to use *who* and *whom* (page 95)
- How to use reflexive pronouns (page 97)
- How to use pronouns in comparison (page 98)
- How to make pronouns agree (page 99)

Pronouns substitute for nouns and work as nouns in a sentence. Because pronouns have specific jobs, they are divided into cases or groups. This chapter will teach you about the different cases, so you will use the right pronoun for each job.

PRONOUNS		
Subject Pronouns	**Object Pronouns**	**Possessive Pronouns**
I	me	my, mine
you	you	your, yours
he	him	his
she	her	her, hers
it	it	its
we	us	our, ours
they	them	their, theirs
who	whom	whose
whoever	whomever	—

HINT

As you go through this chapter, read the examples and correct answers aloud many times. If you practice saying the pronouns correctly, you will be more likely to write them correctly.

Subject Pronouns

Subject pronouns have two main jobs. They are used for the subject of a sentence and for subject complements.

Note that compound subjects or compound subject complements follow the same rule. If compound parts confuse you, write two separate sentences and then choose the correct pronoun.

SUBJECT PRONOUNS
(*I, you, he, she, it, they, who, whoever*)

Jobs	Examples
Subject	They are best friends. Kim and I are going for pizza. He left the price tags on the gifts. Who won the game?
Subject Complement (follows a linking verb and renames the subject)	It was only he at the door. The best plumber was who? The teacher of the year will be Seon or she.

Examples

Read these examples aloud.

1. Kathy and I are going to buy bikes.
   Kathy is going to buy a bike. I am going to buy a bike.
2. She and he went for a picnic in the park on Sunday.
   She went for a picnic in the park.
   He went for a picnic in the park.
3. The top-rated doctors are Khan and she.
   The top-rated doctor is Khan. The top-rated doctor is she.

EXERCISE 1

For each sentence, underline the correct pronoun. Check your work, and read the correct answers aloud.

1. (She, Her) and Russ are moving into their new house today.

2. (They, Them) will have a lot of work to do in the next few days.

3. Rhea and (I, me) will bring dessert on Thursday.

4. (He, Him) and Nancy will provide most of the food and drinks.

5. The best person for the job is (he, him).

6. (He, Him) and (she, her) are Native Americans.

7. Is (she, her) the world class painter?

8. (She, Her) and John will bring the children with them.

9. The workers from the store are (they, them).

10. Which actress is (she, her)?

Answers are on page 324.

REMEMBER

Remember these facts about subject pronouns:

- Subject pronouns are used for subjects and subject complements, which follow a linking verb and rename the subject.

- If compound parts confuse you, write two sentences and then choose the correct pronoun.

Object Pronouns

Object pronouns have two main jobs. They are used for the object of a verb and the object of a preposition.

OBJECT PRONOUNS (*me, you, him, her, it, us, them, whom, whomever*)	
Jobs	**Examples**
Object of the Verb	The ball hit <u>him</u> hard. My wife gave <u>me</u> new hockey skates. Our boss gave <u>her</u> and me a raise. Jared kicked <u>whom</u>?
Object of a Preposition	Dad built a tree house for <u>us</u>. My mom sat between <u>them</u> and <u>me</u>. This gift is from <u>whom</u>?

As you can see, compound objects follow the same rule. If compound objects confuse you, focus on one part of the object at a time.

Examples

Read these examples aloud.

1. Rick drove <u>him</u> and <u>me</u> to the mall.
   Rick drove <u>him</u> to the mall. Rick drove <u>me</u> to the mall.
2. The judge gave <u>her</u> and <u>him</u> a tough sentence.
   The judge gave <u>her</u> a tough sentence.
   The judge gave <u>him</u> a tough sentence.

EXERCISE 2

For each sentence, underline the correct pronoun. Check your work, and read the correct answers aloud.

1. The little girl with the hose sprayed (I, me) with cold water.
2. The manager promised (her, him) and (I, me) a good job.
3. Congress sent (he, him) a bill on welfare reform.
4. Right now, this is the best choice for (we, us).
5. Did you give (he, him) and (she, her) enough paint to finish the job?
6. I want this secret to stay between you and (I, me).
7. Why did Nga tell (he, him) and (she, her) that story?
8. Two actors from the movie were sitting behind Dade and (I, me).
9. The press caught Di and (he, him) off guard.
10. Tyrone wrote his last novel about him and (she, her).

Answers are on page 325.

> **REMEMBER**
>
> Remember these <u>facts about object pronouns</u>:
>
> - Object pronouns are used for an object of a verb or an object of a preposition.
> - Compound objects follow the same rules.
> - If compound objects confuse you, write two sentences and then choose the correct pronoun.

Possessive Pronouns

Possessive pronouns show ownership of a noun, and they substitute for a noun.

HINT

Keep in mind, possessive pronouns never have an apostrophe.

POSSESSIVE PRONOUNS *(my, mine, your, yours, his, her, hers, its, our, ours, their, theirs, whose)*	
Jobs	**Examples**
Show Ownership of a Noun	<u>My</u> dog ate <u>their</u> wedding cake. <u>His</u> car is parked in <u>her</u> parking space.
Substitute for a Noun	The bike in the garage is <u>mine</u>. That book is not <u>hers</u>. <u>Theirs</u> is the yard with the tall grass.

EXERCISE 3

Underline the correct pronoun for each of the following sentences. Check your work, and read the correct answers aloud.

1. The red backpack with black handles is (her's, hers).

2. (Me, My) mom and dad want to see us for the holidays.

3. The high winds and driving rain flooded (he, his) basement and destroyed (her, hers) patio.

4. Jihaye chews gum with (his, him, he) mouth open.

5. I need to find my ticket, but he has (his', his).

6. (They, Their) lived in Guam, France, and Greece when she was in the military.

7. If he wants to be a pro golfer, he will have to improve (he, him, his) putting.

8. That is a nice table, but (it's, its) finish is fading in the sun.

9. Jihye has her own car, but she wants (their's, theirs).

10. Before Shantae runs for office, he will have to improve (he, him, his) speaking.

REMEMBER

Remember these facts about possessive pronouns:

- Possessive pronouns show ownership of nouns and substitute for nouns. (<u>Her</u> book. The book is <u>hers</u>.)

- Possessive pronouns never have an apostrophe.

Answers are on page 325.

Who and *Whom*

Who and *whoever* are subject pronouns. They work as subjects and subject complements. On the other hand, *whom* and *whomever* are object pronouns. They work as objects of prepositions and objects of verbs.

Subject Pronouns (*who, whoever*)	Object Pronouns (*whom, whomever*)
<u>Who</u> is in charge? <u>Whoever</u> wins this game will be in first place.	You gave <u>whom</u> the money? We can give the ticket to <u>whomever</u>.

Examples

Read these examples aloud.

1. <u>Who</u> caught the fly ball? <u>He</u> caught the fly ball? *subject*
2. The best lawyer in town is <u>who</u>?
   The best lawyer in town is <u>he</u>? *subject complement*
3. The FBI charged <u>whom</u> with the crime? The FBI charged <u>him</u> with the crime? *object of the verb*
4. The clerk gave <u>whom</u> the money?
   The clerk gave <u>him</u> the money? *object of the verb*
5. Jake bought this gift for <u>whom</u>?
   Jake bought this gift for <u>him</u>? *object of the preposition*

Unfortunately, not all sentences are this easy. For example, questions that begin with *who* or *whom* often confuse students. Rewording these questions can make them easier.

Examples

Read these examples aloud.

1. <u>Whom</u> do you want for the band?
   You do want <u>whom</u> for the band. *object of the verb*
2. <u>Whom</u> did you send cards to? You did send cards to <u>whom</u>. *object of the preposition*

EXERCISE 4

For each sentence underline the correct pronoun. Check your work, and read the correct answers aloud.

1. (Who, Whom) asked for more food?
2. Lee gave money to (who, whom)?
3. (Who, Whom) was elected president in Haiti?
4. (Who, Whom) should we send to the training program?
5. Cal gave (who, whom) the game ball?
6. (Who, Whom) did Brazil defeat to win the World Cup?
7. (Who, Whom) will be hurt by the new law?
8. (Whoever, whomever) thought we would travel to the moon?
9. The volunteers at the shelter help (whoever, whomever).
10. (Who, Whom) did Jack pay?

Answers are on page 325.

Some sentences have clauses, which are groups of words with a subject and a predicate. Clauses can act like nouns, verbs, and adjectives. They also can work as any part in the sentence. Note the clauses in the following examples.

Examples

Read these examples aloud.

1. The guard knew <u>who escaped</u>.
   Who *escaped* is a clause. *Who* is the subject of the clause, and *escaped* is the verb. The entire clause acts like a noun and is the object of the verb in the sentence. It answers the question, the guard knew who or what?
2. <u>Whoever built this road</u> deserves an award.
   Whoever built this road is the subject of the sentence. It answers the question who or what deserves? In the clause, *whoever* is the subject, *built* is the verb, and *this road* is the object of the verb.
3. The man <u>who filed an appeal</u> won his case.
   Who filed an appeal is an adjective that describes *the man*. It answers the question which man? In the clause, *who* is the subject, *filed* is the verb, and *an appeal* is the object of the verb.
4. She will give the job to <u>whomever her boss recommends</u>.

   Whomever her boss recommends is the object of the preposition *to*. It answers the question to whom or what? In the clause, *her boss* is the subject, *recommends* is the verb, and *whomever* is the object of the verb.

> **NOTE**
>
> A *clause* is a group of words within a sentence that has a subject and a predicate. Clauses can act like nouns, verbs, and adjectives, and they can work as any part of the sentence.

EXERCISE 5

For each sentence, underline the correct pronoun. Check your work, and read the correct answers aloud.

1. The donor gave his blood to (whoever, whomever) had the greatest need.
2. The person (who, whom) granted the money did not give her name.
3. The person (who, whom) we just met has been here before.
4. Three people saw (who, whom) took the new sign on Main Street.
5. (Whoever, Whomever) committed the war crimes in Bosnia will be brought to trial.
6. Dr. Hawk treats children (who, whom) are injured.
7. Kate will give the bonus to (whoever, whomever) she chooses.
8. (Whoever, Whomever) wins the war will have to rebuild the nation.
9. I did not see (who, whom) she saved from the burning car.
10. Many people (who, whom) come to America work hard to learn English.

Answers are on page 326.

Answers are on page 326.

Special Situations

REFLEXIVE PRONOUNS

Reflexive pronouns show that someone did something alone or to himself or herself.

REFLEXIVE PRONOUNS			
myself	himself	itself	yourselves
yourself	herself	ourselves	themselves

Examples

Read the examples aloud.

1. Jay built the house <u>himself</u>.
   Jay built the house without any help.
2. Nasser hit <u>himself</u> with the car door.
   Nasser performed the action and received it.

A reflexive pronoun must refer to another noun or pronoun in the sentence.

REMEMBER

Remember these <u>facts about who and whom</u>:

- *Who* is a subject pronoun, and *whom* is an object pronoun.
- *Who* and *he* have the same jobs. Likewise, *whom* and *him* have the same jobs.
- When the pronoun is the subject of a clause, use *who* or *whoever*. When the pronoun is an object of a clause, use *whom* or *whomever*.
- Rewording a sentence or clause may help you choose the correct pronoun.

NOTE

A reflexive pronoun must refer to another noun or pronoun in the sentence. To see <u>yourself</u> in the mirror, <u>you</u> must stand in front.

Right	Wrong
Katy traveled the world by <u>herself</u>.	<u>Herself</u> traveled the world.
Lee sent letters for Kim and <u>me</u>.	Lee sent letters to Kim and <u>myself</u>.
The finalists were Tisha, Li, and <u>me</u>.	The finalists were Tisha, Li, and <u>myself</u>.
I bumped <u>myself</u> on the head.	I bumped <u>me</u> on the head.

EXERCISE 6

Decide whether or not the underlined pronoun is used correctly. If the pronoun is correct, write a *C* in the space provided. If the pronoun is incorrect, cross it out and write the correct pronoun in the space provided. Check your work, and read the correct answers aloud.

SAMPLE: Abdul sent cards to Jake and ~~myself~~. me

1. Mom planned the whole trip <u>herself</u>. _____

2. You <u>yourself</u> need to get the job done. _____

3. The waiter spilled hot coffee on Megan, Mike, and <u>myself</u>. _____

4. I tripped <u>me</u> with the jump rope. _____

5. The scholarship winners were Brianna, Kaila, and <u>myself</u>. _____

Answers are on page 326.

PRONOUNS IN COMPARISON

Sometimes we do not actually write all of the verbs in a sentence. For example, when we compare two people or things using *than* or *as*, the second verb often is left out of the sentence.

Examples

1. Lee is <u>as</u> tall as I (am).
2. These children have better reading skills <u>than</u> they (do).

When you see a comparison with *than* or *as*, write in the second verb. Then choose the correct pronoun.

REMEMBER

Remember these facts about special situations:

- A reflexive pronoun must refer to another noun or pronoun in the sentence.
- When you see a comparison with *than* or *as*, write in the second verb. Then choose the correct pronoun.

EXERCISE 7

For each of the following sentences, underline the correct pronoun. Check your work, and read the correct answers aloud.

1. Mr. Pyo is as careful with the car as (I, me).

2. Sasha bikes more often than (her, she).

3. Shane skates as well as (he, him).

4. If we work hard, we can play as well as (them, they).

5. Beth and Phil are good athletes, but they are not better than (us, we).

Answers are on page 326.

Pronoun Agreement

Pronouns and their related nouns must send the same message. They must agree in number and gender.

Examples

Read these examples aloud.

1. <u>Carl</u> brought <u>his</u> lunch.
   Carl and *his* show that the sentence is about one man.
2. <u>The students</u> are proud of <u>their</u> art.
   The students and *their* shows that the sentence is about more than one person.

Generally pronoun agreement is easy, but some situations need more thought.

> **PRONOUN AGREEMENT**
> 1. Pronouns must agree in number and gender.
> 2. When *and* joins the related nouns, the pronoun is plural.
> 3. When *or* joins the related nouns, the pronoun agrees with the noun closest to the verb.
> 4. Indefinite pronouns and their related nouns must agree in number.

Examples

Read these examples aloud.

1. <u>Miguel and Ria</u> planned <u>their</u> vacation.
   Miguel and Ria and *their* show that the sentence is about two people.
2. Either <u>the car or the trucks</u> blew <u>their</u> tires on the highway.
   Their agrees with the noun that is closest to the verb.
3. <u>Each</u> of the drivers maintains <u>his</u> own rig.
   His refers to *each*. (See indefinite pronouns on page 85.)
4. <u>Some</u> of the women were upset about <u>their</u> wages.
   Their refers to *some* which is plural in this sentence. (See indefinite pronouns on page 85.)

RULES FOR PRONOUNS

1. Subject pronouns are used for subjects and subject complements.

2. Object pronouns are used for objects of the verb and objects of the preposition.

3. *Who* is a subject pronoun. *Whom* is an object pronoun.

4. Possessive pronouns show ownership of nouns and substitute for nouns.

5. A reflexive pronoun must refer to another noun or pronoun in the sentence.

6. Pronouns and their related nouns must agree in number and gender.

EXERCISE 8

For each of the following sentences, underline the correct pronoun. Check your work, and read the correct answers aloud.

1. Juan or Carlos sends money to (his, their) family in Puerto Rico.

2. Isabelle and Condi were swamped at work. (They, She) had to work late into the night.

3. Few people think that (his, their) bad habits are easy to break.

4. Kerry and Katherine played well with (her, their) toys.

5. Many people try to save (his, their) money, but saving is hard work.

6. None of the pilots thought that (his, their) planes would go down.

7. Everyone wants (his, their) children to live a good life.

8. Each driver parks (his, their) car in the shade on hot days.

9. Nobody thinks (his, their) house will be robbed.

10. Several birds washed (his, their) feathers in the bath by my window.

Answers are on page 326.

REMEMBER

Remember that pronouns must agree in number and gender with their related nouns.

IN THIS CHAPTER YOU HAVE LEARNED:

- How to use subject pronouns (page 91)
- How to use object pronouns (page 93)
- How to use possessive pronouns (page 94)
- How to use *who* and *whom* (page 95)
- How to use reflexive pronouns (page 97)
- How to use pronouns in comparison (page 98)
- How to make pronouns agree (page 99)

Review sections that are difficult for you.

Chapter Review

<u>Questions 1 through 9</u> refer to the following passage.

(1) Everybody who comes to America brings their hopes for a better life. (2) For example, Juan and Rose always believed in the American dream. (3) When they arrived, Juan and Rose promised to work hard for whomever gave them a job. (4) Juan's brothers gave Rose and he money to get started, but it was not enough. (5) Juan often thought that no one ever worked as hard as him. (6) In time, life slowly improved for Rose and him. (7) Working for the future paid off. (8) Before too long, they earned fair wages and provided a good home for them children. (9) Juan told whoever he met about his new life. (10) He was proud of him. (11) Us native-born Americans can learn a lot from these new arrivals.

1. Sentence 1: **Everybody who comes to America brings their hopes for a better life.**

    What correction should be made to this sentence?
    (1) replace <u>who</u> with <u>whom</u>
    (2) replace <u>their</u> with <u>his</u>
    (3) replace <u>Everybody</u> with <u>Nobody</u>
    (4) no correction necessary

2. Sentence 3: **When they arrived, Juan and Rose promised to work hard for whomever gave them a job.**

    What correction should be made to this sentence?
    (1) replace <u>whomever</u> with <u>whoever</u>
    (2) replace <u>they</u> with <u>them</u>
    (3) replace <u>whomever</u> with <u>whom</u>
    (4) no correction necessary

3. Sentence 4: **Juan's brothers gave Rose and he money to get started, but it was not enough.**

    What correction should be made to this sentence?
    (1) replace <u>it</u> with <u>their</u>
    (2) replace <u>he</u> with <u>him</u>
    (3) replace <u>he</u> with <u>who</u>
    (4) no correction necessary

4. Sentence 5: **Juan often thought that no one ever worked as hard as him.**

    What correction should be made to this sentence?
    (1) replace <u>him</u> with <u>he</u>
    (2) replace <u>no one</u> with <u>everybody</u>
    (3) replace <u>him</u> with <u>whom</u>
    (4) no correction necessary

5. Sentence 6: **In time, life slowly improved for Rose and him.**

   What correction should be made to this sentence?
   (1) replace <u>him</u> with <u>he</u>
   (2) replace <u>him</u> with <u>whom</u>
   (3) replace <u>Rose and him</u> with <u>everyone</u>
   (4) no correction necessary

6. Sentence 8: **Before too long, they earned fair wages and provided a good home for them children.**

   What correction should be made to this sentence?
   (1) replace <u>they</u> with <u>everyone</u>
   (2) replace <u>them</u> with <u>their</u>
   (3) replace <u>they</u> with <u>themselves</u>
   (4) no correction necessary

7. Sentence 9: **Juan told whoever he met about his new life.**

   What correction should be made to this sentence?
   (1) replace <u>his</u> with <u>him</u>
   (2) replace <u>whoever</u> with <u>whomever</u>
   (3) replace <u>he</u> with <u>him</u>
   (4) no correction necessary

8. Sentence 10: **He was proud of him.**

   What correction should be made to this sentence?
   (1) replace <u>he</u> with <u>they</u>
   (2) replace <u>him</u> with <u>them</u>
   (3) replace <u>him</u> with <u>himself</u>
   (4) no correction necessary

9. Sentence 11: **Us native-born Americans can learn a lot from these new arrivals.**

   What correction should be made to this sentence?
   (1) replace <u>Us</u> with <u>We</u>
   (2) replace <u>these new arrivals</u> with <u>they</u>
   (3) replace <u>Us</u> with <u>them</u>
   (4) no correction necessary

Answers are on page 326.

UNIT 3

MECHANICS

Punctuation

IN THIS CHAPTER YOU WILL LEARN:

Punctuation marks are like road signs. They tell the reader where to go and how to get there. If you want the reader to go in the right direction, you need to use the correct signs. Otherwise, the reader and your message will be lost. The next two chapters will teach you how to use punctuation marks correctly. As you read the chapters, keep in mind that each punctuation mark is used for specific reasons.

End Marks

End marks are like stop signs. They end sentences and tell the reader to stop—for a moment. There are three different types of end marks: periods (.), question marks (?), and exclamation points (!).

All end marks appear at the end of the sentence.

Period
1. a statement
2. a polite command
3. an indirect question

Question mark
1. a direct question

Exclamation point
1. an emotional command
2. a statement that needs emphasis
3. emotional interjections (Wow!)

PERIODS

Periods have three basic jobs; they end statements, polite commands, and indirect questions. A statement is a sentence that gives information. A polite command kindly tells someone what to do. An indirect question is a question that has been reworded or is not meant to be answered.

Examples

1. We need to learn more about science.
   This statement gives information.
2. Please call me before noon.
   This polite command kindly asks someone to call.
3. The judge asked him why he was late for court.
   This indirect question rewords the judge's question.
4. Our teacher wondered who would finish the test first.
   This indirect question is not meant to be answered.

QUESTION MARKS

NOTE

Question marks and exclamation points work alone. They are not used with other end marks or commas.

Question marks end sentences that ask questions. These sentences are called direct questions because they ask for something specific.

Examples

1. Whom should we hire to replace Kim?
   This question asks for a specific person.
2. Jake asked, "Who will be the new track coach?"
   This question is quoted directly.

EXCLAMATION POINTS

Exclamation points show emotion. Use an exclamation point after emotional commands, statements, and interjections (Wow!).

NOTE

An **interjection** is one word that bursts with emotion. It can begin a sentence or stand alone. Hey! No! Wow! Ouch!

Examples

1. Ted shouted, "Watch out!"
   This command shows emotion.
2. This is a great game!
   This statement shows emotion.
3. Ouch! That hurt!
   Ouch! is an emotional interjection. *That hurt* is a statement that needs emphasis.

Keep in mind, exclamation points should be used rarely. In addition, they should not be used with other end marks or commas.

EXERCISE 1

Write the correct end mark in the space provided.

1. Change the oil in your car every three months or three thousand miles _____

2. When will you finish that book _____

3. Leave me alone _____

4. The plumber asked me how long the sink has been leaking _____

5. Hey _____ I am not done yet!

6. Pat wondered who watered her plants while she was gone _____

7. Please print your name _____

8. Look at me when I talk to you _____

9. What kind of cake do you want for the party _____

10. Many adults take classes at night _____

Answers are on page 327.

Answers are on page 327.

Commas

Commas are like speed bumps. When they are placed properly, the reader slows down at the right time. However, when they are misplaced, the reader becomes frustrated, and the message is lost. Commas are used to separate words, phrases, and clauses. They are used for specific jobs that are listed in the following box.

THE MAIN USES OF COMMAS

1. Separate items in a series (three or more items).
2. Separate independent clauses that are joined by coordinating conjunctions (see page 141).
3. Separate adjectives that describe the same noun.
4. Set apart appositives, phrases, and clauses that are not necessary.
5. Set apart opening words, clauses, and phrases.
6. Separate a speaker from a quotation.
7. Punctuate dates, addresses, and numbers.
8. Prevent misreading.

REMEMBER

Remember these facts about end marks:

- End marks are punctuation marks that end sentences.
- Periods end statements, polite commands, and indirect questions.
- Question marks end sentences that ask direct questions.
- Exclamation points end emotional commands, statements, and interjections (Wow!).
- Exclamation points should not be used with other end marks or commas.

INDEPENDENT CLAUSES AND ITEMS IN A SERIES

Commas are used before conjunctions to separate independent clauses. Commas also are used to separate items in a series. A series, which has three or more items, can include nouns, verbs, modifiers, and phrases.

Examples

NOTE

A comma is <u>not</u> placed after the last item in the series.

1. She packed shorts, jeans, and a skirt for the trip.
   The comma separates nouns in a series.
2. Beth wants to relax more, but she needs to work two jobs.
   The comma separates two independent clauses that are joined by a coordinating conjunction. It is placed before the conjunction.
3. I coughed, sneezed, and shivered all day.
   The comma separates verbs in a series.
4. My clothes are old, tattered, and boring.
   The comma separates modifiers in a series.
5. The dog ran under the fence, through the garden, and into the park.
   The comma separates phrases in a series.

EXERCISE 2

Write commas where they are needed in the following sentences. Some sentences may not need commas.

1. Kim wants to travel with her family but they cannot afford to take a trip this year.

2. Meg bought clothes toys and food for the children at the shelter.

3. The sitter cares for four children during the day and goes to school at night.

4. She sang danced and acted like the star of the show.

5. The house was big clean and costly.

6. I will work longer hours and Fred will help more at home.

7. Jong missed his train yet he did not call for a ride.

8. The gloves hats and scarves make a mess in the hall closet.

9. They played all day and laughed all night.

10. The trial will be delayed so both sides will have more time to gather evidence.

Answers are on page 327.

ADJECTIVES

Commas are used instead of *and* to separate adjectives that describe the same noun or pronoun. First, find which word is being described. Then, decide if the adjectives are equally important. If they are, insert a comma between them.

Examples

1. The soft, white, billowy clouds drifted in the sky.
   Soft, white, and *billowy* are adjectives that describe *clouds.* They are equally important. If you reversed the adjectives, the sentence would have the same meaning.
2. Ray's red sports car needs repairs. *Ray's, red,* and *sports* are adjectives that describe *car,* but they are not equally important. If you reversed the adjectives, the sentence would not have the same meaning.

Commas are not used when numbers combine with adjectives.

Example

The four rusty buckets are full of junk. *Four* and *rusty* are adjectives that describe buckets, but numbers do not follow the rule for adjectives.

EXERCISE 3

Place commas where they are needed in the following sentences. Some sentences will not need commas.

1. The clear blue sky did not have a cloud.
2. Three soup bowls need to be cleaned.
3. Thick black smoke from the fire filled the room.
4. Dr. Lee's shiny new dental chair scares many patients.
5. They searched the woods for five straight days.
6. The new brick building will be our town hall.
7. Fresh white paint will help the shabby old shelves.
8. The old bathroom sink is cracked.
9. It is hard to find good low-cost health care.
10. We filled six large bags with sand.

Answers are on page 327.

NONRESTRICTIVE WORDS, PHRASES, AND CLAUSES

Nonrestrictive words, phrases, and clauses are like extras; they add to the sentence, but they are not necessary. Without the word group, the sentence still makes sense. Nonrestrictive word groups are set apart with commas.

Examples

1. Sean, a struggling artist, needs money.
   The commas set apart the appositive, *a struggling artist.* The appositive is nonrestrictive, because it is not important. Without *a struggling artist,* the reader still knows who needs money, and the sentence makes sense.
2. The band, tired from the concert, took a break.
   Tired from the concert is a nonrestrictive phrase that describes *band.* Without *tired from the concert,* the sentence still makes sense.
3. Vera, who is a great athlete, plays many sports.
   Who is a great athlete is a nonrestrictive clause that describes *Vera.* Without *who is a great athlete* the reader knows who plays many sports, and the sentence makes sense.

Restrictive words, phrases, and clauses do not have commas. They are so important that they cannot be separated from the noun.

Examples

1. The philosopher Socrates taught by asking questions.
   Socrates is an appositive that is restrictive. If *Socrates* were deleted, the reader would not know who taught by asking questions, and the sentence would not make sense.
2. The laws against drug use are being questioned.
   Against drug use is a phrase that is restrictive. If the phrase were deleted, the reader would not know which laws are being questioned.
3. The books that we returned today were due last week.
   That we returned today is a clause that is restrictive. If the clause were deleted, the reader would not know which books were due.

EXERCISE 4

Place commas where they are needed in the following sentences. Some sentences do not need commas.

1. Ty weary from the long trip drank coffee to wake himself.

2. The waiter who spilled soup down my back still got a tip.

3. The hiker cold and alone tried to find help.

4. Nate a lawyer has won some hard cases.

5. The artist Renoir painted many works.

6. Judge Car who is on my case is strict.

7. The judge who is on my case is strict.

8. The ratings that are used for TV shows are vague.

9. Jake tired of reading the same books went to the library to find something new.

10. *American Idol* a great show has aired for many years.

Answers are on page 328.

OPENING WORDS, PHRASES, AND CLAUSES

Commas are used after opening words, phrases, and clauses. These word groups begin sentences, and they usually work as adjectives or adverbs. Interjections that are not emotional also are set apart by commas.

Examples

1. Unfortunately, we need to train more workers.
   The comma sets apart *unfortunately,* an opening word that works as an adverb.
2. Tired, Lee went straight to bed.
   The commas set apart *tired,* an opening word that works as an adjective and describes Lee.
3. No, I do not want to go to the movies.
   The comma sets apart *no,* an opening word that is an unemotional interjection.
4. Joe, will you get the phone for me?
   The comma sets apart *Joe,* an opening word. *Joe* is a direct address because someone is speaking right to him.
5. When we cut coupons, we save money.
   The comma sets apart *when we cut coupons,* an opening clause.

EXERCISE 5

Place commas where they are needed in the following sentences. Some sentences may not need commas.

1. After the rain came the streams overflowed and the streets flooded.

2. Yes I will work a few extra hours.

3. Once the food arrives we can serve the children.

4. Bob leave the flashlight in the car.

5. Scared of the wind and noise Rick hid under the bed during the storm.

6. As soon as we get to the beach I will jump in the water.

7. Between the seat and the door of the car Rita found some loose change.

8. I checked the lights and turned down the heat before we left.

9. Juan did you learn to swim when you were a child?

10. For example some movies have good sound tracks.

Answers are on page 328.

QUOTATIONS

Commas are used to separate speakers from quotations. Commas are placed right after the "talking" word (said, whispered, shouted, announced, etc.) and inside the quotation marks.

Examples

1. The boss said, "A few workers will be laid off."
   The comma is placed right after *said.*
2. "A few workers will be laid off," the boss said.
   The comma is placed inside the quotation mark.
3. "A few workers will be laid off," the boss said, "because the strike lasted so long."
   This quotation is divided into two parts. The commas are placed inside the quotation mark and after *said.*

Commas are not used when the speaker follows a quotation that ends with an exclamation point or question mark.

Examples

1. "Look out!" the foreman called.
   Do not use a comma to set apart the speaker. Exclamation marks work alone.
2. "Why do I have to do the dishes?" her son moaned.
   Do not use a comma to set apart the speaker. Question marks work alone.

EXERCISE 6

Place commas where they are needed in the following sentences. Some sentences do not need commas.

1. He sang "We shall be free."
2. "It's just a job" Tom said "I need the money."
3. "Watch your language!" my mom scolded.
4. "Once we finish this project" he said "I will take a few days off."
5. "When can we go home?" Jane asked.
6. Ned shouted "We need to win this game!"
7. "When I was a boy" he declared "I had to walk to school in the snow."
8. "The ballot is stronger than the bullet" Abraham Lincoln said.
9. "Why will they fire so many workers?" Rose asked.
10. "Stay out of the water!" the lifeguard yelled.

Answers are on page 329.

INTERRUPTIONS

Sometimes the flow of the sentence is interrupted by a word or group of words. Direct addresses, words that connect ideas, and words that explain things often interrupt sentences. Commas separate these words from the rest of the sentence so that the reader will not get confused. If the interruption causes the reader to pause, use commas.

COMMON INTERRUPTERS

I believe	in fact	nonetheless
therefore	I hope	too
perhaps	for example	by the way
I think	also	on the other hand
however	of course	

Examples

1. Will you, Jen, buy milk on your way home from work?
   Jen is a direct address that interrupts the flow of the sentence.
2. We will, however, discuss this problem at a later date.
   However interrupts the sentence and tells the reader to pause.
3. The judge, in fact, delayed our case.
   In fact interrupts the sentence and connects ideas.
4. My main concern, besides paying too much, is finding the right car.
   Besides paying too much interrupts the sentence and provides explanation.

Keep in mind, commas are like speed bumps. In each case above, the commas tell the reader to pause so that the meaning of the sentence will be clear.

EXERCISE 7

Place commas where they are needed in the following sentences. Some sentences may not need commas.

1. The best sales I think are at the malls.

2. Are you sure Jeff that this car is safe?

3. Meat on the other hand should be refrigerated right away.

4. Singers who top the charts can make a lot of money.

5. Sue in fact works hard to save money.

6. You along with your doctor need to take care of your health.

7. Her wrist that had the cast is pale.

8. I hope Kay that we can hire more waiters.

9. The judge ruled of course that Dale should stand trial.

10. Surgeons besides making a lot of money earn respect.

Answers are on page 329.

DATES, ADDRESSES, AND LONG NUMBERS

Commas are used to punctuate dates and addresses. Note the rules in the box that follows.

> **PLACE A COMMA**
>
> 1. between the date and the year
> 2. after a day, date, and year that is used in a sentence
> 3. between items in an address—except for the state and zip code
> 4. at the end of an address that is used in a sentence
> 5. between a city and state and after the state
> 6. in long numbers after every three numbers counting from the right (1,000,000)
>
> *If a specific date is not given, do not use a comma*

Examples

1. May 28, 1992
   A comma is placed between the date and the year.
2. On January 17, 1991, the air war against Iraq began.
   When a date is used in a sentence, an additional comma is placed after the year.
3. Monday, March 11, 1996, was the day my daughter was born.
   A comma is placed after the day, the date, and the year.
4. Send your comments to 55 Lake Drive, Portland, Maine 09845.
   A comma is placed between items in the address—except for the state and zip code.
5. Use Box 10, Red Bank, New Jersey, for all letters.
   A comma is placed between items and at the end of the address.

If a specific date is not given, do not use a comma.

Examples

1. The project will be done by June 2012.
   No comma is used.
2. We need to make a decision by spring 2014.
   No comma is used.

Commas are used to divide long numbers into groups of three. Place a comma after every three numbers counting from the right.

Examples

1. A mile is 5,280 feet.
2. Many houses in this town cost over $200,000.

EXERCISE 8

Place commas where they are needed in the following sentences. Some sentences may not need commas.

1. On December 7 1941 the Japanese bombed Pearl Harbor.

2. We sent all of the cards to 10 King Street Wilton Maine 12543.

3. Many babies were born in September 1996, nine months after the big snow storm.

4. Carl spent over $40000 for that car.

5. We may have some bad luck on Friday May 13.

6. Please send our mail to Box 12 Rush New York 54693 after June 4 1997.

7. The moon is about 240000 miles from the earth.

8. I arrived in Glens Falls New York at three o'clock.

9. Sayre will have the book done by June 1997.

10. On Friday March 15 Ruth will have her birthday party.

Answers are on page 329.

COMMAS CLARIFY SENTENCES

Commas force readers to pause so that they will understand a sentence.

Examples

1. Shortly before seven people will start to arrive.
   Shortly before seven, people will start to arrive.
   Without the comma, the reader may think that the sentence is about seven people.
2. Soon after she bought the dress.
   Soon after, she bought the dress.
   Without the comma, the reader may wonder what happened soon after she bought the dress.

EXERCISE 9

Place commas in the following sentences to prevent misreading.

1. To Jen Laura was a great friend.

2. In baseball fans are a key part of the game.

3. For some dogs help cure loneliness.

4. Before nine guests had to leave.

5. Though sad Meg put a smile on her face for all to see.

Answers are on page 330.

> **REMEMBER**
>
> Remember these facts about commas:
>
> - Commas tell the reader to slow down.
> - Commas separate words, phrases, and clauses. They should be used for specific jobs. (See the chart on page 114.)

Apostrophe (')

> ## THE MAIN USES OF THE APOSTROPHE
>
> 1. shows possession   2. forms contractions

POSSESSION

The apostrophe (') has specific jobs. First, the apostrophe shows ownership or possession.

Examples

1. The teacher read <u>Carl's</u> essay to the class.
   Carl owns the essay.
2. The <u>children's</u> toys are all over the house.
   The children own the toys.
3. <u>Everyone's</u> goal is to finish this job.
   Everyone possesses the goal.

Look at the box below to see how nouns are made possessive.

USING APOSTROPHES (') FOR POSSESSION			
Noun	**Add**	**Examples**	**Sentences**
Singular noun	's	Charles + 's boy + 's	<u>Charles's</u> book won an award. The <u>boy's</u> shoes were lost.
Plural noun that does not end in *-s*	's	children + 's	The <u>children's</u> eyes were wide open.
Indefinite pronoun that does not end in *-s*	's	everyone + 's	<u>Everyone's</u> dream is to succeed.
Plural noun that does end in *-s*	'	nurses + '	The <u>nurses'</u> shifts were changed.

Possessive pronouns (his, her, theirs, its, ours, yours) never have apostrophes.

EXERCISE 10

In the space provided, write the possessive form of the word that is in parentheses.

1. (Lori) plane will land in a few hours. _____

2. We do not want to leave (anyone) things behind. _____

3. Both (lawyers) legal pads were filled with notes during the trial. _____

4. I don't like her plan, so let's go with (his). _____

5. The (voters) minds were made up long before the election. _____

6. The notebook must be (hers). _____

7. Make sure that (Jake) car has enough gas. _____

8. Check (children) toys to be sure that they are safe. _____

9. Why did they need to take (ours)? _____

10. The (baby) cries filled the house. _____

11. (Everybody) needs are different. _____

12. I am not sure if this car is (theirs). _____

13. We need to fix (it) wheel before the race. _____

14. It was hard to judge the (people) mood during the debate. _____

15. (Jen Stephens) job keeps her busy. _____

Answers are on page 330.

There are some special situations for apostrophes. Note the rules in the box below.

SPECIAL SITUATIONS FOR POSSESSION

Situation	Rule	Examples
compound word or word groups	add 's to the last word	My <u>sister-in-law's</u> car is red. This is <u>somebody else's</u> problem.
individual ownership with two or more	add 's to each individual	<u>Mike's</u> and <u>Jim's</u> cars are fast. (Each person owns a car. Note that cars is plural.)
joint ownership with two or more	add 's to the last word	Mom and <u>Dad's</u> house sits on a hill. (They share the same house. Note that house is singular.)

EXERCISE 11

In the space provided, write the possessive form of the words that are in parentheses.

1. (Gale and Myleen) trip to Greece was cut short by the bad weather. _____

2. I will have my (step-sister) room when she goes to college. _____

3. (Kristin and Pat) son works after school. _____

4. (Kay and Phil) writing skills have helped them get great jobs. _____

5. My (brother-in-law) job is in New York. _____

6. (Brian, Rachel, Deena, and David) day-care center is near where I work. _____

7. My (mother-in-law) advice is helpful. _____

8. (Greg and Rye) bad habits got them in trouble. _____

9. The judge did not accept (Erin and Doris) reasons. _____

10. Someone stole (Rose and Juan) car from the lot. _____

Answers are on page 330.

CONTRACTIONS

Apostrophes also are used to form contractions. The apostrophe shows that one or more letters have been left out of the word. Note the common contractions that are listed in the box.

Many people confuse contractions with personal pronouns (their, its, your, whose). Keep in mind, personal pronouns show ownership, and they never have apostrophes.

Examples

1. <u>It's</u> going to be a great day.
   It is going to be a great day.
2. <u>They're</u> running to catch the bus.

COMMON CONTRACTIONS			
Full Words	**Contraction**	**Full Words**	**Contraction**
did not	didn't	they are	they're
do not	don't	we are	we're
does not	doesn't	it is	it's
were not	weren't	there is	there's
can not	can't	who is	who's
could not	couldn't	class of 2009	class of '09
is not	isn't	of the clock	o'clock
you are	you're		

Use contractions for speech and informal writing, but do not use them in formal writing.

EXERCISE 12

Underline the correct word for each of the following sentences.

1. Fix (your, you're) hair before we go on stage.

2. (Whose, Who's) car did you borrow last night?

3. (It's, Its) a bad habit that you need to break.

4. (They're, Their) check bounced at the food store.

5. (Whose, Who's) the lead actor in this play?

6. I want to be sure that (you're, your) ready on time.

7. Jim just heard that (they're, their) moving.

8. Kay wants to ride her bike, but I need to fix (its, it's) back wheel.

9. (Whose, Who's) toys are out in the rain?

10. (It's, Its) a great day to go to the zoo.

11. (We're, Were) you at the concert last night?

12. Hoa needs to fix (it's, its) program before noon.

13. Our leaders (don't, dont) tell the truth.

14. (We're, were) going to class now.

15. (You're, your) ready to board the plane.

Answers are on page 331.

EXERCISE 13

Read the following passage and find ten errors in apostrophe use. Cross out the incorrect words and write the correct words in the margin.

My children came home with their report cards yesterday. Although I was pleased with their grades, I was surprised by the teachers' comments. On Zacks' report card, the teacher noted that he wasnt very focused in math.   Normally, math is his' favorite subject. Taylor, on the other hand, earned high marks in reading. Last year Taylors' reading scores were quite low. We worked on Taylors' reading over the summer, but I still cant understand how his scores improved so much.   Jacob's report card doesnt make sense at all. Jacob earned good grades, but the teacher commented that he isn't working very hard. Its very confusing.   I will e-mail the teachers so they can explain the childrens' report cards. If that doesnt work, we will have to arrange some conferences.

Answers are on page 331.

REMEMBER

Remember these facts about apostrophes:

- To show possession, add an apostrophe and an *s* ('s) to singular nouns, indefinite pronouns, and plural nouns that do not end in *-s*.
- To show possession, add an apostrophe (') to plural nouns that do end in *-s*.
- Possessive pronouns (his, her, theirs, its, ours, yours) never have apostrophes.
- Apostrophes form contractions. The apostrophe shows that one or more letters have been left out of a word.

EXERCISE 14

Read the following passage and find ten errors in apostrophe use. Cross out the incorrect words and write the correct words in the margin.

We accidently left Shantels laptop in the airport last weekend. At first, we didnt even know it was missing. On Monday, Shantel tried to get some work done, but he couldnt find the computer anywhere. Eventually, Shantel realized that he had left it on the ticket counter. Of course, we called the airline right away, and the agents' simply stated that theyre not responsible for lost or stolen items. In other words, its not their fault. We borrowed my brother-in-laws car and drove back to the airport, which took over two hours. Fortunately, we found the computer right away. Shantel has good security on his laptop, so we dont think anyone accessed his data. Nonetheless, theres always a chance that someone could have gotten into the system. In the future, were going to be much more careful.

Answers are on page 332.

Quotation Marks (" ")

THE MAIN USES OF QUOTATION MARKS

1. set off someone's exact words (direct quotations)
2. set off the title of something that is part of a larger work (song, short story, poem, essay, episode of a TV or radio program, part of a book)
3. set off special words

There are two types of quotation, direct and indirect. Direct quotations quote someone word-for-word. Indirect quotations tell what someone has said, but they do not use the person's exact words. Thus, indirect quotations often begin with *that*. Quotation marks are used only for direct quotations. They set the quotation apart from the rest of the sentence.

Examples

1. Abraham Lincoln said, "In giving freedom to the slave, we assure freedom to the free."
   These are Lincoln's exact words. Direct quotations need quotation marks.
2. Lincoln said that when the slaves are free, we will all be free.
   Lincoln's words have been changed. Do not use quotation marks for indirect quotations. Note the quotation begins with *that*.
3. "Put all your eggs in one basket," Mark Twain wrote, "and — watch that basket."
   These are Mark Twain's exact words. Quotation marks are placed before and after each part of the quotation.

EXERCISE 15

Place quotation marks where they are needed. Some sentences may not need quotation marks.

1. Golf is good walk spoiled, said Mark Twain.

2. Our boss announced that we will have fewer hours this year.

3. I don't want much, he said, I just want to spend more time with my family.

4. I remain just one thing, and one thing only—and that is a clown, said Charlie Chaplin.

5. John said that he wants to take a trip to Greece.

6. The day has just begun, she sang.

7. He argued that we spent too much time on this project.

8. During the speech Barb whispered, If we all put our heads down, maybe he will stop talking, and we will go home.

9. Will Rogers said that he didn't know jokes, he just watched the government and reported the facts.

10. I need a break! he yelled.

Answers are on page 332.

LESSER TITLES AND DEFINITIONS

Use quotation marks to set off the title of something that is part of a larger work. For example, quotation marks are used for songs, short poems, and short stories because they are part of something larger. Quotation marks also are used for episodes of TV or radio programs, essays, articles in periodicals (magazines), and parts of books.

Examples

1. "Friends in Low Places" is a song title.
2. "Great Men" by Ralph Waldo Emerson is a short poem.
3. "Courage" by John Galsworthy is a short story.
4. "The Man Who Made Things Happen" in *Golf Digest* is an article in a periodical.
5. "Faith," Chapter 10 of *The Book of Virtues* is part of a book.

Quotation marks or italics may be used to set apart words that are being defined.

Example

When I say "hurry," I mean come here right away.
Hurry is being defined.

EXERCISE 16

Place quotation marks where they are needed.

1. The article New Toys for Fishermen appeared in the last issue of *Field and Stream.*

2. Billy Joel's song Goodnight My Angel will put her to sleep.

3. Chapter 7 which is titled What We Live By made me think about many things in my life.

4. The Stone in the Road is a short story that you will like.

5. In my view, discipline means setting limits.

6. Have you read the poem titled The Busy Man?

Answers are on page 332.

PUNCTUATION WITH QUOTATION MARKS

Keep in mind, punctuation marks are like road signs. If road signs are not placed in the right order, drivers get lost. The same is true with punctuation marks. When quotation marks are used with other forms of punctuation, you need to put the marks in the correct order. Note the rules that are listed.

1. Place periods and commas inside the quotation marks (." or ,")
2. If the whole sentence is a question or exclamation, place the question mark or exclamation point outside the quotation marks ("! or "?)
3. If only the quotation is a question or exclamation, place the question mark or exclamation point inside the quotation marks (!" or ?")
4. Question marks and exclamation points work alone. They are not used with other end marks or commas.

Examples

1. Van yelled, "Ready or not, here I come."
   The period is inside the quotation marks.
2. When she says we "will be here at 5 am sharp," she is serious.
   The comma is inside the quotation marks.
3. "Do I have to?" she cried.
   Only the quotation is a question. The question mark is inside the quotation marks, and it works alone.
4. Who asked, "Where can I find a good plumber"?
   The whole sentence is a question. The question mark is outside the quotation marks, and it works alone.
5. That man called me "crazy"!
   The whole sentence is an exclamation. The exclamation point is outside of the quotation marks, and it works alone.

EXERCISE 17

Insert quotation marks where they are needed in the following sentences. Make sure that all punctuation marks are placed correctly inside or outside the quotation marks.

1. When he shouted, Ump, you are crazy! he was thrown out of the game.

2. The sign says, You must be as tall as my hand to go on this ride.

3. He shouted, You're out!

4. Are you sure he said, We need to hire four more drivers?

5. She said, We need to talk.

Answers are on page 333.

IN THIS CHAPTER YOU HAVE LEARNED:

- How to use periods, question marks, and exclamation points (page 105)
- How to use commas with independent clauses and items in a series (page 108)
- How to use commas with adjectives (page 109)
- How to use commas with non-restrictive words, phrases, and clauses (page 110)
- How to use commas with opening words, phrases, and clauses (page 111)
- How to use commas with quotation marks (page 112)
- How to use commas with interrupters (page 113)
- How to use commas with dates, addresses, and long numbers (page 114)
- How to use commas to prevent misreading (page 115)
- How to use apostrophes (page 116)
- How to use quotation marks (page 116)

Review sections that are difficult for you.

REMEMBER

Remember the following <u>facts about quotation marks</u> (" "):

- Quotation marks are used for direct quotations, lesser titles, and words that are being defined.

- Quotation marks set the quotation apart from the rest of the sentence.

- When quotation marks are used with other forms of punctuation, you need to put the marks in the correct order. (See the chart on page 122.)

Chapter Review

EXERCISE 1

Add commas and apostrophes where they are needed.

We have moved many times but moving doesnt get much easier with experience. When we search for a new home, we look for a nice neighborhood excellent schools and a decent commute. Generally we have moved into a home that we have enjoyed but finding a nice home in a new town is hard. One needs to learn about the town which can vary from one neighborhood to another, and the schools. Although the meetings with real estate agents seem endless, a good agent can help make the move a little easier. Every move is hard. Its important to take the time to do it right.

Answers are on page 333.

EXERCISE 2

<u>Questions 1 through 8</u> refer to the passage below. Read the passage, and answer the questions that follow.

(1) By now everyone knows that eating right and exercising are important. (2) However life is not that easy. (3) Every time I see the doctor, she asks How often do you exercise? (4) Not often enough I respond. (5) People who travel struggle to find decent meals and a place to work out. (6) Parents' schedules are hectic because of work trips to the doctor and kids' activities. (7) Students even have trouble fitting good food and exercise into their lives. (8) We all need to step back and look at our priorities. (9) If we dont take care of ourselves, who will? (10) Even though its hard, we need to take the frustrations out of our lives and put the healthy habits back in.

1. Sentence 1: **By now everyone knows that eating right and exercising are important.**

    What change should be made to this sentence?
    (1) replace <u>knows</u> with <u>knows'</u>
    (2) insert a comma after <u>right</u>
    (3) replace <u>important.</u> with <u>important?</u>
    (4) no correction necessary

2. Sentence 3: **Every time I see the doctor, she <u>asks How often do you exercise?</u>**

    What is the best way to write the underlined part of the sentence? If you think the original is best, choose option 1.
    (1) asks How often do you exercise?
    (2) asks, "How often do you exercise?"
    (3) asks "How often do you exercise"?
    (4) asks. "How often do you exercise"?

3. Sentence 4: **Not often enough I respond.**

   What is the best way to write this sentence? If you think the original is best, choose option 1.
   (1) Not often enough I respond.
   (2) "Not often enough I respond."
   (3) "Not often enough", I respond.
   (4) "Not often enough," I respond.

4. Sentence 5: **People who travel struggle to find decent meals and a place to work out.**

   What correction should be made to this sentence?
   (1) insert a comma after <u>people</u>
   (2) replace <u>meals</u> with <u>meals'</u>
   (3) insert a comma after <u>meals</u>
   (4) no correction necessary

5. Sentence 6: **Parents' schedules are hectic because of <u>work trips to the doctor and kids' activities.</u>**

   What is the best way to write the underlined part of the sentence? If you think that the original is best, choose option 1.
   (1) work trips to the doctor and kids' activities.
   (2) work, trips to the doctor, and kids' activities.
   (3) work, trips to the doctor, and kids activities.
   (4) work trips to the doctor and kids activities.

6. Sentence 7: **Students even have trouble fitting good food and exercise into their lives.**

   What correction should be made to this sentence?
   (1) replace <u>Students</u> with <u>Students'</u>
   (2) insert a comma after <u>food</u>
   (3) replace <u>their</u> with <u>their'</u>
   (4) no correction necessary

7. Sentence 9: **If we dont take care of ourselves, who will?**

   What correction should be made to this sentence?
   (1) replace <u>dont</u> with <u>don't</u>
   (2) remove the comma after <u>ourselves</u>
   (3) replace <u>who will?</u> with <u>who will.</u>
   (4) no correction necessary

8. Sentence 10: **Even though its hard, we need to take the frustrations out of our lives and put the healthy habits back in.**

   What correction should be made to this sentence?
   (1) remove the comma after <u>hard</u>
   (2) insert a comma after <u>lives</u>
   (3) replace <u>its</u> with <u>it's</u>
   (4) no correction necessary

Answers are on page 333.

EXERCISE 3

Questions 1 through 5 refer to the passage below. Read the passage, and answer the following questions.

(1) Looking for a job is hard but there are ways to get help. (2) Most people will change jobs many times during their lives so it is important to learn job search skills. (3) The public library has helpful books articles and computer programs. (4) High schools and colleges have career counselors who aid students in the job market. (5) For a fee employment services will help workers find jobs in a particular field. (6) There even is information online. (7) If resumes applications and interviews are in your future get the help you need. (8) Makes this job search your last one.

1. Sentence 1: **Looking for a job is hard but there are ways to get help.**

   What is the best way to write the underlined part of this sentence?
   If you think the original is best, choose option 1.
   (1) job is hard but there are
   (2) job is hard, but there are
   (3) job is hard. But there are
   (4) job is hard! But there are

2. Sentence 2: **Most people will change jobs many times during their lives so it is important to learn job search skills.**

   What is the best way to write the underlined part of the sentence?
   If you think the original is best, choose option 1.
   (1) their lives so it is important
   (2) their lives! So it is important
   (3) their lives, so it is important
   (4) their lives? So it is important

3. Sentence 3: **The public library has helpful books articles and computer programs.**

   What is the best way to write the underlined part of the sentence?
   If you think the original is best, choose option 1.
   (1) helpful books articles and computer programs
   (2) helpful, books, articles, and computer programs
   (3) helpful books, articles, and computer programs
   (4) helpful books, articles, and computer programs,

4. Sentence 4: **High schools and colleges have career counselors who aid students in the job market.**

   What is the best way to write the underlined part of the sentence?
   If you think the original is best, choose option 1.
   (1) have career counselors who aid students
   (2) have career, counselors who aid students
   (3) have career counselors, who aid, students
   (4) have, career counselors who aid students

5. Sentence 5: <u>**For a fee employment services will**</u> help workers find jobs in a particular field.

What is the best way to write the underlined part of the sentence?
If you think the original is best, choose option 1.
(1) For a fee employment services will
(2) For a fee employment, services will
(3) For a fee employment services will,
(4) For a fee, employment services will

Answers are on page 334.

Capitalization

CHAPTER 7

IN THIS CHAPTER YOU WILL LEARN:

- When to capitalize letters (page 129)

Capital letters are used for certain jobs. By now you know most of these jobs. For example, you know to capitalize the first word in a sentence and the pronoun *I*. However, capital letters are used in other situations, as well.

CAPITALIZE THE FOLLOWING:

1. the first word in a sentence
2. the pronoun *I*
3. major words in titles
4. proper nouns, which are names for specific people, places, or things
5. abbreviations for proper nouns

Quotations

When you quote someone, capitalize the first word of that person's sentence.

Example

Hoa said, "<u>S</u>ome teachers want more students."

Titles

Capitalize major words in titles. Major words include the first and last word of the title. Do not capitalize articles (a, an, the), conjunctions (and, but, so), or prepositions (about, between, etc.) unless they are the first or last word of the title.

Examples

1. Titles of books: *The Bridges of Madison County, Green Eggs and Ham, Winds of War*
2. Titles of songs: "Take It Easy," "Over There," "Beautiful Day"

Capitalize the titles that appear before a person's name. If the title comes after a person's name, do not capitalize it.

Examples

1. Dr. Kathy Hawkins
   Kathy Hawkins, a doctor
2. Professor Tran Lee
   Tran Lee, a professor

EXERCISE 1

For each of the following sentences, cross out letters that should be capitalized, and write the capital letter in the space above.

1. my boss said, "we need a longer lunch break. a half hour is not enough time."

2. I wrote a letter about health care to senator Robb, and i sent a copy to Vi Rus, my doctor.

3. Kate wants to take a class with Ted Jones, a professor with great teaching skills.

4. in her book, Jan wrote, "meeting friends is hard for some people."

5. dr. Seuss's book, *the cat in the hat,* is a big hit with children.

6. Susan said, "we get more conservative as we age."

7. Mark Beauchamp, our mayor, has done great things for this town.

8. The song "let's give them something to talk about" reminds me of you.

9. Some people want the mayor to create a center for day laborers.

10. Ellen's music box plays "ring around the rosie."

Answers are on page 334.

Common Nouns and Proper Nouns

Common nouns are nouns that name general groups of people, places, or things (park, street, father, time). However, common nouns can be used as part of a name (Park Street, Father Time). Capitalize common nouns only when they are used to name specific people, places, or things.

Examples

1. <u>Mother</u>, will you please sit with Brie?
    Mother is used as a name.
2. My <u>mother</u> will sit with Brie.
    My mother is not used as a name.
3. The food store is on <u>Main Street</u>.
    Main Street is the name of the street.
4. The food store is on the <u>main street</u> in town.
    Main street is not used as a name. It simply describes where the store is.
5. In the next election, <u>Governor</u> Dean may run for <u>president</u>.
    Governor is a title. *President* is a position; it is not used to name anyone in particular.
6. A few years ago, the <u>governor</u> of Texas became <u>President</u> Bush.
    Governor is used to describe a position. *President* is used as a title before a name.

Capitalize proper nouns, which are words that name specific persons, places, or things.

PROPER NOUNS	
Specific Person or Thing	Barack Obama; Nobel Peace Prize
Geographic Names	Paris, France; Alabama Avenue the South (the place, not the direction)
Peoples and Languages	Americans; English; Farsi
Religions, Their Worshippers, Holy Days,	Judaism; Muslims; Christmas
Holy Books, and Holy Beings	Bible; Koran; God
Days of the Week, Months, Holidays	Tuesday; January; Labor Day
Historic Events, Periods, or Documents	Korean War; the Ice Age; the Bill of Rights
Government Agencies and Organizations	State Department; Red Cross Fairfax High School
Abbreviations of Proper Nouns	CIA (Central Intelligence Agency); CNN (Cable News Network)

Note: Do *not* capitalize seasons—winter, spring, summer, and fall.

REMEMBER

Remember these facts about capitalization:

- Capitalize the first word in a sentence, major words in titles, proper nouns, and the pronoun *I*.
- Capitalize a title that appears before a person's name.
- Capitalize proper nouns.

EXERCISE 2

Cross out letters that should be capitalized, and write the capital letter in the spaces above.

1. On monday, hope church will open a new soup kitchen at park street and king street.

2. Blair high school held classes on veterans' day, but the students were off for labor day.

3. Christians read the bible, and jews read the talmud.

4. my mom came all the way from france to see me.

5. the purple heart and the bronze star are meaningful awards.

6. The renaissance was a time of great art and music.

7. Aunt Sue and uncle Peter are from the south, but they enjoyed traveling to vermont and new york.

8. Dad studied russian and spanish when he worked for the fbi.

9. Many lakes, such as lake champlain and squam lake, attract tourists in the summer.

10. Did you know that grandma liked nike's commercials that aired during the super bowl?

Answers are on page 334.

IN THIS CHAPTER YOU HAVE LEARNED:

- When to capitalize letters (page 129)

Review sections that are difficult for you.

Chapter Review

EXERCISE 1

Capitalize as needed. Likewise, cross out capital letters where they don't belong.

Every so often an author writes a book or a series that is really popular. years ago, young children loved *Little House On the Prairie*. The authors, Laura Ingalls Wilder and Garth Williams, created a number of books that eventually became the basis of a successful television series. Many young children today enjoy books by Mary Pope Osborne. My Son read *The Knight at Dawn* and *Midnight on the moon* over and over again. Recently, many older readers have focused on *The Lightning Thief*, which began a successful series by Rick Riordan. Likewise, *Twilight* by Stephenie Meyer was a popular book that went on to become a hit movie with young Teens. Fortunately, authors continue to write books that all ages can enjoy.

Answers are on page 335.

EXERCISE 2

Capitalize as needed. Likewise, cross out capital letters where they don't belong.

Art, music, and literature touch our lives. A french playwright said, "a work of art is above all an adventure of the mind." Some people travel the world to see great works, such as *David* or the *Mona lisa*. Other people simply go to the library or turn on the radio to find great works. Books, such as *The Road Less Traveled*, make us think about our lives. Songs, such as "My Hometown," describe our feelings. We all can't travel to see art from the renaissance or hear great music, but we can enjoy the simple works that reach us every day.

Answers are on page 335.

EXERCISE 3

Questions 1 through 5 refer to the following paragraph.

(1) Reading is a part of life. (2) we read road signs, recipes, directions, and newspapers daily. (3) Your Mother may be able to prepare dinner without a recipe, but the rest of us depend on *Dinner in No Time* or some other cookbook for help. (4) Likewise, when we program the radio, we read the directions. (5) We check the listings for TV shows such as *American idol* or our favorite movies. (6) At the health club, some people read *The New York Times* while they ride the bike. (7) We even read our Junk mail. (8) Reading doesn't just get Us through the day; it opens up a whole new world.

1. Sentence 2: **we read road signs, recipes, directions, and newspapers daily.**

   What correction should be made to this sentence?
   (1) replace <u>we</u> with <u>We</u>
   (2) replace <u>directions</u> with <u>Directions</u>
   (3) replace <u>road</u> with <u>Road</u>
   (4) no correction necessary

2. Sentence 3: **Your Mother may be able to prepare dinner without a recipe, but the rest of us depend on Dinner in No Time or some other cookbook for help.**

   What correction should be made to this sentence?
   (1) replace <u>Dinner in No Time</u> with <u>Dinner In No Time</u>
   (2) replace <u>cookbook</u> with <u>Cookbook</u>
   (3) replace <u>Mother</u> with <u>mother</u>
   (4) no correction necessary

3. Sentence 5: **We check the listings for TV shows such as American idol or our favorite movies.**

   What correction should be made to this sentence?
   (1) replace <u>TV</u> with <u>tv</u>
   (2) replace <u>American idol</u> with <u>American Idol</u>
   (3) replace <u>We</u> with <u>we</u>
   (4) no correction necessary

4. Sentence 7: **We even read our Junk mail.**

   What correction should be made to this sentence?
   (1) replace <u>We</u> with <u>we</u>
   (2) replace <u>mail</u> with <u>Mail</u>
   (3) replace <u>Junk</u> with <u>junk</u>
   (4) no correction necessary

5. Sentence 8: **Reading doesn't just get Us through the day; it opens up a whole new world.**

   What correction should be made to this sentence?
   (1) replace <u>Us</u> with <u>us</u>
   (2) replace <u>day</u> with <u>Day</u>
   (3) replace <u>world</u> with <u>World</u>
   (4) no correction necessary

Answers are on page 336.

Word Choice

IN THIS CHAPTER YOU WILL LEARN:

- Which words are often confused (page 135)
- How to use these words correctly (page 135)

Remember, you are the boss, and words are your workers. You need to choose the right word for the job. This chapter will teach you not only which words cause problems but also how to use these words correctly.

COMMONLY CONFUSED WORDS		
Words	**Definitions**	**Sentences**
accept **except**	to receive something not including	Granny <u>accepted</u> a ride. Everyone saw <u>except</u> Megan.
affect **effect**	to influence; to cause change result	Frost <u>affects</u> the apples. The layoffs will have an <u>effect</u> on everyone.
already **all ready**	by now everyone is/was prepared	We <u>already</u> biked ten miles. We are <u>all ready</u> for dinner.
board **bored**	piece of wood tired of something	The <u>board</u> needs paint. Sue's job <u>bored</u> her.
borrow **lend**	to receive something that will be returned to give something that will be returned	Laura <u>borrowed</u> a book from Jen. She will <u>lend</u> me a pencil.
by **buy**	through, next to, not later than to purchase	We ran <u>by</u> the store. Where did you <u>buy</u> those shoes?
desert (noun) **desert (verb)** **dessert**	dry, sandy region to leave or abandon sweet food at the end of a meal	The Gobi <u>Desert</u> is in Asia. Did the soldier <u>desert</u> his post? He likes pie and ice cream for <u>dessert</u>.
hear **here**	listen to a place	We <u>hear</u> sounds. We put things <u>here</u> and there.
hole **whole**	an opening complete or full	There is a <u>hole</u> in your shirt. He ate the <u>whole</u> cake.
know **no**	to understand a negative response or an adjective that means "not one"	I <u>know</u> that you are upset. <u>No</u>, I won't do it. There is <u>no</u> way.

MORE COMMONLY CONFUSED WORDS

Words	Definitions	Sentences
brake break	to slow down to destroy a rest	<u>Brake</u> when you go downhill. Do not <u>break</u> the vase. We need a <u>break</u> from work.
hour our	time shows possession	Be ready in one <u>hour</u>. We need <u>our</u> worksheets.
knew new	understood latest different	She <u>knew</u> the assignment. That car is the <u>new</u> model. This is a <u>new</u> approach.
learn teach	to understand educate	He wants to <u>learn</u> about science. She will <u>teach</u> math to the class.
meat meet	animal product one can eat to gather, to greet, to touch	We eat <u>meat</u>. I will <u>meet</u> you at noon.
passed past	went by approved earlier time	Kay <u>passed</u> the food store. Congress <u>passed</u> the bill. That was in the <u>past</u>.
principle principal	rule or law head of school main	Our policy is based on <u>principles</u>. Ms. Marino is a school <u>principal</u>. The <u>principal</u> cause was bad wiring.
quiet quit quite	silence to give up, to stop very	Be <u>quiet</u> in the library. He <u>quit</u> the team. It is <u>quite</u> loud in here.
right write	correct record, inscribe	You have the <u>right</u> answer. I need to <u>write</u> a letter.
their there they're	shows possession a place contraction for *they are*	We need <u>their</u> notes. The book is over <u>there</u>. <u>They're</u> moving in June.
to too two	a preposition part of a verb in its infinitive form also extremely the number 2	He ran <u>to</u> the store. She wanted <u>to</u> run. Do you want dessert, <u>too</u>? He was driving <u>too</u> fast. I need <u>two</u> tires for my car.
weak week	not strong Sunday through Saturday (or 7 consecutive days)	He is a <u>weak</u> swimmer. The appointment is this <u>week</u>. The thief was caught a <u>week</u> later.)
wear where	put on a place	She will <u>wear</u> a sweater. <u>Where</u> is the book?
your you're	shows possession contraction for *you are*	We need <u>your</u> car. <u>You're</u> going to be late.

EXERCISE 1

Underline the correct word in each of the following sentences.

1. Rick will (except, accept) the award for best actor.
2. The doctor (all ready, already) gave me a blood test.
3. Will this witness (affect, effect) the trial?
4. His speech (bored, board) some people.
5. Will you (borrow, lend) me ten dollars for the movies?
6. I don't want to (by, buy) a new car now.
7. Do you want some ice cream for (desert, dessert)?
8. Did you (hear, here) the news?
9. A (desert, dessert) has few plants and little rainfall.
10. No one has a key to the safe, (accept, except) the owner.
11. The (whole, hole) team will go to the game.
12. Do you (know, no) how to fix a flat tire?

Answers are on page 336.

EXERCISE 2

Underline the correct word in each of the following sentences.

1. Please (teach, learn) me how to change the oil in my car.
2. What type of (meet, meat) is in this dish?
3. Smoking is the (principal, principle) reason for lung cancer.
4. People should be (quiet, quit, quite) in a movie theater.
5. I thought we parked the car (their, they're, there) by the light.
6. The lawyer is (to, two, too) confident that he will win this case.
7. Juan wants to buy (to, two, too) more tickets for the show.
8. Are you sure (their, there, they're) done with dinner?
9. Shantae wants to (learn, teach) Tara a new dance.
10. Dee wants to (quiet, quit, quite) the team and focus on her schoolwork.
11. Kate, make sure (your, you're) room is clean before you leave the house.
12. He had wanted a (brake, break) after working all night.
13. Nila needs to finish the proposal in one (our, hour).
14. The manager needs a (knew, new) training program.
15. For the (passed, past) two hundred years, our family has farmed this land.
16. Shantae will (right, write) another essay.
17. We need to borrow (their, there, they're) shovel.

18. Danzel is too (weak, week) to leave the hospital.

19. What are you going to (wear, where) to the dance?

20. (Your, You're) standing in my way.

Answers are on page 336.

IN THIS CHAPTER YOU HAVE LEARNED:

- Which words are often confused (page 135)
- How to use these words correctly (page 135)

Review sections that are difficult for you.

Chapter Review

EXERCISE 1

The following paragraph has words that are used incorrectly. Cross out the wrong words and write the right words in the margin.

Buying a car takes time and effort. First, the buyer must teach about the different cars that are on the market and decide what type of car she wants. She may need to lend money and get insurance, two. After the preparations, the buyer and salesperson meat to agree upon a price. If the buyer all ready nos a lot about the car, she may get a better deal. After the sale, even more paperwork is done. Many people are glad when the hole process is finally over.

Answers are on page 337.

EXERCISE 2

The following paragraph has words that are used incorrectly. Cross out the wrong words and write the right words in the margin.

Many boating accidents could be avoided if boaters learned important safety measures. Too often, motorboats dash buy shallow areas wear people are swimming. As a result, some states have all ready restricted boat traffic on lakes and rivers to protect not only swimmers, but also wildlife and shorelines. Many states also require instruction courses that cover piloting techniques, proper boater behavior, and important safety information. Boaters who no this material should be able two pilot there boats safely. Whether one is slowly navigating through a narrow strait or racing in the open seas, safety measures are important.

Answers are on page 337.

UNIT 4

SENTENCES AND PARAGRAPHS

Writing Clear Sentences

As a writer, you need to be sure that you express your thoughts clearly. Writing sentences is like giving someone directions. Sometimes what is obvious to you may not be so plain to the reader. This chapter will help you send a clear message. In addition, it will teach you to express ideas in many different ways.

Independent and Dependent Clauses

A clause is simply a group of words with a subject and a predicate. An independent clause expresses a complete thought and can be a sentence. A dependent clause does not express a complete thought and cannot be a sentence.

NOTE

Place a comma before a conjunction that joins two independent clauses.

Sample Sentences	**Independent Clauses** An **independent clause** expresses a complete thought.	**Dependent Clauses** A **dependent clause** does not express a complete thought.
Before Braden opened the gift, he read the card.	he read the card	before Braden opened the gift
Keegan ran to catch the train when he heard the whistle.	Keegan ran to catch the train	when he heard the whistle
Whenever I study hard, I do well on my tests.	I do well on my tests	whenever I study hard
Our boss announced the raise, and everyone cheered.	our boss announced the raise everyone cheered	—

Compound Sentences

A compound sentence can use a conjunction to combine two or more independent clauses.

Compound Sentences	Independent Clauses
Nu worked hard, so she could save her money.	Nu worked hard she could save her money
Claire moved out of her apartment, and she bought a house.	Claire moved out of her apartment she bought a house
Donzel wanted to go to school, but he couldn't leave work early.	Donzel wanted to go to school he couldn't leave work early

Keep in mind that not all conjunctions are the same. Note how they are used in the following table.

Conjunctions	Jobs	Compound Sentences
and	adds two equal statements	Dee worked two jobs, <u>and</u> she raised three children.
but, yet	show a difference, a contrast, or something unexpected	Kim wants to help, <u>but</u> she doesn't know how. Lee broke his arm, <u>yet</u> he still had fun.
or	shows an option	Jong won the lottery, <u>or</u> he got a huge raise.
for, so	• shows why something happened • shows cause and effect	Jack worked hard, <u>so</u> he could pay off his loans.

EXERCISE 1

Use a conjunction to combine the following clauses and form a compound sentence. Make sure you add a comma before the appropriate conjunction. Write your sentence in the space provided. There may be more than one correct answer.

SAMPLE: Kim wants to help her son with his homework. She doesn't know how to read.

<u>Kim wants to help her son with his homework, but she doesn't know how to read.</u>

1. Kira came to this country as an adult. She learned English as quickly as she could.

   _____

   _____

2. Lou wanted to buy a new car. He saved his money.

   _____

   _____

3. Snakes are not cuddly pets. Some people love them.

   _____

   _____

4. Many people order pizza for the Super Bowl. They prepare food before the game.

   _____

   _____

5. Yang is a great cook. She does not like to have friends over for dinner.

   _____

   _____

Answers are on page 337.

COMPOUND SENTENCES WITH SEMICOLONS

A compound sentence also can use a semicolon to combine two or more independent clauses. Use a semicolon, instead of a coordinating conjunction, to join independent clauses that are closely related.

Compound Sentences	Independent Clauses
Some people worship often; others do not.	some people worship often others do not
We ordered more food, drinks, and supplies; we still didn't have enough.	we ordered more food, drinks, and supplies we still didn't have enough
Many people went home; the true fans stayed to the end.	many people went home the true fans stayed to the end
We wore life jackets on the boat; the water was rough, and we are not good swimmers.	we wore life jackets on the boat the water was rough we are not good swimmers

EXERCISE 2

Use a semicolon to combine the following clauses and form a compound sentence. Write your sentence in the space provided.

SAMPLE: It is hard to stay in school. I work two jobs to pay my bills.
<u>It is hard to stay in school; I work two jobs to pay my bills.</u>

1. Junk food causes many problems. Obesity is a major issue for children and adults.

    _____

    _____

2. I need to save more money. My grocery bills and car payments are high these days.

    _____

    _____

3. Many fatal reactions occur every year. Food allergies are a big issue today.

    _____

    _____

4. Gas prices have skyrocketed. Many people are now walking or riding their bikes.

_____

_____

5. All states require car seats. They help keep children safe.

_____

_____

Answers are on page 338.

COMPOUND SENTENCES WITH CONJUNCTIVE ADVERBS

When you want to show the relationship between two independent clauses, use a conjunctive adverb. Semicolons are placed before the conjunctive adverb, and commas are placed after them.

Conjunctive Adverbs	Jobs	Compound Sentences
although even though however instead nonetheless	shows comparison or contrast	We had fun; however, we lost the game. Kedar didn't like the doctor's suggestions; nonetheless, he started to exercise more often.
besides in fact	gives more information	We didn't have enough supplies; in fact, our tour guide went back to get more food.
eventually finally meanwhile now still then	shows time relationship	Fakih saved enough money; now, he can afford a nice house. The driver took two wrong turns; meanwhile, we scrambled to find better directions.
as a result for example therefore thus	gives example or result	Many children do not play outside; as a result, obesity is a national problem. Some adults skip breakfast; for example, my friend rarely eats a decent meal in the morning.

EXERCISE 3

Use a conjunctive adverb to combine the following clauses and form a compound sentence. Make sure you add a semicolon before and a comma after the appropriate conjunctive adverb. Write your sentence in the space provided. There may be more than one correct answer.

SAMPLE: Iron pills can poison children. Adults must store the pills safely.
<u>Iron pills can poison children; therefore, adults must store the pills safely.</u>

1. The detective searched the crime scene, traced phone calls, and questioned suspects. No arrests have been made.

   _____

   _____

2. We were ready for a bad rush hour. The snow never came.

   _____

   _____

3. We wanted to go to the beach. We stayed home.

   _____

   _____

4. For years people thought that smoking was safe. We know that it causes cancer.

   _____

   _____

5. The game was delayed because of rain. The fans waited patiently.

   _____

   _____

6. Asthma is much more common these days. Almost 6 million children in America have asthma.

   _____

   _____

7. Many schools have reduced recess time. Children are often restless and distracted during class.

_____

_____

Answers are on page 338.

Complex Sentences

A complex sentence combines an independent clause with one or more dependent clauses. A dependent clause begins with a subordinating conjunction and gives information about the independent clause. When a dependent clause begins a sentence, use a comma after the last word in the clause.

Complex Sentences	Independent Clause	Dependent Clause
Russell broke the window **when** he banged on the door.	Russell broke the window	when he banged on the door
Katherine plays with Brie **whenever** they are together.	Katherine plays with Brie	whenever they are together
I bought milk **so that** Andrew could have a good breakfast.	I bought milk	so that Andrew could have a good breakfast
Jack will go to the game **if** it is raining.	Jack will go to the game	if it is raining
Since Vincent broke his leg, we have not traveled.	We have not traveled	since Vincent broke his leg

Subordinating conjunctions are used for specific situations. Note how they are used in the box below.

Subordinating Conjunctions	Jobs	Complex Sentences
after, before, once, since, until, when, whenever, while	time	<u>After</u> we went to the store, I remembered that we needed milk.
in order that, who, whose, whom, which, that, where, wherever	additional information	Jamie cancelled the party <u>that</u> we had planned for weeks.
although, even though, than, though, unless	contrast	<u>Even though</u> Kaila was exhausted, she couldn't fall asleep.
as, as if, as well as, as much as	comparison	Zeon wrote <u>as much as</u> he could remember.
because, so that	cause and effect	Locken studied hard <u>because</u> he wanted to pass his math test.

EXERCISE 4

Use a subordinate conjunction to combine the following clauses and form a complex sentence. Remember to use a comma when a dependent clause begins a sentence. Write your answer in the space provided. There may be more than one correct answer to a question.

SAMPLE: We have plenty of food and drinks. More people come.
Unless more people come, we have plenty of food and drinks.
or
We have plenty of food and drinks unless more people come.

1. I paid my debts. I felt a sense of relief.

   _____

   _____

2. Rose works two jobs. Juan will have to do more housework.

   _____

   _____

3. Kate is smart. She still needs to work hard.

   _____

   _____

4. I don't pass this test. I will not get my driver's license.

   _____

   _____

5. Salma will plant her garden. The soil and sunlight are good.

   _____

   _____

6. The landlord needs to fix our heat. The cold weather comes.

   _____

   _____

Answers are on page 338.

Run-On Sentences

A run-on sentence has two or more independent clauses that could stand alone. Instead, they form one sentence with improper punctuation.

There are five basic ways to fix a run-on sentence.

Run-on Sentences	Correction	Correct Sentences
Kit and Jenna rushed back home, they forgot the movie.	**Write two sentences.**	Kit and Jena rushed back home. They forgot the movie.
Kaila served the food, Allison cleaned up the mess.	**Use a coordinating conjunction after a comma.**	Kaila served the food, and Allison cleaned up the mess.
The concert lasted for hours the band even played in the rain.	**Use a semicolon between the clauses.**	The concert lasted for hours; the band even played in the rain.
We already covered this material the test was last week.	**Use a semicolon, conjunctive adverb, and comma between the clauses.**	We already covered this material; in fact, the test was last week.
The hikers will have to turn around they can't reach the summit by dark.	**Create one dependent clause and one independent clause.**	If they can't reach the summit by dark, the hikers will have to turn around.

EXERCISE 5

Rewrite the following run-on sentences to form new, correct sentences. There may be more than one correct answer for each question. In addition, correct sentences may have different meanings.

SAMPLE: We need to leave for the game, finish your lunch.

We need to leave for the game; finish your lunch.
or
Finish your lunch before we need to leave for the game.

1.   The housing crisis is hard on many families foreclosures are difficult.

_____

_____

2.   Save your energy it is a long walk.

_____

_____

3. Colin's leg is broken, we need to get help immediately.

_____

_____

4. Put on bug spray you go into the woods.

_____

_____

5. Make sure you are taking the medicine properly some medicines must be taken with food.

_____

_____

6. Flu shots are recommended for many people, the flu can be quite serious.

_____

_____

7. Jacob struggles with reading school is hard for him.

_____

_____

8. The candidates have different views on the issues, the debate should be interesting.

_____

_____

9. Karim dropped the heavy box it landed on his foot.

_____

_____

10. Gas prices have gone up, I can't pay my bills.

_____

_____

Answers are on page 339.

Parallel Structure

Parallel structure means that words with similar jobs in a sentence have the same form. Sentences with parallel structure are clear and easy to read. Check for parallel structure every time you have items in a series.

Not Parallel	Series	Parallel
Our boss <u>praises</u> workers, <u>giving</u> raises, and <u>allows</u> vacations.	**Verbs**	Our boss <u>praises</u> workers, <u>gives</u> raises, and <u>allows</u> vacations.
The resort has <u>good</u> food, <u>live</u> entertainment, and a <u>pool that is heated</u>.	**Adjectives**	The resort has <u>good</u> food, <u>live</u> entertainment, and a <u>heated</u> pool.
Parents must teach values <u>consciously</u>, <u>openly</u>, and <u>with consistence</u>.	**Adverbs**	Parents must teach values <u>consciously</u>, <u>openly</u>, and <u>consistently</u>.
Our friends will decide <u>to buy</u> a car, <u>to save</u> their money, or <u>go</u> on a trip. Clean <u>under the hood</u>, <u>behind the wheels</u>, and <u>the part in between the doors</u>.	**Phrases**	Our friends will decide <u>to buy</u> a car, <u>to save</u> their money, or <u>to go</u> on a trip. Clean <u>under the hood</u>, <u>behind the wheels</u>, and <u>between the doors</u>.

EXERCISE 6

Rewrite the following sentences. Make sure you use parallel structure.

SAMPLE: Before Brie got on the bus, she jumped out of bed, ate breakfast, and she got her backpack organized.
Before Brie got on the bus, she jumped out of bed, ate breakfast, and organized her backpack.

1. Max dressed up because he wanted to charm his girlfriend, to impress his friends, and please his parents.

_____

_____

2. Food that was free, great music, and good weather made the state fair a big hit.

_____

_____

3. People should save their money carefully, regularly, and with wisdom.

   _____

   _____

4. Tran who wants a quiet, bright place that is relaxing to study needs to look hard.

   _____

   _____

5. When you go to the food store, drive through town, over the bridge, and drive past the town pool.

   _____

   _____

6. Before they admitted that nicotine is addictive, cigarette manufacturers ignored scientific research, testified before Congress, and fighting lawsuits against them.

   _____

   _____

7. Many people in the community volunteer happily, repeatedly, and with kindness.

   _____

   _____

8. Many students look for a college with a good reputation, athletic programs, and a tuition that is reasonable.

   _____

   _____

9. Various books, online computers, and materials that are for children help the public libraries attract many different people.

   _____

   _____

10. Athletes who want a large, open gym that is well designed should go to the health club around the corner.

_____

_____

Answers are on page 339.

CONSISTENT VERB TENSE

The verb tense, which tells when something happens, generally should be the same throughout a sentence or paragraph.

Example

Confusing	Consistent Verb Tense
On Fridays, Wolf <u>went</u> for a stroll, and he <u>stops</u> by the bread store.	On Fridays, Wolf <u>goes</u> for a stroll, and he <u>stops</u> by the bread store.
Whenever a comet <u>appears</u>, many people <u>bought</u> telescopes.	Whenever a comet <u>appears</u>, many people <u>buy</u> telescopes.

EXERCISE 7

Choose the correct tense for the underlined verb. Write your answer in the space provided.

1. Every Friday, Jake orders pizza, and he <u>watched</u> a movie. _____

2. Next week, Kim will clean the basement, and she <u>cut</u> the lawn. _____

3. Lee bought a new computer and <u>will have moved</u> his office last month. _____

4. Next year, Congress <u>passed</u> a welfare reform bill, and the president will sign it. _____

5. On Monday, she walked into the store and <u>acts</u> like she owned the place. _____

6. Last week, leaders of the warring nations signed a peace treaty, and the fighting <u>ends</u>. _____

7. In the next few years, business leaders <u>invested</u> more money downtown and will bring more jobs to the region. _____

8. Jamestown, the first permanent English settlement in America, lures various tourists and <u>attracted</u> many historians every year. _____

9. In Haiti, a military group overturned the democratic government and <u>establishes</u> a dictatorship. _____

10. Chi's parents took her out of the public school and <u>teach</u> her at home last year. _____

Answers are on page 340.

Misplaced Modifiers

A modifier is a word or group of words that describes something else in the sentence. When modifiers are misplaced, sentences are confusing. To keep sentences clear, always place modifiers near the words that they describe.

Misplaced Modifier	Issue	Clear Sentence
After we searched for a sitter, we found a nice woman to care for our children <u>frantically</u>.	Is the nice woman frantically caring for the children?	After we <u>frantically</u> searched for a sitter, we found a nice woman to care for the children.
Rachel wanted to buy a safe car <u>with a child on the way</u>.	Does the car have a child on the way?	<u>With a child on the way</u>, Rachel wanted to buy a safe car.
Our coach yelled at the umpire <u>who rarely loses his temper</u>.	Does the coach or the umpire rarely lose his temper?	Our coach, <u>who rarely loses his temper</u>, yelled at the umpire.
<u>Soaring toward the goal</u>, Kaila stopped a hard shot.	Was Kaila or the shot soaring?	Kaila stopped a hard shot that was <u>soaring toward the goal</u>.
Jenna <u>almost</u> read 200 pages.	How do you *almost* read?	Jenna read <u>almost</u> 200 pages.
Colin <u>nearly</u> ate an entire pizza.	How do you *nearly* eat?	Colin ate <u>nearly</u> an entire pizza.

EXERCISE 8

Rewrite the following sentences so that the meaning is clear. Some questions have more than one possible answer.

SAMPLE: Haley <u>nearly saw</u> twenty deer when she was walking in the woods.
Haley <u>saw nearly</u> twenty deer when she was walking in the woods.

1. Luke barely drove the car 1,000 miles before the transmission died.

_____

_____

2. Children often watch TV until their parents come home after school.

   _____

   _____

3. Homes are being moved to higher ground with flood damage.

   _____

   _____

4. The working poor often cannot afford good health care struggling to pay the bills.

   _____

   _____

5. I called in sick to work tired from the flu.

   _____

   _____

6. Lim found a good plumber to fix his sink unintentionally.

   _____

   _____

> **NOTE**
>
> Place *almost, nearly, only, just, hardly, barely, even,* and *often* near the words they describe.

7. Dr. Tim tells people to eat a low-fat diet and exercise with weight problems.

   _____

   _____

8. Some people are frustrated with HMOs who want to choose their own doctors.

   _____

   _____

9. The Chair of the Federal Reserve will raise interest rates concerned about the risk of inflation.

   _____

   _____

10. Trained to help the visually impaired, some people use dogs.

_____

_____

Answers are on page 340.

Dangling Modifiers

A dangling modifier has nothing to describe. You must reword the sentence to give the modifier meaning.

Dangling Modifier	Issue	Clear Sentence
Driving to the store, a deer ran across the road.	Was the deer driving?	When we were driving to the store, a deer ran across the road.
Sailing on the lake, a beautiful sunset filled the sky.	Was the sunset sailing?	While we were sailing on the lake, a beautiful sunset filled the sky.

EXERCISE 9

Rewrite the following sentences so that the meaning is clear. Each question has more than one correct answer.

1. While climbing up the mountain face, my backpack slipped.

_____

_____

2. Searching for clues to the crime, the police car was stolen.

_____

_____

3. Tired and hungry, our museum tour ended.

_____

_____

4. Checking my watch, the sun came out from behind the clouds.

   _____

   _____

5. Frustrated with campaign funding, reform bills quickly passed through Congress.

   _____

   _____

REMEMBER

Remember these <u>facts about modifiers</u>:

- Always place modifiers near the words that they describe.
- Sentences with misplaced or dangling modifiers must be reworded.

6. Annoyed by Jamel's attitude, the raises stopped.

   _____

   _____

7. With steady hours and good pay, Ty searched the want ads for a job.

   _____

   _____

8. Running to catch the bus, my briefcase spilled all over the sidewalk.

   _____

   _____

9. Angered by the slow response, the ambulance finally arrived at the scene.

   _____

   _____

10. Fresh off the delivery truck, the salesperson showed us the new cars.

   _____

   _____

Answers are on page 341.

Confusing Pronouns

Pronouns substitute for nouns. When you write, make sure the reader clearly understands which word the pronoun references. An antecedent is simply the word that the pronoun replaces.

Confusing Pronouns	Issue	Clear Sentences
When Anwar entered the classroom, he was nervous. <u>They</u> were watching him.	**unclear antecedent** Who was watching?	When Anwar entered the classroom, he was nervous. <u>The students</u> were watching him.
The staff asked me about the program that has great graphics. <u>They</u> should help with the account.	**unclear antecedent** Does *they* refer to the staff or the graphics?	The staff asked me about the program that has great graphics. <u>It</u> should help with the account.
Before Ms. Tran hired the new clerks, <u>they</u> interviewed each person.	**pronoun shift** *Ms. Tran* is singular, while *they* is plural. It seems unlikely that the new clerks did the interviewing.	Before Ms. Tran hired the new clerks, <u>she</u> interviewed each person.

EXERCISE 10

Rewrite the following sentences. Make sure that the pronouns are used correctly and the sentences are clear. Some questions have more than one correct answer.

1. Many parents are concerned about gangs. They have teamed up with the local police and schools to improve safety.

   _____

   _____

2. Our food store caters to busy lives. They open early, close late, and carry prepared meals.

   _____

   _____

3. When Katrina wore her new uniform to the soccer match, she knew it would be exciting.

_____

_____

4. Before one interviews for a job, you need to learn about the company.

_____

_____

5. In 1846, James Smithson gave a fortune to help form the Smithsonian Institution. Today, they operate many museums in Washington, DC.

_____

_____

Answers are on page 341.

Rewriting Sentences

Rewriting sentences is like reorganizing a closet. Using the same space, you need to reorganize the items effectively. The GED will test your ability to rewrite sentences. Although the words may change, the meaning of the new sentence must be the same.

STEPS FOR REWRITING SENTENCES

1. Find the main idea(s).
2. Find the relationship between ideas.
3. Rewrite the sentence. (Some words may be changed or omitted in the new sentence.)
4. Make sure that the new sentence sends the same message as the original.
5. Check the grammar in the new sentence.

Practice will make rewriting sentences easier.

Original Sentence	New Sentence
The store was flooded by shoppers with bags in hand.	Shoppers with bags in hand flooded the store.
Children's toys, car seats, and cribs are safer because of federal safety guidelines.	Federal safety guidelines have made children's toys, car seats, and cribs safer.

EXERCISE 11

Rewrite the following sentences as directed. Some sentences have more than one correct answer.

1. Hunters slaughter elephants whose ivory tusks are valuable.
   Rewrite the sentence beginning with <u>Because ivory tusks are valuable</u>

   _____

   _____

2. Wildlife groups work hard to save the endangered species, but some animals may not survive.
   Rewrite the sentence beginning with <u>Although wildlife groups work hard to save</u>

   _____

   _____

3. Children are affected by the violence that they see on TV.
   Rewrite the sentence beginning with <u>TV violence</u>

   _____

   _____

4. Car owners must be prepared to spend a lot of money; gas, maintenance, and insurance are expensive.
   Rewrite the sentence beginning with <u>Gas, maintenance, and insurance are expensive</u>

   _____

   _____

5. Back support is important whenever one lifts something heavy.
   Rewrite the sentence beginning with <u>Whenever one lifts something heavy</u>

   _____

   _____

6. Sometimes persons are infected by rabid animals.
   Rewrite the sentence beginning with <u>Rabid animals</u>

   _____

   _____

7. Some persons earn bad credit ratings because they do not pay their bills on time.
   Rewrite the sentence beginning with <u>Because they do not pay</u>

   _____

   _____

8. Financial planners help people with bad debts.
   Rewrite the sentence beginning with <u>People with bad debts</u>

   _____

   _____

9. Over time, alcoholism can destroy the liver and other organs.
   Rewrite the sentence beginning with <u>The liver and other organs</u>

   _____

   _____

10. Jim and Pat saved money each year so their child would go to college.
    Rewrite the sentence beginning with <u>Because their child</u>

    _____

    _____

11. Because many women do not receive appropriate prenatal care, their babies do not get the medical treatment that they need.
    Rewrite this sentence beginning with <u>Babies do</u>

    _____

    _____

12. In an effort to track terrorists internationally, American officials tried to cooperate more effectively with other world leaders.
    Rewrite the sentence beginning with <u>American officials</u>

    _____

    _____

13. Physicians across the nation are trying to address the poor eating habits and sedentary lifestyles that have made childhood obesity an epidemic in America.
Rewrite the sentence beginning with <u>Because childhood obesity is an epidemic in America</u>

_____

_____

14. Hospitals are struggling to recruit and retain nurses because of a severe nursing shortage, which is expected to worsen in the next few years.
Rewrite the sentence beginning with <u>As a result of</u>

_____

_____

15. Many students work hard to balance different aspects of their lives: school, work, and family life demand a great amount of the students' time and energy.
Rewrite the sentence beginning with <u>School, work, and family life</u>

_____

_____

Answers are on page 342.

Combining Sentences

The GED will ask you to combine two sentences and form one new sentence. Combining sentences is like reorganizing a closet, as well. However, you generally need to send the same message with fewer words.

COMBINING SENTENCES PART I

One way to combine sentences is to use connectors. Coordinating conjunctions (and, but, nor, or), conjunctive adverbs (therefore, now), and semicolons connect independent clauses. Sentences are combined in different ways to keep the original meaning. Note the jobs for connectors that are listed below.

CONNECTORS

Coordinating Conjunctions	Conjunctive Adverbs	Job
and	also, likewise, moreover, besides, in addition, furthermore	Add two equal statements.
but, yet	nonetheless, however, still, instead, nevertheless, though, although	Show a difference, a contrast, or something unexpected.
for, so	thus, therefore, consequently	Show why something happens, connect cause and effect.
____	now, next, when, finally, meanwhile	Show when something happens.
or	_____	Show an option or choice.
nor	_____	Show that neither option or choice is good.

Conjunctive adverbs *now, next, then, finally,* and *meanwhile* show when something happens.
A semicolon (;) shows that the two statements are related.
Insert a comma before a coordinating conjunction (, but).
Insert a semicolon before and a comma after a conjunctive adverb (; however,).

Examples

Original Sentences	Relationship	New Sentence
Tran wants to get her eyes checked. She needs new glasses.	**additional information**	Tran wants to get her eyes checked; she needs new glasses.
Phil wants to buy a house. He cannot afford a down payment.	**difference or contrast**	Phil wants to buy a house, **but** he cannot afford a down payment.
Juan's car would not start. He had to walk to work.	**cause and effect**	Juan's car would not start, **so** he had to walk to work.
Max called home. Mirabel e-mailed her parents at the same time.	**when something happened**	Max called home; **meanwhile,** Mirabel e-mailed her parents.
Haley can pick up the report before work. Faith can pick up the report on the way home, as well.	**an option or choice**	Haley can pick up the report before work, **or** Faith can pick it up on the way home.

EXERCISE 12

In the following exercises, combine two sentences to form one new sentence.

SAMPLE: We bought a lot of food at the store. We forgot to buy milk.

We bought a lot of food at the store, **but** we forgot to buy milk.
or
We bought a lot of food at the store; **however**, we forgot to buy milk.

1. Kay was struggling to pay her bills. She took an extra job on weekends.

   _____

   _____

2. Han wants to let her daughter play outside. There is too much violence in their neighborhood.

   _____

   _____

3. Tim drops Greg off at daycare in the morning. Shavone picks Greg up after work.

   _____

   _____

4. Ray wants to star in the school play. He has not learned his lines.

   _____

   _____

5. Eve wants to learn a new software program by Friday. She needs to prepare for her presentation, which is tomorrow.

   _____

   _____

6. Credit card debt can destroy a family's finances. It is better to buy only what one can afford to pay in cash.

   _____

   _____

7. Most people know the dangers of smoking. Teenage tobacco use continues to increase.

   _____

   _____

8. Politicians keep talking about cutting government spending. Few people want to give up the government services that they use.

   _____

   _____

9. The tax code in America is complex. Many Americans must pay a professional to do their taxes.

   _____

   _____

10. Faith needs more training for her job. She is taking a computer class on weekends.

    _____

    _____

Answers are on page 342.

COMBINING SENTENCES PART II

Sometimes you will use phrases or dependent clauses to combine two sentences. After you have found the relationship between the two sentences, write a new sentence that sends the same message. Note that some words may be changed or deleted to make the new sentence clear.

Original Sentences	Relationship	New Sentence
The train rates change. They drop after rush hour.	**time**	After rush hour, the train rates drop.
Some cars are easy targets for thieves. They are stolen more often than other cars.	**additional information**	Some cars that are easy targets for thieves are stolen more often than other cars.
Most people know that seat belts save lives. Many drivers still do not wear them.	**contrast**	Although most people know that seat belts save lives, many drivers still do not wear them.
Greg likes to visit the zoo. Vera likes the zoo just as much.	**comparison**	Vera likes to visit the zoo as much as Greg does.
Industrial waste poured into rivers for years. We need to spend time and money cleaning up the environment.	**cause and effect**	Because industrial waste poured into rivers for years, we have to spend time and money cleaning up the environment.

COMMON SIGNAL WORDS FOR CLAUSES	
Relationship	**Subordinating Conjunctions**
Time	after, before, once, since, until, when, whenever, while
Additional Information	in order that, who, whose, whom, which, that, where, wherever
Contrast	although, even though, than, though, unless
Comparison	as, as if, as well as, as much as
Cause and Effect	because, so that

EXERCISE 13

For each question, combine the sentences using phrases or dependent clauses. Write the new sentence in the space provided. There is more than one correct answer for each question.

1. Matt's mom came home from work. He was excited to see her.

    _____

    _____

2. We were sitting at the stoplight, and we could hear music blaring from another car. The car was across the street.

    _____

    _____

3. Salma had a bad cold. Salma's mother could not leave her at day-care.

    _____

    _____

4. Anh finished his test in less than thirty minutes. He did not have many correct answers.

    _____

    _____

5. The lights on a school bus flash. Cars must stop so that students can exit the bus safely.

    _____

    _____

6. Nathan paints landscapes well. Kaila can paint them just as well.

    _____

    _____

7. The tornado whipped through the town. People huddled in their basements hoping they would be safe.

    _____

    _____

8. Very few people voted in the primary elections. The elections will determine the Republican candidates.

    _____

    _____

9. Wolf wanted to swim to cool off from the hot weather. The water in the pool was too cold.

    _____

    _____

10. Many people in the Midwest desperately need flood relief. The politicians promised to give the relief a month ago.

    _____

    _____

11. Jenna struggled to complete her assignments for school. She needed to work two jobs to help support her younger siblings.

    _____

    _____

12. Maharan traveled to India to visit his family for several weeks. He decided to live there permanently.

    _____

    _____

13. Before Colin filed the suit, he tried to settle his complaint with the store owner. The owner refused to give Colin a refund—even a partial one.

    _____

14. Americans are concerned about terrorism, the economy, and the threat of war. The stock market is down, and investors are getting nervous.

    _____

    _____

15. Life-threatening food allergies are much more prevalent today than they were twenty years ago. Doctors still do not understand completely how food allergies develop or how to prevent them.

    _____

    _____

Answers are on page 343.

Who, Which, and *That*

Who, which, and *that* have specific jobs. Note how they are used in the chart below.

Signal Words	Job	Examples
Who, Whom, Whose	refer to people	Lee, <u>who</u> won the race, trained for years.
Which	refers to things and animals (nonrestrictive clauses)	My car, <u>which</u> is falling apart, needs new tires.
That	refers to things and animals (restrictive clauses)	The house <u>that</u> I want to buy is for sale.

Some clauses simply give more information. Other clauses help identify the noun. A clause that helps to identify the noun is called a restrictive clause. The information is so important that it cannot be separated from the noun. *Restrictive clauses do not use commas.*

Examples

Restrictive Clauses

1. The doctor <u>who performed my surgery</u> was great.

   There are many doctors. *Who performed my surgery* restricts the noun and tells which doctor was great.

2. The light <u>that burned out</u> needs to be replaced.

   There are many lights. *That burned out* restricts the noun and tells which light needs to be replaced.

Nonrestrictive Clauses

3. My house, <u>which I just painted</u>, is in great shape.

   The fact that the house was painted is not important in identifying the house. The reader knows which house it is—*my house.*

EXERCISE 14

Underline the correct signal word for the following sentences. Check your work and read the correct answers aloud.

1. The lawyer (who, which) took my case is an old friend.

2. The geese (who, that) live in the park damage the grass.

3. Farmer Rick's barn, (which, that) needs repair, is partly on my land.

4. Lynne, (who, which) is my parents' friend, lives in New York.

5. Khan wants to find a job (which, that) will pay him more money.

6. Ahmed needs a friend (that, whom) he can trust.

7. Lung cancer (that, which) kills many people, often can be prevented.

8. I told Dave a joke (which, that) he had not heard before.

9. Some soldiers (that, who) served in the Persian Gulf War are sick.

10. Joe wants to buy a dog (that, which) will be good with children.

Answers are on page 344.

IN THIS CHAPTER YOU HAVE LEARNED:

- How to write sentences with independent and dependent clauses (page 141)
- How to write compound sentences (page 142)
- How to use conjunctions (page 142)
- How to use conjunctive adverbs (page 145)
- How to write complex sentences (page 147)
- How to correct run-on sentences and comma splices (page 149)
- How to create parallel structure (page 151)
- How to use consistent verb tense (page 153)
- How to correct misplaced and dangling modifiers (page 154)
- How to correct confusing pronouns (page 158)
- How to rewrite sentences (page 159)
- How to combine sentences (page 162)
- How to use *who, which,* and *that* (page 170)

Review sections that are difficult for you.

Chapter Review

EXERCISE 1

Read the paragraphs and answer the questions that follow.

<u>Items 1 through 11</u> refer to the following paragraphs.

(1) Across the nation, developers are discovering rural areas and create new communities. (2) Where farms and orchards once stood, townhouses and strip malls now dominate the land. (3) Although these new developments delight some people, they frustrate others. (4) New housing changes property values, crowds schools, and local services are burdened.

(5) Some government leaders are working hard to balance the need for more housing with the desire to preserve a rural setting. (6) In Montgomery County, Maryland, county leaders established a preservation project. (7) The project protects over 93,000 acres of land from development. (8) Many people want the preservation project to continue, but others want it to end. (9) Farmers, who own much of the land, are losing money that is preserved. (10) Meanwhile, developers want to use the land to create new housing, office space, and stores for retail. (11) They insist that effective use of the land could bring jobs and money to the county. (12) This debate will rage for years between developers and preservationists.

1. Sentence 1: **Across the nation, developers are discovering rural <u>areas and create</u> new communities.**

   What is the best way to write the underlined portion of the sentence? If you think the original is the best way, choose option (1).

   (1) areas and create
   (2) areas will create
   (3) areas and creating
   (4) areas; create
   (5) areas and had created

2. Sentence 2: **Where farms and orchards once stood, townhouses and strip malls now dominate the land.**

   If you rewrote the sentence beginning with

   <u>Townhouses and strip malls</u>

   the next word should be

   (1) land
   (2) farms
   (3) where
   (4) now
   (5) once

3. Sentence 3: **Although these new developments delight some people, they frustrate others.**

   If you rewrote the sentence beginning with

   <u>These new developments delight some people</u>

   the next word(s) should be

   (1) , but
   (2) , nor
   (3) ; now,
   (4) ; therefore,
   (5) , so

4. Sentence 4: **New housing changes property values, crowds schools, and <u>local services are burdened.</u>**

   Which of the following is the best way to write the underlined portion of the sentence? If you think that the original is best, choose option (1).

   (1) local services are burdened.
   (2) local services are burdening.
   (3) burdening local services.
   (4) burdened local services.
   (5) burdens local services.

5. Sentence 5: **Some government leaders are working hard to balance the need for more housing with the desire to preserve a rural setting.**

   What correction should be made to this sentence?

   (1) insert a comma after *housing*
   (2) replace *are working* with *worked*
   (3) insert a comma after *leaders*
   (4) move *with the desire* after *setting*
   (5) no correction necessary

6. Sentences 6 and 7: **In Montgomery County, Maryland, county leaders established a preservation project. The project protects over 93,000 acres of land from development.**

   The most effective combination of sentences 6 and 7 would include which of the following word groups?

   (1) ; however, the
   (2) , but the
   (3) , which protects
   (4) who protects
   (5) ; nonetheless, the

7. Sentence 8: **Many people want the preservation project to continue, but others want it to end.**

   If you rewrote sentence 8 beginning with

   <u>Although many people</u>

   the next word(s) should be

   (1) however
   (2) it
   (3) but
   (4) others
   (5) want

8. Sentence 9: **Farmers, who own much of the land, are losing money that is preserved.**

   What correction should be made to this sentence?

   (1) move *that is preserved* after *land*
   (2) remove the comma after *Farmers*
   (3) insert a comma after *money*
   (4) change *own* to *owns*
   (5) no correction necessary

9. Sentence 10: **Meanwhile, developers want to use the land to create new housing, office space, and stores for retail.**

   What correction should be made to this sentence?

   (1) remove the comma after *meanwhile*
   (2) remove the comma after *space*
   (3) change *stores for retail* to *retail stores*
   (4) change *want* to *wants*
   (5) no correction necessary

10. Sentence 11: **They insist that effective use of the land could bring jobs and money to the county.**

    What correction should be made to this sentence?

    (1) insert a comma after *jobs*
    (2) change *they* to *it*
    (3) change *insist* to *insists*
    (4) move *to the county* after *land*
    (5) no correction necessary

11. Sentence 12: **This debate will rage for years between developers and preservationists.**

    What correction should be made to this sentence?

    (1) insert a comma after *developers*
    (2) move *between developers and preservationists* after *debate*
    (3) change *rage* to *rages*
    (4) move *for years* after *developers*
    (5) no correction necessary

Answers are on page 345.

EXERCISE 2

Read the paragraphs and answer the questions that follow.

<u>Questions 1 through 9</u> refer to the following paragraphs.

(1) Home parties are making a comeback. (2) These parties are used to sell products. (3) In the traditional home party, a sales representative invites people to purchase goods with friends and neighbors while socializing. (4) Tupperware has sold its products through home parties for years, but now many different companies use this technique to market their goods. (5) At home parties today, sales representatives peddle everything from baskets to computers.

(6) This sales trend has developed for a number of reasons. (7) The trend started in the early nineties. (8) Many parents became sales representatives to supplement their family income. (9) Busy lifestyles have encouraged some people to shop in these social settings. (10) Likewise, an increasing inventory of goods have made home parties more inviting. (11) Whatever the reason, this is a trend that will continue.

1. Sentences 1 and 2: **Home parties are making a comeback. These parties are used to sell products.**

   The most effective combination of sentences 1 and 2 would include which of the following word groups?

   (1) comeback, but
   (2) comeback; however,
   (3) parties that are used
   (4) home, which parties are
   (5) Although home parties are

2. Sentence 3: **In the traditional home party, a sales representative invites people to purchase goods with friends and neighbors while socializing.**

   What correction should be made to this sentence?

   (1) insert a comma after *friends*
   (2) move *with friends and neighbors* after *socializing*
   (3) remove the comma after *party*
   (4) replace *invites* with *invited*
   (5) replace *socializing* with *socializes*

3. Sentence 4: **Tupperware has sold its products through home parties for years, but now many different companies use this technique to market their goods.**

   If you rewrote this sentence beginning with

   Although Tupperware has sold its products through home parties for years

   the next word(s) should be

   (1) use this
   (2) , but now
   (3) ; however, now
   (4) , now many
   (5) because many

4. Sentence 5: **At home parties today, sales representatives peddle everything from baskets to computers.**

   What correction should be made to this sentence?

   (1) remove the comma after *today*
   (2) replace *parties* with *party's*
   (3) insert a comma after *baskets*
   (4) replace *peddle* with *will peddle*
   (5) no correction necessary

5. Sentences 6 and 7: **This sales trend has developed for a number of reasons. The trend started in the early nineties.**

   The most effective combination of these sentences would include which of the following word groups?

   (1) trend, which started
   (2) reasons, but
   (3) reasons; therefore,
   (4) Even though this sales
   (5) reasons, so the

6. Sentence 8: **Many <u>parents became sales</u> representatives to supplement their family income.**

   Which of the following is the best way to write the underlined portion of the sentence? If you think that the original is best, choose option (1).

   (1) parents became sales
   (2) parents, became sales
   (3) parents will become sales
   (4) parents' became sales
   (5) parents have become

7. Sentence 9: **Busy lifestyles have encouraged some people to shop in these social settings.**

   If you rewrote this sentence beginning with

   <u>Some people who have busy lifestyles</u>

   the next word(s) would be

   (1) , and
   (2) ; nonetheless
   (3) have been encouraged
   (4) shop
   (5) social settings

8. Sentence 10: **Likewise, an increasing inventory of goods have made home parties more inviting.**

   What correction should be made to this sentence?

   (1) remove the comma after *likewise*
   (2) replace *parties* with *party's*
   (3) insert a comma after *goods*
   (4) replace *have* with *has*
   (5) no correction necessary

9. Sentence 11: **Whatever the reason, this is a trend that will continue.**

   What correction should be made to this sentence?

   (1) remove the comma after *reason*
   (2) replace *is* with *was*
   (3) replace *that* with *which*
   (4) replace *will continue* with *continued*
   (5) no correction necessary

Answers are on page 345.

Chapters 1 Through 9

Overview

The setup for this practice section is similar to an actual GED exam. However, this practice section will test only what you learned in Chapters 1 through 9. The actual GED exam will test all of the information in this book. (See the Pretest on page 7 and the Posttest on page 279.)

DIRECTIONS

1. This practice test has five passages with numbered sentences. The sentences may have errors, or they may be correct as written. First, read the paragraph. Then, answer the related questions. Choose the best answer for each question. The best answer should be consistent with the point of view and verb tense that is used throughout the paragraph.

2. Answer every question. If you are not sure of the answer, make a logical guess.

3. Write your answers to the questions on the answer grid. For each question, mark the number that matches the answer you chose.

EXAMPLE

Sentence 1: Parents need to give there children a lot of attention.

What correction should be made to this sentence?

(1) replace *Parents* with *Parents'*

(2) change *there* to *their*

(3) replace *need* with *needed*

(4) insert a comma after *children*

(5) no correction necessary

1. ① ● ③ ④ ⑤

In this sentence, *their* is the correct word to use.

Answer Sheet

PRACTICE

1. ① ② ③ ④ ⑤	26. ① ② ③ ④ ⑤
2. ① ② ③ ④ ⑤	27. ① ② ③ ④ ⑤
3. ① ② ③ ④ ⑤	28. ① ② ③ ④ ⑤
4. ① ② ③ ④ ⑤	29. ① ② ③ ④ ⑤
5. ① ② ③ ④ ⑤	30. ① ② ③ ④ ⑤
6. ① ② ③ ④ ⑤	31. ① ② ③ ④ ⑤
7. ① ② ③ ④ ⑤	32. ① ② ③ ④ ⑤
8. ① ② ③ ④ ⑤	33. ① ② ③ ④ ⑤
9. ① ② ③ ④ ⑤	34. ① ② ③ ④ ⑤
10. ① ② ③ ④ ⑤	35. ① ② ③ ④ ⑤
11. ① ② ③ ④ ⑤	36. ① ② ③ ④ ⑤
12. ① ② ③ ④ ⑤	37. ① ② ③ ④ ⑤
13. ① ② ③ ④ ⑤	38. ① ② ③ ④ ⑤
14. ① ② ③ ④ ⑤	39. ① ② ③ ④ ⑤
15. ① ② ③ ④ ⑤	40. ① ② ③ ④ ⑤
16. ① ② ③ ④ ⑤	41. ① ② ③ ④ ⑤
17. ① ② ③ ④ ⑤	42. ① ② ③ ④ ⑤
18. ① ② ③ ④ ⑤	43. ① ② ③ ④ ⑤
19. ① ② ③ ④ ⑤	44. ① ② ③ ④ ⑤
20. ① ② ③ ④ ⑤	45. ① ② ③ ④ ⑤
21. ① ② ③ ④ ⑤	46. ① ② ③ ④ ⑤
22. ① ② ③ ④ ⑤	47. ① ② ③ ④ ⑤
23. ① ② ③ ④ ⑤	48. ① ② ③ ④ ⑤
24. ① ② ③ ④ ⑤	49. ① ② ③ ④ ⑤
25. ① ② ③ ④ ⑤	50. ① ② ③ ④ ⑤

Directions: Choose the best answer for each question.

Questions 1 through 11 refer to the following passage.

(A)

(1) For the past few decades, Americans neglect to save enough money. (2) People who struggle to pay their bills each month can't imagine saving a little extra for the future but they must. (3) A down payment for a home, college tuition, and retirement are major milestones in many peoples lives. (4) Likewise, a job loss or disability are an awful financial burden. (5) Unfortunately, many Americans need to save more to meet his financial goals and to weather difficult situations.

(B)

(6) With discipline and careful financial planning, Americans can save more money. (7) First, they must create an emergency fund. (8) This fund holds enough money to cover expenses for three to six months. (9) Next, they should pay off credit card debts which have high interest rates. (10) Instead of saving for the future many people are trapped paying their bills. (11) The high interest rates for credit cards deplete potential savings and make it difficult to get ahead. (12) Once an emergency fund is created and credit card debts are eliminated, Americans can focus on long-term goals such as a home college, or retirement. (13) Some financial planners offer free counseling that learns people to make saving a way of life.

1. Sentence 1: **For the past few decades, Americans neglect to save enough money.**

   Which of the following is the best way to write the underlined portion of the sentence? If you think the original is best, choose option (1)

   (1) neglect
   (2) will neglect
   (3) have neglected
   (4) will have neglected
   (5) had neglected

2. Sentence 2: **People who struggle to pay their bills each month can't imagine saving a little extra for the future but they must.**

   Which of the following is the best way to write the underlined portion of the sentence? If you think the original is the best way, choose option (1).

   (1) future but
   (2) future; But
   (3) future. But
   (4) future: but
   (5) future, but

3. Sentence 3: **A down payment for a home, college tuition, and retirement are major milestones in many peoples lives**.

   What correction should be made to this sentence?

   (1) insert a comma after retirement
   (2) replace are with is
   (3) remove the comma after home
   (4) replace peoples with people's
   (5) no correction is necessary

4. Sentence 4: **Likewise, a job loss or disability are an awful financial burden.**

   What correction should be made to this sentence?

   (1) remove the comma after likewise
   (2) replace are with is
   (3) insert a comma after loss
   (4) replace job with Job
   (5) no correction is necessary

5. Sentence 5: **Unfortunately, many Americans need to save more to meet his financial goals and to weather difficult situations.**

   What correction should be made to this sentence?

   (1) remove the comma after Unfortunately
   (2) replace Americans with American's
   (3) insert a comma after goals
   (4) replace his with their
   (5) no correction necessary

6. Sentence 6: **With discipline and careful financial planning, Americans can save more money.**

What correction should be made to this sentence?

(1) remove the comma after <u>planning</u>
(2) replace <u>can</u> with <u>cans</u>
(3) replace <u>Americans</u> with <u>Americans'</u>
(4) insert a comma after <u>discipline</u>
(5) no correction necessary

7. Sentences 7 and 8: **First, they must create an emergency fund. This fund holds enough money to cover expenses for three to six months.**

The most effective combination of sentences 7 and 8 would include which of the following word groups?

(1) fund, but holds
(2) fund, and which holds
(3) fund however holds
(4) fund that holds
(5) fund, this fund holds

8. Sentence 9: **Next, they should pay off credit card <u>debts which</u> have high interest rates.**

Which of the following is the best way to write the underlined portion? If you think the original is the best way, choose option (1).

(1) debts which
(2) debts, that
(3) debts, which
(4) debts. Which
(5) debts: that

9. Sentence 10: **Instead of saving for the future many people are trapped paying their bills.**

What correction should be made to this sentence?

(1) insert comma after <u>future</u>
(2) replace <u>are</u> with <u>is</u>
(3) replace <u>their</u> with <u>there</u>
(4) insert a comma after <u>trapped</u>
(5) no change is necessary

10. Sentence 11: **The high interest rates for credit cards deplete potential savings and make it difficult to get ahead.**

What correction should be made to this sentence?

(1) replace <u>make</u> with <u>makes</u>
(2) insert a comma after <u>cards</u>
(3) replace <u>deplete</u> with <u>depletes</u>
(4) insert <u>have</u> before <u>deplete</u>
(5) no change is necessary

11. Sentence 12: **Once an emergency fund is created and credit card debts are eliminated, Americans can focus on long-term goals such as a home college, or retirement.**

What correction should be made to this sentence?

(1) replace <u>is</u> with <u>are</u>
(2) remove the comma after <u>eliminated</u>
(3) replace <u>can focus</u> with <u>focused</u>
(4) insert a comma after <u>home</u>
(5) no correction is necessary

12. Sentence 13: **Some financial planners offer free counseling that learns people to make saving a way of life.**

What correction should be made to this sentence?

(1) replace <u>learns</u> with <u>teaches</u>
(2) insert a comma after <u>counseling</u>
(3) replace <u>planners</u> with <u>planners'</u>
(4) replace <u>offer</u> with <u>offers</u>
(5) no change is necessary

<u>Questions 13 through 19</u> refer to the following passage.

(1) Families with young children have to make many difficult decisions about child care work, and lifestyle changes. (2) Many parents' make child care arrangements and continue working full time while their children are young. (3) Some individuals continue working because they enjoy there jobs, which may be particularly exciting or rewarding. (4) Other parents are concerned that their careers will suffer if they take time off to raise children. (5) Likewise, many households simply need the money. (6) Some families depend on two incomes to

pay the bills. (7) For these parents, finding good child care are a major concern not only for their families, but also for their careers.

(8) On the other hand, many parents want to decrease their hours work from home, or stop working altogether once their children are born. (9) In some families, the cost of child care, commuting, and services may outweigh the benefit of a second income. (10) In other situations, parents simply may want too be home while the children are young. (11) Parents need to evaluate their concerns carefully. (12) Parents have to choose the best options for themselves and their children. (13) Fortunately, new options for work and child care emerged every day.

13. Sentence 1: **Families with young children have to make many difficult decisions about child care work, and lifestyle changes.**

    What correction should be made to this sentence?

    (1) insert a comma after <u>children</u>
    (2) remove the comma after <u>work</u>
    (3) replace <u>have</u> with <u>has</u>
    (4) insert a comma after <u>care</u>
    (5) no correction necessary

14. Sentence 2: **Many parents' make child care arrangements and continue working full time while their children are young.**

    What correction should be made to this sentence?

    (1) replace <u>parents'</u> with <u>parents</u>
    (2) insert a comma after <u>care</u>
    (3) replace <u>their</u> with <u>there</u>
    (4) replace <u>are</u> with <u>is</u>
    (5) no correction necessary

15. Sentence 3: **Some individuals continue working because they enjoy there jobs, which may be particularly exciting or rewarding.**

    What correction should be made to this sentence?

    (1) replace <u>there</u> with <u>their</u>
    (2) remove the comma after <u>jobs</u>
    (3) replace <u>continue</u> with <u>continues</u>
    (4) replace <u>may be</u> with <u>will be</u>
    (5) no correction necessary

16. Sentence 4: **Other parents are concerned that their careers will suffer if they take time off to raise children.**

    What correction should be made to this sentence?

    (1) replace <u>are</u> with <u>is</u>
    (2) insert a comma after <u>concerned</u>
    (3) replace <u>their</u> with <u>there</u>
    (4) replace <u>to</u> with <u>too</u>
    (5) no correction necessary

17. Sentences 5 and 6: **Likewise, many households simply need the money. Some families depend on two incomes to pay the bills.**

    The best combination of sentences 5 and 6 would include which group of words?

    (1) money; nonetheless, some families
    (2) money; some families
    (3) money; therefore, some families
    (4) money, so some families
    (5) money, or some families

18. Sentence 7: **For these parents, finding good child care are a major concern not only for their families, but also for their careers.**

    What correction should be made to this sentence?

    (1) remove the comma after <u>parents</u>
    (2) replace <u>but also</u> with <u>and</u>
    (3) remove the comma after <u>families</u>
    (4) replace <u>are</u> with <u>is</u>
    (5) no correction necessary

19. Sentence 8: **On the other hand, many parents want to decrease their hours work from home, or stop working altogether once their children are born.**

    What correction should be made to sentence 8?

    (1) remove the comma after <u>hand</u>
    (2) replace <u>their</u> with <u>there</u>
    (3) insert a comma after <u>hours</u>
    (4) replace <u>want</u> with <u>wants</u>
    (5) no correction necessary

20. Sentence 9: **In some families the cost of child care, commuting, and services may outweigh the benefit of a second income.**

    If you rewrote this sentence beginning with

    The cost of child care, commuting, and services

    the next words should be

    (1) the benefit of
    (2) some families
    (3) may outweigh
    (4) second income
    (5) in however

21. Sentence 10: **In other situations, parents simply may want too be home while the children are young.**

    What correction should be made to this sentence?

    (1) insert a comma after home
    (2) replace too with to
    (3) remove the comma after situations
    (4) replace parents with parent's
    (5) no correction is necessary

22. Sentences 11 and 12: **Parents need to evaluate their concerns carefully. Parents have to choose the best options for themselves and their children.**

    The most effective combination of sentences 11 and 12 would include which of the following word groups?

    (1) carefully and choose the best
    (2) concerns, lasting influence
    (3) carefully, but parents
    (4) concerns that will have
    (5) carefully; however

23. Sentence 13: **Fortunately, new options for work and child care emerged every day.**

    What is the best way to write the underlined portion of the sentence? If you think the original is best, choose option (1).

    (1) emerged
    (2) had emerged
    (3) emerge
    (4) will have emerged
    (5) were emerging

Questions 24 through 31 refer to the following paragraphs.

(1) Police Departments in major cities across the nation are taking new steps to fight crime. (2) In the past police officers focused on major crimes while letting minor offenses go unnoticed. (3) Now, they will be working harder to enforce all of the laws. (4) Traffic violations and crimes, such as disorderly conduct, panhandling, loitering, and prostitution is getting much more attention. (5) Some people are thrilled with the new approach, others are concerned that it may cause new problems.

(6) When all laws are upheld the quality of life for the city improves. (7) Some neighborhoods become safer, more pleasant places to live. (8) Businesses often has more customers and fewer problems with shoplifting or other crimes. (9) Likewise, many police officials believe that enforcing minor laws actually prevents major crimes from happening.

(10) This approach to public safety has reduced crime in some cities but not everyone is happy. (11) The American Civil Liberties Union (ACLU), that works to protect people's rights, notes that complaints against officers have increased. (12) Some community leaders feel that police officers target they're neighborhoods unfairly. (13) Likewise, some police officials complain that they do not have enough officers to enforce all of the laws well. (14) In spite of these concerns, the new focus on enforcing all laws probably will continue.

24. Sentence 1: **Police Departments in major cities across the nation are taking new steps to fight crime.**

    What correction should be made to this sentence?

    (1) replace are to were
    (2) replace nation with Nation
    (3) insert a comma after cities
    (4) replace Departments with departments
    (5) no correction necessary

25. Sentence 4: **Traffic violations and crimes, such as disorderly conduct, panhandling, loitering, and prostitution is getting much more attention.**

What correction should be made to this sentence?

(1) insert a comma after <u>prostitution</u>
(2) replace <u>is</u> with <u>are</u>
(3) remove the comma after <u>loitering</u>
(4) insert a comma after <u>violations</u>
(5) no correction necessary

26. Sentence 5: **Some people are thrilled with the <u>new approach, others are</u> concerned that it may cause new problems.**

What is the best way to write the underlined sections of the sentence? If you think that the original is best, choose option (1).

(1) new approach, others are
(2) new approach, but others are
(3) new approach, so others are
(4) new approach, because others are
(5) new approach. Therefore, others are

27. Sentence 6: **When all laws are upheld the quality of life for the city improves.**

What correction should be made to this sentence?

(1) replace <u>improves</u> with <u>improved</u>
(2) insert a comma after <u>life</u>
(3) change <u>are</u> to <u>will be</u>
(4) insert a comma after <u>upheld</u>
(5) no correction necessary

28. Sentence 8: **Businesses often has more customers and fewer problems with shoplifting or other crimes.**

What correction should be made to this sentence?

(1) insert a comma after <u>customers</u>
(2) replace <u>Businesses</u> with <u>Businesses'</u>
(3) insert a comma after <u>shoplifting</u>
(4) replace <u>has</u> with <u>have</u>
(5) no correction necessary

29. Sentence 10: **This approach to public safety has reduced crime in some cities but not everyone is happy.**

What correction should be made to this sentence?

(1) replace <u>is</u> with <u>was</u>
(2) insert a comma after <u>cities</u>
(3) replace <u>has</u> with <u>have</u>
(4) replace <u>cities</u> with <u>cities'</u>
(5) no correction necessary

30. Sentence 11: **The American Civil Liberties Union (ACLU), that works to protect people's rights, notes that complaints against officers have increased.**

What correction should be made to this sentence?

(1) replace <u>that</u> with <u>which</u>
(2) remove the comma after <u>rights</u>
(3) replace <u>ACLU</u> with <u>aclu</u>
(4) replace <u>notes</u> to <u>will note</u>
(5) no correction necessary

31. Sentence 12: **Some community leaders feel that police officers target they're neighborhoods unfairly.**

What correction should be made to this sentence?

(1) replace <u>they're</u> with <u>their</u>
(2) replace <u>officers</u> with <u>officers'</u>
(3) insert a comma after <u>leaders</u>
(4) replace <u>target</u> with <u>targets</u>
(5) no correction necessary

<u>Questions 32 through 41</u> refer to the following passage.

(A)

(1) Many factors help schools meet their students' needs, however, one characteristic clearly marks a successful school—parental involvement. (2) When parents participate regularly in school activities children excel. (3) Active parents send a clear message to their children. (4) Education matters. (5) Involved parents monitor homework, attend athletic events, and organize extracurricular activities. (6) They get to know their childrens classmates and friends while working with teachers to reinforce key values. (7) Involved parents understand the concerns of there local schools, and they address problems quickly.

(B)

(8) Many educators which stress parental involvement have developed innovative ways to get parents into the schools. (9) Conferences, meetings, and athletic events are scheduled at night so that working parents can attend. (10) Some schools encourage parents to attend classes eat lunch, and go on field trips with their children. (11) In some school districts, parents even sign contracts that state exactly how parents should supervise homework, encourage good behavior, and support their child's teachers. (12) Likewise, many parents pledge to volunteer during the school year and to assist whomever needs help. (13) While some people wait for the federal government to help our schools, others work to improve the schools now.

32. Sentence 1: **Many factors help schools meet their students' needs however one characteristic clearly marks a successful school—parental involvement.**

    What correction should be made to this sentence?

    (1) replace <u>students'</u> with <u>student's</u>
    (2) replace <u>however</u> with <u>; however,</u>
    (3) replace <u>help</u> with <u>were helping</u>
    (4) replace <u>their</u> with <u>there</u>
    (5) no correction necessary

33. Sentence 2: **When parents participate regularly in school activities children excel.**

    What correction should be made to this sentence?

    (1) replace <u>children</u> with <u>child</u>
    (2) insert a comma after <u>activities</u>
    (3) change <u>excel</u> to <u>excels</u>
    (4) replace <u>regularly</u> with <u>regular</u>
    (5) no correction necessary

34. Sentences 3 and 4: **Active parents send a clear message to their children. Education matters.**

    The most effective combination of sentences 3 and 4 would include which of the following word groups?

    (1) children: education
    (2) children; however, education
    (3) children, and
    (4) children; nonetheless
    (5) children, but

35. Sentence 6: **They get to know their childrens classmates and friends while working with teachers to reinforce key values.**

    What correction should be made to this sentence?

    (1) replace <u>their</u> with <u>there</u>
    (2) insert a comma after <u>classmates</u>
    (3) replace <u>childrens</u> with <u>children's</u>
    (4) replace <u>get</u> with <u>got</u>
    (5) no correction necessary

36. Sentence 7: **Involved parents understand the concerns of there local schools, and they address problems quickly.**

    What correction should be made to this sentence?

    (1) remove the comma after <u>schools</u>
    (2) replace <u>there</u> with <u>their</u>
    (3) replace <u>parents</u> with <u>parents'</u>
    (4) replace <u>quickly</u> with <u>quick</u>
    (5) no correction necessary

37. Sentence 8: **Many educators which stress parental involvement have developed innovative ways to get parents into the schools.**

    What correction should be made to this sentence?

    (1) insert a comma after <u>educators</u>
    (2) replace <u>have developed</u> with <u>will have developed</u>
    (3) replace <u>which</u> with <u>who</u>
    (4) replace <u>parents</u> with <u>parents'</u>
    (5) no correction necessary

38. Sentence 10: **Some schools encourage parents to attend classes eat lunch, and go on field trips with their children.**

    What correction should be made to this sentence?

    (1) remove the comma after <u>lunch</u>
    (2) replace <u>encourage</u> with <u>encourages</u>
    (3) insert a comma after <u>classes</u>
    (4) replace <u>their</u> with <u>they're</u>
    (5) no correction necessary

39. Sentence 11: **In some school districts, parents even sign contracts which state exactly how parents should supervise homework, encourage good behavior, and support their child's teachers.**

    What correction should be made to this sentence?

    (1) remove the comma after <u>districts</u>
    (2) replace <u>their</u> with <u>they're</u>
    (3) replace <u>which</u> with <u>that</u>
    (4) replace <u>child's</u> with <u>childs</u>
    (5) no correction necessary

40. Sentence 12: **Likewise, many parents pledge to volunteer during the school year and to assist whomever needs help.**

    What correction should be made to this sentence?

    (1) replace <u>whomever</u> with <u>whoever</u>
    (2) insert a comma after <u>year</u>
    (3) change the spelling of <u>parents</u> to <u>parents'</u>
    (4) insert a comma after <u>assist</u>
    (5) no correction necessary

41. Sentence 13: **While some people wait for the federal government to help our schools, others work to improve the schools now.**

    What correction should be made to this sentence?

    (1) remove the comma after <u>schools</u>
    (2) replace <u>work</u> with <u>works</u>
    (3) insert a comma after <u>wait</u>
    (4) replace <u>our</u> with <u>are</u>
    (5) no correction necessary

<u>Questions 42 through 50</u> refer to the following letter.

Mr. Colin Joseph
Outdoor Living
1250 King Street
Panther Valley, NJ 29273

Dear Mr. Joseph:

(A)

(1) Three weeks ago, I purchased patio furniture from your store. (2) After reviewing many different brands and styles I decided to buy the Blue Sky package from Summerset, which happened to be on sale. (3) Luke Owen, the Salesperson, told me that this is a very popular package because it comes with a five-year warranty.

(B)

(4) When the furniture was delivered, I noticed right away that too of the chairs were damaged. (5) The delivery men took the chairs back, and they told me they would bring replacement chairs the following monday. (6) The replacement chairs never arrived. (7) On Tuesday, I called you're customer service center, and a representative told me that replacement chairs are not available because the Blue Sky package has been discontinued. (8) She told me that I could choose two new chairs from other Summerset products. (9) Obviously I don't want two different chairs. (10) They will not match my patio set. (11) I want a complete patio set with matching chairs at the sale price I originally paid.

(C)

(12) As a result, I would like to return the patio set, at your expense and I would like to purchase a new, complete set of furniture at the sale price. (13) Outdoor Living has been in business for many years thus, I am sure you understand how important it is to handle customer concerns appropriately.

Sincerely,
Jenna Hogan

42. Sentence 2: **After reviewing many different brands and styles I decided to buy the Blue Sky package from Summerset, which happened to be on sale.**

What correction should be made to this sentence?

(1) replace <u>decided</u> with <u>decide</u>
(2) remove the comma after <u>Summerset</u>
(3) replace <u>which</u> with <u>that</u>
(4) insert a comma after <u>styles</u>
(5) no correction necessary

43. Sentence 3: **Luke Owen, the Salesperson, told me that this is a very popular package because it comes with a five-year warranty.**

What correction should be made to this sentence?

(1) replace <u>Salesperson</u> with <u>salesperson</u>
(2) insert a comma after <u>me</u>
(3) replace <u>is</u> with <u>are</u>
(4) replace <u>comes</u> with <u>come</u>
(5) no correction necessary

44. Sentence 4: **When the furniture was delivered, I noticed right away that too of the chairs were damaged.**

What correction should be made to this sentence?

(1) remove the comma after <u>delivered</u>
(2) replace <u>were</u> with <u>was</u>
(3) insert a comma after <u>away</u>
(4) replace <u>too</u> with <u>two</u>
(5) no correction necessary

45. Sentence 5: **The delivery men took the chairs back, and they told me they would bring replacement chairs the following monday.**

What correction should be made to this sentence?

(1) remove the comma after <u>back</u>
(2) replace <u>monday</u> with <u>Monday</u>
(3) replace <u>took</u> with <u>take</u>
(4) replace <u>bring</u> with <u>brought</u>
(5) no correction necessary

46. Sentence 7: **On Tuesday, I called you're customer service center, and a representative told me that replacement chairs are not available because the Blue Sky package has been discontinued.**

What correction should be made to this sentence?

(1) remove the comma after <u>center</u>
(2) replace <u>are</u> with <u>is</u>
(3) insert a comma after <u>me</u>
(4) replace <u>you're</u> with <u>your</u>
(5) no correction necessary

47. Sentences 9 and 10: **Obviously I don't want two different chairs. They will not match my patio set.**

What is the best way to combine sentences 9 and 10?

(1) Obviously I don't want two different chairs, they will not match my patio set.
(2) Obviously I don't want two different chairs; therefore, they will not match my patio set.
(3) Obviously I don't want two different chairs because they will not match my patio set.
(4) Obviously I don't want two different chairs; however, they will not match my patio set.
(5) Obviously I don't want two different chairs, nonetheless they will not match my patio set.

48. Sentence 11: **I want a complete patio set with matching chairs at the sale price I originally paid.**

What correction should be made to this sentence?

(1) insert a comma after <u>set</u>
(2) replace <u>want</u> with <u>wants</u>
(3) replace <u>paid</u> with <u>pay</u>
(4) insert a comma after <u>price</u>
(5) no correction necessary

49. Sentence 12: **As a result, I would like to return the patio set, at your expense and I would like to purchase a new, complete set of furniture at the sale price.**

What correction should be made to this sentence?

(1) insert a comma after <u>expense</u>
(2) replace <u>your</u> with <u>you're</u>
(3) remove the comma after <u>new</u>
(4) replace <u>to purchase</u> with <u>purchased</u>
(5) no correction necessary

50. Sentence 13: **Outdoor Living has been in business for many <u>years thus, I am</u> sure you understand how important it is to handle customer concerns appropriately.**

What is the best way to write the underlined section of sentence 13? If you think the original sentence is best, choose option (1).

(1) years thus, I am
(2) years. However, I am
(3) years; thus, I am
(4) years while I am
(5) years. Nonetheless, I am

Answers on page 346.

Writing Paragraphs ^{CHAPTER} 10

Paragraphs are like scenes from a movie. Each paragraph focuses on one topic. Together, paragraphs present all of the information to the reader.

Topic Sentences

A topic sentence is like a movie preview. It summarizes the paragraph and tells the reader what to expect. Every sentence in the paragraph must be related to the topic sentence. In most paragraphs, the topic sentence is the first sentence.

Examples

1. <u>Children are fascinated by animals.</u> From infancy onward, children enjoy seeing animals in zoos, farms, pet shops, and parks. Books and videos about animals also stimulate a child's interest. Some children prefer soft, cuddly animals, such as rabbits; others are attracted to monkeys, elephants, and even snakes. Clearly, creatures large and small capture children's attention.

2. <u>Campaign finance reform has become a major issue since the last election.</u> Fund-raising abuses by both major parties have alarmed voters. Unfortunately, many Americans do not trust political leaders to fix the system. Why should they? Everyone seems to benefit from fund-raising abuses—except the American public.

3. Employees who pursue additional training generally land higher-paying jobs, which may also have better benefits. <u>Unfortunately, many employees do not take advantage of job-training opportunities.</u> Some are struggling to balance their responsibilities at work and at home. Others simply do not recognize how important job training is. Employers offer special classes and information sessions to improve their workforce as a whole and to identify skilled, motivated individuals. As a result, workers who do not continue their training are often overlooked when new job opportunities develop.

> **TOPIC SENTENCE**
> 1. Summarizes the paragraph.
> 2. Relates to every sentence in the paragraph.
> 3. Pulls all of the information together.
> 4. Usually begins the paragraph.

EXERCISE 1

In the space provided, write topic sentences for each of the following paragraphs. Make sure that every sentence in the paragraph is related to the topic sentence. Each question has more than one correct answer.

Dan insists that he is working hard, but his grades have dropped. He is often late to class, and he has been disciplined many times by his teacher. Dan rarely does any homework. Even his track coach has noticed a change. If Dan turns himself around soon, he will still be able to pursue his college dreams.

1. _____

   _____

Farms and homes were destroyed. Roads and bridges were washed away. Our town has had many floods, but most people cannot remember the last time that the river was this high. In spite of the devastation, the townspeople will rebuild on this land. These families have lived here for generations.

2. _____

   _____

Many parents want their children to be involved in several different activities. These parents believe that active children are less likely to get into trouble. However, this belief can be taken to an extreme. These days, even young children have full schedules. By the end of the week, some parents and children are exhausted.

3. _____

   _____

Just a few years ago, few people knew much about aggressive driving. Now it is a national problem. Drivers who ignore the speed limit, run red lights, and recklessly pass other cars are causing numerous fatal accidents. Like drunk drivers, aggressive drivers pose a risk for everyone on the road.

4. _____

   _____

In France, strict labor laws make it difficult for companies to lay off workers. Although this may sound great, it actually hurts the economy. Because French businesses are unable to close factories or relocate workers, they lose money. Many French companies simply cannot compete with other international businesses. As a result, France has a high unemployment rate, which just keeps growing.

5. _____

_____

No one expected that two feet of snow would fall on April 1, but it did. Schools, roads, and airports closed. Trains stopped in their tracks, and people were left without power for days. It took some time for life to get back to normal. This was one April Fool's joke that we could have done without.

6. _____

_____

Appendicitis can be devastating. Initially, patients experience abdominal pain, nausea, and a fever. However, within twelve hours the pain becomes more intense in the lower right side, and the abdomen swells. Anyone who experiences these symptoms should contact a doctor.

7. _____

_____

> **REMEMBER**
>
> Remember these facts about topic sentences:
>
> - Topic sentences summarize the paragraph and tell the reader what to expect.
> - Every sentence in a paragraph must relate to the topic sentence.

For years, children took their first few steps in walkers, which are baby seats with wheels. Now many pediatricians speak out against walkers. Every year thousands of children are injured while using these toys. Often these injuries occur when the child falls down a flight of stairs. Some of the accidents are even fatal. Walkers, which were once a right of passage, have become a genuine safety concern.

8. _____

_____

Americans used to enjoy steaks regularly. A steak on the grill in the summertime was almost an American tradition. Now, Americans consume much less red meat. Fish and poultry have become more popular. While some people avoid meat for health reasons, others are simply looking for less expensive meals.

9. _____

_____

Girls and boys enjoy watching bulldozers, excavators, and dump trucks working the land. Perhaps they are attracted to the size of the equipment or the noise that it makes. Whatever the reason, few children can stroll by a construction site without stopping.

10. _____

_____

Answers are on page 349.

Supporting Details

Supporting details are like the actors' lines in a film. The topic sentence summarizes the paragraph, and the supporting details provide more specific information. Remember, every sentence in the paragraph must be related to the topic sentence.

Example

Parents need to provide a safe home for their children. Every year children are injured by accidents that could have been prevented. Even before a baby is brought home from the hospital, parents should do a safety check. Cribs, playpens, and highchairs must meet federal safety guidelines. Car seats, which are crucial, should fit securely in the backseat of the car. Small objects, medicines, knives, cleaning products, and cords must be kept out of reach. Bathtubs, toilets, and buckets should be off-limits; children, in fact, can drown in only a few inches of water. If parents inspect their homes carefully, they can prevent many accidents.

In this paragraph, every sentence supports that idea that parents need to provide a safe home for their children.

TEST FOR SUPPORTING DETAILS

1. Find the topic sentence.
2. Read each supporting detail along with the topic sentence.
3. Decide if each supporting detail agrees with the topic sentence.

Example

In the following paragraph, one sentence is not related to the topic sentence.

Fireworks can be very dangerous when they are not handled properly. Many children and young adults are injured by fireworks every year. Guns are also dangerous for children. Because of the danger, fireworks are illegal in some states. However in many areas of the country, fireworks are easy to get. If parents allow their children to use fireworks, they must provide constant supervision.

TOPIC SENTENCE: *Fireworks can be very dangerous when they are not handled properly.* Clearly this paragraph is about the danger of fireworks.

MISPLACED SENTENCE: *Guns are also dangerous for children.* This sentence has nothing to do with the danger of fireworks.

EXERCISE 2

Read the following paragraphs. Underline the topic sentence. Cross out sentences that are not related to the topic sentence.

1. Searching for a new job requires a lot of hard work and patience. In some areas of the country, few jobs are available. As a result, one must be persistent. Job applicants have to write many letters and research companies. Likewise, completing applications and going on interviews takes time. Congress recently increased the minimum wage. In addition, many people have to look for a new job while they are still working. Although a job search is demanding, the results can be quite rewarding.

2. Soccer has become a popular sport in America. Parents generally like soccer because every child has a chance to participate actively. As a result, recreational leagues and competitive teams abound in many regions. Some soccer leagues cannot keep up with the demand for new teams, equipment, and playing fields. Likewise, many college athletic directors have worked hard to develop their soccer programs for both men and women. Because players run for long periods of time, leg injuries are common in soccer. It is too early to tell how long this enthusiasm for soccer will last.

3. Americans need to take food poisoning more seriously. Overeating and high-fat diets contribute to many health problems in the United States. Poorly processed or undercooked meats, as well as contaminated water supplies, often cause food poisoning, which affects thousands of people every year. Some cases of food poisoning are fatal. Everyone should take precautions to make sure that their food is safe to eat.

4. It is hard for some individuals to save and invest money. Many people prefer mutual funds to stocks, which demand more research and attention. Baby boomers are using mutual funds to save for retirement. People in their twenties and thirties use mutual funds to save for a home or their children's education. As a result, more Americans are investing in mutual funds now than ever before.

5. Many people simply are not interested in caring for young children. Other jobs offer higher wages and better benefits. As a result, a good babysitter is hard to find. In an effort to improve child care, some local hospitals offer babysitting classes, which teach teenagers to care for young children. However, even teenagers often prefer other types of employment. Likewise, parents are having fewer children these days. Instead of hiring a sitter, many parents simply choose to stay home.

Answers are on page 350.

DEVELOPING SUPPORTING DETAILS

Good supporting details are critical. Without them, a paragraph is pointless. The topic sentence provides a preview, but the supporting details give the key information. These details may include personal experiences, knowledge, and observations.

DEVELOPING SUPPORTING DETAILS

Type	Description	Example
Personal Experience	An event or emotion that the writer has lived through.	In my family, TV time is restricted to one hour a day.
Knowledge	A fact that can be proved true. Think of information from the news, magazines, or books. Consider people, events, or activities that illustrate your thoughts.	Most Americans watch television every day.
Observations	Things you have noticed or your thoughts and feelings on a topic.	My friends are allowed to watch as much television as they want.

Example

TV viewing habits vary greatly. Most Americans watch some television every day (knowledge). While some people simply watch the news or sports, others tune into daytime drama or talk shows (knowledge and observation). In my family, TV time is restricted to one hour a day (personal experience). My friends, however, are allowed to watch as much television as they want (observation). As a result, they often watch TV for almost five hours a day (observation). People should turn off the television and start doing more positive things (observation).

A good paragraph has <u>at least</u> three sentences with supporting details. These sentences may include personal experiences, knowledge, and observations.

EXERCISE 3

For each topic sentence, write three supporting details. Include personal experience, knowledge, and an observation. Make sure each detail relates to the topic sentence. Each question has more than one correct answer.

1. Movie rentals are a major form of entertainment.

   PERSONAL EXPERIENCE: _____

   KNOWLEDGE: _____

   OBSERVATION: _____

2. Parenting is exciting, but it is hard work.

   PERSONAL EXPERIENCE: _____

   KNOWLEDGE: _____

   OBSERVATION: _____

3. We often view life differently as we get older.

   PERSONAL EXPERIENCE: _____

   KNOWLEDGE: _____

   OBSERVATION: _____

4. A great teacher can change your life.

   PERSONAL EXPERIENCE: _____

   KNOWLEDGE: _____

   OBSERVATION: _____

5. Many Americans do not save enough money.

   PERSONAL EXPERIENCE: _____

   KNOWLEDGE: _____

   OBSERVATION: _____

Answers are on page 351.

REMEMBER

Remember these facts about supporting details:

- Supporting details provide specific information about the topic sentence.

- Each supporting detail must relate to the topic sentence.

- A paragraph should have at least three sentences with supporting details.

- Supporting details may be personal experience, knowledge, or observations.

Organization

When watching a movie, most people want the scenes to flow smoothly. Certainly, no one expects the surprise ending to occur halfway through the film. Likewise, moviegoers usually don't want scenes from two different movies to be mixed together. The same is true for paragraphs.

Paragraphs have to be organized effectively. The information must be related, and the sentences should flow smoothly from one point to the next. You have already learned how to include supporting details that are related to the topic sentence. Now it is time to focus on organizing the information appropriately.

Read the following paragraph, and note how disorganized the sentences are.

Example

Kaila and I bought a DVD player from a local electronics store two weeks ago. Last Saturday, I decided to return it. When we brought the DVD player home, we struggled to connect it to our current entertainment system. When we turned on the DVD player, the television stopped working. The next day we called the manufacturer, and a representative informed us that the particular DVD player we bought is not compatible with our television. After working on the problem for hours, we finally managed to get the new equipment installed. I wish we had known that ahead of time.

It is hard for the reader to determine what happened when.

The following paragraph explains the situation more clearly.

Last Saturday, I decided to return a DVD player. Kaila and I bought it from a local electronics store two weeks ago. When we brought the DVD player home, we struggled to connect it to our current entertainment system. After working on the problem for hours, we finally managed to get the new equipment installed. However, when we turned on the DVD player, the television stopped working. The next day we called the manufacturer, and a representative informed us that the particular DVD player we bought is not compatible with our television. I wish we had known that ahead of time.

EXERCISE 4

In each of the following paragraphs, one sentence is misplaced. Circle the misplaced sentence, and draw an arrow to where it should be. There may be more than one appropriate location for the misplaced sentence.

1. In addition to providing critical medical care, many pediatricians try to focus on safety and developmental issues. Now when children visit the doctor, they are often encouraged to use seat belts in vehicles and helmets when riding a bike. Checkups include much more than a physical exam. Likewise, parents are often prompted to childproof their homes and monitor their children carefully. Many physicians also instruct parents to provide stimulating toys and read to their children daily. Doctors hope that this comprehensive approach will help children with their physical, emotional, and intellectual development.

2.   Some people prepare their taxes on their own, using tax preparation software or materials from the Internal Revenue Service (IRS). Paying taxes is a frustrating experience for many Americans. However, many people, who find tax preparation too complicated or time consuming, hire accountants to prepare their taxes. Whatever method one uses, the result is often the same; taxpayers can expect either a tax bill or a refund sometime after April 15.

3.   The computer, which I recently purchased, is not functioning properly. I have examined the cables and determined that it is set up correctly. However, I am still unable to run the printer. When I select "print" from the pull-down menu, an error message appears. I contacted the printer manufacturer, and the technician assured me that the printer should be working properly. She insisted that the computer must be causing the problem. Usually the message says that the computer is having a communication problem with the printer, but I have had other error messages as well. At this point, I am so frustrated that I am ready to return everything to the store.

4.   The American space program has been so successful that most people take it for granted—until an accident occurs. When the space shuttle *Columbia* was lost in 2003, some people questioned whether the NASA program should be continued. After the *Challenger* explosion in 1986, seventeen years and more than eighty successful missions passed before Americans were awakened by another tragedy. However, most people recognized that space travel is now part of the American dream, a new frontier that we will explore. Certainly our nation needs time to mourn and examine what went wrong; nonetheless, we will learn from this experience and move on to even greater things.

5.   Parents are a child's first teachers. Critical phases of a child's education begin long before kindergarten, or even preschool. Children learn a tremendous amount by watching their parents or caregivers and interacting with them. Parents help children develop not only academically, but also socially. Children who are nurtured, disciplined, and read to tend to make a much smoother transition to school than those who are not. Many of us have heard that phrase before, but few people truly understand what it means. Whether children are at home with a parent or in a child care situation, they are constantly learning about themselves and the world around them.

Answers are on page 351.

Sentence Variety

Sentences are like food; variety is key. No one wants to eat the same food daily. Likewise, no one wants to read the same sentence style repeatedly. In the last chapter, you learned to rewrite sentences. Now it is time to use what you have learned in a new way. Paragraphs need to have sentences with different lengths and styles. Note how frustrating it is to read a paragraph without a variety of sentences.

Example

WITHOUT SENTENCE VARIETY

Americans take space travel for granted these days. We know astronauts can travel to the moon. We use space satellites daily. We often do not pay attention when a space shuttle launches. We are not even excited about Americans living on a Russian space station. Maybe future space missions will generate more enthusiasm.

This paragraph needs help. Too many sentences begin with *we*, and most sentences are simple sentences. Note the improvements that follow:

WITH SENTENCE VARIETY

Americans take space travel for granted these days. We know astronauts can travel to the moon, and we use space satellites daily. When a space shuttle launches, few people pay attention. Even Americans living on a Russian space station does not excite many people. Maybe future space missions will generate more enthusiasm.

A few simple changes can make a big difference.

EXERCISE 5

Improve each of the following paragraphs by rewriting the underlined sentences. You may change the sentence length or style, but you must keep the message the same. Each question has more than one correct answer.

1. Technology changes very quickly. Forty-five years ago a costly fax machine would fill an entire room. <u>It would take ten minutes to transmit one page. That page would be hard for the recipient to read. Some fax machines are now the size of a large book. They can send multiple pages in minutes.</u> By next year, fax machines will be smaller, faster, and cheaper.

    _____

    _____

    _____

    _____

    _____

    _____

2.   Many young athletes dream of turning professional. <u>They often focus on improving their athletic ability. They neglect their education. Very few athletes turn pro. Those who do often have short careers.</u> Athletes need an excellent education so that they will be prepared for whatever the future brings.

_____

_____

_____

_____

_____

_____

3.   Early science education is getting more attention. Television programs such as *The Magic School Bus* and *Bill Nye, the Science Guy* interest children at a young age. <u>More schools are introducing science topics to students who are in elementary school. Second and third graders now learn about basic biology. They also learn about physics.</u> Future scientists will spring from these new educational efforts.

_____

_____

_____

_____

_____

_____

4.   Computers have created new privacy issues. <u>Many features make computers helpful and easy to use. These same features often expose private information. People use computers for banking and investments. Hackers enter their files and learn personal information.</u> Computer users need to protect their privacy.

_____

_____

_____

_____

_____

_____

5. When buying a car, you need to follow several steps. <u>Obviously, you will need to check the car carefully. You may want to hire a good mechanic to inspect the car for you. You need to get insurance. You may need to arrange for a loan.</u> Once all the arrangements are made, simply drive your new car home.

_____

_____

_____

_____

_____

_____

Answers are on page 353.

Word Choice

Use words that leave an image in the reader's mind. Sometimes changing one or two words in a sentence can make a big difference.

Examples

Changing the verb does not change the meaning of the sentence. In each case, Tim went to the store. However, the various verbs leave different images in the reader's mind.

1. Tim <u>walked</u> to the store.
2. Tim <u>rushed</u> to the store.
3. Tim <u>limped</u> to the store.
4. Tim <u>skipped</u> to the store.
5. Tim <u>ran</u> to the store.

Specific words throughout a paragraph create a clear mental picture.

Example

WITHOUT SPECIFIC WORDS

We **go** downtown **often** to visit the shops, get something to eat, and enjoy different events. The local bakery offers free slices of **good** bread. Sylvana's, a restaurant, has **great** food and a **nice** atmosphere. On Friday nights, there are free concerts on the town green. Most of the bands play **good** music. The downtown area has something for everyone.

WITH SPECIFIC WORDS

We **stroll** downtown **weekly** to visit the shops, get something to eat, and enjoy different events. The local bakery offers free slices of **soft, warm** bread. Sylvana's, a **Greek** restaurant, has **healthy, inexpensive** food and a **relaxing** atmosphere. On Friday nights, there are free concerts on the town green. Most of the bands play **upbeat** music. The downtown area has something for everyone.

Remember, you want to create an image in the reader's mind. Describe how things look, smell, taste, and feel. Likewise, answer the questions *why, when,* and *how.* Why is something good or bad? When does an event occur? How is an action done?

EXERCISE 6

For each sentence, think of three or more words that could replace the underlined word without changing the basic meaning of the sentence. Write your answers in the space provided. There is more than one correct set of answers.

1. Phebe <u>said</u>, "This class is boring."

   _____

2. We had a <u>good</u> day.

   _____

3. We saw a <u>big</u> cow in the road.

   _____

4. This is a <u>small</u> problem for us.

   _____

5. Today is a <u>bad</u> day.

   _____

6. The food was <u>great</u>.

   _____

7. The truck <u>hit</u> the car.

   _____

8. The waves <u>landed</u> on the beach.

   _____

9. I go to the food store <u>often</u>.

   _____

10. The traffic was <u>annoying</u>.

   _____

Answers are on page 353.

> **REMEMBER**
>
> Remember to use words that create an image in the reader's mind.

CHECKLIST FOR PARAGRAPHS

☐ Does the paragraph have a good topic sentence?

☐ Does the paragraph have <u>at least</u> three sentences with supporting details?

☐ Do all of the supporting details relate to the topic sentence?

☐ Does the paragraph have sentences with different lengths and styles?

☐ Do the verbs and adjectives create an image in the reader's mind?

IN THIS CHAPTER YOU HAVE LEARNED:

- How to write a topic sentence (page 191)
- How to write supporting details (page 194)
- How to organize information effectively (page 198)
- How to vary sentences (page 200)
- How to choose specific words (page 202)

Review sections that are difficult for you.

Chapter Review

Each paragraph below needs a topic sentence. Write a topic sentence in the space provided. Each question has more than one possible answer.

A recent study by the National Institute of Child Health and Human Development focused on young children in daycare. According to the study, children in good daycare programs learn to speak and think as well as children who are cared for by their mothers. However, the research also showed that very young children who are in daycare for many hours each week have weaker bonds with their mothers. As daycare becomes increasingly popular, researchers will continue to study how daycare affects children and their parents.

1. _____

_____

Many roads and bridges in our country have not been well maintained. Routine maintenance is expensive, but necessary. Large, dangerous potholes are damaging cars and causing accidents. Aging structural supports are weakening bridges and endangering motorists. We need to focus on making roads and bridges safe for everyone.

2. _____

_____

The associations regulate solicitation. Homeowners' associations set standards for landscaping, maintenance, and additions to homes. They even decide what color paint may be used for each house. Some homeowners like the structure of associations; others think that the associations are too heavy handed.

3. _____

_____

The longer days make it easier for people to get outside after work or school. Green grass and flowers add color to the landscape. Everyone finally gets a chance to open their windows and enjoy the fresh air. Even spring cleaning lifts some people's spirits.

4. _____

_____

Some people save a little bit of money from each paycheck. Others write a check for savings when they pay the rent or mortgage. A few people put money in savings before they pay their bills. Whatever the technique, it is important to create a good savings account.

5. _____

   _____

When children are young, they want to do many things when they grow up. A child may insist that she wants to be a doctor, a dancer, and an artist. Unfortunately as children age, these wonderful dreams often fade away. Parents and teachers need to work hard to keep children's dreams alive so that today's children will be tomorrow's leaders.

6. _____

   _____

Major purchases, such as cribs, strollers, and high chairs, are expensive. Even disposable items are costly. Formula for babies can cost $150 dollars a month. Diapers cost about $600 a year. Parents need to be prepared for the financial responsibilities of having children.

7. _____

   _____

TV sets, radios, and telephones have more features than they had years ago. Likewise, answering machines, VCRs, and microwaves are common in homes today. Many older Americans think that these objects are luxuries and a waste of money. To younger generations, however, these items seem necessary for everyday life.

8. _____

   _____

By law, school districts must provide transportation for their students. However, many parents on their way to work simply drive their children to school. As a result, school buses in many towns are almost empty. These empty buses cost taxpayers a lot of money. There must be a better way to provide transportation for the students.

9. _____

   _____

Most people have a favorite station on the radio. However, there are many other rhythms around us. Dishwashers and washing machines hum as they clean. Construction equipment beats out a rhythm. The wind whistles through the trees, and birds sing wonderful melodies. Once in a while, we should turn off our radios and listen to the other music in our lives.

10. _____

_____

Answers are on page 353.

EXERCISE 2

Add two supporting details to each of the following paragraphs. Write your answers in the space provided. Each question has more than one possible answer.

1. Maintaining a home takes a lot of work. Carpets need to be vacuumed. Floors must be washed, and bathrooms need to be cleaned regularly.

   a. _____

   b. _____

2. Biking is a great form of exercise. Some exercise programs are hard to learn, but most people already know how to ride a bike. Biking also does not need a lot of fancy equipment; any bike will work.

   a. _____

   b. _____

3. Pets become part of the family. Some pets protect the home while others simply provide friendship. When a pet dies, many people feel a great sense of loss.

   a. _____

   b. _____

4. Many different items travel through the mail. Bills and payments are just one form of mail. Advertisements and special offers, which are commonly called junk mail, fill mailboxes everywhere.

   a. _____

   b. _____

5. Fire engines capture children's attention. The lights and sirens are exciting for some children. Likewise, the size of the trucks and the powerful equipment interest others.

   a. _____

   b. _____

6. Computers have changed our lives. They help us get information faster and easier than ever before. Computers enable people to communicate around the world.

   a. _____

   b. _____

7. Many new services have developed to help people with their busy lives. Dry cleaners pick up clothes right where people work. Taxi services that are specially designed for busy parents transport children to various activities.

   a. _____

   b. _____

8. Parents can be involved in their children's education in many ways. Checking homework is just one way. Parents can take their children to museums, zoos, and aquariums, which stimulate learning.

   a. _____

   b. _____

9. Advertisers use many gimmicks to capture our attention. Catchy songs and slogans help us remember products. Clothing, such as T-shirts and hats, make the products seem fashionable.

   a. _____

   b. _____

10. There are many ways to save money. Cutting coupons can help reduce grocery bills. Turning off lights that are not being used can save on electricity.

    a. _____

    b. _____

Answers are on page 354.

EXERCISE 3

Write a paragraph on the following topic:

Describe the qualities of a great leader.

_____

_____

_____

_____

_____

_____

_____

_____

_____

_____

_____

_____

Answer is on page 355.

UNIT 5

THE GED ESSAY

Planning the Essay CHAPTER **11**

> **IN THIS CHAPTER YOU WILL LEARN:**
>
> - How the Language Arts, Writing Test, Part II is organized (page 213)
> - How to manage your time (page 214)
> - How to read the instructions (page 214)
> - How to write a thesis statement (page 215)
> - How to brainstorm (page 217)
> - How to organize the information into main ideas and details (page 218)

Essays are like exercise routines. To have a good workout, you need to warm up, exercise, and cool down. If you neglect any one of these stages, your workout will suffer. The same is true with an essay. To write a good essay, you need to plan, write, and revise. Writers who pay attention to each step in the process write stronger essays.

Overview of the Essay

In Part II of the Language Arts, Writing Test, you will be asked to write an essay. In 45 minutes, you will need to discuss your views on a particular topic. You will not need to know any special information about the topic, but you will need to write a clear, organized, well-developed essay. You will be encouraged to organize your thoughts on scratch paper. However, *your final product must be written on two lined pages in the official answer book.* The evaluators will not read any additional pages.

Sample Essay Topics

1. Some inventions dramatically change the way we live our lives. Choose one invention from your lifetime and discuss how it has made life different. Your response may include personal experiences, knowledge, and observations.

2. Describe the qualities of a good teacher. Your response should include personal experiences, knowledge, and observations.

The essay will be scored holistically (see the grading chart that follows on page 264). In other words, the evaluators will look at your essay as a whole; they will focus mostly on how well you explain your ideas. A few minor errors will not drastically affect your score. Nonetheless, it is important to check your writing carefully. If errors make your essay hard to understand, you will earn a lower score.

Time Management

The following chapters will teach you how to write a solid five-paragraph essay. Writing a good essay includes more than just putting words on paper. There are three important steps to the writing process: planning, writing, and revising. Taking the time to complete each step will help you write a better essay.

You will have 45 minutes to complete the essay. The following chart suggests how your time should be divided.

TIME MANAGEMENT

Planning (10 Minutes)
1. Read the instructions and the topic.
2. Write a thesis statement.
3. Brainstorm.
4. Create an outline.

Writing (25 Minutes)
1. Review your notes.
2. Write an introduction, body, and conclusion.

Revising (10 Minutes)
1. Compare your essay and notes.
2. Check and revise for the information: organization, content, and clarity.
3. Check and revise for the rules: grammar, usage, mechanics, and capitalization.

Understanding Instructions

The basic instructions for the essay question are always the same. You will be expected to do the following:

1. Read the entire question carefully.
2. Plan your response before you write.
3. Write only about the assigned topic.
4. Make notes on the blank pages of the test booklet or scratch paper. Your notes will not be scored.
5. Write your essay on two lined pages in the answer book.
6. Carefully read your essay and make changes that will improve it.
7. Use correct paragraphing, sentence structure, usage, punctuation, and capitalization.
8. Use a ballpoint pen and write legibly.

REMEMBER

Remember these facts about the essay:

- You will have 45 minutes to write an essay.
- Even though your essay will be graded holistically, you should pay attention to organization and grammar.
- There are three steps to writing a good essay: planning, writing, and revising.
- Allow about 10 minutes for planning, 25 minutes for writing, and 10 minutes for revising.

REMEMBER

Remember, carefully read all of the instructions before you begin the essay.

NOTE

You **must** write about the assigned topic. Essays that are on a different topic cannot be scored. As a result, a Language Arts, Writing Test composite score will not be reported.

Thesis Statements

The thesis statement is like an arrow that points a lost writer in the right direction. In an essay, the thesis statement summarizes what you want to write and organizes your thoughts.

We have already discussed how a topic sentence is like a movie preview: it summarizes the paragraph and tells the reader what to expect. Likewise, a thesis statement is like the plan for a series of movies. It tells the reader what the main issue is for the entire essay. The thesis statement pulls all of the paragraphs together using a common thread or idea.

Examples

1. **Essay topic:** Some inventions dramatically change the way we live our lives. Choose one invention from your lifetime and discuss how it has made life different. Your response may include personal experiences, knowledge, and observations.

   Thesis statement: Cell phones help people in many ways, but they also have drawbacks.

2. **Essay topic:** Describe the qualities of a good teacher. Your response should include personal experiences, knowledge, and observations.

   Thesis statement: A good teacher knows the subject and understands how to teach students effectively.

3. **Essay topic:** Many high schools across the country have made community service a graduation requirement. Should high schools have community service requirements? Your response may include personal experiences, knowledge, and observations.

   Thesis statement: High schools should require community service because it helps students become more thoughtful, responsible citizens.

The thesis statement of an essay depends on the writer's thoughts. Some writers like to brainstorm before writing a thesis statement. If this may describe you, read the next section before completing Exercise 1.

> **HINT**
>
> Do not use the phrases "In my opinion," "I believe," or "I think." Simply state your thoughts.
>
> WRONG: In my opinion, the telephone has been beneficial.
>
> RIGHT: The telephone has been beneficial.

EXERCISE 1

Read each essay topic. In the space provided, write your thesis statement for the essay. Each question has more than one correct answer.

1. **Topic:** What makes someone a hero? Write an essay describing the characteristics of a hero. Your response may include personal experiences, knowledge, and observations.

   Thesis statement: _____

   _____

2. **Topic:** Should teenagers be allowed to drink alcohol, or should more efforts be made to stop teenage drinking? In an essay, explain your views. Your response may include personal experiences, knowledge, and observations.

   Thesis statement: _____

   _____

3. **Topic:** Has television made our lives better or worse? In an essay, explain your views. Your response may include personal experiences, knowledge, and observations.

   Thesis statement: _____

   _____

4. **Topic:** What is the best way to teach new drivers before they get a license? Write an essay that explains your views. Your response may include personal experiences, knowledge, and observations

   Thesis statement: _____

   _____

5. **Topic:** If you knew that you only had a few months to live, how would your life change? In an essay, explain your thoughts. Your response may include personal experiences, knowledge, and observations.

   Thesis statement: _____

   _____

Answers are on page 356.

Brainstorming

Brainstorming is like emptying all of your thoughts onto a piece of paper. When you brainstorm, do not worry about grammar; simply write your ideas as quickly as you can. In addition, do not separate the good ideas from the bad ones; let them all spill out. A "bad" idea may actually help you think of more "good" information. After you have emptied all of your thoughts, cross out the ones that you do not want to include.

Good Effects	Drawbacks
emergency calls	can be expensive
I called for help when my car broke down	employers can contact you anytime, anywhere
talk to friends and relatives	don't always want to talk to other people
kids can call their parents when they need a ride	some people talk on their phones too much
~~don't need landline~~	my friend got in an accident when she was on the phone
portable	don't always want people to take pictures of me
~~come in many different styles~~	students use phones to cheat
can talk anytime, anywhere	don't always work in emergencies
call husband when he travels	people talk on their phones instead of with the people who are around them
can access Web, e-mail	~~many different cell phone plans~~
phones take pictures, play music	

Example

Essay topic: Some inventions dramatically change the way we live our lives. Choose one invention from your lifetime, and discuss how it has made life different. Your response may include personal experiences, knowledge, and observations.

Thesis statement: Cell phones have helped people in many ways, but they also have drawbacks.

HINT

To get your thoughts flowing, ask yourself the following questions about the topic: How? When? Where? What? Who?

EXERCISE 2

Brainstorm ideas for the following essay topic. Use the space provided or a separate sheet of paper.

Essay topic: Describe the qualities of a good teacher. Your response should include personal experiences, knowledge, and observations.

_____

_____

_____

_____

_____

_____

_____

_____

Answers are on page 356.

Main Ideas and Details

After you have brainstormed, you need to separate your thoughts into main ideas and details. Main ideas work like boxes that group the details together. Eventually, main ideas will become topic sentences for your paragraphs.

T-LISTS AND WEBS

T-lists and webs are two basic ways to organize your thoughts into main ideas and details. For a T-list, the paper is divided into two columns. Main ideas are listed on the left side, and supporting details are listed on the right. Web groups relate information in different areas of the paper.

Example

Essay topic: Some inventions dramatically change the way we live our lives. Choose one invention from your lifetime and discuss how it has made life different. Your response may include personal experiences, knowledge, and observations.

Thesis statement: Cell phones have helped people in many ways, but they also have drawbacks.

T-LIST

Main Ideas	Details
Cell phones help people stay in touch.	talk to friends and relatives kids can call their parents when they need a ride can talk anytime, anywhere
Cell phones are practical.	emergency calls I called for help when my car broke down portable can access Web, e-mail, take pictures, play music
Cell phones have drawbacks.	can be expensive employers can contact you anytime, anywhere don't always want to talk to other people some people talk on their phones too much my friend got in an accident when she was on the phone students use phones to cheat people talk on their phones instead of with the people who are around them

WEB

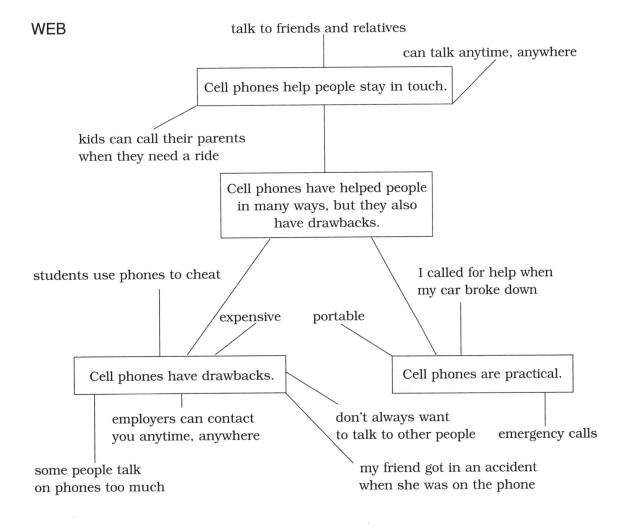

EXERCISE 3

Read the essay topic, thesis statement, and supporting details that follow. Using the T-list chart or a separate sheet of paper, group the supporting details according to three different main ideas.

Essay topic: Describe the qualities of a good teacher. Your response should include personal experiences, knowledge, and observations.

Thesis statement: A good teacher knows the subject and understands how to teach students effectively.

DETAILS

- a good teacher knows the subject very well
- my math teacher makes the class interesting
- teachers should understand basic psychology
- my brother's history teacher just reads out of the textbook
- good teachers show how the subject relates to our lives
- good teachers give extra help
- good teachers should have teacher training
- teachers should have high expectations
- good teachers treat the students fairly
- good teachers believe everyone can learn
- teachers should care about their students
- teachers need a sense of humor
- when I was little, no one cared that I couldn't read

Main Ideas	Details

Answers are on page 356.

EXERCISE 4

Read the essay topic, thesis statement, and supporting details that follow. Using the web diagram or a separate sheet of paper, group the supporting details according to three different main ideas.

Essay topic: Many high schools across the country have made community service a graduation requirement. Should high schools have community service requirements? Your response may include personal experiences, knowledge, and observations.

Thesis statement: High schools should require community service because it helps students become more thoughtful, responsible citizens.

DETAILS

- students can volunteer in programs that interest them
- teenagers become more interested in community issues
- my sister decided to become a nurse after helping in a clinic
- students help in nursing homes or daycare centers
- community service improves many students' self-esteem
- students learn to work with other adults
- teens work as tutors and hospital aides
- students learn how important it is to volunteer
- when people volunteer as teens, they are more likely to volunteer as adults
- I learned important job skills when I volunteered
- our high school students cleaned up the local playground and repaired the equipment
- high school community service programs have made students more active in college volunteer programs

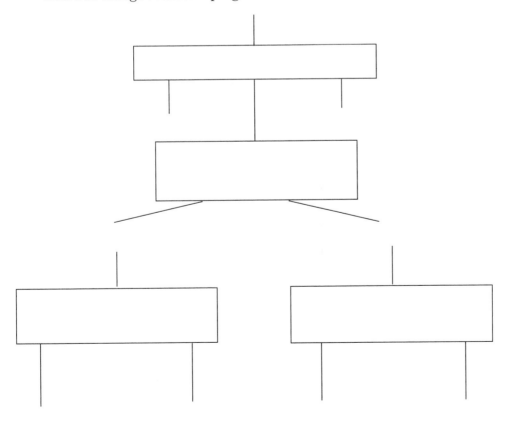

Answers are on page 357.

EXERCISE 5

Brainstorm ideas for each of the following topics. Try to come up with at least ten ideas. After you brainstorm, organize your thoughts into main ideas and details. Write in the space provided or on a separate sheet of paper. Use whichever organizational method works well for you. Each question has many possible answers.

1. **Topic:** What makes someone a hero? Write an essay describing the characteristics of a hero. Your response may include personal experiences, knowledge, and observations.

2. **Topic:** Should teenagers be allowed to drink alcohol or should more efforts be made to stop teenage drinking? In an essay, explain your views. Your response may include personal experiences, knowledge, and observations.

3. **Topic:** Has television made our lives better or worse? In an essay, explain your views. Your response may include personal experiences, knowledge, and observations.

4. **Topic:** What is the best way to teach new drivers before they get a license? Write an essay that explains your views. Your response may include personal experiences, knowledge, and observations.

REMEMBER

Remember these facts about organizing the information:

- Separate your thoughts into main ideas and details.
- Main ideas will eventually become topic sentences for your paragraphs.
- The details will become the supporting details for your topic sentences.

REMEMBER

Remember, outlines organize information for the essay.

5. **Topic:** If you knew that you only had a few months to live, how would your life change? In an essay, explain your thoughts. Your response may include personal experiences, knowledge, and observations.

Answers are on page 358.

THE PLANNING STAGE

1. Read the instructions carefully, and make sure that you understand them before you begin.
2. Write a thesis statement that will point your thoughts in the right direction.
3. Brainstorm ideas for your essay.
4. Cross out ideas that you will not use.
5. Separate your main ideas and details.
6. Organize the information.

IN THIS CHAPTER YOU HAVE LEARNED:

- How the Language Arts, Writing Test, Part II is organized (page 213)
- How to manage your time (page 214)
- How to read the instructions (page 214)
- How to write a thesis statement (page 215)
- How to brainstorm (page 217)
- How to organize the information (page 218)

Review sections that are difficult for you.

Chapter Review

EXERCISE 1

For the following essay, complete each step in the planning stage as directed. You may need to use a separate sheet of paper. There is more than one correct answer.

Essay topic: If you could meet anyone (living or dead), whom would you choose and why? In an essay, explain your thoughts. Your response may include personal experiences, knowledge, and observations.

Step 1: Thesis statement:

_____

_____

_____

Step 2: Brainstorm ideas for your essay. Make sure you have *at least* ten good ideas. After brainstorming, cross out ideas that you will not use.

Step 3: Organize your thoughts into main ideas and details. Use a T-list, web, or another systematic approach. You may need to use a separate sheet of paper.

Answers are on page 360.

EXERCISE 2

For the following essay, complete each step in the planning stage as directed. You may need to use a separate sheet of paper. There is more than one correct answer.

> **Essay topic:** Americans need better public schools. Write an essay describing how we can improve public schools in America. Your response may include personal experiences, knowledge, and observations.

Step 1: Thesis statement:

_____

_____

_____

Step 2: Brainstorm ideas for your essay. Make sure you have *at least* ten good ideas. After brainstorming, cross out ideas that you will not use.

Step 3: Organize your thoughts into main ideas and details. Use a T-list, a web, or another systematic approach. You may need to use a separate sheet of paper.

Answers are on page 361.

Writing the Essay

- How to organize a five-paragraph essay (page 229)
- How to write the introductory paragraph (page 230)
- How to write the body paragraphs (page 233)
- How to use transitional words and phrases (page 237)
- How to write the concluding paragraph (page 240)

Remember, essays are like exercise routines. A good workout includes a warm-up, an exercise, and a cool down. The writing stage of essay writing is like the exercise phase of a workout. Now that your mind is warmed up from the planning stage, you can actually write your essay.

During this stage, do not worry about spelling, punctuation, or grammar. You can correct your mistakes later. First let the information flow. Then write about your ideas. After you have completed the first two steps, revise your work.

Overview

Now it is time to learn how to write a five-paragraph essay. Each paragraph in the essay has a job. Note the jobs that are listed in the following box.

THE FIVE-PARAGRAPH ESSAY

Introductory Paragraph
Provides background material.
Gives the essay direction.
Includes the thesis statement.

Body Paragraph 1
Develops the thesis statement.
Includes a topic sentence.
Includes supporting details.

Body Paragraph 2
Develops the thesis statement.
Includes a topic sentence.
Includes supporting details.

Body Paragraph 3
Develops the thesis statement.
Includes a topic sentence.
Includes supporting details.

Concluding Paragraph
Summarizes the essay.
Provides an insightful statement.

Writing the Introductory Paragraph

The introductory paragraph is like an advertisement for a movie. It grabs the reader's attention. An advertisement does not show all the good scenes or tell the ending of a film. Likewise, a good introduction does not provide details about the topic. Instead, it encourages the reader to continue.

> ### INTRODUCTORY PARAGRAPH
> 1. Review your outline and thesis statement.
> 2. Write 1–2 general sentences about the topic.
> 3. Write 1–2 more specific sentences about the topic.
> 4. Write your thesis statement.

Your introductory paragraph should move from general information to more specific material. You may write your thesis statement anywhere in the introduction. However, if you write the thesis statement last, it will help point your thoughts in the right direction.

Example

Essay topic: Some inventions dramatically change the way we live our lives. Choose one invention from your lifetime and discuss how it has made life different. Your response may include personal experiences, knowledge, and observations.

Introductory paragraph: Throughout history, new inventions have changed people's lives. Inventions often make our lives easier or our work more productive. Sometimes, however, they seem to make life more difficult. The cell phone is one invention that has had mixed results. Cell phones have helped people in many ways, but they also have had drawbacks.

The introduction starts off with a general statement about all inventions and ends with a thesis statement about the positive and negative effects of the cell phone. The reader clearly knows what to expect from this essay.

EXERCISE 1

Read each essay topic. Review the thesis statements that you wrote on page 216 and the information that you brainstormed on page 222. Then write an introductory paragraph for each topic. Use the space provided or a separate sheet of paper. Each question has more than one correct answer.

1. **Topic:** What makes someone a hero? Write an essay describing the characteristics of a hero. Your response may include personal experiences, knowledge, and observations.

    Introductory paragraph: _____

    _____

    _____

    _____

    _____

    _____

    _____

    _____

    _____

2. **Topic:** Should teenagers be allowed to drink alcohol, or should more efforts be made to stop teenage drinking? In an essay, explain your views. Your response may include personal experiences, knowledge, and observations.

    Introductory paragraph: _____

    _____

    _____

    _____

    _____

    _____

    _____

    _____

3. **Topic:** Has television made our lives better or worse? In an essay, explain your views. Your response may include personal experiences, knowledge, and observations.

Introductory paragraph: _____

_____

_____

_____

_____

_____

_____

_____

REMEMBER

Remember these facts about the introductory paragraph:

- The introductory paragraph provides background material and the thesis statement.
- Start the introductory paragraph with general information and end with more specific material.
- Make your thesis statement the last sentence in the paragraph.

4. **Topic:** What is the best way to teach new drivers before they get a license? Write an essay that explains your views. Your response may include personal experiences, knowledge, and observations.

Introductory paragraph: _____

_____

_____

_____

_____

_____

_____

_____

5. **Topic:** If you knew that you only had a few months to live, how would your life change? In an essay, explain your thoughts. Your response may include personal experiences, knowledge, and observations.

Introductory paragraph: _____

_____

_____

_____

_____

_____

_____

_____

Answers are on page 362.

Body Paragraphs

Paragraphs are like scenes from a movie. Each paragraph focuses on one topic. Together, the paragraphs present all of the information to the reader. Once you have organized your thoughts into an outline, the body paragraphs are fairly easy to write. The main ideas in your outlines become topic sentences for the paragraphs. Likewise, the details for each main idea become the supporting details for each paragraph.

The topic sentence can be placed anywhere in the paragraph. However, if you write the topic sentence first, it will direct your thoughts. In addition, it will be easier to check that every supporting detail relates to the topic sentence.

THE BODY PARAGRAPHS

1. Review your outline and thesis statement.
2. Choose the order for your main ideas.
3. Focus on one main idea at a time.
4. Rewrite the main idea as a topic sentence.
5. Rewrite the details as supporting sentences.
6. Add more information as needed.

Example

Essay topic: Some inventions dramatically change the way we live our lives. Choose one invention from your lifetime and discuss how it has made life different. Your response may include personal experiences, knowledge, and observations.

Introductory paragraph:

Throughout history, new inventions have changed people's lives. Inventions often make our lives easier or our work more productive. Sometimes, however, they seem to make life more difficult. The cell phone is one invention that has had mixed results. Cell phones have helped people in many ways, but they also have had drawbacks.

Body paragraphs:

Cell phones help people stay in touch. With a cell phone, I can talk to family and friends anytime and anywhere. When my husband travels for work, it is easy for us to communicate. Likewise, my children can call me when their plans have changed. Last week, my son called me on his cell phone because practice ended early and he needed a ride.

Cell phones are practical. In an emergency, I can get help quickly with a cell phone. When my car broke down last spring, I easily called for help. Drivers often use their cell phones to report accidents or dangerous conditions. With my cell phone, I have everything I need. I can access the Web, send e-mail, take pictures, and play music.

Although cell phones can be helpful in many ways, they also can be expensive and annoying. Monthly bills, which may have unexpected charges, can be costly. In addition, cell phones help people contact you— even when you do not want them to call. For example, my boss often calls me on my day off. Some people talk on their cell phones too much; they forget that other people can hear their conversations. In addition, cell phones are distracting. My friend got into a car accident when she was on the phone.

The writer added some information that was not in the outline on page 219. If new thoughts come to you while you are writing, include them.

> **REMEMBER**
>
> It is important to add specific examples and details to support your thoughts. Ask yourself the following questions to get your thoughts flowing about the topic: How? When? Where? What? Who? Why?

EXERCISE 2

Read the essay topic. Review the brainstorming that you did on page 222 and write the body paragraphs for this topic. If you need more space, use an additional sheet of paper. There is more than one correct answer.

Essay topic: What makes someone a hero? Write an essay describing the characteristics of a hero. Your response may include personal experiences, knowledge, and observations.

_____

_____

_____

_____

_____

_____

_____

_____

_____

_____

_____

_____

_____

_____

_____

_____

_____

_____

_____

_____

_____

_____

_____

_____

_____

_____

_____

_____

_____

_____

_____

_____

_____

_____

_____

_____

_____

_____

_____

_____

_____

_____

_____

_____

Answers are on page 363.

Transitions

When a movie jumps from one scene to another, the story is hard to follow. The same is true with an essay. When you write, you need to make sure that your writing flows smoothly. Transitional words and phrases will help your thoughts flow.

TRANSITIONS BETWEEN SENTENCES

Transitional words and phrases form connections; they show the relationship between one thought and another. You may use transitional words in the beginning or middle of a sentence. Wherever they are located, transitional words should be set apart with commas.

TRANSITIONAL WORDS AND PHRASES		
Transitions	**Job**	**Example**
also, in addition, likewise, too, furthermore	Connect similar ideas.	Running can help you lose weight. <u>Likewise,</u> biking has health benefits.
because, as a result, therefore, thus, so that, consequently	Connect a cause to an effect.	Airbags have killed children. <u>As a result,</u> children under twelve should be in the back seat.
for instance, for example, such as	Connect specific examples to a general idea.	Smoking causes illnesses. <u>For example,</u> lung cancer kills many Americans each year.
although, even though, instead, however, yet, on the other hand, nonetheless	Connect ideas that are different.	Many foods provide nutrients. Junk food, <u>however,</u> has no nutritional value.
first, second, next, then, later, after, now, finally	Connect ideas according to time.	<u>First,</u> melt the butter and add the spices. <u>Then</u> brush the mixture on the fish. <u>Finally,</u> broil the fish for five minutes.

EXERCISE 3

Read the sentence pairs below. Then write an appropriate transitional word or phrase in the space provided. Include the correct punctuation. Each question has more than one correct answer.

1. His new book is full of suspense and intrigue. The violence _____ is overwhelming.

2. Many species are protected by the Endangered Species Act. _____ the snail darter and the spotted owl have been protected for years.

3. The move from middle school to high school is difficult for some students. _____ the transition from high school to college is challenging.

4. _____ find a spot where the fish are biting. _____ make a few casts and reel in some dinner.

5. Many people cannot afford to go to college or a vocational school. _____ many students do not get the education that they need.

6. We wanted to go to a fancy restaurant downtown. _____ we went to a fast food place around the corner.

7. For years women were expected to stay home and raise children. _____ they have many options for their careers and their families.

8. Many immigrants work hard to start a new life in America. Some adults _____ work two or three jobs to provide for their families.

9. We thought that we were buying the home of our dreams. _____ what we bought was one big nightmare.

10. Children need immunizations for protection from serious diseases. _____ many children in America are not immunized properly.

Answers are on page 363.

TRANSITIONS BETWEEN PARAGRAPHS

Transitional words and phrases are also used to connect paragraphs.

Example

Even though health clubs can provide a great workout, I prefer exercising outdoors. Health clubs can be expensive. On the other hand, for the cost of a pair of running shoes I can get all the exercise I need. Likewise, I do not need to drive to a health club or workout during certain times of the day. Instead, I can walk out my front door and exercise wherever or whenever I want.

I do not want to exercise with other people. I am around many people all day. When I work out, I want to be alone so that I have some time to myself. I also like to exercise by myself so that I can set my own pace; I do not like being rushed or slowed down. Health clubs are great for a lot of people, but for me the best workouts are outdoors.

Both paragraphs show the advantages of exercising outside instead of in a health club. Each of the following transitions could be used to show this relationship:

1. In addition, I do not want to exercise with other people.
2. Likewise, I do not want to exercise with other people.
3. Furthermore, I do not want to exercise with other people.
4. I also do not want to exercise with other people.

EXERCISE 4

After you have read the following essay, underline the transitional words that will connect the ideas effectively.

Over the past ten years, computer use has increased significantly. Like many inventions, computers have changed our lives. Although computers have had some negative effects, most of the changes have been positive.

1. (Likewise, For example) computers help us communicate faster and easier. Computer networks help coworkers, family members, and friends send e-mail or faxes. 2. (As a result, Nonetheless) people who used to drive to an office can now use their computers to telecommute. 3. (Likewise, Instead) companies can use computers to hold meetings without actually getting people together in the same room.

4. Computers (however, also) help people learn more easily. Computer programs can teach everything from Spanish to anatomy. Computers give students individualized instruction; each student can learn the material at his or her own pace. 5. (In addition, Therefore) through the Internet, computer users can tour museums or foreign countries.

REMEMBER

Remember these facts about the body paragraphs:

- Each body paragraph should have one topic sentence and at least three sentences with supporting details.

- Use your outline as a guide for writing the body paragraphs.

- Use transitional words and phrases to show the relationship between ideas. Transitional words can connect sentences and paragraphs.

6. (On the other hand, For instance) computers isolate people. Some people play computer games rather than socialize with others. Students use computers to get class notes without ever actually going to class. 7. (Likewise, Thus) employees who work from home may never even meet their coworkers.

Computers have had positive and negative effects. Computers have improved communication and made learning easier, but they also have isolated people. 8. (Nonetheless, Because) they will continue to be an important invention.

Answers are on page 363.

Concluding Paragraph

The conclusion is like a quick review of your essay. It summarizes your main points and ends with an insightful statement.

WRITING A CONCLUDING PARAGRAPH

1. Review your essay.
2. In 1 sentence, rewrite your thesis statement.
3. In 1–2 sentences, summarize your topic sentences.
4. In 1–2 sentences, write a general statement about the topic.

HINT

You should rewrite your thesis statement. However, if you cannot think of a new sentence, write *clearly* in front of your original thesis statement.

Example

Clearly, cell phones can be both beneficial and frustrating. Cell phones help people communicate, and they have many practical uses. However, they also are expensive and annoying. Like many inventions, the cell phone is a great tool when it is used wisely.

EXERCISE 5

Read the thesis statement and topic sentences for each question. Then write a concluding paragraph for each item. If you need more space, use an additional sheet of paper. Each question has more than one correct answer.

1. **Thesis statement:** A hero sacrifices himself or herself to help other people.

   Topic sentences:
   Heroes share certain characteristics.
   There are many different types of heroes.
   Everyday people can be heroes.

   Concluding paragraph:

   _____

   _____

   _____

   _____

   _____

   _____

   _____

   _____

   _____

   _____

   _____

   _____

   _____

   _____

   _____

   _____

   _____

   _____

2. **Thesis statement:** As a nation, we must work harder to stop teenage drinking.

   Topic sentences:
   Many teens don't understand the dangers of alcohol.
   Teens need to learn to be responsible with alcohol.
   There are ways to prevent teen alcohol use and abuse.

   Concluding paragraph:

   _____

   _____

   _____

   _____

   _____

   _____

   _____

   _____

   _____

   _____

   _____

   _____

   _____

   _____

   _____

   _____

   _____

   _____

   _____

   _____

   _____

3. **Thesis statement**: Televisions have helped Americans learn more about themselves and the world.

   Topic sentences:
   Television shows can be educational.
   Television is a great form of entertainment.
   Television has drawbacks.

   Concluding paragraph:

REMEMBER

Remember, the concluding paragraph summarizes the main points in the essay.

---

4. **Thesis statement:** Drivers should experience many different driving situations before they get a license.

Topic sentences:
People who get licenses must be safe drivers.
Students should gradually earn their licenses.
Students need practical driving experience.

Concluding paragraph:

_____

_____

_____

_____

_____

_____

_____

_____

_____

_____

_____

_____

_____

_____

_____

_____

_____

_____

_____

_____

_____

_____

5. **Thesis statement:** If I knew that I only had a few months to live, I would focus more on the important things in life, particularly my faith, family, and friends.

Topic sentences:

If I knew I didn't have much time to live, I would try new things and focus on my faith.

In my last days, I would focus on my family and plan for their future without me.

Before dying, I would want to have fun with my friends and reconnect with some people.

Concluding paragraph:

_____

_____

_____

_____

_____

_____

_____

_____

_____

_____

_____

_____

_____

_____

_____

Answers are on page 364.

IN THIS CHAPTER YOU HAVE LEARNED:

- How to organize a five-paragraph essay (page 229)
- How to write the introductory paragraph (page 230)
- How to write the body paragraphs (page 233)
- How to use transitional words and phrases (page 237)
- How to write the concluding paragraph (page 240)

Review sections that are difficult for you.

Chapter Review

EXERCISE 1

Read the essay topic. Review the thesis statement and the outline that you created on page 225. Then write your essay. If you need more space, use additional paper. Each question has more than one correct answer.

Essay topic: If you could meet anyone (living or dead), whom would you choose and why? In an essay, explain your thoughts. Your response may include personal experiences, knowledge, and observations.

_____

_____

_____

_____

_____

_____

_____

_____

_____

_____

_____

_____

_____

_____

_____

_____

_____

_____

Answers are on page 364.

EXERCISE 2

Read the essay topic. Review the thesis statement and the outline that you created on page 226. Then write your essay. If you need more space, use additional paper. Each question has more than one correct answer.

Essay topic: Americans need better public schools. Write an essay describing how we can improve public schools in America. Your response may include personal experiences, knowledge, and observations.

_____

_____

_____

_____

_____

_____

_____

_____

_____

_____

_____

_____

_____

_____

_____

_____

_____

_____

_____

_____

_____

_____

_____

_____

_____

_____

_____

_____

_____

_____

_____

_____

_____

_____

_____

_____

_____

_____

_____

_____

_____

_____

Answers are on page 365.

Revising the Essay

CHAPTER 13

IN THIS CHAPTER YOU WILL LEARN:

- How to check the information in your essay (page 253)
- How to check grammar, usage, mechanics, and capitalization in your essay (page 257)
- How to make corrections in your essay (page 254)

Keep in mind, essays are like exercise routines. A good workout includes three stages: a warm-up, an exercise, and a cool down. The revision stage of essay writing is like the cool down phase of a workout. During this stage, review your work and make necessary changes.

The revision stage has two main steps. In the first step, focus on the information in your essay. In the second step, concentrate on the rules: grammar, usage, mechanics, and capitalization. Once you have finished both steps, your essay will be complete.

> **NOTE**
>
> Even though the revision stage focuses on corrections, you may make changes at any point in the writing process. If you notice an error, fix it.

Step One: The Information

ORGANIZATION, CONTENT, AND CLARITY

The first step focuses on the information in your essay. Are your thoughts well organized? Did you include good information to support your ideas? Is the information clearly presented? The checklist that follows will give you a systematic way to review your essay.

CHECKLIST FOR INFORMATION

ORGANIZATION

- ☐ Does the introductory paragraph have a thesis statement that gives the essay direction?
- ☐ Does each body paragraph have a topic sentence and supporting details?
- ☐ Does each body paragraph relate to the thesis statement?
- ☐ Does the concluding paragraph summarize the main points of your essay?

CONTENT

☐ In each paragraph, do the supporting details relate to the topic sentence?

☐ Does the essay include all appropriate information from the outline?

☐ Does each body paragraph have <u>at least</u> three sentences with supporting details?

CLARITY

☐ Is each idea clearly written?

☐ Do transitional words connect the information smoothly?

☐ Does the essay have different types of sentences?

After you have reviewed the information, make necessary corrections. Add supporting details, and reword awkward sentences. Likewise, cross out material that is not related to the topic.

HOW TO MAKE CORRECTIONS

1. Cross out unwanted words with a single line.
2. Use a caret (^) or asterisk (*) to insert words or sentences.
3. Use the margins or spaces between lines to add ideas or make corrections.
4. Use the symbol ¶ to show that a paragraph should be indented.
5. Rewrite any section that is too sloppy to read.

Do not rewrite your whole essay unless it is absolutely necessary.

Example

New inventions are created every day. Often they make our lives easier, but sometimes they can be frustrating.

for instance,
The cellular phone, ^ has changed the way people communicate. However not all of the changes have been helpfull. Cellular phones have had positive and negative effects on modern life.

For example,
^ cell phones help people stay in touch with family, friends, and employers. If a child has a problem, he or she can always call a parent. Some children regularly call their parents after school. ~~Parents want to be sure that their children are safe.~~ *Likewise, adults can call home or work when they is going to be late.*

Cellular phones also are convenient. It is easy to make a phone call in an emergency. Many people keep the phones in their cars, but others take them jogging, biking, or walking to make themselves feel safer. Cell phones also are more convenient than pay phones; sometimes it is hard to find a pay phone that works.

Nonetheless, cellular phones do have drawbacks. Some studies show that cell phone use while driving actually causes accidents. Even basic cellular phone rates can be expensive, and other people can listen into your conversations.

In addition, cell phones may make it to easy for people to contact you; there are times when you do not want phone calls.

Clearly, cell phones have affected our lives in positive and negative ways. Even though cell phones are helpful and convenient, they do cause some problems. Like many inventions, cell phones can make our lives easier. ~~After all, computers have made our lives easier.~~. We simply need to use them wisely.

The writer crossed out information that was not related to the topic and added transitional words to the first and second paragraphs.

EXERCISE 1

Revise the following essay using these steps:

1. Read the essay once.

2. Read the essay a second time while completing the checklist for information.

3. Make necessary changes in the margins or spaces between the lines. You may need to cross out some material and add new sentences.

CHECKLIST FOR INFORMATION

ORGANIZATION
- ☐ Does the introductory paragraph have a thesis statement that gives the essay direction?
- ☐ Does each body paragraph have a topic sentence and supporting details?
- ☐ Does each body paragraph relate to the thesis statement?
- ☐ Does the concluding paragraph summarize the main points of your essay?

CONTENT
- ☐ In each paragraph, do the supporting details relate to the topic sentence?
- ☐ Does the essay include all appropriate information from the outline?
- ☐ Does each body paragraph have <u>at least</u> three sentences with supporting details?

CLARITY
- ☐ Is each idea clearly written?
- ☐ Do transitional words connect the information smoothly?
- ☐ Does the essay have different types of sentences?

ESSAY TOPIC 1

Public education is an important part of American society. Many public schools in America do not educate children well. As a result, too many students do not have the skills they need.

First, parents and educators need to set higher expectations for students. Children learn more when they are challenged. High school students should take at least three years of English, math, science, social studies, and physical education. Courses for high school students should prepare them for college, job training, or both. Adults in the community can serve as mentors.

Likewise, parents need to get more involved in the schools and show their children that education matters. Parents should attend parent-teacher conferences and volunteer in the schools. Parents must improve their own education to show their children that learning does not stop at the school door.

The community also needs to support the local schools. Community leaders can donate equipment to the schools and arrange for more afterschool activities for students. Often teachers live in the community. The community as a whole can work together to make sure that school buildings are well maintained.

Higher standards, greater parental involvement, and more local support can make the public schools more successful. If we work together, public schools can help students develop their skills and achieve their dreams.

ESSAY TOPIC 2

In America many people are described as heroes. Athletes, soldiers, and even politicians get labeled as heroes sometimes. A real hero is more than just a famous person.

Heroes share certain characteristics. Most importantly, heroes sacrifice themselves to help others. Generally, heroes are caring, brave, and thoughtful. They are willing to try things that others are afraid to try. Explorers and astronauts, for example, go places other people can't imagine. My brother's special education teacher really works hard to help him in school and to prepare him for the outside world. Often heroes just do what comes naturally to them; they don't even think their actions are heroic.

There are many different types of heroes. Usually when we think of heroes, we think of police officers, firefighters, and soldiers. Every year on 9/11, Americans remember the many heroes who died trying to save others. Throughout history, soldiers have risked their lives to protect our country as well as others. There are doctors who travel to dangerous places to help people in need. Although athletes are often called heroes, most are not. Athletes are only heroes if they use their fame and fortune to help others.

Some heroes are famous, but everyday people can be heroes, as well. Recently, my friend organized a fundraiser to help a needy family. To that family, my friend was a hero. Likewise, teachers who put in extra hours to help their students are heroes.

More than most people, a hero sacrifices himself or herself to help others.

Answers are on page 366.

Step Two: The Rules

GRAMMAR, USAGE, MECHANICS, AND CAPITALIZATION

The second step, which is often called editing or proofreading, focuses on the rules of English. Are pronouns and verbs used correctly? Are punctuation marks used properly? The checklist that follows will give you a systematic way to review your essay.

CHECKLIST FOR RULES

- ☐ Is every sentence a complete sentence?
- ☐ Are pronouns and verbs used correctly?
- ☐ Are punctuation marks used correctly?
- ☐ Are words capitalized correctly?
- ☐ Are words used appropriately?

Example

Now, the writer has completed the second step with the essay on cellular phones. Note the corrections that are in color.

New inventions are created every day. Often they make our lives easier, but sometimes they can be frustrating.

The cell phone, ^ *for instance,* *has changed the way people communicate. However not all of the changes have been* ~~*helpfull*~~ *helpful. Cell phones have had positive and negative effects on modern life.*

^ *For example, cell* ~~*Cellular*~~ *phones help people stay in touch with family, friends, and employers. If a child has a problem, he or she can always call a parent. Some children regularly call their parents after school.* ~~*Parents want to be sure that their children are safe.*~~

Likewise, adults can call home or work when they ~~*is*~~ *are going to be late.*

Cell phones also are convenient. It is easy to make a phone call in an emergency. Many people keep cell phones in their cars, but others take them jogging, biking, or walking to make themselves feel safer. Cell phones also are more convenient than pay phones; sometimes it is hard to find a pay phone that works.

Nonetheless, cell phones do have drawbacks. Some studies show that cell phone use while driving actually causes accidents. Even basic cell phone rates can be expensive, and other people can listen in to your conversations. In addition, cell phones may make it ~~to~~ *too* easy for people to contact you; there are times when you do not want phone calls.

Clearly, cell phones have affected our lives in positive and negative ways. Even though cell phones are helpful and convenient, they do cause some problems. Like many inventions, cell phones can make our lives easier. ~~After all, computers have made our lives easier.~~ We simply need to use them wisely.

EXERCISE 2

Revise the following essay using these steps.

1. Read the essay once.

2. Read the essay a second time while completing the checklist for rules.

3. Make necessary changes in the margins or spaces between the lines.

CHECKLIST FOR RULES

☐ Is every sentence a complete sentence?
☐ Are pronouns and verbs used correctly?
☐ Are punctuation marks used correctly?
☐ Are words capitalized correctly?
☐ Are words used appropriately?

In every profession, you need certain skills to succeed. Teaching is no different. Teachers have the power and the responsibility to change peoples' lives. Therefore, it is important that they have certain attributes. A good teacher knows the subject and understands how to teach students effectively.

Perhaps most importantly, a good teacher is well educated. Teachers need to know there subject area well, and they should understand basic psychology. In addition, a teacher must have training so as to develop good classroom management skills.

Good teachers know how to make a class interesting. Unfortunately, a lot of teachers are like my brother's history teacher, who just reads out of the textbook. A good teacher on the other hand has a sense of humor and shows how the subject relates to the students' lives. When students have a great teacher, they is eager to work hard and learn as much as they can.

Students also know that a good teacher really cares about them. Strong teachers have high expectations for their students and treat everyone fairly. When I was younger, no one cared that I couldn't read. Eventually, I got a great teacher who knew I could learn and gave me extra help. By just reaching out, she made a difference in my life.

People choose to become teachers for many different reasons. However, great teachers stand out because she has the necessary training, skills, and dedication. As students sometimes we don't appreciate how hard these teachers work to help us learn. Therefore, when we have great teachers, it is important to thank them.

Answers are on page 367.

EXERCISE 3

Revise the following essay using these steps:

1. Read the essay once.

2. Read the essay a second time while completing the checklist for information and rules.

3. Make necessary changes in the margins or spaces between the lines. You may need to cross out some material and add new sentences.

CHECKLIST FOR INFORMATION AND RULES

ORGANIZATION
☐ Does the introductory paragraph have a thesis statement that gives the essay direction?
☐ Does each body paragraph have a topic sentence and supporting details?
☐ Does each body paragraph relate to the thesis statement?
☐ Does the concluding paragraph summarize the main points of your essay?

CONTENT
☐ In each paragraph, do the supporting details relate to the topic sentence?
☐ Does the essay include all appropriate information from the outline?
☐ Does each body paragraph have <u>at least</u> three sentences with supporting details?

RULES
☐ Is every sentence a complete sentence?
☐ Are pronouns and verbs used correctly?
☐ Are punctuation marks used correctly?
☐ Are words capitalized correctly?
☐ Are words used appropriately?

Many people are active in volunteer activities. These projects not only get people involved in they're communities but also help people in need. Some people want to make community service a high school graduation requirement; others think that schools should not force students to "volunteer." High schools should require community service because it helps students become more thoughtful, responsible adults.

Students discover different careers that might interest them, such as medicine or teaching. Teens develop important job skills that will help them in the future. They learn to be on time, to follow directions, and to complete projects. People who volunteer as teens are more likely to volunteer as adults.

Students also get involved in many different types of community service. Teenagers can choose volunteer programs that interest them.

Likewise, when students are involved in community service, they develop into more active confident adults. Community service makes teens more self-assured. High school community service programs have made students more active in college volunteer programs. In addition, teenagers who are involved in community programs are more interested in local issues.

Clearly community service can be an important part of one's high school education. Community service programs positively effect students not only when they are teens but also when they become adults.

Answers are on page 368.

IN THIS CHAPTER YOU HAVE LEARNED:

- How to check the information in your essay (page 253)
- How to check grammar, usage, mechanics, and capitalization in your essay (page 257)
- How to make corrections in your essay (page 254)

Review sections that are difficult for you.

Chapter Review

In Chapter 12, you wrote about the following essay topics. Use the checklist for information and the checklist for rules to revise the essays, which you have already written. Share your revised essay with a teacher or another student.

Essay topic 1: If you could meet anyone (living or dead), whom would you choose and why? In an essay, explain your thoughts. Your response may include personal experiences, knowledge, and observations.

Essay topic 2: Americans need better public schools. Write an essay describing how we can improve public schools in America. Your response may include personal experiences, knowledge, and observations.

Evaluating the Essay CHAPTER **14**

Two GED evaluators will read your essay once and score it holistically. The evaluators will focus mostly on your ability to support a good, clear thesis statement. Even though a few minor errors will not significantly affect your score, check your writing carefully. If errors make your essay hard to understand, you will earn a lower score.

REMEMBER

Remember the following points:

- In 45 minutes, you will need to discuss your views on a particular topic. You will not need to know any special information about the topic, but you will need to write a clear, organized, well-developed essay.

- Your final product must be written on two lined pages in the official answer book. The evaluators will not read any additional pages.

- Two trained evaluators will read your essay and grade it based on their view of the essay as a whole. The evaluators' scores will be averaged.

- You need an essay score of 2 or higher to pass. If your essay earns at least a 2, your essay score will be combined with the multiple-choice score to form a composite score for the GED Language Arts, Writing Test. However, if your essay earns a 1 or 1.5, you will not receive a composite score. Instead, you will need to retake both the multiple-choice and essay portions of the test.

- A "0" or asterisk (*, **) on your transcript indicates that you did not earn a passing score.

DEFINITION OF DESCRIPTORS*

The GED Testing Service defines the descriptors as follows:

- **Response to prompt** refers to how well the candidate responded to the topic, including whether or not the focus of the response shifted.

- **Organization** refers to whether or not there is evidence that the candidate had a clear idea about what he or she would write and was able to establish a definable plan for writing the essay.

- **Development and details** refers to the candidate's ability to expand on initial concepts or statements through the use of examples and specific details rather than using lists or reiterating the same information.

*Reprinted with permission from GED® Testing Service of the American Council on Education®

- **Conventions of Edited American English** refers to the candidate's ability to use appropriately edited written English, including the application of the basic rules of grammar, such as sentence structure, mechanics, usage, and so forth.
- **Word choice** refers to the candidate's ability to use appropriate words to express an idea.

SCORING CHART

For some students, a chart is easier to understand. Each column shows the characteristics of a particular essay.

GED OFFICIAL ESSAY-SCORING GUIDE*			
1 **Inadequate**	**2** **Marginal**	**3** **Adequate**	**4** **Effective**
Reader has difficulty indentifying or following the writer's ideas.	Reader occasionally has difficulty understanding or following the writer's ideas.	Reader understands writer's ideas.	Reader understands and easily follows the writer's expression of ideas.

	1 Inadequate	**2** Marginal	**3** Adequate	**4** Effective
Response to the Prompt	Attempts to address the prompt but with little or no success in establishing a focus.	Addresses the prompt, though the focus may shift.	Uses the writing prompt to establish a main idea.	Presents a clearly focused main idea that addresses the prompt.
Organization	Fails to organize ideas.	Shows some evidence of an organizational plan.	Uses an identifiable organizational plan.	Establishes a clear and logical organization.
Development and Ideas	Demonstrates little or no development; usually lacks details or examples or presents irrelevant information.	Has some development but lacks specific details; may be limited to a listing, repetitions, or generalizations.	Has focused but occasionally uneven development; incorporates some specific detail.	Achieves coherent development with specific and relevant details and examples.
Conventions of EAE	Exhibits minimal or no control of sentence structure and the conventions of Edited American English (EAE).	Demonstrates inconsistent control of sentence structure and the conventions of Edited American English (EAE).	Generally controls sentence structure and the conventions of Edited American English (EAE).	Consistently controls sentence structure and the conventions of Edited American English (EAE).
Word Choice	Exhibits weak and/or inappropriate words.	Exhibits a narrow range of word choice, often including inappropriate selections.	Exhibits appropriate word choice.	Exhibits varied and precise word choice.

*Reprinted with permission from GED® Testing Service of the American Council on Education®

IN OTHER WORDS...	
Response to Prompt	Write only on the assigned topic. Establish a main idea and stick to it.
Organization	Use a clear, logical plan to organize your thoughts.
Development and Details	Develop the topic thoroughly. Use many specific, relevant details.
Conventions of EAE	Use proper English.
Word Choice	Use a variety of words that are appropriate.

Example

Essay topic: Are music, art, and athletic programs in the public schools important? In an essay, explain your thoughts. Your response may include personal experiences, knowledge, and observations.

SAMPLE ESSAY

Programs for art, music, and athletics are important. These programs help keep some students in school. Even if schools don't have a lot of money, they should keep art, music, and athletics.

Many students like art, music, and sports. Even people who don't want to go to school like going to these classes. They get bored in there other classes, but in these classes they get to do things that they want to do. These classes are more relaxed then other classes.

In these programs students learn things that they can't learn in there other classes. Some people work hard in school so they can stay in these programs. Art, music, and athletics help people become better students.

In my opinion, programs for art, music, and athletics should not be cut. Students need these programs.

This essay probably would receive a 2. It has some organization, but it does not have enough supporting details. In addition, there are a few errors—mostly in word choice.

Your Turn

The following pages have sample essays for you to evaluate. Use the Checklist for Evaluating an Essay and the Scoring Chart as guides. After you have evaluated the essays independently, check your scores against those on page 369. In addition, have a teacher or student review the scores that you assigned. Follow these steps:

1. Read the essay once to get an overall impression.
2. Read the essay a second time to evaluate the information. Complete the first three sections of the checklist.
3. Read the essay a third time to evaluate how well it follows the rules. Complete the last section of the checklist.
4. Review your answers to the checklist. Look on the chart to find the numbered column that best describes the essay. Assign an essay score.
5. Compare the essay score that you assigned with the scores on page 369.

ESSAY TOPIC

Essay topic: Are music, art, and athletic programs in the public schools important? In an essay, explain your thoughts. Your response may include personal experiences, knowledge, and observations.

SAMPLE ESSAY 1

I think that art, music, and sports are important. Kids like them. They are a lot easier than other classes. They are more relaxing. You get to do things that you like to do and you can have fun. These classes teach students things that they can't learn in there other classes. Some students are really interested in these classes. They may want to be artists, musisians or atheletes. When they get older. If these classes are cut some kids won't want to go to school. Schools should cut other things that aren't as important.

CHECKLIST FOR EVALUATING AN ESSAY

ORGANIZATION
- ☐ Does the introductory paragraph have a thesis statement that gives the essay direction?
- ☐ Does each body paragraph have a topic sentence and supporting details?
- ☐ Does each body paragraph relate to the thesis statement?
- ☐ Does the concluding paragraph summarize the main points of the essay?

CONTENT
- ☐ In each paragraph, do the supporting details relate to the topic sentence?
- ☐ Does the essay include all appropriate information from the outline?
- ☐ Does each body paragraph have <u>at least</u> three sentences with supporting details?

CLARITY
☐ Is each idea clearly written?
☐ Do transitional words connect the information smoothly?
☐ Does the essay have different types of sentences?

THE RULES
☐ Is every sentence a complete sentence?
☐ Are pronouns and verbs used correctly?
☐ Are punctuation marks used correctly?
☐ Are words capitalized correctly?
☐ Are words used appropriately?

SCORE
◯ *   ◯ 1   ◯ 2   ◯ 3   ◯ 4

SAMPLE ESSAY 2

Art! everybody like art. Music to and sports. Long time ago people think that artrists are famous like monet and now they want to not spend money on art classess. Even music classess. Where will all the new artrists come from? Oh no! who will paint pictures and make music? We need sports to. Some kids, they liked sports. where will they play? what will they did if they don't play sports? who will played on pro teams? These classess keep kids off drugs. big problem. Theyll do more drugs. Keep art and music in school. Sports to! Kids want to go to school and go to these classess and learn lots about art and music. some kids wont go. who will teach them? Art is great!

CHECKLIST FOR EVALUATING AN ESSAY

ORGANIZATION
☐ Does the introductory paragraph have a thesis statement that gives the essay direction?
☐ Does each body paragraph have a topic sentence and supporting details?
☐ Does each body paragraph relate to the thesis statement?
☐ Does the concluding paragraph summarize the main points of the essay?

CONTENT
☐ In each paragraph, do the supporting details relate to the topic sentence?
☐ Does the essay include all appropriate information from the outline?
☐ Does each body paragraph have <u>at least</u> three sentences with supporting details?

CLARITY
☐ Is each idea clearly written?
☐ Do transitional words connect the information smoothly?
☐ Does the essay have different types of sentences?

THE RULES

☐ Is every sentence a complete sentence?
☐ Are pronouns and verbs used correctly?
☐ Are punctuation marks used correctly?
☐ Are words capitalized correctly?
☐ Are words used appropriately?

SCORE

○ *   ○ 1   ○ 2   ○ 3   ○ 4

SAMPLE ESSAY 3

Schools should work hard to keep their art, music, and athletic programs.

Art, music, and athletics are important for many students. Some enjoy the more relaxed atmosphere that these classes offer because it is different than their other classes. Other students want to learn more about these subjects so that they can study them in college or use them for jobs. For some students, these classes are the only reason they want to go to school. Schools that cut these classes may end up with a higher dropout rate.

These programs give students a better education. They learn to be creative, to appreciate other people's skills, to relax, to explore, and to take care of their health. They also learn to think better. For example, students who are involved in music often do well in math.

Some schools may want to cut these programs because they don't have enough money, but they should cut something else instead, like Spanish or something. Art, music, and athletics are important in the schools. They make education more interesting.

CHECKLIST FOR EVALUATING AN ESSAY

ORGANIZATION

☐ Does the introductory paragraph have a thesis statement that gives the essay direction?
☐ Does each body paragraph have a topic sentence and supporting details?
☐ Does each body paragraph relate to the thesis statement?
☐ Does the concluding paragraph summarize the main points of your essay?

CONTENT

☐ In each paragraph, do the supporting details relate to the topic sentence?
☐ Does the essay include all appropriate information from the outline?
☐ Does each body paragraph have <u>at least</u> three sentences with supporting details?

CLARITY
☐ Is each idea clearly written?
☐ Do transitional words connect the information smoothly?
☐ Does the essay have different types of sentences?

THE RULES
☐ Is every sentence a complete sentence?
☐ Are pronouns and verbs used correctly?
☐ Are punctuation marks used correctly?
☐ Are words capitalized correctly?
☐ Are words used appropriately?

SCORE
○ *   ○ 1   ○ 2   ○ 3   ○ 4

SAMPLE ESSAY 4

Schools have many different programs. Some give extra help to students, and others make school more interesting. However, when money is tight, some programs have to be eliminated. The art, music, and athletics programs should not be cut.

Art, music, and athletics add variety to the school day. These classes are set up differently than other subjects. My art class, for example, is less structured than math or science. Likewise, in physical education classes students are active. Some students need these subjects so that they can get through the rest of the day.

Art, music, and athletics also are an important part of an education. These classes help students learn more about different types of art and music. Otherwise the only music some students would hear would be on the radio. Athletics help students learn more about their bodies and how to keep themselves healthy.

In addition, these programs help students develop a variety of skills. Some people use these skills to pursue hobbies such as photography and drawing. Others play in bands or sell paintings to earn money. Through sports, students develop athletic skills that they can use there entire lives.

Art, music, and athletics are an important part of our schools. These educational programs add variety to the school day. They also help students develop useful skills.

CHECKLIST FOR EVALUATING AN ESSAY

ORGANIZATION
☐ Does the introductory paragraph have a thesis statement that gives the essay direction?
☐ Does each body paragraph have a topic sentence and supporting details?
☐ Does each body paragraph relate to the thesis statement?
☐ Does the concluding paragraph summarize the main points of your essay?

CONTENT
☐ In each paragraph, do the supporting details relate to the topic sentence?
☐ Does the essay include all appropriate information from the outline?
☐ Does each body paragraph have <u>at least</u> three sentences with supporting details?

CLARITY
☐ Is each idea clearly written?
☐ Do transitional words connect the information smoothly?
☐ Does the essay have different types of sentences?

THE RULES
☐ Is every sentence a complete sentence?
☐ Are pronouns and verbs used correctly?
☐ Are punctuation marks used correctly?
☐ Are words capitalized correctly?
☐ Are words used appropriately?

SCORE
○ *   ○ 1   ○ 2   ○ 3   ○ 4

SAMPLE ESSAY 5

School leaders have to make difficult decisions. Some programs are easy to eliminate, but most are hard to cut. No one wants to lose a good program. The art, music, and athletic programs should not be reduced, because they are too important.

Art, music, and athletics often attract students' attention. Many students struggle in their academic classes. For these children, special programs provide an opportunity to develop skills that they enjoy using. Some students would not even attend school if these special programs were eliminated.

When students learn about art, music, and athletics, they also have a more general education. Students learn to be more creative and innovative. They learn more about themselves and other people. Through sports, students learn to keep their bodies healthy. According to some studies, these classes actually help students do better in math, science, and English. Without these programs, one's education is limited.

The special programs help students interact better. In some schools, students are grouped in academic classes according to their abilities. They often spend most of the school day with the same students. In the special programs, however, students are more likely to be mixed together. Therefore, they learn to get along with a variety of people, and they learn that everybody has different talents.

Clearly, art, music, and athletics programs are necessary. These programs interest students and develop their general education. In addition, these programs help students interact better. Most budget decisions are hard, but this is one is easy.

CHECKLIST FOR EVALUATING AN ESSAY

ORGANIZATION

☐ Does the introductory paragraph have a thesis statement that gives the essay direction?

☐ Does each body paragraph have a topic sentence and supporting details?

☐ Does each body paragraph relate to the thesis statement?

☐ Does the concluding paragraph summarize the main points of your essay?

CONTENT

☐ In each paragraph, do the supporting details relate to the topic sentence?

☐ Does the essay include all appropriate information from the outline?

☐ Does each body paragraph have <u>at least</u> three sentences with supporting details?

CLARITY

☐ Is each idea clearly written?

☐ Do transitional words connect the information smoothly?

☐ Does the essay have different types of sentences?

THE RULES

☐ Is every sentence a complete sentence?

☐ Are pronouns and verbs used correctly?

☐ Are punctuation marks used correctly?

☐ Are words capitalized correctly?

☐ Are words used appropriately?

SCORE

○ *   ○ 1   ○ 2   ○ 3   ○ 4

Answers are on page 369.

IN THIS CHAPTER YOU HAVE LEARNED:

- How essays are scored (page 264)
- What you can do to improve your essay score (page 265)

Review sections that are difficult for you.

Chapter Review

In Chapter 12, you wrote about the following essay topics. Evaluate your essays using the Checklist for Evaluating and the Scoring Chart as guides. After you have evaluated the essays independently, have a teacher or another adult review the scores that you assigned. Follow these steps:

1. Read the essay once to get an overall impression.
2. Read the essay a second time to evaluate the information. Complete the first three sections of the checklist.
3. Read the essay a third time to evaluate how well it follows the rules. Complete the last section of the checklist.
4. Review your answers to the checklist. Look on the chart to find the numbered column that best describes the essay. Assign an essay score.

Essay topic 1: If you could meet anyone (living or dead), whom would you choose and why? In an essay, explain your thoughts. Your response may include personal experiences, knowledge, and observations.

Essay topic 2: Americans need better public schools. Write an essay describing how we can improve public schools in America. Your response may include personal experiences, knowledge, and observations.

Practice Essays

Overview

This practice section includes one essay with step-by-step instructions that guide you through the writing process. It also includes simulated tests you should complete independently. When you are done, check your essays against those on page 371. In addition, have a teacher or another adult read your work.

GUIDED SAMPLE ESSAY

This practice essay is designed to guide you through the entire writing process. Before you begin the essay, make sure that you have plenty of scratch paper and a copy of the answer sheet on page 277. Do not time yourself for this particular essay.

DIRECTIONS

1. Read the entire question carefully.

2. Plan your response before you write.

3. Write only about the assigned topic. You will receive no credit for writing on a different topic.

4. Make notes on scratch paper. Your notes will not be scored.

5. Write your essay on a copy of the answer sheet on page 277 or a separate sheet of paper.

6. Carefully read your essay and make changes that will improve it.

7. Use correct paragraphing, sentence structure, usage, punctuation, and capitalization.

8. Use a ballpoint pen and write legibly.

Essay topic: If you could live anywhere in America, where would you live and why? In an essay, explain your thoughts. Your response may include personal experiences, knowledge, and observations.

> **NOTE**
>
> The practice topics are similar to real GED essay topics. To maintain the integrity of the test, actual GED essays are not published.

STEP-BY-STEP INSTRUCTIONS

Check off each completed step.

Planning

☐ 1. Read the essay topic. In the space provided or on a separate sheet of paper, write your thesis statement.

Thesis Statement ➡ _____

_____

☐ 2. On a separate sheet of paper, brainstorm ideas for the essay. Make sure you have <u>at least</u> ten good ideas.

☐ 3. Separate your ideas into main ideas and details.

☐ 4. Organize your ideas into an outline. Use either a T-list or web.

Writing

☐ 5. Write your introductory paragraph.
   a. Review your outline.
   b. Write 1–2 general statements about the topic.
   c. Write 1–2 more specific statements about the topic.
   d. Write your thesis statement.

☐ 6. Write your body paragraphs.
   a. Review your outline and thesis statement.
   b. Choose the order for your main ideas.
   c. Focus on one main idea at a time.
   d. Rewrite the main idea as a topic sentence.
   e. Rewrite the supporting details as supporting sentences.
   f. Add more information as needed.

☐ 7. Write your conclusion.
   a. Review your essay.
   b. In 1 sentence, rewrite your thesis statement.
   c. In 1–2 sentences, summarize your topic sentences.
   d. In 1–2 sentences, write a general statement about the topic.

Revising

☐ 8. Complete the checklist and make changes as necessary.

CHECKLIST FOR EVALUATING AN ESSAY

ORGANIZATION

☐ Does the introductory paragraph have a thesis statement that gives the essay direction?

☐ Does each body paragraph have a topic sentence and supporting details?

☐ Does each body paragraph relate to the thesis statement?

☐ Does the concluding paragraph summarize the main points of your essay?

CONTENT
☐ In each paragraph, do the supporting details relate to the topic sentence?
☐ Does the essay include all appropriate information from the outline?
☐ Does each body paragraph have <u>at least</u> three sentences with supporting details?

CLARITY
☐ Is each idea clearly written?
☐ Do transitional words connect the information smoothly?
☐ Does the essay have different types of sentences?

THE RULES
☐ Is every sentence a complete sentence?
☐ Are pronouns and verbs used correctly?
☐ Are punctuation marks used correctly?
☐ Are words capitalized correctly?
☐ Are words used appropriately?

Evaluating

☐ 9. Use the essay checklist and scoring chart on page 264 to evaluate your essay.
☐ 10. After you have evaluated your essay independently, have a teacher or student review your writing and the score that you assigned.

SIMULATED TESTS

For these tests, it is important to simulate the actual testing conditions as much as possible. For each essay, assemble your materials (pens, paper, etc.) before you begin, and set a timer for 45 minutes. Start the timer as soon as you begin reading the instructions.

    After you have completed your essay, evaluate it. First, complete the evaluation process independently. Then, ask your teacher or another adult to evaluate your essay.

REMINDER

Time Management

Planning (10 Minutes)
1. Figure out the instructions and the topic.
2. Write the thesis statement.
3. Brainstorm.
4. Create an outline.

Writing (25 Minutes)
1. Review your notes.
2. Write the introduction, body, and conclusion.

Revising (10 Minutes)
1. Compare your essay and notes.
2. Check and revise for the information: organization, content, and clarity.
3. Check and revise for the rules: grammar, usage, mechanics, and capitalization.

SAMPLE TEST A

Directions

Part II of the Language Arts, Writing Test examines your ability to write well. In 45 minutes, write an essay on the assigned topic. Follow the steps below:

1. Read the entire question carefully.
2. Plan your response before you write.
3. Write only about the assigned topic. You will receive no credit for writing on a different topic.
4. Make notes on scratch paper. Your notes will not be scored.
5. Write your essay on a copy of the answer sheet on page 277 or a separate sheet of paper.
6. Carefully read your essay and make changes that will improve it.
7. Use correct paragraphing, sentence structure, usage, punctuation, and capitalization.
8. Use a ballpoint pen and write legibly.

Essay topic: What are the characteristics of a good role model? In an essay, explain your thoughts. Your response may include personal experiences, knowledge, and observations.

SAMPLE TEST B

Directions

Part II of the Language Arts, Writing Test examines your ability to write well. In 45 minutes, write an essay on the assigned topic. Follow the steps below:

1. Read the entire question carefully.
2. Plan your response before you write.
3. Write only about the assigned topic. You will receive no credit for writing on a different topic.
4. Make notes on scratch paper. Your notes will not be scored.
5. Write your essay on a copy of the answer sheet on page 277 or a separate sheet of paper.
6. Carefully read your essay and make changes that will improve it.
7. Use correct paragraphing, sentence structure, usage, punctuation, and capitalization.
8. Use a ballpoint pen and write legibly.

Essay topic: What can be done to prevent teen violence? In an essay, explain your thoughts. Your response may include personal experiences, knowledge, and observations.

Answers are on page 372.

ANSWER SHEET FOR PRACTICE ESSAYS

Name _____

Class _____

Date _____

Topic _____

Start Time _____

Finish Time _____

_____

_____

_____

_____

_____

_____

_____

_____

_____

_____

_____

_____

_____

_____

_____

_____

_____

_____

_____

_____

_____

_____

_____

_____

_____

_____

_____

_____

_____

_____

_____

_____

_____

_____

_____

_____

_____

_____

_____

_____

_____

_____

_____

_____

_____

_____

(Continue practice essay on additional sheets of paper.)

Posttest 1

DIRECTIONS

1. This test has five passages with numbered sentences. The sentences may have errors, or they may be correct as written. First read the passage. Then answer the related questions. Choose the best answer for each question. The best answer should be consistent with the point of view and verb tense that is used throughout the passage.

2. Answer every question. If you are not sure of the answer, make a logical guess.

3. Allow yourself 75 minutes to answer the 50 questions. When the time is up, underline the last item that you completed. Then finish the test. This will help you monitor your time for the actual GED test.

4. Write your answers to the questions on the answer grid. For each question, mark the number that matches the answer you chose.

5. After you have completed the test, check your answers and complete the Skills Chart to see which sections are difficult for you.

EXAMPLE

Sentence 1: **Parents need to give there children a lot of attention.**

What correction should be made to this sentence?

(1)   replace *Parents* with *Parents'*

(2)   replace *there* with *their*

(3)   replace *need* with *needed*

(4)   insert a comma after *children*

(5)   no correction necessary

1.   ① ● ③ ④ ⑤

In this sentence, *there* should be replaced with *their.*

Answer Sheet
POSTTEST 1

1. ① ② ③ ④ ⑤
2. ① ② ③ ④ ⑤
3. ① ② ③ ④ ⑤
4. ① ② ③ ④ ⑤
5. ① ② ③ ④ ⑤
6. ① ② ③ ④ ⑤
7. ① ② ③ ④ ⑤
8. ① ② ③ ④ ⑤
9. ① ② ③ ④ ⑤
10. ① ② ③ ④ ⑤
11. ① ② ③ ④ ⑤
12. ① ② ③ ④ ⑤
13. ① ② ③ ④ ⑤
14. ① ② ③ ④ ⑤
15. ① ② ③ ④ ⑤
16. ① ② ③ ④ ⑤
17. ① ② ③ ④ ⑤
18. ① ② ③ ④ ⑤
19. ① ② ③ ④ ⑤
20. ① ② ③ ④ ⑤
21. ① ② ③ ④ ⑤
22. ① ② ③ ④ ⑤
23. ① ② ③ ④ ⑤
24. ① ② ③ ④ ⑤
25. ① ② ③ ④ ⑤

26. ① ② ③ ④ ⑤
27. ① ② ③ ④ ⑤
28. ① ② ③ ④ ⑤
29. ① ② ③ ④ ⑤
30. ① ② ③ ④ ⑤
31. ① ② ③ ④ ⑤
32. ① ② ③ ④ ⑤
33. ① ② ③ ④ ⑤
34. ① ② ③ ④ ⑤
35. ① ② ③ ④ ⑤
36. ① ② ③ ④ ⑤
37. ① ② ③ ④ ⑤
38. ① ② ③ ④ ⑤
39. ① ② ③ ④ ⑤
40. ① ② ③ ④ ⑤
41. ① ② ③ ④ ⑤
42. ① ② ③ ④ ⑤
43. ① ② ③ ④ ⑤
44. ① ② ③ ④ ⑤
45. ① ② ③ ④ ⑤
46. ① ② ③ ④ ⑤
47. ① ② ③ ④ ⑤
48. ① ② ③ ④ ⑤
49. ① ② ③ ④ ⑤
50. ① ② ③ ④ ⑤

Directions: Choose the best answer for each question.

<u>Questions 1 through 9</u> refer to the following passage.

(A)

(1) Once again, teenage smoking has become a national issue. (2) At the same time that adult smoking has declined, teenage smoking will have increased. (3) Teenagers are smoking not only cigarettes, but also cigars. (4) Many teens argue that they smoke because of peer pressure. (5) Others insist that they simply like to smoke. (6) Unfortunately, scientific studies have shown that the nicotine in cigarettes are addictive for many people. (7) Persons who sell tobacco products to underage smokers may be punished more severely. (8) Thus, teens which start smoking are likely to continue their habit into adulthood.

(B)

(9) Across the nation and around the world, various efforts to stop teenage smoking is now under way. (10) As a result of pressure from the federal government and various lawsuits even cigarette manufacturers have created ads that are designed to discourage teenage smoking. (11) People who want to buy tobacco products in stores or restaurants often have to show photo identification. (12) This identification proves they are at least 18 years old. (13) Likewise, vending machines may no longer be accessible to teenage smokers. (14) These actions will not eliminate teenage smoking but they should stop some teens from picking up a dangerous habit.

1. Sentence 2: **At the same time that adult smoking has declined, teenage smoking will have increased.**

   What correction should be made to this sentence?

   (1) replace <u>will have increased</u> with <u>has increased</u>
   (2) replace <u>has declined</u> with <u>will decline</u>
   (3) remove the comma after <u>declined</u>
   (4) replace <u>that</u> with <u>which</u>
   (5) no correction necessary

2. Sentences 4 and 5: **Many teens argue that they smoke because of peer pressure. Others insist that they simply like to smoke.**

   The best combination of sentences 4 and 5 would include which group of words?

   (1) pressure others insist
   (2) pressure; others insist
   (3) pressure. And others insist
   (4) pressure because others insist
   (5) pressure others, insist

3. Sentence 6: **Unfortunately, scientific studies have shown that the nicotine in cigarettes are addictive for many people.**

   What correction should be made to this sentence?

   (1) remove the comma after <u>Unfortunately</u>
   (2) move <u>for many people</u> after <u>nicotine</u>
   (3) replace <u>are</u> with <u>is</u>
   (4) replace <u>have shown</u> with <u>will show</u>
   (5) no correction necessary

4. Sentence 7: **Persons who sell tobacco products to underage smokers may be punished more severely.**

What change should be made to the placement of sentence 7?

(1) move sentence 7 to follow sentence 2
(2) move sentence 7 to follow sentence 4
(3) move sentence 7 to follow sentence 12
(4) move sentence 7 to the end of paragraph B
(5) move sentence 7 to follow sentence 5

5. Sentence 8: **Thus, teens which start smoking are likely to continue their habit into adulthood.**

What correction should be made to this sentence?

(1) replace <u>their</u> with <u>they're</u>
(2) remove the comma after <u>thus</u>
(3) replace <u>are</u> with <u>is</u>
(4) replace <u>which</u> with <u>who</u>
(5) no correction necessary

6. Sentence 9: **Across the nation and around the world, various efforts to stop teenage smoking is now under way.**

What correction should be made to this sentence?

(1) replace <u>is</u> with <u>are</u>
(2) remove the comma after <u>world</u>
(3) insert a comma after <u>smoking</u>
(4) replace <u>to stop</u> with <u>will stop</u>
(5) no correction necessary

7. Sentence 10: **As a result of pressure from the federal government and various lawsuits even cigarette manufacturers have created ads that are designed to discourage teenage smoking.**

What correction should be made to this sentence?

(1) replace <u>have created</u> with <u>has created</u>
(2) replace <u>are</u> with <u>is</u>
(3) replace <u>that</u> with <u>which</u>
(4) insert a comma after <u>lawsuits</u>
(5) no correction necessary

8. Sentences 11 and 12: **People who want to buy tobacco products in stores or restaurants often have to show photo identification. This identification proves they are at least 18 years old.**

The most effective combination of sentences 11 and 12 would include which of the following groups of words?

(1) photo identification, but proves
(2) photo identification; nonetheless proves
(3) photo identification; therefore, proves
(4) photo identification that proves
(5) photo identification; however, proves

9. Sentence 14: **These actions will not eliminate teenage <u>smoking but they</u> should stop some teens from picking up a dangerous habit.**

What is the best way to write the underlined portion of the sentence? If you think that the original is correct, choose option (1).

(1) smoking but they
(2) smoking. And they
(3) smoking, but they
(4) smoking; therefore, they
(5) smoking: because they

Questions 10 through 19 refer to the following passage.

How to Install Child Safety Seats

(A)

(1) Many parents struggle for their children to install car seats safely. (2) However, a correctly installed safety seat can reduce the risk of death in an accident by 71 percent. (3) For each stage of development, there is different child safety seats. (4) Parents must be careful when installing children's seats. (5) They should follow the guidelines for car-seat safety.

(B)

(6) Even though safety guidelines vary, there are recommendations that most states share. (7) Newborns should be placed in a rear-facing car-seat until there one year of age and at least 20 pounds. (8) After that stage, a child should sit in a forward-facing car seat which is designed for children between 20 and 40 pounds. (9) Children over 40 pounds should sit in a booster, which works with the seat belt in the car. (10) Many safety experts recommend that children remain in a booster until they are at least 65 pounds or approximately eight years old but some states allow children to sit in a standard seat when they are as young as four.

(C)

(11) These guidelines do vary somewhat from state to state, so it is important to get the latest information on car-seat safety from one's physician or the local police department. (12) Parents must check regularly to make sure that they are positioned properly. (13) Safety seats always should be placed in the backseat of the car. (14) In addition, car seats should be secured tightly to the car the seat should not move more than one inch when tugged. (15) Many local police departments will assist whomever needs help with car-seat installation. (16) Safely installed car seats provide a sense of security for the child and the parent.

10. Sentence 1: **Many parents struggle for their children to install car seats safely.**

    What correction should be made to this sentence?

    (1) insert a comma after <u>seats</u>
    (2) move <u>for their children</u> after <u>safely</u>
    (3) replace <u>parents</u> with <u>parent's</u>
    (4) replace <u>their</u> with <u>they're</u>
    (5) no correction necessary

11. Sentence 3: **For each stage of development, there is different child safety seats.**

    What correction should be made to this sentence?

    (1) remove the comma after <u>development</u>
    (2) replace <u>there</u> with <u>they're</u>
    (3) replace <u>is</u> with <u>are</u>
    (4) insert a comma after <u>stage</u>
    (5) insert a semicolon after <u>development</u>

12. Sentences 4 and 5: **Parents must be careful when installing children's seats. They should follow the guidelines for car-seat safety.**

    The best combination of sentences 4 and 5 would include which group of words?

    (1) children's seats: nonetheless, they should
    (2) children's seats because they should
    (3) children's seats; however, they should
    (4) children's seats, but they should
    (5) children's seats; they should

13. Sentence 7: **Newborns should be placed in a rear-facing car-seat until there one year of age and at least 20 pounds.**

    What correction should be made to this sentence?

    (1) replace <u>Newborns</u> with <u>Newborns'</u>
    (2) replace <u>pounds</u> with <u>Pounds</u>
    (3) insert a comma after <u>car seat</u>
    (4) replace <u>there</u> with <u>they're</u>
    (5) no correction necessary

14. Sentence 8: **After that stage, a child should sit in a forward-facing safety seat which is designed for children between 20 and 40 pounds.**

    What correction should be made to this sentence?

    (1) remove the comma after <u>stage</u>
    (2) replace <u>which</u> with <u>that</u>
    (3) replace <u>is</u> with <u>are</u>
    (4) insert a comma after <u>safety</u>
    (5) no correction necessary

15. Sentence 10: **Many safety experts recommend that children remain in a booster until they are at least 65 pounds or approximately eight years old but some states allow children to sit in a standard seat when they are as young as four.**

    What correction should be made to this sentence?

    (1) replace <u>that</u> with <u>who</u>
    (2) replace <u>experts</u> with <u>experts'</u>
    (3) insert a comma after <u>old</u>
    (4) insert a comma after <u>recommend</u>
    (5) no correction necessary

16. Sentence 11: **These guidelines do vary somewhat from state to state, so it is important to get the latest information on car-seat safety from one's physician or the local police department.**

    What change should be made to the placement of sentence 11?

    (1) move sentence 11 to follow sentence 3
    (2) move sentence 11 to the beginning of paragraph A
    (3) move sentence 11 to follow sentence 14
    (4) move sentence 11 to the end of paragraph C
    (5) move sentence 11 to follow sentence 5

17. Sentence 12: **Parents must check regularly to make sure that they are positioned properly.**

    What correction should be made to this sentence?

    (1) move <u>sure</u> after <u>check</u>
    (2) replace <u>check</u> with <u>checks</u>
    (3) replace <u>they</u> with <u>car seats</u>
    (4) insert a comma after <u>check</u>
    (5) no correction necessary

18. Sentence 14: **In addition, car seats should be secured tightly <u>to the car the seat should</u> not move more than one inch when tugged.**

    What is the best way to write the underlined portion of the sentence? If you think that the original is best, choose option (1).

    (1) to the car the seat should
    (2) to the car, but the seat should
    (3) to the car; the seat should
    (4) to the car, the seat should
    (5) to the car; however, the seat should

19. Sentence 15: **Many local police departments will assist whomever needs help with car-seat installation.**

    What correction should be made to this sentence?

    (1) replace <u>whomever</u> with <u>whoever</u>
    (2) replace <u>police departments</u> with <u>Police Departments</u>
    (3) insert a comma after <u>help</u>
    (4) replace <u>needs</u> with <u>needed</u>
    (5) no correction necessary

Questions 20 through 28 refer to the following passage.

(A)

(1) Women who do not have a private physician can often find appropriate care through a hospital clinic or women's medical center. (2) Even before women become pregnant, she should consider prenatal treatment. (3) Many doctors prescribe vitamins to women who want to have children. (4) Physicians also encourage women to focus on proper nutrition exercise, and childbirth classes, which will help prepare new mothers for the delivery.

(B)

(5) In the past decade, doctors have emphasized the importance of good prenatal care, which focuses on the expectant mother and her developing baby. (6) During checkups throughout the pregnancy, the developing baby's health and the mother's condition are monitored by doctors. (7) Doctors listen to the baby's heartbeat and observe its growth. (8) They also perform tests that provide information about the baby's physical development. (9) Physicians focus on the mother's nutrition health and emotional well-being as well. (10) Doctors help expectant mothers understand not only the physical, but also the emotional changes that they are experiencing. (11) Likewise, doctors teach expectant parents about childbirth and newborn care. (12) Women generally deliver healthier babies who have good prenatal care. (13) As a result, prenatal care should be part of every womans pregnancy.

20. Sentence 1: **Women who do not have a private physician can often find appropriate care through a hospital clinic or women's medical center.**

    What correction should be made to sentence 1?

    (1) replace <u>who</u> with <u>which</u>
    (2) insert a comma after <u>clinic</u>
    (3) replace <u>do</u> with <u>does</u>
    (4) insert a comma after <u>care</u>
    (5) no correction necessary

21. Sentence 2: **Even before women become pregnant, she should consider prenatal treatment.**

    What correction should be made to this sentence?

    (1) remove the comma after <u>pregnant</u>
    (2) replace <u>become</u> with <u>became</u>
    (3) insert a comma after <u>prenatal</u>
    (4) replace <u>she</u> with <u>they</u>
    (5) no correction necessary

22. Sentence 4: **Physicians also encourage women to focus on proper nutrition exercise, and childbirth classes, which will help prepare new mothers for the delivery.**

    What correction should be made to sentence 4?

    (1) replace <u>Physicians</u> with <u>Physician's</u>
    (2) remove the comma after <u>exercise</u>
    (3) insert a comma after <u>nutrition</u>
    (4) replace <u>which</u> with <u>that</u>
    (5) no correction necessary

23. Sentence 5: **In the past decade, doctors have emphasized the importance of good prenatal care, which focuses on the expectant mother and her developing baby.**

    Which change should be made to the placement of sentence 5?

    (1) move sentence 5 to the beginning of paragraph A
    (2) move sentence 5 to follow 3
    (3) move sentence 5 to follow 7
    (4) move sentence 5 to follow 9
    (5) move sentence 5 to the end of paragraph B

24. Sentence 6: **During checkups throughout the pregnancy, the developing baby's health and the mother's condition are monitored by doctors.**

If you rewrote sentence 4 beginning with

During checkups throughout the pregnancy, doctors

the next words would be

(1) condition are
(2) baby's health
(3) monitor the
(4) mother's condition
(5) monitored by

25. Sentences 7 and 8: **Doctors listen to the baby's heartbeat and observe its growth. They also perform tests that provide information about the baby's physical development.**

The best combination of sentences 7 and 8 would include which group of words?

(1) heartbeat and observe its growth and perform tests
(2) heartbeat and observe its growth because they perform tests
(3) heartbeat and observe its growth; therefore, they also perform tests
(4) heartbeat, observe its growth; nonetheless, they perform tests
(5) heartbeat, observe its growth, and perform tests

26. Sentence 9: **Physicians focus on the mother's nutrition exercise and emotional well-being as well.**

What is the best way to write the underlined portion of the sentence? If you think that the original is best, choose option (1).

(1) mother's nutrition exercise and emotional well-being
(2) mothers nutrition exercise and emotional well-being
(3) mother's nutrition; exercise; and emotional, well-being
(4) mother's nutrition exercise, and emotional well-being
(5) mother's nutrition, exercise, and emotional well-being

27. Sentence 12: **Women generally deliver healthier babies who have good prenatal care.**

What correction should be made to this sentence?

(1) move who have good prenatal care after women
(2) change babies to baby's
(3) replace who with which
(4) insert a comma after healthier
(5) no correction necessary

28. Sentence 13: **As a result, prenatal care should be part of every womans pregnancy.**

What correction should be made to this sentence?

(1) replace womans with woman's
(2) remove the comma after result
(3) insert a comma after care
(4) replace should be with was
(5) no correction necessary

Questions 29 through 38 refer to the following letter.

March 31, 2009

Mr. John M. Fallon, President
A-1 Construction, Inc.
230 Main Street
Herndon, VA 20172

Dear Mr. Fallon:

(A)

(1) On February 12 2009, I hired your company to repair the roof on my house. (2) At the time, I had several small leaks, which was causing water spots on the bedroom ceilings. (3) You told me that your workers could fix the leaks and prevent further water damage at the same time. (4) The contract we both signed clearly stated that the project would cost $4,000. (5) The contract also stated that the project would be completed by March 21, 2009.

(B)

(6) The roof continues to leak in the original areas, and the workers creates new leaks in some spots. (7) As a result, recent rain storms have caused major damage in all three bedrooms.

(C)

(8) However, your company still has not finished the repair job properly. (9) When I discussed the situation with Christopher James, the project foreman, it was told to me that the original job was complete, and that the new damage was unrelated. (10) He even suggested that I pay more money to have you're company repair the new leaks and fix the damage to the bedrooms.

(D)

(11) Instead, I have hired a different contractor to fix the roof and repair the bedrooms. (12) However, I certainly expect that A-1 Construction will reimburse me for the original repair costs and the damage that your workers caused. (13) I have enclosed a detailed estimate of $8,000 for damage. (14) You can pay me for my losses. (15) In addition, I have already contacted the Better Business Bureau about this issue. (16) If you do not pay me by April 15, 2009, I will contact a lawyer as well for the damages.

Sincerely,

Katya Murdy

29. Sentence 1: **On February 12 2009, I hired your company to repair the roof on my house.**

What correction should be made to sentence 1?

(1) remove the comma after 2009
(2) replace your with you're
(3) insert a comma after February 12
(4) replace hired with will be hiring
(5) no correction necessary

30. Sentence 2: **At the time, I had several small leaks, which was causing water spots on the bedroom ceilings.**

What correction should be made to this sentence?

(1) remove the comma after time
(2) replace which with that
(3) remove the comma after leaks
(4) replace was with were
(5) no correction necessary

31. Sentences 4 and 5: **The contract we both signed clearly stated that the project would cost $4,000. The contract also stated that the project would be completed by March 21, 2009.**

The best combination of sentences 4 and 5 would include which of the following groups of words?

(1) would cost $4,000, and that it would be completed
(2) would cost $4,000, but it would be completed
(3) would cost $4,000; therefore, it would be completed
(4) would cost $4,000, because it would be completed
(5) would cost $4,000; since, it would be completed

32. Sentence 6: **The roof continues to leak in the original areas, and the workers creates new leaks in some spots.**

What correction should be made to this sentence?

(1) replace workers with workers'
(2) remove the comma after areas
(3) replace continues with continue
(4) replace creates with have created
(5) no correction necessary

33. Sentence 8: **However, your company still has not finished the repair job properly.**

What change should be made to the placement of sentence 8?

(1) move sentence 8 to follow sentence 4
(2) move sentence 8 to the beginning of paragraph B
(3) move sentence 8 to follow sentence 11
(4) move sentence 8 to follow sentence 12
(5) move sentence 8 to the end of paragraph C

34. Sentence 9: **When I discussed the situation with Christopher James, the project foreman, it was told to me that the original job was complete, and that the new damage was unrelated.**

    What correction should be made to this sentence?

    (1) remove the comma after <u>Christopher James</u>
    (2) replace <u>was complete</u> with <u>were complete</u>
    (3) remove the comma after <u>foreman</u>
    (4) replace <u>it was told to me</u> with <u>he told me</u>
    (5) no correction necessary

35. Sentence 10: **He even suggested that I pay more money to have you're company repair the new leaks and fix the damage to the bedrooms.**

    What correction should be made to this sentence?

    (1) replace <u>pay</u> with <u>will have paid</u>
    (2) insert a comma after <u>suggested</u>
    (3) replace <u>you're</u> with <u>your</u>
    (4) replace <u>that</u> with <u>which</u>
    (5) no correction necessary

36. Sentence 12: **However, I certainly expect that A-1 Construction will reimburse me for the original repair costs and the damage that your workers caused.**

    What correction should be made to this sentence?

    (1) replace <u>workers</u> with <u>worker's</u>
    (2) remove the comma after <u>However</u>
    (3) replace <u>A-1 Construction</u> with <u>a-1 construction</u>
    (4) insert a comma after <u>me</u>
    (5) no correction necessary

37. Sentences 13 and 14: **I have enclosed a detailed estimate of $8,000 for the damage. You can pay me for my losses.**

    The best combination of sentences 13 and 14 would include which group of words?

    (1) the damage; although you can pay me
    (2) the damage, so you can pay me
    (3) the damage, or you can pay me
    (4) the damage; likewise, you can pay me
    (5) the damage; otherwise, you can pay me

38. Sentence 16: **If you do not pay me by April 15, 2009, I will contact a lawyer as well for the damages.**

    What correction should be made to this sentence?

    (1) remove the comma after <u>2009</u>
    (2) replace <u>will contact</u> with <u>contacted</u>
    (3) move <u>for the damages</u> to follow <u>pay me</u>
    (4) insert a comma after <u>contact</u>
    (5) no correction necessary

<u>Questions 39 through 50</u> refer to the following letter.

Cova University

Mr. Kedar Warner
440 Park Avenue
Stally, TX 50402

Dear Mr. Warner:

(A)

(1) It is pleasing to us that you are interested in the nursing program at Cova University. (2) As you know nursing is a growing field with many opportunities for men and women. (3) Our program will prepare you to enter nursing with solid medical training and exceptional hands-on experience. (4) Nurses from Cova University move strait to the top of their field locally and across the nation.

(B)

(5) The medical community needs more nurses with your enthusiasm. (6) It also needs more highly trained nurses. (7) As a result of changes in the workforce many nurses are expected to retire in the near future. (8) At the same time, Americans are demanding more medical care. (9) A nursing career offers many benefits for men and women. (10) We has an aging population, an emphasis on preventive medicine, and many medical advances, which all require well-trained nurses. (11) Clearly, you will have enter a growing field that is full of opportunities for skilled, motivated workers.

(C)

(12) Flexible schedules, a variety of work environments, advanced job-training programs, and good pay is just a few of the rewards. (13) Nurses have even more employment options who continue their education.

(D)

(14) The nursing program at Cova University will prepare you for this exciting career. (15) Simply complete the enclosed application and you will be on your way to a better job and a rewarding future.

Sincerely,
Madeline Hamm
Admissions Director

39. Sentence 1: **It is pleasing to us that you are interested in the nursing program at Cova University.**

    What correction should be made to this sentence?

    (1) replace <u>Cova University</u> with <u>cova university</u>
    (2) insert a comma after <u>us</u>
    (3) replace <u>It is pleasing to us</u> with <u>We are pleased</u>
    (4) replace <u>you are</u> with <u>you is</u>
    (5) no correction necessary

40. Sentence 2: **As you know nursing is a growing field with many opportunities for men and women.**

    What correction should be made to this sentence?

    (1) insert a comma after <u>know</u>
    (2) move <u>with many opportunities</u> after <u>women</u>
    (3) replace <u>is</u> with <u>are</u>
    (4) insert a comma after <u>men</u>
    (5) no correction necessary

41. Sentence 3: **Our program will prepare you to enter nursing with solid medical training and exceptional hands-on experience.**

    What correction should be made to this sentence?

    (1) insert a comma after <u>training</u>
    (2) move <u>with solid medical training</u> after <u>experience</u>
    (3) replace <u>will prepare</u> with <u>prepared</u>
    (4) replace <u>Our</u> with <u>Are</u>
    (5) no correction necessary

42. Sentence 4: **Nurses from Cova University move strait to the top of their field locally and across the nation.**

    What correction should be made to this sentence?

    (1) replace <u>their</u> with <u>they're</u>
    (2) insert a comma after <u>locally</u>
    (3) replace <u>strait</u> with <u>straight</u>
    (4) replace <u>move</u> with <u>moves</u>
    (5) no correction necessary

43. Sentences 5 and 6: **The medical community needs more nurses with your enthusiasm. (6) It also needs more highly trained nurses.**

    The best combination of sentences 5 and 6 would include which group of words?

    (1) needs more highly trained nurses with your enthusiasm
    (2) with your enthusiasm; therefore, it also
    (3) with your enthusiasm, so it also
    (4) needs more highly trained nurses; however, your enthusiasm
    (5) more nurses and more enthusiasm

44. Sentence 7: **As a result of changes in the workforce many nurses are expected to retire in the near future.**

    What correction should be made to sentence 7?

    (1) replace <u>are expected</u> with is <u>expected</u>
    (2) insert a comma after <u>workforce</u>
    (3) move <u>in the workforce</u> after <u>future</u>
    (4) replace <u>to retire</u> with <u>retired</u>
    (5) no correction necessary

45. Sentence 9: **A nursing career offers many benefits for men and women.**

    What change should be made to the placement of sentence 9?

    (1) move sentence 9 to the beginning of paragraph B
    (2) move sentence 9 to follow sentence 6
    (3) move sentence 9 to follow sentence 4
    (4) move sentence 9 to the beginning of paragraph C
    (5) move sentence 9 to the end of paragraph D

46. Sentence 10: **We has an aging population, an emphasis on preventive medicine, and many medical advances, which all require well-trained nurses.**

    What correction should be made to sentence 10?

    (1) remove the comma after <u>medicine</u>
    (2) replace <u>has</u> with <u>have</u>
    (3) insert a comma after <u>aging</u>
    (4) replace <u>which</u> with <u>that</u>
    (5) no correction necessary

47. Sentence 11: **Clearly, you will have enter a growing field that is full of opportunities for skilled, motivated workers.**

    What correction should be made to this sentence?

    (1) remove the comma after <u>skilled</u>
    (2) replace <u>that</u> with <u>which</u>
    (3) insert a comma after <u>field</u>
    (4) replace <u>will have enter</u> with <u>will enter</u>
    (5) no correction necessary

48. Sentence 12: **Flexible schedules, a variety of work environments, advanced job-training programs, and good pay is just a few of the rewards.**

    What correction should be made to this sentence?

    (1) replace <u>is</u> with <u>are</u>
    (2) remove the comma after <u>schedules</u>
    (3) move <u>of the rewards</u> after <u>programs</u>
    (4) insert a comma after <u>pay</u>
    (5) no correction necessary

49. Sentence 13: **Nurses have even more employment options who continue their education.**

    What correction should be made to this sentence?

    (1) replace <u>have</u> with <u>has</u>
    (2) move <u>who continue their education</u> after <u>nurses</u>
    (3) replace <u>their</u> with <u>there</u>
    (4) insert a comma after <u>options</u>
    (5) no correction necessary

50. Sentence 15: **Simply complete the enclosed application and you will be on your way to a better job and a rewarding future.**

    What correction should be made to this sentence?

    (1) insert a comma after <u>application</u>
    (2) replace <u>will be</u> with <u>were</u>
    (3) insert a comma after <u>job</u>
    (4) move <u>on your way</u> after <u>application</u>
    (5) no correction necessary

Answers are on page 374.

Posttest 1 Skills Chart

DIRECTIONS

Check your answers to Posttest 1 and circle the items that you got wrong. While studying for the actual GED, focus particularly on the topics that are difficult for you. Keep in mind that many questions focus on more than one category.

TOPICS	QUESTION NUMBERS
Sentence Structure	
Combining Sentences	2, 8, 12, 25, 31, 37, 43
Rewriting Sentences	9, 24, 39
Active Voice	34
Misplaced Modifier	10, 27, 38, 49
Grammar and Usage	
Subject-Verb Agreement	3, 6, 11, 30, 46, 48
Who, Whom, Which, That	14, 19
Word Choice	13, 35, 42
Pronouns	5, 17, 21
Verb Tense	1, 32, 47
Organization	
Sentence Placement	4, 16
Paragraph Organization	23, 33, 45
Mechanics	
Commas	7, 15, 22, 26, 29, 40, 44, 50
Apostrophes	28
Semicolons	18
No Correction	20, 36, 41

Posttest 2

DIRECTIONS

1. This test has five passages with numbered sentences. The sentences may have errors, or they may be correct as written. First read the passage. Then answer the related questions. Choose the best answer for each question. The best answer should be consistent with the point of view and verb tense that is used throughout the passage.

2. Answer every question. If you are not sure of the answer, make a logical guess.

3. Allow yourself 75 minutes to answer the 50 questions. When the time is up, underline the last item that you completed. Then finish the test. This will help you monitor your time for the actual GED test.

4. Write your answers to the questions on the answer grid. For each question, mark the number that matches the answer you chose.

5. After you have completed the test, check your answers and complete the Skills Chart to see which sections are difficult for you.

EXAMPLE

Sentence 1: **Parents need to give there children a lot of attention.**

What correction should be made to this sentence?

(1) replace *Parents* with *Parents'*

(2) replace *there* with *their*

(3) replace *need* with *needed*

(4) insert a comma after *children*

(5) no correction necessary

1. ① ● ③ ④ ⑤

In this sentence, *there* should be replaced with *their.*

Answer Sheet

POSTTEST 2

1. ① ② ③ ④ ⑤
2. ① ② ③ ④ ⑤
3. ① ② ③ ④ ⑤
4. ① ② ③ ④ ⑤
5. ① ② ③ ④ ⑤
6. ① ② ③ ④ ⑤
7. ① ② ③ ④ ⑤
8. ① ② ③ ④ ⑤
9. ① ② ③ ④ ⑤
10. ① ② ③ ④ ⑤
11. ① ② ③ ④ ⑤
12. ① ② ③ ④ ⑤
13. ① ② ③ ④ ⑤
14. ① ② ③ ④ ⑤
15. ① ② ③ ④ ⑤
16. ① ② ③ ④ ⑤
17. ① ② ③ ④ ⑤
18. ① ② ③ ④ ⑤
19. ① ② ③ ④ ⑤
20. ① ② ③ ④ ⑤
21. ① ② ③ ④ ⑤
22. ① ② ③ ④ ⑤
23. ① ② ③ ④ ⑤
24. ① ② ③ ④ ⑤
25. ① ② ③ ④ ⑤

26. ① ② ③ ④ ⑤
27. ① ② ③ ④ ⑤
28. ① ② ③ ④ ⑤
29. ① ② ③ ④ ⑤
30. ① ② ③ ④ ⑤
31. ① ② ③ ④ ⑤
32. ① ② ③ ④ ⑤
33. ① ② ③ ④ ⑤
34. ① ② ③ ④ ⑤
35. ① ② ③ ④ ⑤
36. ① ② ③ ④ ⑤
37. ① ② ③ ④ ⑤
38. ① ② ③ ④ ⑤
39. ① ② ③ ④ ⑤
40. ① ② ③ ④ ⑤
41. ① ② ③ ④ ⑤
42. ① ② ③ ④ ⑤
43. ① ② ③ ④ ⑤
44. ① ② ③ ④ ⑤
45. ① ② ③ ④ ⑤
46. ① ② ③ ④ ⑤
47. ① ② ③ ④ ⑤
48. ① ② ③ ④ ⑤
49. ① ② ③ ④ ⑤
50. ① ② ③ ④ ⑤

Directions: Choose the best answer for each question.

Questions 1 through 9 refer to the following passage.

Ms. Kaila Marie,

(A)

(1) The best way to ensure your child's success in school is inexpensive and fun. (2) Reading aloud to children makes her better prepared for school. (3) Listening to stories helps children develop better language skills longer attention spans, and a greater interest in learning. (4) Now that parents have to compete with television and video games reading is often dismissed as old-fashioned or even boring. (5) However, books are entertaining and educational.

(B)

(6) For young children, review the letters in the title of the book. (7) Even before your child can identify all of the letters, discuss the sound each letter makes. (8) Ask questions while reading the book, and in your child's life relate the story to experiences. (9) Use different voices for the characters in the book, and create mental images of the story. (10) There are a number of techniques that can help make reading time more enjoyable and instructive. (11) Likewise, encourage your child to continue the story or produce a different ending. (12) These simple techniques help children develop there reading skills.

(C)

(13) Once the child has learned to read independently continue reading more advanced stories aloud. (14) For example, if the child can read picture books independently, read a good chapter book to the child. (15) With more advanced stories, the child will improve his vocabulary and hear more complex sentences. (16) Perhaps more importantly, the more advanced books kept the child interested in reading.

(D)

(17) If you need additional resources for your child, please contact me. (18) I want to make sure that every child is successful in our program.

Sincerely,

Cesar Moran

Reading Specialist

1. Sentence 2: **Reading aloud to children makes her better prepared for school.**

   What correction should be made to this sentence?

   (1) replace <u>makes</u> with <u>made</u>
   (2) replace <u>her</u> with <u>them</u>
   (3) insert a comma after <u>prepared</u>
   (4) move <u>for school</u> after <u>children</u>
   (5) no correction necessary

2. Sentence 3: **Listening to stories helps children develop better language skills longer attention spans, and a greater interest in learning.**

   What correction should be made to this sentence?

   (1) insert a comma after <u>skills</u>
   (2) replace <u>helps</u> with <u>helped</u>
   (3) replace <u>stories</u> with <u>stories'</u>
   (4) insert a comma after <u>interest</u>
   (5) no correction necessary

3. Sentence 4: **Now that parents have to compete with television and video games reading is often dismissed as old-fashioned or even boring.**

   What correction should be made to this sentence?

   (1) replace <u>to</u> with <u>too</u>
   (2) replace <u>is</u> with <u>are</u>
   (3) replace <u>parents</u> with <u>parents'</u>
   (4) insert a comma after <u>games</u>
   (5) no correction necessary

4. Sentence 7: **Even before your child can identify all of the letters, discuss the sound each letter makes.**

If you rewrote sentence 7 beginning with

<u>Discuss the sound each letter makes</u>

the next words would be

(1) can identify all
(2) even before your child
(3) of the letters
(4) your child can
(5) child can identify

5. Sentence 8: **Ask questions while reading the book, and in your child's life relate the story to experiences.**

What correction should be made to this sentence?

(1) replace <u>child's</u> with <u>childs</u>
(2) remove the comma after <u>book</u>
(3) replace <u>Ask</u> with <u>Asked</u>
(4) move <u>in your child's life</u> after <u>experiences</u>
(5) no correction necessary

6. Sentence 10: **There are a number of techniques that can help make reading time more enjoyable and instructive.**

What change should be made to the placement of sentence 10?

(1) move sentence 10 to the start of paragraph B
(2) move sentence 10 to the end of paragraph C
(3) move sentence 10 to follow sentence 7
(4) move sentence 10 to follow sentence 3
(5) no change necessary

7. Sentence 12: **These simple techniques help children develop there reading skills.**

What correction should be made to this sentence?

(1) replace <u>help</u> with <u>helps</u>
(2) replace <u>skills</u> with <u>skills'</u>
(3) insert a comma after <u>techniques</u>
(4) replace <u>there</u> with <u>their</u>
(5) no correction necessary

8. Sentence 13: **Once the child has learned to read independently continue reading more advanced stories aloud.**

What correction should be made to this sentence?

(1) replace <u>has</u> with <u>have</u>
(2) insert a comma after <u>independently</u>
(3) insert a comma after <u>more</u>
(4) replace <u>stories</u> with <u>stories'</u>
(5) no correction necessary

9. Sentence 16: **Perhaps more importantly, the more advanced books kept the child interested in reading.**

What correction should be made to this sentence?

(1) remove the comma after <u>importantly</u>
(2) move <u>in reading</u> after <u>books</u>
(3) replace <u>kept</u> with <u>keep</u>
(4) insert a comma after <u>interested</u>
(5) no correction necessary

<u>Questions 10 through 20</u> refer to the following passage.

(A)

(1) When many young adults start living on their own they know very little about personal finance. (2) Budgeting, saving and investing are activities that many people simply do not understand. (3) However, in order to survive in today's economy, Americans needed to know not only how to earn money, but also how to manage it.

(B)

(4) First, many people need to learn how to control their spending. (5) In the old days of easy credit and good economic times, many people lost track of how much money they were wasting on unneeded items. (6) Over time, even small unnecessary purchases add up to a significant expense. (7) As a good guideline, consider how much an item will cost over the course of a year. (8) For example, two dollars a day spent on coffee or a donut adds up to $730 in a year. (9) That's a lot of money.

(C)

(10) Next, Americans should focus on saving more money. (11) Obviously, many families struggle to pay their bills. (12) For them, saving money seems impossible. (13) However, every bit helps. (14) Many families save to create an emergency fund. (15) When a car breaks down, they are ready. (16) If a family member becomes ill or an appliance needs replacing, these families are prepared. (17) Likewise, families often focus on saving for particular items such as a vacation, college, or retirement. (18) If most people cut down on expenses and put aside a little each month, they can save a significant amount of money.

(D)

(19) Finally, young adults need to learn how to invest their money. (20) There are many different types of investments which are appropriate for various situations. (21) Expensive cars, large televisions, and fancy clothes may be nice, but are they necessary? (22) For some people, investing is overwhelming. (23) Fortunately on money management and investing many books, magazines, and web sites have good tips. (24) Even simple investments help. (25) For example, a $1000 investment with a 5 percent interest rate would earn $276 in five years. (26) A higher interest rate would earn even more money. (27) Learning to save and invest at a young age is important. (28) It is never too late to start.

10. Sentence 1: **When many young adults start living on their own they know very little about personal finance.**

    What correction should be made to this sentence?

    (1) replace <u>their</u> with <u>they're</u>
    (2) insert a comma after <u>own</u>
    (3) replace <u>they know </u>with <u>he knows</u>
    (4) move <u>on their own</u> after <u>finance</u>
    (5) no correction necessary

11. Sentence 2: **Budgeting, saving and investing are activities that many people simply do not understand.**

    What correction should be made to this sentence?

    (1) replace <u>are</u> with <u>is</u>
    (2) replace <u>do</u> with <u>does</u>
    (3) insert a comma after <u>saving</u>
    (4) insert a comma after <u>activities</u>
    (5) no correction necessary

12. Sentence 3: **However, in order to survive in today's economy, Americans needed to know not only how to earn money but also how to manage it.**

    What correction should be made to this sentence?

    (1) remove the comma after <u>economy</u>
    (2) insert a comma after <u>know</u>
    (3) replace <u>manage it</u> with <u>manage them</u>
    (4) replace <u>needed</u> with <u>need</u>
    (5) no correction necessary

13. Sentence 6: **Over time, even small unnecessary purchases add up to a significant expense.**

    What correction should be made?

    (1) insert a comma after <u>small</u>
    (2) replace <u>add</u> with <u>adds</u>
    (3) replace <u>to</u> with <u>two</u>
    (4) replace <u>purchases</u> with <u>purchases'</u>
    (5) no correction necessary

14. Sentence 7: **As a good guideline, consider how much an item will cost over the course of a year.**

    What correction should be made to this sentence?

    (1) remove the comma after <u>guideline</u>
    (2) replace <u>will cost</u> with <u>had cost</u>
    (3) replace <u>consider</u> with <u>had considered</u>
    (4) insert a comma after <u>cost</u>
    (5) no correction necessary

15. Sentences 15 and 16: **When a car breaks down, they are ready. If a family member becomes ill or an appliance needs replacing, these families are prepared.**

    The best combination of sentences 15 and 16 would include which group of words?

    (1) Before a car breaks down, these families
    (2) a car breaks down, a family member becomes ill,
    (3) if these families are prepared, the car won't break
    (4) they are ready and prepared
    (5) instead, an appliance needs replacing

16. Sentence 18: **If most people cut down on expenses and put aside a little each month, they can save a significant amount of money.**

    What corrections should be made to this sentence?

    (1) insert a comma after <u>expenses</u>
    (2) move <u>on expenses</u> after <u>month</u>
    (3) remove the comma after <u>month</u>
    (4) replace <u>expenses</u> with <u>expenses'</u>
    (5) no correction necessary

17. Sentence 20: **There are many different types of investments which are appropriate for various situations.**

    What correction should be made to this sentence?

    (1) replace <u>there</u> with <u>their</u>
    (2) replace <u>are</u> with <u>is</u>
    (3) insert a comma after <u>types</u>
    (4) replace <u>which</u> with <u>that</u>
    (5) no correction necessary

18. Sentence 21: **Expensive cars, large televisions, and fancy clothes may be nice, but are they necessary?**

    What change should be made to the placement of sentence 21?

    Move sentence 21

    (1) after sentence 28
    (2) after sentence 5
    (3) to the start of paragraph C
    (4) after sentence 2
    (5) to the start of paragraph D

19. Sentence 23: **Fortunately on money management and investing many books, magazines, and web sites have good tips.**

    What correction should be made to this sentence?

    (1) move <u>on money management and investing</u> after <u>tips</u>
    (2) remove the comma after <u>magazines</u>
    (3) insert a comma after <u>web sites</u>
    (4) replace <u>have</u> with <u>has</u>
    (5) no correction necessary

20. Sentences 27 and 28: **Learning to save and invest at a young age is important. It is never too late to start.**

    The best combination of sentences 27 and 28 would include which group of words?

    (1) important, and it is
    (2) important; therefore,
    (3) important, so it
    (4) important; however,
    (5) important, which it

Questions 21 through 29 refer to the following passage.

Ms. H. Krynicki, Director
Good Day Preschool
145 Main Street
Herndon, VA 20890

Dear Ms. Krynicki:

(1) When we spoke last week you asked for additional information about fire safety. (2) We have a number of brochures and we have videos that focus on safety measures for adults and children. (3) The following points are important to discuss with the children and adults in your program.

- (4) Make sure that children do not have access to matches and lighters. (5) Even a two-year-old can strike a match and start a fire.
- (6) Children should never have been left alone near an operating stove, a burning candle, or a lit fire.
- (7) Smoke alarms should be installed in every level of the home. (8) They must be cleaned regularly, and the batteries should be replaced at least once a year.
- (9) Families should plan at least two escape routes from their home and a meeting place. (10) Children and adults should practice the routes. (11) They will be prepared if a fire occurs.
- (12) Children must be taught that when there is a fire, he should get out of the house—and stay out. (13) Children often want to go back into the home to retrieve a pet or favorite toy.
- (14) Make sure children know how and when to dial 9-1-1.

(15) I hope the enclosed brochures help you educate the families in your school. (16) In addition, we would be happy to stop buy to show the children our trucks and equipment. (17) We have a number of firefighters whom love to put on their gear for the kids. (18) Please call or stop by the station if you have any more questions or concerns.

Sincerely,
Colin Joseph
Station 4

21. Sentence 1: **When we spoke last week you asked for additional information about fire safety.**

    What correction should be made to this sentence?

    (1) replace spoke with spokes
    (2) insert a comma after week
    (3) move for additional information after spoke
    (4) replace asked with ask
    (5) no correction necessary

22. Sentence 2: **We have a number of brochures and we have videos that focus on safety measures for adults and children.**

    What is the best way to write the underlined portion of the sentence? If you think that the original is best, choose option 1.

    (1) a number of brochures and we have videos
    (2) a number of brochures, videos
    (3) a number of brochures and videos
    (4) a number of brochures; and videos
    (5) a number of brochures or we have videos

23. Sentences 4 and 5: **Make sure that children do not have access to matches and lighters. Even a two-year-old can strike a match and start a fire.**

    The best combination of sentences 4 and 5 would include which group of words?

    (1) matches and lighters; however, even a two-year-old
    (2) matches and lighters, and even a two-year-old
    (3) matches and lighters, but even a two-year-old
    (4) matches and lighters; even a two-year-old
    (5) matches and lighters; as a result, even a two-year-old

24. Sentence 6: **Children should never have been left alone near an operating stove, a burning candle, or a lit fire.**

    What correction should be made to this sentence?

    (1) remove the comma after <u>candle</u>
    (2) replace <u>should never have been</u> with <u>never should be</u>
    (3) replace <u>operating stove</u> with <u>stove that is being used</u>
    (4) insert a comma after <u>near</u>
    (5) no correction necessary

25. Sentences 10 and 11: **Children and adults should practice the routes. They will be prepared if a fire occurs.**

    The best combination of sentences 10 and 11 would include which group of words?

    (1) the routes, so they
    (2) the routes; nonetheless, they will
    (3) the routes, but they will
    (4) the routes; however, they will
    (5) the routes when they will

26. Sentence 12: **Children must be taught that when there is a fire, he should get out of the house—and stay out.**

    What correction should be made to this sentence?

    (1) remove the comma after <u>fire</u>
    (2) replace <u>that</u> with <u>which</u>
    (3) insert a comma after <u>taught</u>
    (4) replace <u>he</u> with <u>they</u>
    (5) no correction necessary

27. Sentence 16: **In addition, we would be happy to stop buy to show the children our trucks and equipment.**

    What correction should be made to this sentence?

    (1) remove the comma after <u>addition</u>
    (2) replace <u>buy</u> with <u>by</u>
    (3) insert a comma after <u>trucks</u>
    (4) replace <u>our</u> with <u>hour</u>
    (5) no correction necessary

28. Sentence 17: **We have a number of firefighters whom love to put on their gear for the kids.**

    What correction should be made to this sentence?

    (1) replace <u>We</u> with <u>They</u>
    (2) replace <u>their</u> with <u>they're</u>
    (3) insert a comma after <u>gear</u>
    (4) replace <u>whom</u> with <u>who</u>
    (5) no correction necessary

29. Sentence 18: **Please call or stop by the station if you have any more questions or concerns.**

    If this sentence began with

    <u>If you have any more questions</u>

    the next words would be

    (1) or concerns, please call
    (2) by the station
    (3) if you have any
    (4) please, stop
    (5) the station or concerns

<u>Questions 30 through 40</u> refer to the following passage.

(A)

(1) For many families, dinnertime can be a hectic experience. (2) School, sports, and work schedules, make life complicated. (3) Sometimes simply preparing dinner can seem overwhelming. (4) Nonetheless, family meals are important. (5) They are a great way to reconnect and encourage healthy eating habits.

(B)

(6) These children are less likely to eat fast food and unhealthy snacks compared to their peers. (7) Instead, they eat more fruits and vegetables as part of a balanced diet. (8) Likewise, when children eat family meals regularly, there social skills develop. (9) Simple discussions around a family dinner table helps children become more confident and outgoing with their peers.

(C)

(10) Family meals help teenagers, as well. (11) Children who have regular family meals tend to have good eating habits and better social skills. (12) Teens who have regular family meals generally engage in less risky behavior. (13) They develop good eating habits. (14) They are less inclined to have eating disorders. (15) Even though a teenagers schedule may make family meals hard to plan, the extra effort is worthwhile.

(D)

(16) Starting at an early age, parents can encourage their children to help plan and prepare meals. (17) Even a young child can browse through a cookbook or prepare a salad. (18) Many parents try to avoid bringing their children to the food store. (19) Trips to the store are an opportunity to teach a child about nutrition and making good choices. (20) In addition, when a child helps prepare a meal, they is more likely to eat it.

(E)

(21) In an age of busy schedules, it is hard to plan a family meal. (22) However, the evidence is clear. (23) Family meals help children become healthy, confident adults.

30. Sentence 2: **School, sports, and work schedules, make life complicated.**

    What correction should be made to this sentence?

    (1) replace <u>make</u> with <u>makes</u>
    (2) insert a comma after <u>work</u>
    (3) replace <u>schedules</u> with <u>schedules'</u>
    (4) remove the comma after <u>schedules</u>
    (5) no correction necessary

31. Sentences 4 and 5: **Nonetheless, family meals are important. They are a great way to reconnect and encourage healthy eating habits.**

    The best combination of sentences 4 and 5 would include which group of words?

    (1) important because they
    (2) important; nonetheless, they
    (3) important, but they
    (4) important; however, they
    (5) important, yet they

32. Sentence 6: **These children are less likely to eat fast food and unhealthy snacks compared to their peers.**

    What correction should be made to this sentence?

    (1) replace <u>are</u> with <u>is</u>
    (2) insert a comma after <u>food</u>
    (3) move <u>compared to their peers</u> before <u>these children</u>
    (4) replace <u>their</u> with <u>they're</u>
    (5) no correction necessary

33. Sentence 8: **Likewise, when children eat family meals regularly, there social skills develop.**

    What correction should be made to this sentence?

    (1) remove the comma after <u>regularly</u>
    (2) replace <u>skills</u> with <u>skills'</u>
    (3) insert a comma after <u>social</u>
    (4) replace <u>there</u> with <u>their</u>
    (5) no correction necessary

34. Sentence 9: **Simple discussions around a family dinner table helps children become more confident and outgoing with their peers.**

    What correction should be made to this sentence?

    (1) insert a comma after <u>family</u>
    (2) replace <u>their</u> with <u>there</u>
    (3) replace <u>helps</u> with <u>help</u>
    (4) move <u>with their peers</u> after <u>discussions</u>
    (5) no correction necessary

35. Sentence 11: **Children who have regular family meals tend to have good eating habits and better social skills.**

    Where is the best placement for sentence 11? If you think that the original is best, choose option 1.

    (1) after sentence 10
    (2) before sentence 6
    (3) after sentence 13
    (4) before sentence 20
    (5) after sentence 3

36. Sentence 12: **Teens who have regular family meals generally engage in less risky behavior.**

    What correction should be made to this sentence?

    (1) replace <u>have</u> with <u>had</u>
    (2) insert a comma after <u>regular</u>
    (3) replace <u>who</u> with <u>whom</u>
    (4) move <u>in less risky behavior</u> after <u>teens</u>
    (5) no correction necessary

37. Sentences 13 and 14: **They develop good eating habits. They are less inclined to have eating disorders.**

    The best combination of these two sentences would include which group of words?

    (1) habits, but they
    (2) habits, and they
    (3) habits; nonetheless they
    (4) habits, unfortunately they
    (5) habits; however, they

38. Sentence 15: **Even though a teenagers schedule may make family meals hard to plan, the extra effort is worthwhile.**

    What correction should be made to this sentence?

    (1) remove the comma after <u>plan</u>
    (2) replace <u>make</u> with <u>made</u>
    (3) insert a comma after <u>though</u>
    (4) replace <u>teenagers</u> with <u>teenager's</u>
    (5) no correction necessary

39. Sentences 18 and 19: **Many parents try to avoid bringing their children to the food store. Trips to the store are an opportunity to teach a child about nutrition and making good choices.**

    The best combination of sentences 18 and 19 would include which of the following word groups?

    (1) store; however, trips
    (2) store because trips
    (3) store, so trips
    (4) store; as a result,
    (5) store, and trips

40. Sentence 20: **In addition, when a child helps prepare a meal, they is more likely to eat it.**

    What correction should be made to this sentence?

    (1) remove the comma after <u>meal</u>
    (2) replace <u>helps</u> with <u>will help</u>
    (3) insert a comma after <u>likely</u>
    (4) replace <u>they</u> with <u>he or she</u>
    (5) no correction necessary

<u>Questions 41 through 50</u> refer to the following passage.

Ms. Jennifer C. Hogie
Speech Therapy Center
Lakeside, NH 17830

Dear Ms. Hogie,

(A)

(1) Thank you for sending me the full documentation regarding my account. (2) I received outstanding speech therapy for my children and I have recommended your program to a number of people. (3) However, the billing situation have been frustrating. (4) I am fully prepared to pay the bill. (5) I want accurate information before I write a check. (6) This invoice is the first to show my payment for $220 on July 9 2011. (7) In addition, earlier invoices charged me twice for therapy on August 19. (8) Fortunately, I have kept accurate records. (9) I know exactly what my payment should be.

(B)

(10) I contact your office several times over the past few weeks to take care of this situation. (11) Your receptionist insisted that you would send me a more detailed invoice. (12) Instead of more information, I got late fees which I am not going to pay. (13) Clearly, there is a communication gap between you and I.

(C)

(14) For your business to succeed you must provide not only excellent speech therapy but also accurate invoices. (15) Now that I have the information I need, I will mail you a check for $600, which should cover my outstanding balance. (16) The check will arrive in the next day or two.

Sincerely,
Kit Marino

41. Sentence 2: **I received outstanding speech therapy for my children and I have recommended your program to a number of people.**

    What correction should be made to this sentence?

    (1) insert a comma after <u>children</u>
    (2) move <u>to a number of people</u> after <u>therapy</u>
    (3) replace <u>your</u> with <u>you're</u>
    (4) insert a comma after <u>speech</u>
    (5) no correction necessary

42. Sentence 3: **However, the billing situation have been frustrating.**

    What correction should be made to this sentence?

    (1) remove the comma after <u>However</u>
    (2) replace <u>have been</u> with <u>has been</u>
    (3) insert a comma after <u>billing</u>
    (4) replace <u>have been</u> with <u>will have been</u>
    (5) no correction necessary

43. Sentences 4 and 5: **I am fully prepared to pay the bill. I want accurate information before I write a check.**

    The best combination of sentences 4 and 5 would include which of the following word groups?

    (1) bill because I want
    (2) bill; fortunately, I want
    (3) bill, but I want
    (4) bill; instead, I want
    (5) bill when I want

44. Sentence 6: **This invoice is the first to show my payment for $220 on July 9 2011.**

    What correction should be made to this sentence?

    (1) replace <u>is</u> with <u>are</u>
    (2) insert a comma after <u>July 9</u>.
    (3) move <u>on July 9 2011</u> before <u>This</u>
    (4) replace <u>to show</u> with <u>to have shown</u>
    (5) no correction necessary

45. Sentence 7: **In addition, earlier invoices charged me twice for therapy on August 19.**

    What correction should be made to this sentence?

    (1) remove the comma after <u>addition</u>
    (2) replace <u>me</u> with <u>I</u>
    (3) insert a comma after <u>August</u>
    (4) replace <u>charged</u> with <u>charge</u>
    (5) no correction necessary

46. Sentences 8 and 9: **Fortunately, I have kept accurate records. I know exactly what my payment should be.**

    The best combination of sentences 8 and 9 would include which of the following word groups?

    (1) records when I know
    (2) records; nonetheless, I know
    (3) records; as a result, I know
    (4) records, yet I know
    (5) records after I know

47. Sentence 10: **I contact your office several times over the past few weeks to take care of this situation.**

    What correction should be made to this sentence?

    (1) replace <u>contact</u> with <u>contacted</u>
    (2) move <u>over the past few weeks</u> after <u>situation</u>
    (3) replace <u>weeks</u> with <u>weeks'</u>
    (4) replace <u>your</u> with <u>you're</u>
    (5) no correction necessary

48. Sentence 12: **Instead of more information, I got late fees which I am not going to pay.**

    What correction should be made to this sentence?

    (1) remove the comma after <u>information</u>
    (2) replace <u>got</u> with <u>will get</u>
    (3) insert a comma after <u>Instead</u>
    (4) replace <u>which</u> with <u>that</u>
    (5) no correction necessary

49. Sentence 13: **Clearly, there is a communication gap between you and I.**

    What correction should be made to this sentence?

    (1) replace <u>there</u> with <u>their</u>
    (2) insert a comma after <u>you</u>
    (3) replace <u>I</u> with <u>me</u>
    (4) replace <u>is</u> with <u>will be</u>
    (5) no correction necessary

50. Sentence 14: **For your business to succeed you must provide not only excellent speech therapy but also accurate invoices.**

    What correction should be made to this sentence?

    (1) replace <u>your</u> with <u>you're</u>
    (2) replace <u>provide</u> with <u>provides</u>
    (3) insert a comma after <u>succeed</u>
    (4) replace <u>business</u> with <u>Business</u>
    (5) no correction necessary

Answers are on page 378.

Posttest 2 Skills Chart

DIRECTIONS

Check your answers to Posttest 2 and circle the items that you got wrong. While studying for the actual GED, focus particularly on the topics that are difficult for you. Keep in mind that many questions focus on more than one category.

TOPICS	QUESTION NUMBERS
Sentence Structure	
Combining Sentences	20, 23, 25, 31, 37, 39, 43, 46
Rewriting Sentences	4, 15, 22, 29
Misplaced Modifier	5, 19, 32
Grammar and Usage	
Subject-Verb Agreement	34, 42
Who, Whom, Which, That	17, 28, 48
Word Choice	7, 27, 33
Pronouns	1, 26, 40, 49
Verb Tense	9, 12, 24, 47
Organization	
Sentence Placement	6, 35
Paragraph Organization	18
Mechanics	
Commas	2, 3, 8, 10, 11, 13, 21, 30, 41, 44, 50
Apostrophes	38
No Correction	14, 16, 36, 45

Answers to Exercises

CHAPTER 1: PARTS OF SPEECH

EXERCISE 1: *page 32.*

1. SUBJECT: **The girl** PREDICATE: **ate a donut.**
2. SUBJECT: **Some people** PREDICATE: **cannot afford health care.**
3. SUBJECT: **Lions, tigers, elephants, and horses** PREDICATE: **perform tricks at the circus.**
4. SUBJECT: **Mr. Po** PREDICATE: **read the poem to the class.**
5. SUBJECT: **The flu** PREDICATE: **strikes many people in the winter.**
6. SUBJECT: **Some workers** PREDICATE: **have to develop their skills.**
7. SUBJECT: **Cal** PREDICATE: **caught the ball, ran to second base, and tagged the runner.**
8. SUBJECT: **Juan** PREDICATE: **dreams of playing in the pros.**
9. SUBJECT: **Parents** PREDICATE: **want decent jobs, safe streets, and good schools.**
10. SUBJECT: **Some people** PREDICATE: **come to America to start a new life.**

EXERCISE 2: *page 33.*

1. **manager, store** Both nouns follow *the,* which is an article.
2. **coach, Saul, medal** *The* is an article that comes before *coach. Saul* is a person's name. *A* is an article that comes before *medal.*
3. **judge, Chris, car** *A* is an article that comes before *judge. Chris* is a person's name. *The* is an article that comes before *car.*
4. **coffee, notebook** *The* comes before *coffee. My* is an adjective that describes *notebook.*
5. **fire, house** *The* comes before *fire. Our* is an adjective that describes *house.*
6. **Sean, letters, computer** *Sean* is a person. *Three* is an adjective that describes how many *letters. The* is an article that comes before *computer.*
7. **Lynn, sitter, baby** *Lynn* is a person. *A* comes before *sitter,* and *the* comes before *baby.*
8. **Ty, job, hours, pay** *Ty* is a person. *A* comes before *job. Decent* describes *hours,* and *good* describes *pay. Hours* and *pay* are things.
9. **landlord, leaks, ceiling** *Paul* is a person. *The* comes before *leaks* and *ceiling.*
10. **Students, success, school** *Students* are people. *Success* is an idea. *School* is a place.

EXERCISE 3: *page 34.*

1. **it** *It* substitutes for *the wallet.*
2. **whomever, they** *Whomever* is used because we do not know who will be questioned. *They* substitutes for *FBI.*
3. **Who** *Who* substitutes for the volunteer. The volunteer is unknown.
4. **himself, he** *Himself* and *he* refer to Nate.
5. **Everybody** *Everybody* substitutes for the people.
6. **They, themselves** *They* and *themselves* substitute for the people who were hurt on the field.
7. **I, this** *I* refers to a person. *This* refers to a thing.
8. **you, you** *You* refers to a person.
9. **It, her, herself** *It* refers to a thing. *Her* and *herself* refer to a person.
10. **Which** *Which* refers to a thing.

EXERCISE 4: *page 37.*

1. That band <u>seems</u> awful. *Seems* is a linking verb.
2. Juan <u>stayed</u> in the hospital for days. *Stayed* is an action verb.
3. Ahmed <u>felt</u> the hot sun on his back. *Felt* is a linking verb.
4. My soup <u>tastes</u> salty. *Tastes* is a linking verb.
5. She <u>smells</u> the flowers on the table. *Smells* is a linking verb.
6. Carl <u>grew</u> three inches last year. *Grew* is an action verb.
7. <u>Taste</u> the cheesecake. *Taste* is an action verb.
8. After the lawsuit, Ray <u>remained</u> angry for months. *Remained* is a linking verb.
9. Kaila <u>appeared</u> sick after lunch. *Appeared* is a linking verb.
10. We <u>grew</u> tired of his empty promises. *Grew* is an action verb.

EXERCISE 5: *page 37.*

1. Jenna wanted **to study** really hard for her exam.
2. no change
3. Mirabel tried **to bake** a cake quickly before her guests arrived.
4. no change
5. While doing medical research, scientists try **to monitor** their experiments carefully.

EXERCISE 6: *page 39.*

1. Jim and Alice <u>are</u> at the beach. *Are* is a linking verb.
2. The two lawyers <u>were arguing</u> about the case. *Were* is a helping verb, and *arguing* is the main verb.
3. Mike and Joe <u>could have eaten</u> better food. *Could* and *have* are helping verbs. *Eaten* is the main verb.
4. Khan <u>should have thought</u> about his future. *Should* and *have* are helping verbs. *Thought* is the main verb.
5. In two weeks, we <u>will be going</u> on vacation. *Will* and *be* are helping verbs. *Going* is the main verb.
6. Who <u>is</u> the best worker? *Is* is a linking verb.
7. Pam <u>has been working</u> from home. *Has* and *been* are helping verbs. *Working* is the main verb.
8. Keith's mom <u>will watch</u> the two children. *Will* is a helping verb. *Watch* is the main verb.
9. Jan <u>moved</u> to a new home. *Moved* is an action verb.
10. The judge <u>could have asked</u> the jury. *Could* and *have* are helping verbs. *Asked* is the main verb.

EXERCISE 7: *page 39.*

1. **three, her, new** *Three* describes how many companies. *Her* describes whose job. Remember, when a noun or pronoun is possessive, it works like an adjective. *New* describes what type of job.
2. **My, small, monthly** *My* describes whose paycheck. *Small* describes what type of paycheck. *Monthly* describes what type of bills.
3. **kind, our, poor** *Kind* describes what type of friends. *Our* and *poor* describe *family.*
4. **old, brick, violent** *Old* and *brick* describe what type of building. *Violent* describes what type of earthquake.
5. **hard** *Hard* describes what type of language.
6. **best, final** *Best* describes which team. *Final* describes which round.
7. **his, right, hard** *His* describes whose elbow. *Right* describes which elbow. *Hard* describes what type of ground.
8. **good, child, expensive** *Good, child,* and *expensive* describe what type of care. Normally *child* is a noun. However, if it works like an adjective, it is an adjective.
9. **Many, more, their** *Many* describes how many parents. *More* describes how much time. *Their* describes whose children.
10. **high-paying, good** *High-paying* describes which jobs. *Good* describes what kind of education.

EXERCISE 8: *page 41.*

1. **brave** Susan is the only person mentioned.
2. **best** A football team has more than three people.
3. **more** The new phone is compared to the old one.
4. **most** A staff most likely has three or more people.
5. **easier** Spanish is compared to one other language, French.
6. **more** Wayne is compared to one other person, his partner.
7. **best** Most likely the company has three or more people.
8. **shortest** The sophomore class probably has three or more people.
9. **worst** *I* probably has seen at least three movies.
10. **better** *You* is compared to one other person, *Ken.*

EXERCISE 9: *page 42.*

1. **very, hard** *Hard* explains how the crew worked. *Very* tells to what extent for the adverb *hard.*
2. **often, late** *Often* tells when the bills are paid. *Late* tells how the bills are paid.
3. **today, beautifully** *Today* tells when the chorus sang. *Beautifully* tells how the chorus sang.
4. **never** *Never* tells when we told. (We told at no time.)
5. **quite** *Quite* tells to what extent for the adjective *talented.*
6. **quickly** *Quickly* tells how the dog ate his food. *Friendly* is an adjective that describes the dog.
7. **really, soon** *Really* tells to what extent Jay wants a raise. *Soon* tells when he wants a raise.
8. **truly** *Truly* tells to what extent the plumber fixed the problem.
9. **away, yesterday** *Away* tells where the cat ran. *Yesterday* tells when the cat ran.
10. **promptly, straight, home** *Promptly* and *straight* tell how she walked. (In this sentence, *straight* means directly.) *Home* tells where she walked.

11. **too, late, never** *Too* and *late* tell when he arrived, and *never* describes when he met.
12. **not** *Not* tells how or when she would leave.

EXERCISE 10: *page 43.*

1. **faster** The hiker entered the cave twice.
2. **harder** The team played twice, yesterday and today.
3. **most** There were six speakers.
4. **best** There are at least three dressed women in Hollywood.
5. **more** Eve ran twice, today and Friday.
6. **most** The store probably has at least three colorful shirts.
7. **louder** Ted yelled at two people, his secretary and me.
8. **worse** Two speakers, Guy and you, ramble.
9. **more** Two buildings were destroyed, this one and that one.
10. **less** Two types of annoying calls are compared.

EXERCISE 11: *page 44.*

Remember, there are many correct answers. This is just one option.

Last night, a bird flew **about** our house. We chased the bird **around** the kitchen and **through** the living room. Everyone was helping— **except for** the dog. Her barking scared the bird so much, it wouldn't fly **out** the open windows. Eventually, the dog followed the bird **into** our garage and forced it **under** the car right **behind** the front wheel. The bird stayed **underneath** the car **throughout** the night. Finally **in** the morning **before** I went **to** work, the bird flew **out** the garage door.

EXERCISE 12: *page 46.*

1. **with the red hat** *With the red hat* describes *the student.*
   to her class *To her class* tells where the student is running.
2. **after the storm** *After the storm* tells when the rainbow appeared.
   across the sky *Across the sky* tells where the rainbow stretched.
3. **In spite of her broken arm** *In spite of her broken arm* tells how she rode.
   into town *Into town* tells where she rode.
4. **During spring break** *During spring break* tells when she went.
   to Florida *To Florida* tells where she went.
   with her friends *With her friends* tells with whom she went.
5. **Before noon** *Before noon* shows when the president will tell.
   about his new staff *About his new staff* describes *something.*
6. **up the steps** *Up the steps* tells where Jong climbed.
   behind me *Behind me* shows where Jong sat.
7. **Because of the cramp** *Because of the cramp* tells how she will run.
   in her leg *In her leg* shows where the cramp is.
   as far as that tree *As far as that tree* tells where she will run.
8. **on many issues** *On many issues* describes how the parties differ.
   besides crime *Besides crime* describes which issues.
9. **below the shelf** *Below the shelf* tells where you will find the box.
   in the basement *In the basement* describes which shelf.
10. **Because of her hard work** *Because of her hard work* tells how Rose earned more vacation.
    with pay *With pay* describes what type of *days.*

CHAPTER REVIEW

EXERCISE 1: *page 47.*

1. **4 looked** promising *Were* is a linking verb. In this sentence, one could substitute *looked* and keep the same meaning.
2. **3 better** Two proposals are compared, so *better* is the correct form.
3. **2 more flexible** *More* is used when two options are compared and the adjective has three or more syllables.
4. **3 are** Use the correct form of *be*.
5. **3 pay for the work** This sentence needs the preposition *for* to make sense.
6. **1 will contact** *Will* is a helping verb for the main verb *contact*.

ADDITIONAL HELP

If you can easily make comparisons using adjectives and adverbs, move on to Chapter 2. On the other hand, if you need more practice with comparisons, complete the following exercise.

Read the following paragraph. Underline the correct adjective or adverb for each situation.

Many children get involved in competitive sports programs at a very young age. Years ago, most kids didn't even play organized sports until second or third grade. Nowadays, children at that age try out for select teams, which only take the (best, more better)[1] players. When two kids are competing for a position, it's easy to determine who is (faster, fastest) or (stronger, strongest).[2] However, it's much harder to decide which player will be (better, more better)[3] in the long run. Likewise, with a large group of players, it's hard to determine who is the (more, most)[4] motivated. Sometimes (weak, weakest) players who are motivated develop into (great, greatest)[5] athletes as they get older. It's important for children to be (active, activer) in sports. However, we need to remember that athletes progress at different rates.

1. **best**—Many players try out. Only the best are chosen. *More* should not be used with *better*.
2. **faster** and **stronger**—Two players are compared.
3. **better**—Two players are compared. *More* should not be used with *better*.
4. **most**—Three or more players are compared.
5. **weak** and **great**—Both adjectives describe *players*. No one is being compared.
6. **active**—*Activer* is not a word.

CHAPTER 2: PARTS OF A SENTENCE

EXERCISE 1: *page 50.*

There is more than one correct revision for each fragment.
1. **F** The women with the pink shirt missed the train.
2. **C** The subject is *the tall man in the red hat*, and the predicate is *asked me for directions*.
3. **C** This is a command. The subject, *you*, is implied.
4. **F** This group of words does not have a verb. *The coaches, teams, and officials were frustrated with the rain delays* is a complete sentence.
5. **F** This group of words does not have a verb. *Before the drop in the stock market and the accounting scandals, many Americans were confident about their investments* is a complete sentence.
6. **C** This is a command. The subject, *you*, is implied.

7. **F** This group of words does not have a verb. *After water skiing at the lake house, Katherine, Russell, and Andrew were exhausted* is a complete sentence.
8. **C** This is a command. The subject, *you*, is implied.
9. **C** What about *the man in charge of payroll. The man in charge of payroll has many friends on Fridays.*
10. **C** This is a command. The subject, *you*, is implied.

EXERCISE 2: *page 51.*

1. This past winter was terrible. **C**
2. The snow buried **F** This group of words does not express a complete thought. What did the snow bury?
3. Schools were closed for several days, and many people could not get to work. **C**
4. Pipes froze. **C**
5. Some roofs collapsed. **C**
6. Luckily, no one was **F** This group of words does not express a complete thought. No one was what?
7. Next winter may be even worse. **C**
8. Watch out! **C** This sentence is a command. The subject, *you*, is implied.

EXERCISE 3: *page 53.*

1. **her baby** Jasmine bathed whom? Her baby. *Her* is an adjective that describes *baby*.
2. **X** *Across the sky* is a prepositional phrase that shows where *the thunder rolled.*
3. **his math test** Abdul passed what? His math test. *His* and *math* are adjectives that describe *test*.
4. **X** *Hard* is an adverb that tells how she tried.
5. **the sunrise** I saw what? The sunrise.
6. **a helmet** Amal straps what? A helmet.
7. **X** *around the bend* and *over the hill* are prepositional phrases that show where *Brian, Steven, and Patrick raced.*
8. **their college savings** Many people lost what? Their college savings. *Their* and *college* are adjectives that describe *savings.*
9. **the defendant** The prosecutor charged whom? The defendant.
10. **a new house** Megan and Andy bought what? A new house. *Near their relatives* and *close to work* are prepositional phrases that describe *house.*

EXERCISE 4: *page 55.*

1. **free tickets, me** Doyle offered what? Free tickets. Doyle offered free tickets to whom? Me.
2. **The check.** We mailed what? The check. *Yesterday* is an adverb that tells when the check was mailed.
3. **the mail, us** The post office sent what? The mail. The post office sent the mail to whom? Us.
4. **award, Mansi** The coach gave what? An award. The coach gave an award to whom? Mansi.
5. **the cookies** Kim baked what? The cookies. *Friday* tells when the cookies were baked.
6. **a great lead pass, Brianna** Ian gave what? A great lead pass. Ian gave a great lead pass to whom? Brianna.

7. **thank-you notes, teachers** Kaila and Logan wrote what? Thank-you notes. Kaila and Logan wrote thank-you notes to whom? Their teachers.

8. **a worried look, the manager** The bank teller gave what? A worried look. The bank teller gave a worried look to whom? The manager.

9. **their resumes** Colin and Luke submitted what? Their resumes. *To several companies* is a prepositional phrase that shows where they submitted their resumes.

10. **the blazing fire** Jenna extinguished what? The blazing fire. *At the scene* is a prepositional phrase that describes where she arrived.

EXERCISE 5: *page 57.*

1. Those flowers **are lilacs**. Those flowers ↔ lilacs.
2. The cars **seem costly**. The cars ↔ costly.
3. The water **appears deep**. The water ↔ deep.
4. He **will remain** a **lawyer**. He ↔ a lawyer.
5. Megan **will be thrilled**. Megan ↔ thrilled.
6. Courtney **looks sad**. Courtney ↔ sad.
7. Gas prices **are high**. Gas prices ↔ high.
8. The milk **smells sour**. The milk ↔ sour.
9. My ride for work **is late**. My ride for work ↔ late.
10. Groceries **are** more **expensive**. Groceries ↔ expensive.

CHAPTER REVIEW

EXERCISE 1: *page 59.*

1. **3 remains a difficult time** The original passage contains two incomplete sentences. Option (3) forms one complete sentence. The other options do not create complete sentences.

2. **2 organizations educate people about hurricane preparations** Whom do the organizations educate? People. The original sentence does not make sense.

3. **3 insert supplies after gather** What do people gather? Supplies.

4. **3 insert to evacuate after residents** What do leaders urge residents? To evacuate.

5. **4 no correction necessary** Sentence 5 is a complete sentence.

6. **1 insert assistance after provide** What do government agencies provide? Without *assistance* the sentence in incomplete.

7. **4 no correction necessary** The sentence is complete.

CHAPTER 3: VERB USAGE

EXERCISE 1: *page 65.*

1. **bakes** Every Monday shows that the action happens repeatedly.
2. **helped, played** *Last week* shows that the action happened in the past.
3. **will receive** *Next Monday* shows that the action will take place in the future.
4. **will start** *Next fall* shows that the action will happen in the future.
5. **ripped** *Yesterday* shows that the action happened in the past.
6. **will show** *Tomorrow night* shows the action will happen in the future.
7. **bloom or will bloom** This action happens repeatedly. However, *in the spring* does suggest that the action will happen in the future.

8. **exploded** *Noticed* is in the past tense. *He exploded* when *he noticed.* Both actions happened in the past.
9. **rows** *Often* shows that the action happens repeatedly.
10. **raved** *Last night* shows that the action happened in the past.

EXERCISE 2: *page 67.*

1. **had considered** *Last year* and *before running for office* show that the action was completed before another action in the past. The past perfect tense is used.
2. **will have** *By tomorrow* shows that the action will be completed by a specific time in the future. The future perfect tense is used.
3. **has jogged** *Since last week* and *every day* show that the action began in the past and continues into the present. The present perfect tense is used.
4. **has studied** *Already* shows that the action was just completed. The present perfect tense is used.
5. **will have finished** *By next spring* shows that the action will be completed by a specific time in the future. The future perfect tense is used.
6. **have painted** *Already* shows that the action was just completed. The present perfect tense is used.
7. **had dreamed** *Before July 4, 1776* shows that the action was completed before a specific time in the past. The past perfect tense is used.
8. **will have traveled** *By 2050* shows that the action will be completed by a specific time in the future. The future perfect tense is used.
9. **had destroyed** *Before...last year,* shows that the action was completed before a specific time in the past. The past perfect tense is used.
10. **will have applied** *By next fall* shows that the action will be completed by a specific time in the future. The future perfect tense is used.

EXERCISE 3: *page 69.*

1. **am working** *Right now* shows that the verb should be in the present continuing tense.
2. **were watching** *Yesterday* shows that the verb should be in the past continuing tense.
3. **will be living** *Next year* shows that the verbs should be in the future continuing tense.
4. **were shoveling** *Last Friday* shows that the verb should be in the past continuing tense.
5. **will be playing** *Next fall* shows that the verb should be in the future continuing tense.
6. **were barking** *This morning* shows that the verb should be in the past continuing tense.
7. **will be studying** *Next spring* shows that the verbs should be in the future continuing tense.
8. **was trying** *All morning yesterday* shows that the verb should be in the past continuing tense.
9. **will be struggling** *In the spring next year* shows that the verb should be in the future continuing tense.
10. **are putting** *At present* shows that the verb should be in the present continuing tense.

EXERCISE 4: *page 70.*

1. *be* Last week she <u>was</u>
   This week she <u>is</u>
2. *be* Last week they <u>were</u>
   This week they <u>are</u>
3. *be* Last week it <u>was</u>
   This week it <u>is</u>
4. *be* Last week I <u>was</u>
   This week I <u>am</u>
5. *be* Last week he <u>was</u>
   This week he has <u>been</u>
6. *be* Last week they <u>were</u>
   This week they have <u>been</u>
7. *be* Last week I <u>was</u>
   This week I have <u>been</u>
8. *be* Last week Tim <u>was</u>
   This week Tim has <u>been</u>

EXERCISE 5: *page 71.*

1. For the past week, Karim has (are, were, <u>been</u>) late for work.
2. This year Colin (<u>is</u>, was, am) ready for kindergarten.
3. The presidential candidates have (are, were, <u>been</u>) running attack ads for months.
4. Our math teacher (was, <u>is,</u> been) making the work harder now.
5. I (<u>am</u>, is, were) exhausted today.
6. We have (are, were, <u>been</u>) working on this project for two weeks.
7. The mayor (<u>is</u>, be, been) in trouble for tax evasion.
8. Food allergies (<u>are</u>, was, been) a bigger problem than they used to be.
9. Yesterday, Jackson (<u>was</u>, be, been) injured during the football game.
10. Kit has (is, are, <u>been</u>) hospitalized many times.

EXERCISE 6: *page 72.*

1. *bring* Last week I **brought.** This week I have **brought.**
2. *buy* Last week I **bought.** This week I have **bought.**
3. *come* Last week I **came.** This week I have **come.**
4. *do* Last week I **did**. This week I have **done.**
5. *go* Last week I **went.** This week I have **gone.**
6. *have* Last week I **had.** This week I have **had.**
7. *run* Last week I **ran.** This week I have **run.**
8. *see* Last week I **saw.** This week I have **seen.**

EXERCISE 7: *page 72.*

1. **seen** *Have* signals the perfect tenses. The past participle *seen* must be used.
2. **went** *Yesterday,* shows that the action happened in the past.
3. **run** *Have* signals the perfect tenses. The past participle *run* must be used.
4. **come** *Have* signals the perfect tenses. The past participle *come* must be used.
5. **done** *Has* signals the perfect tenses. The past participle *done* must be used.
6. **bought** *Have* signals the perfect tenses. The past participle *bought* must be used.

7. **had** *Have* signals the perfect tenses. The past participle *had* must be used.
8. **brought** *Last Friday* signals the past tense.
9. **gone** *For the past two days* and *has* signal the present perfect tense. The past participle *gone* must be used.
10. **came** *Last night* signals the past tense.

EXERCISE 8: *page 73.*

1. *begin* Last week I **began.** This week I have **begun.**
2. *drink* Last week I **drank.** This week I have **drunk.**
3. *win* Last week I **won.** This week I have **won.**

EXERCISE 9: *page 73.*

1. **begun** *By nine o'clock tomorrow* and *will have* signal that the action will be completed by a specific time in the future. The future perfect tense needs the past participle *begun.*
2. **won** *Have* signals the present perfect tenses. The past participle *won* must be used.
3. **drunk** *Had* and *before the race* signal that this action was completed before another action in the past. The past participle *drunk* must be used for the past perfect tense.
4. **began** *Yesterday* signals the past.
5. **won** *Has* signals the present perfect tense. The past participle *won* must be used.

EXERCISE 10: *page 74.*

1. *choose* Last week I **chose.** This week I have **chosen.**
2. *eat* Last week I **ate.** This week I have **eaten.**
3. *get* Last week I **got.** This week I have **gotten.**
4. *give* Last week I **gave.** This week I have **given.**
5. *know* Last week I **knew.** This week I have **known.**
6. *write* Last week I **wrote.** This week I have **written.**

EXERCISE 11: *page 75.*

1. **chosen** *By nine o'clock last night* and *had* signal the past perfect tense. The past participle is needed.
2. **ate** *Last year* signals the past tense.
3. **given** *Have* signals the present perfect tense.
4. **written** *Have* and *just* signal the present perfect tense. The past participle is needed.
5. **knew** *Yesterday* signals the past tense.
6. **gotten** *Has* signals the present perfect tense. The past participle is needed.

EXERCISE 12: *page 76.*

1. **rises** The subject, *Jong,* moves. *Every morning* shows that the action is repeated, and the present tense should be used.
2. **laid** Rose placed her notes.
3. **raised** *Flowers* is the object of the verb. The subject handles *flowers.*
4. **lay** I reclined for just a few minutes. *Yesterday* shows that the verb is in the past tense. The past tense of *lie* is *lay.*
5. **rose** José stood quickly.
6. **laid** The workers will have placed the new roof.

CHAPTER REVIEW

EXERCISE 1: *page 77.*

Yesterday I **decided** to change my study habits. I **want** to be more successful in school. I *always* work hard, but my hard work does not pay off. I **will study** differently *from now on. Tomorrow,* I will go to my teacher, and I **will ask** her for advice. *Then* I **will list** all of the changes that I will make. I *will put* that list on my desk, and I **will look** at it at night when I study. The list **will frustrate** me sometimes, but I know it *will help* me *in the long run.* If I **improve** my skills *now,* I **will study** better *in the future.*

EXERCISE 2: *page 77.*

Brie has **gone** through a major change. *Last year,* she **was** in terrible shape. She could not run a mile, and she **had** bad eating habits. *Recently* Brie has **been** training for a triathlon. *For the past six months,* she has **gone** to the gym *every day.* In February, she **saw** a great bike in a store window, and she **bought** it. *Now* she *rides* her bike and **runs** as often as she can. I **saw** her last week, and I **did** not even know her. She **is** so different *now.* She **came** up to me and *introduced* herself. This new lifestyle has **been** good for her.

EXERCISE 3: *page 77.*

1. **2 have found** This research started in the past and continues into the present.
2. **1 replace <u>were</u> with <u>are</u>** This sentence describes television shows in the present.
3. **4 no correction necessary** This sentence is about the present.
4. **2 has seen** This describes violent acts that an American child sees on television from birth to 18. The violent acts on television started in the past and continue into the present.
5. **2 are blaming** Researchers are blaming excessive television for these problems right now.
6. **3 need** The rest of the sentence is in the present tense.
7. **4 no correction necessary** *Should avoid* is in the present tense.
8. **2 replace <u>discussing</u> with <u>discuss</u>** *View* and *discuss* should be in the same tense.
9. **1 can create** *Can create* should be in the present tense. This is a general truth.
10. **3 replace <u>was</u> with <u>is</u>** This sentence is a general truth. It should be in the present tense.

CHAPTER 4: SUBJECT-VERB AGREEMENT

EXERCISE 1: *page 82.*

1. **itches** *Skin* is singular.
2. **read** When *you* is the subject, the verb does not have an *-s.*
3. **look** When *I* is the subject, the verb does not have an *-s.*
4. **practice** *Players* is plural.
5. **think** *They* is a plural pronoun.
6. **wants** *Ted* is one person.
7. **open** *Children* is plural.

8. **fall** *Peaches* is plural.
9. **wears** *Kay* is one person.
10. **dress** *The girls* is plural.

EXERCISE 2: *page 83.*

1. **were** *We* is plural.
2. **has** *Megan* is one person.
3. **have** *Children* is plural.
4. **are** *They* is plural.
5. **is** *He* is singular.
6. **Are** When *you* is the subject, the verb does not end in *-s*. If in doubt, reword the question as a statement. *You are sure that the movie starts at 7 o'clock.*
7. **were** *The boys* is plural.
8. **have** When *I* is the subject, the verb does not end in *-s*.
9. **is** *Steve* is one person.
10. **Is** If in doubt, reword the question as a statement. *The last flight to New York is about to leave. Last flight* is singular.

EXERCISE 3: *page 84.*

1. **is** Beware of words that are set off by commas, *which,* or *that.* The horse ~~that jumped over four fences~~ is in the lead.
2. **sits** Cross out prepositional phrases. The crate ~~of apples~~ sits next to the pears.
3. **works** Beware of words that make the subject appear plural or are set off by commas. Juan, ~~together with his brothers,~~ works at the paper mill.
4. **needs** Cross out prepositional phrases. The fence ~~in the backyard by the barn~~ needs a repair.
5. **was** Cross out prepositional phrases. Rose, ~~along with her children,~~ was at the mall today.
6. **is** Beware of words that are set off by commas, *which,* or *that.* The desk ~~that has two chairs~~ is mine.
7. **have** Cross out prepositional phrases. The plants ~~on the shelf over by the window~~ have died.
8. **like** Cross out prepositional phrases. The workers ~~with long trips home~~ like to leave early on Fridays.
9. **increases** Beware of words that make the subject sound plural or are set off by commas. Nga's salary, ~~as well as her benefits,~~ increases every fall.
10. **scares** Beware of words that are set off by commas, *which,* or *that.* The haunted house, ~~full of rats and bats,~~ scares many people at night.

EXERCISE 4: *page 85.*

1. **are** My <u>shoes</u> are where?
2. **are** Reword the sentence, and cross out the prepositional phrase. Two reasons ~~for your success~~ are there.
3. **want** <u>You</u> do want more sugar for your coffee.
4. **goes** <u>Khan</u> goes there.
5. **is** <u>Joe</u> is going where on his trip?
6. **are** <u>You</u> are doing what with my new coat?
7. **is** The <u>horse</u> ~~from the stable across the road~~ is here.

8. **Does** Your <u>mother</u> does still drive to the store every day.
9. **do** <u>You</u> do win every time you play chess.
10. **Does** <u>Chad</u> does believe in ghosts.

EXERCISE 5: *page 86.*

1. **wants** *Nobody* is always singular.
2. **Does** *Anyone* is always singular.
3. **likes** *Neither (one)* is always singular.
4. **Has** *Everybody* is always singular.
5. **knits** *Each (one)* is always singular.
6. **cares** *No one* is always singular.
7. **is** *Either (one)* is always singular.
8. **cuts** *Somebody* is always singular. *Everyday* signals that the verb should be in the present tense because the action happens repeatedly.
9. **Does** *Anybody* is always singular.
10. **needs** *Something* is always singular.
11. **are** The verb must be plural. <u>Some</u> of my <u>friends</u>
12. **want** The verb must be plural. <u>Several</u> of my <u>peers</u>
13. **falls** The verb must be singular. <u>All</u> of my <u>change</u>
14. **are** The verb must be plural. <u>None</u> of my <u>siblings</u>
15. **think** The verb must be plural. <u>Both</u> of the <u>coaches</u>

EXERCISE 6: *page 87.*

1. **growls** The tiger or <u>the bear growls</u>. When *or* is the conjunction, the verb agrees with the closest subject.
2. **work** The chef <u>and</u> the waiters work. When *and* is the conjunction, the verb is plural.
3. **know** Neither the coach nor <u>his players know</u>. When *nor* is the conjunction, the verb agrees with the closest subject.
4. **are** Red, blue, <u>and</u> yellow are. When *and* is the conjunction, the verb is plural.
5. **think** The doctor <u>and</u> the nurses think. When *and* is the conjunction, the verb is plural.
6. **join** Carl or <u>his sisters join</u>. When *or* is the conjunction, the verb agrees with the closest subject.
7. **knocks** The cats or <u>the dog knocks</u>. When *or* is the conjunction, the verb agrees with the closest subject.
8. **make** The cold air, snow, <u>and</u> high winds make. When *and* is the conjunction, the verb is plural.
9. **flourishes** The flowers nor <u>the tree</u> flourishes. When *nor* is the conjunction, the verb agrees with the closest subject.
10. **erase** The teacher or the students <u>erase</u>. When *or* is the conjunction, the verb agrees with the closest subject.

EXERCISE 7: *page 88.*

1. **is** The subject is *athlete.*
2. **were** The subject is *cars.*
3. **is** The subject is *interest,* which is singular.
4. **is** The subject is *sight,* which is singular. Don't forget to cross out prepositional phrases. A lovely sight ~~in the fall~~ is ...
5. **are** The subject is *trees.*
6. **is** The subject is *his main concern.*
7. **idea** The subject is *idea.*

8. **were** The compound subject is *a bigger backstop and more bleachers.* When the conjunction *and* is used for a compound subject, the verb must be plural.

9. **were** The compound subject is *a nicer sign or more ads.* When the conjunction *or* is used for a compound subject, the verb must agree with the closest subject, *more ads.*

10. **were** The compound subject is *More voter turnout and better polls.* When the conjunction *and* is used for a compound subject, the verb must be plural.

CHAPTER REVIEW

EXERCISE 1: *page 89.*

1. **1 replace <u>want</u> with <u>wants</u>** The verb must agree with *everybody,* which is always singular.

2. **4 no correction necessary** *Lack* agrees with *poor people and ill people,* which is plural.

3. **1 replace <u>are</u> with <u>is</u>** The verb must agree with *problem,* which is the subject of the sentence.

4. **3 replace <u>promises</u> with <u>promise</u>** The verb must agree with *politicians,* which is plural. Don't be confused by *looking for votes and full of hot air,* which describes *politicians.*

5. **1 replace <u>is</u> with <u>are</u>** In this sentence, the subject, *plans,* is after the verb.

6. **3 replace <u>belong</u> with <u>belongs</u>** The verb must agree with *boss,* which is singular. Don't be confused by *along with some others,* which is a prepositional phrase.

7. **4 no correction necessary** *See* agrees with *many,* which is always plural.

8. **1 replace <u>seems</u> with <u>seem</u>** The verb must agree with *forms,* which is plural. Ignore *that we all complete.*

9. **3 replace <u>is</u> with <u>are</u>** The verb must agree with *Few,* which is always plural.

10. **2 replace <u>is</u> with <u>are</u>** The verb must agree with *plans,* which is plural.

CHAPTER 5: PRONOUNS

EXERCISE 1: *page 92.*

1. **She** Subject
2. **They** Subject
3. **I** Subject
4. **He** Subject
5. **he** Subject Complement
6. **He, she** Subject
7. **she** Subject Complement
8. **She** Subject
9. **they** Subject Complement
10. **she** Subject Complement

EXERCISE 2: *page 93.*

1. **me** *Me* is an object of the verb. The little girl sprayed whom?
2. **him, me** *Him and me* form an object of the verb. The manager promised a good job to whom?
3. **him** *Him* is an object of the verb. Congress sent a bill to whom?
4. **us** *Us* is the object of the preposition *for.* If you need to review the prepositions, see Chapter 1.
5. **him, her** *Him and her* form an object of the verb. Did you give enough paint to whom?
6. **me** *You and me* form the object of the preposition *between.* Many people incorrectly choose *I* because they think it "sounds" right. Practice saying *between you and me.*
7. **him, her** *Him and her* form an object of the verb. Why did Nga tell that story to whom?
8. **me** *Dade and me* form the object of the preposition *behind.* If you need to review prepositions, see Chapter 1.
9. **him** *Di and him* form an object of the verb.
10. **her** *Him and her* form the object of the preposition *about.*

EXERCISE 3: *page 94.*

1. **hers** Possessive pronouns do not have apostrophes.
2. **My** *My* shows ownership.
3. **his, her** *His* and *her* show ownership.
4. **his** *His* shows ownership.
5. **his** Possessive pronouns do not have apostrophes.
6. **They** This pronoun should not be possessive.
7. **his** *Putting* is an *-ing* verb that acts like a noun. Use a possessive pronoun.
8. **its** Possessive pronouns do not have apostrophes.
9. **theirs** Possessive pronouns do not have apostrophes.
10. **his** *Speaking* is an *-ing* verb that acts like a noun. Use a possessive pronoun.

EXERCISE 4: *page 96.*

1. **Who** *Who* is the subject. Who or what asked?
2. **whom** *Whom* is the object of the preposition. Lee gave money to whom or what?
3. **Who** *Who* is the subject. Who or what was elected president?
4. **Whom** We should send whom to the training program?
5. **whom** *Whom* is an object of the verb. Cal gave the game ball to whom or what?
6. **Whom** Brazil did defeat whom to win the World Cup in 1994?
7. **Who** Be careful. You might reword this sentence and make *the new law* the subject. *The new law will hurt whom.* However, *by the new law* is a prepositional phrase; *the new law* cannot be the subject. The subject of the sentence is *who.* Who or what will be hurt?
8. **whoever** *Whoever* is the subject. Who or what thought?
9. **whomever** *Whomever* is an object of the verb. The volunteers help whom or what?
10. **Whom** Jack did pay whom?

EXERCISE 5: *page 97.*

1. **whoever** *Whoever* is the subject of the clause *whoever had the greatest need.*
2. **who** *Who* is the subject of the clause *who granted the money.*
3. **whom** *Whom* is the object of the verb in the clause *whom we just met.* Rewrite the clause *we just met whom.*
4. **who** *Who* is the subject of the clause *who took the new sign.*
5. **Whoever** *Whoever* is the subject of the clause *whoever committed the war crimes.*
6. **who** *Who* is the subject of the clause *who are injured.*
7. **whomever** *Whoever* is the object of the verb in the clause. Try rewording the clause. *She chooses whomever.*
8. **Whoever** *Whoever* is the subject of the clause *whoever wins the war.*
9. **whom** *Whom* is the object of the verb in the clause. Try rewording the clause. *She saved whom.*
10. **who** *Who* is the subject of the clause *who come to America.*

EXERCISE 6: *page 98.*

1. **correct** Mom planned the whole trip without any help.
2. **correct** You need to get the job done alone.
3. **me** *Myself* does not refer to another noun or pronoun in the sentence.
4. **myself** I performed the action on myself.
5. **me** *Myself* does not refer to another noun or pronoun in the sentence. *Me* receives the action.

EXERCISE 7: *page 99.*

1. **I** Mr. Pyo is as careful with the car as <u>I am.</u>
2. **she** Sasha bikes more often than <u>she bikes.</u>
3. **he** Shane skates as well as <u>he skates.</u>
4. **they** If we work hard, we can play as well as <u>they play.</u>
5. **we** Beth and Phil are good athletes, but they are not better than <u>we are.</u>

EXERCISE 8: *page 100.*

1. **his** *His* agrees with *Juan or Carlos.*
2. **They** *They* agrees with *Isabelle and Condi,* which is plural.
3. **their** *Their* agrees with *few people,* which is plural.
4. **their** *Their* agrees with *Kerry and Katherine,* which is plural.
5. **their** *Their* agrees with *many people,* which is plural.
6. **their** *Their* agrees with *none of the pilots,* which is plural because *pilots* is plural.
7. **his** *His* agrees with *everyone,* which is singular.
8. **his** *His* agrees with *each,* which is singular.
9. **his** *His* agrees with *nobody,* which is singular.
10. **their** *Their* agrees with *several birds,* which is plural.

CHAPTER REVIEW

EXERCISE 1: *page 101.*

1. **2 replace <u>their</u> with <u>his</u>** The pronoun must agree with *Everybody,* which is always singular.
2. **1 replace <u>whomever</u> with <u>whoever</u>** *Whoever gave them a job* is a clause, and *whoever* is the subject of that clause. Juan and Rose did not work for *whomever.* They worked for *whoever gave them a job.*
3. **2 replace <u>he</u> with <u>him</u>** Juan's brothers gave *him* money. *Him* is an object of the verb in this sentence.

4. **1 replace <u>him</u> with <u>he</u>** Remember, *Juan often thought that no one worked as hard as he did.*
5. **no correction necessary**
6. **2 replace <u>them</u> with <u>their</u>** Whose children had a good home? Use the possessive form.
7. **2 replace <u>whoever</u> with <u>whomever</u>** Juan told *whomever he met.* In this case, *whomever* is an object in the clause *whomever he met.*
8. **3 replace <u>him</u> with <u>himself</u>** In this sentence, Juan performs the action on himself.
9. **1 replace <u>Us</u> with <u>We</u>** *We* is the subject of the sentence.

CHAPTER 6: PUNCTUATION

EXERCISE 1: *page 107.*

1. ... **miles.** This is a polite command.
2. ... **book?** This is a direct question.
3. ... **alone!** This is an emotional command.
4. ... **leaking.** This is an indirect question. These are not the plumber's exact words.
5. **Hey!** This is an emotional interjection.
6. ... **gone.** This is an indirect question.
7. ... **name.** This is a polite command.
8. ... **you!** This is an emotional command.
9. ... **party?** This is a direct question.
10. ... **night.** This is a statement.

EXERCISE 2: *page 108.*

1. Kim wants to travel with her **family, but** they cannot afford to take a trip this year. The comma and conjunction *but* join independent clauses.
2. Meg bought **clothes, toys, and food** for the children at the shelter. The commas separate items in a series.
3. The sitter cares for four children during the day and goes to school at night. Do not add commas. This sentence has a compound verb.
4. She **sang, danced, and acted** like the star of the show. The commas separate verbs in a series.
5. The house was **big, clean, and costly.** The commas separate adjectives in a series.
6. I will work longer **hours, and** Fred will help more at home. The comma and conjunction *and* join two independent clauses.
7. Jong missed his **train, yet** he did not call for a ride. The comma and the conjunction *yet* join two independent clauses.
8. The **gloves, hats, and scarves** make a mess in the hall closet. The commas separate nouns in a series.
9. They played all day and laughed all night. Do not add commas. *Played* and *laughed* form a compound verb.
10. The trial will be **delayed, so** both sides will have more time to gather evidence. The comma and the conjunction *so* join two independent clauses.

EXERCISE 3: *page 109.*

1. The **clear, blue** sky did not have a cloud. *Clear* and *blue* describe *sky,* and they are equally important.
2. Three soup bowls need to be cleaned. Do not add commas. Numbers should not be separated from other adjectives.

3. **Thick, black** smoke from the fire filled the room. *Thick* and *black* describe *smoke*, and they are equally important.
4. Dr. Lee's **shiny, new** dental chair scares many patients. *Shiny* and *new* both describe dental chair. *Dental* is an adjective, but it is more important than *shiny* and *new*.
5. They searched the woods for five straight days. Do not add commas. Numbers should not be separated from other adjectives.
6. The new brick building will be our town hall. *New* and *brick* are both adjectives that describe *building*, but they are not equally important.
7. **Fresh, white** paint will help the shabby old shelves. *Fresh* and *white* both describe *paint*, and they are equally important.
8. The old bathroom sink is cracked. *Old* and *bathroom* both describe *sink*, but they are not equally important.
9. It is hard to find **good, low-cost** health care. *Good* and *low-cost* describe *health care*, and they are equally important.
10. We filled six large bags with sand. Do not add commas. Numbers should not be separated from other adjectives.

EXERCISE 4: *page 110.*

1. **Ty, weary** from the long **trip, drank** coffee to wake himself. Without the phrase, the reader still knows who drank coffee.
2. The waiter who spilled soup down my back still got a tip. Do not add commas. *Who spilled soup down my back* is a restrictive clause. It tells which waiter.
3. The **hiker, cold** and **alone, tried** to find help. Without the phrase *cold and alone*, the sentence still makes sense.
4. **Nate, a lawyer, has** won some hard cases. Without the appositive, the reader still knows who won some hard cases.
5. The artist Renoir painted many works. Do not add commas. Without *Renoir*, the reader does not know which artist painted many works.
6. Judge **Car, who** is on my **case, is** strict. Without the phrase *who is on my case*, the reader still knows which judge is strict.
7. The judge who is on my case is strict. This time *who is on my case* is important. It tells the reader which judge is strict.
8. The ratings that are used for TV shows are vague. The clause *that are used for TV shows* tells which ratings are vague. *That* is only used with restrictive clauses.
9. **Jake, tired** of reading the same **books, went** to the library to find something new. Without *tired of reading the same books*, the reader still knows who went to the library.
10. **American Idol, a** great **show, has aired** for many years. Without *a great show*, the reader still knows which program aired for many years.

EXERCISE 5: *page 111.*

1. After the rain **came, the** streams overflowed and the streets flooded. Place a comma after introductory clauses.
2. **Yes, I** will work a few extra hours. *Yes* is an introductory word. It is an unemotional interjection.
3. Once the food **arrives, we** can serve the children. Place a comma after introductory clauses.
4. **Bob, leave** the flashlight in the car. Place a comma after a direct address.
5. Scared of the wind and **noise, Rick** hid under the bed during the storm. Place a comma after an introductory phrase.
6. As soon as we get to the **beach, I** will jump in the water. Place a comma after an introductory clause.

7. Between the seat and the door of the **car, Rita** found some loose change. Place a comma after an introductory phrase.

8. I checked the lights and turned down the heat before we left. Do not add commas. *Checked* and *turned* form a compound verb.

9. **Juan, did** you learn to swim when you were a child? Place a comma after a direct address.

10. For **example, some** movies have good soundtracks. Place a comma after opening words.

EXERCISE 6: *page 112.*

1. He **sang, "We** shall be free." Place a comma after the "talking" word *sang* to set apart the speaker.

2. "It's just a **job," Tom said, "I** need the money." Place commas inside the quotation marks and after the "talking" word *said* to set apart the speaker.

3. "Watch your language!" my mom scolded. Do not add commas. Exclamation marks work alone.

4. "Once we finish this **project," he said, "I** will take a few days off." Place commas inside the quotation marks and after the "talking" word *said* to set off the speaker.

5. "When can we go home?" Jane asked. Do not add commas. Question marks work alone.

6. Ned **shouted, "We** need to win this game!" Place a comma after the "talking" word *shouted.*

7. "When I was a **boy," he declared, "I** had to walk to school in the snow." Place commas inside the quotation marks and after the "talking" word *declared.*

8. "The ballot is stronger than the **bullet," Abraham** Lincoln said. Place a comma inside the quotation marks.

9. "Why will they fire so many workers?" Rose asked. Do not add commas. Question marks work alone.

10. "Stay out of the water!" the lifeguard yelled. Do not add commas. Exclamation marks work alone.

EXERCISE 7: *page 113.*

1. The best **sales, I think, are** at the malls. *I think* is an interruption that connects ideas.

2. Are you **sure, Jeff, that** this car is safe? *Jeff* is a direct address.

3. **Meat, on** the other **hand, should** be refrigerated right away. *On the other hand* is an interruption that connects ideas.

4. Singers who top the charts can make a lot of money. Do not add commas. *Who top the charts* is a restrictive clause. Without it, the reader would not know which singers make a lot of money.

5. **Sue, in fact, works** hard to save money. *In fact* is an interruption that connects ideas.

6. **You, along** with your **doctor, need** to take care of your health. *Along with your doctor* is an interruption that provides explanation.

7. Her wrist that had the cast is pale. Do not add commas. *That had the cast* is a restrictive clause that tells which wrist.

8. I **hope, Kay, that** we can hire more waiters. *Kay* is a direct address.

9. The judge **ruled, of course, that** Dale should stand trial. *Of course* is an interruption that connects ideas.

10. **Surgeons, besides** making a lot of **money, earn** respect. *Besides making money* is an interruption that provides explanation.

EXERCISE 8: *page 115.*

1. On December **7, 1941, the** Japanese bombed Pearl Harbor. Don't forget to place a comma after the year.
2. We sent all of the cards to 10 King **Street, Wilton, Maine** 12543. Place a comma between each part of the address, except for the state and zip code.
3. Many babies were born in September 1996, nine months after the big snowstorm. Do not add commas.
4. Carl spent over **$40,000** for that car. Add a comma after every three numbers counting from the right.
5. We may have some bad luck on **Friday, May** 13. Place a comma after the day.
6. Please send our mail to Box **12, Rush, New** York **54693, after** June **4, 1997.** Place a comma between parts of the address, except the state and zip code. Place a comma after the entire address when it is in a sentence. Place a comma between the date and the year.
7. The moon is about **240,000** miles from the earth. Place a comma after every three numbers counting from the right.
8. I arrived in Glens **Falls, New York, at** three o'clock. Place a comma between a city and state and after the state.
9. Sayre will have the book done by June 1997. Do not add commas.
10. On **Friday, March 15, Ruth** will have her birthday party. Place a comma after the day and after the entire date.

EXERCISE 9: *page 115.*

1. To **Jen, Laura** was a great friend. The reader needs to pause after *Jen* to separate it from *Laura.*
2. In **baseball, fans** are a key part of the game. The reader needs to pause after *baseball* to separate it from *fans.*
3. For **some, dogs** help cure loneliness. The reader needs to pause after *some* to separate it from *dogs.*
4. Before **nine, guests** had to leave. The reader needs to pause after *nine* to separate it from *guests.*
5. Though **sad, Meg** put a smile on her face for all to see. The reader needs to pause after *sad* to separate it from *Meg.*

EXERCISE 10: *page 117.*

1. **Lori's** Add *'s* after a singular noun.
2. **anyone's** Add *'s* after an indefinite pronoun.
3. **lawyers'** Add *'* after a plural noun that ends in *-s.*
4. **his** Possessive pronouns do not have apostrophes.
5. **voters'** Add *'* after a plural noun that ends in *-s.*
6. **hers** Possessive pronouns do not have apostrophes.
7. **Jake's** Add *'s* after a singular noun.
8. **children's** Add *'s* to a plural noun that does not end in *-s.*
9. **ours** Possessive pronouns do not have apostrophes.
10. **baby's** Add *'s* to a singular noun.
11. **Everybody's** Add *'s* to an indefinite pronoun.
12. **theirs** Possessive pronouns do not have apostrophes.
13. **its** Possessive pronouns do not have apostrophes.
14. **people's** Add *'s* to a plural noun that does not end in *-s.*
15. **Stephen's** Add *'s* after a singular noun. Some writers will add only an apostrophe to a name that ends in *-s.* In some situations, omitting the *-s* is acceptable. However, adding *'s* after a singular noun is always correct, so you might as well include the *-s.*

EXERCISE 11: *page 118.*

1. **Gale and Myleen's** Gale and Myleen shared one trip. Note that *trip* is singular.
2. **step-sister's** Add *'s* to the last word in the compound.
3. **Kristin and Pat's** Kristin and Pat share a son. Note that *son* is singular.
4. **Kay's and Phil's** Kay and Phil each have their own writing skills.
5. **brother-in-law's** Add *'s* to the last word in the compound.
6. **Brian, Rachel, Deena, and David's** They all share the same day-care center. Note that *center* is singular.
7. **mother-in-law's** Add *'s* to the last word in the compound.
8. **Greg's and Rye's** Greg and Rye each have their own bad habits. Note that *habits* is plural.
9. **Erin's and Doris's** Erin and Doris each have their own reasons. Note that *reasons* is plural.
10. **Rose and Juan's** Rose and Juan share a car. Note that *car* is singular.

EXERCISE 12: *page 119.*

1. **your** *You* owns the hair.
2. **Whose** *Who* owns the car.
   Possessive pronouns do not have apostrophes.
3. **It's** It is a bad habit.
4. **Their** They own the check.
5. **Who's** Who is the lead actor?
6. **you're** I want to be sure that you are ready.
7. **they're** Jim just heard that they are moving.
8. **its** *It* owns the back wheel.
9. **Whose** *Who* owns the toys.
   Possessive pronouns do not have apostrophes.
10. **It's** It is a great day.
11. **Were** Were you at the concert last night?
12. **its** The possessive form does not have an apostrophe.
13. **don't** *Don't* is the contraction for *do not.*
14. **We're** *We're* is the contraction for *we are.*
15. **You're** *You're* is the contraction for *you are.*

EXERCISE 13: *page 119.*

My children came home with their report cards yesterday. Although I was pleased with their grades, I was surprised by the teachers' comments. On **Zack's**[1] report card, the teacher noted that he **wasn't**[2] very focused in math. Normally, math is **his**[3] favorite subject. Taylor, on the other hand, earned high marks in reading. Last year **Taylor's**[4] reading scores were quite low. We worked on **Taylor's**[5] reading over the summer, but I still **can't**[6] understand how his scores improved so much. Jacob's report card **doesn't**[7] make sense at all. Jacob earned good grades, but the teacher commented that he isn't working very hard. **It's**[8] very confusing. I will e-mail the teachers so they can explain the **children's**[9] report cards. If that **doesn't**[10] work, we will have to arrange some conferences.

1. *Zack* is singular. Add *'s.*
2. *Wasn't* is the contraction for *was not.*
3. *His* is a possessive pronoun. Possessive pronouns do not have apostrophes.
4. *Taylor* is singular. Add *'s.*
5. *Taylor* is singular. Add *'s.*
6. *Can't* is the contraction for *can not.*
7. *Doesn't* is the contraction for *does not.*

8. *It's* is the contraction for *it is.*
9. *Children* is a plural noun. Add 's.
10. *Doesn't* is the contraction for *does not.*

EXERCISE 14: *page 120.*

We accidently left **Shantel's**[1] laptop in the airport last weekend. At first, we **didn't** even know it was missing. On Monday, Shantel tried to get some work done, but he **couldn't**[3] find the computer anywhere. Eventually, Shantel realized that he had left it on the ticket counter. Of course, we called the airline right away, and the **agents**[4] simply stated that **they're**[5] not responsible for lost or stolen items. In other words, **it's**[6] not their fault. We borrowed my **brother-in-law's**[7] car and drove back to the airport, which took over two hours. Fortunately, we found the computer right away. Shantel has good security on his laptop, so we **don't**[8] think anyone accessed his data. None-theless, **there's**[9] always a chance that someone could have goten into the system. In the future, **we're**[10] going to be much more careful.

1. *Shantel* is singular. Add 's.
2. *Didn't* is the contraction for *did not.*
3. *Couldn't* is the contraction for *could not.*
4. *Agents* is not possessive. There is no need for an apostrophe.
5. *They're* is the contraction for *they are.*
6. *It's* is the contraction for *it is.*
7. *Brother-in-law's* is possessive. The brother–in-law owns the car.
8. *Don't* is the contraction for *do not.*
9. *There's* is the contraction for *there is.*
10. *We're* is the contraction for *we are.*

EXERCISE 15: *page 121.*

1. **"Golf** is good walk **spoiled,"** said Mark Twain. These are his exact words.
2. Our boss announced that we will have fewer hours this year. This is an indirect quotation. Note *that.* Do not add quotation marks.
3. **"I** don't want **much,"** he said, **"I** just want to spend more time with my **family."** These are his exact words.
4. **"I** remain just one thing, and one thing only — and that is a **clown,"** said Charlie Chaplin. These are his exact words.
5. John said that he wants to take a trip to Greece. This is an indirect quotation. Note *that.* Do not add quotation marks.
6. **"The** day has just **begun,"** she sang. These are her exact words.
7. He argued that we spent too much time on this project. This is an indirect quotation. Note *that.* Do not add quotation marks.
8. During the speech Barb whispered, **"If** we all put our heads down, maybe he will stop talking, and we will go **home."** These are her exact words.
9. Will Rogers said that he didn't know jokes, he just watched the government and reported the facts. This is an indirect quotation. Note *that.* Do not add quotation marks.
10. **"I** need a **break!"** he yelled. These are his exact words.

EXERCISE 16: *page 122.*

1. The article **"New** Toys for **Fishermen"** appeared in the last issue of *Field and Stream. New Toys for Fisherman* is the title of an article in a magazine.
2. Billy Joel's song **"Goodnight** My **Angel"** will put her to sleep. A song is part of a larger work, an album.

3. Chapter 7, which is titled **"What** We Live **By,"** made me think about many things in my life. A chapter is part of a larger work, a book.
4. **"The** Stone in the **Road"** is a short story that you will like. Short stories need quotation marks.
5. In my view, **"discipline"** means setting limits. *Discipline* is defined.
6. Have you read the poem titled **"The Busy Man"**? Poems need quotation marks.

EXERCISE 17: *page 123.*

1. When he **shouted, "Ump,** you are **crazy!" he** was thrown out of the game. Only the quotation needs the exclamation mark.
2. The sign **says, "You** must be as tall as my hand to go on this **ride."** Periods go inside quotation marks.
3. He **shouted, "You're out!"** Only the quotation needs the exclamation point.
4. Are you sure he **said, "we** need to hire four more **drivers"**? The question mark is for the whole sentence.
5. She **said, "We** need to **talk."** Periods are placed inside quotation marks.

CHAPTER REVIEW

EXERCISE 1: *page 124.*

We have moved many **times, but**[1] moving **doesn't**[2] get much easier with experience. When we search for a new home, we look for **a nice neighborhood, excellent schools, and a decent commute.**[3] Generally we have moved into a home that we have **enjoyed, but**[4] finding a nice home in a new town is hard. One needs to learn about the **town, which**[5] can vary from one neighborhood to another, and the schools. Although the meetings with real estate agents seem endless, a good agent can help make the move a little easier. Every move is hard. **It's**[6] important to take the time to do it right.

1. **times, but** The comma separates two independent clauses that are joined by the coordinating conjunction *but.*
2. **Doesn't** is the contraction for *does not.*
3. **A nice neighborhood, excellent schools, and a decent commute** is a series. A comma must separate the items.
4. **enjoyed, but** The comma separates two independent clauses that are joined by the coordinating conjunction *but.*
5. **town, which** *Which* signals a nonrestrictive clause. *Which can vary from one neighborhood to another* should be set off with commas.
6. **It's** is the contraction for *it is.*

EXERCISE 2: *page 124.*

1. **4 no correction necessary**
2. **2 asks, "How often do you exercise?"** This is a direct quotation, so it needs to be set off with quotation marks. A comma is placed after *asks,* and the question mark is placed inside the quotation marks because the whole quote is a question.
3. **4 "Not often enough," I respond.** This is a direct quotation. It must be set apart with quotation marks. Commas go inside quotation marks.
4. **4 no correction necessary** *Who travel* describes *people,* and it is restrictive.
5. **2 work, trips to the doctor, and kids' activities** This sentence has three items in a series, and *kids'* is possessive.

6. **4 no correction necessary**
7. **1 replace *dont* with *don't*** *Don't* is a contraction for *do not*.
8. **3 replace *its* with *it's*** *It's* is a contraction for *it is*.

EXERCISE 3: *page 126.*

1. **2 job is hard, but there are** This sentence has two independent clauses. In this case, a comma with a conjunction is the best way to join the two clauses.
2. **3 their lives, so it is important** This sentence has two independent clauses. In this case, a comma with a conjunction is the best way to join the two clauses.
3. **3 helpful books, articles, and computer programs** *Helpful books, articles, and computer programs* form a series. *Helpful* simply describes *books,* so it should not be set off with a comma. Likewise, you should not place a comma after the last item in a series.
4. **1 have career counselors who aid students** There is no need for commas in this section.
5. **4 For a fee, employment services will** In this case, the comma clarifies the sentence. Without the comma, *For a fee employment services* runs together, and the sentence is confusing.

CHAPTER 7: CAPITALIZATION

EXERCISE 1: *page 130.*

1. **My** boss said, **"We** need a longer lunch break. **A** half hour is not enough time." *My, We* and *A* all begin sentences.
2. I wrote a letter about health care to **Senator** Robb, and **I** sent a copy to Vi Rus, my doctor. *Senator* is a title, and the pronoun *I* is always capitalized. *Doctor* is not capitalized because it appears after the name.
3. **no changes** *A professor* is a title that follows a name. It should not be capitalized.
4. **In** her book, Jan wrote, **"Meeting** friends is hard for some people." *In* is the first word of the sentence. *Meeting* is the first word of a sentence that is a quotation.
5. **Dr.** Seuss's book, ***The Cat** in the **Hat***, is a big hit with children. *Dr.* is a title and the first word of a sentence. *The, cat,* and *hat* should be capitalized because they are major words in a title.
6. Susan said, **"We** get more conservative as we age." *We* is the first word of a sentence that is a quotation.
7. **no changes** The title *mayor* comes after the name.
8. The song **"Let's Give Them Something To Talk About"** reminds me of you. Each word in the title is a major word. *To* is not a preposition; it is part of the infinitive *to talk. About* is a preposition, but it is the last word in the title, so it is a major word.
9. **no changes** *The mayor* is a title, but it is not used before a person's name.
10. Ellen's music box plays **"Ring** around the **Rosie."** *Ring* and *Rosie* are major words. *Around* is a preposition, and *the* is an article.

EXERCISE 2: *page 132.*

1. On **Monday, Hope Church** will open a new soup kitchen at **Park Street** and **King Street.** *Monday* is a day of the week. *Hope Church* is an institution. *Park, King,* and *Street* are common nouns that are part of a name.

2. Blair **High School** held classes on **Veterans' Day,** but the students were off for **Labor Day.** *Blair High School* is an institution. *Veterans' Day* and *Labor Day* are holidays.
3. Christians read the **Bible,** and **Jews** read the **Talmud.** *Christians* and *Jews* are worshippers. The *Bible* and *Talmud* are holy books.
4. **My** mom came all the way from **France** to see me. *My* is the first word of the sentence. *France* is a geographical name. Do not capitalize *mom,* which is a common noun in this sentence.
5. **The Purple Heart** and the **Bronze Star** are meaningful awards. *The Purple Heart* and *Bronze Star* are names of specific awards.
6. The **Renaissance** was a time of great art and music. The Renaissance is a historic period.
7. Aunt Sue and **Uncle** Peter are from the **South,** but they enjoyed traveling to **Vermont** and **New York.** *Uncle* is a common noun that is used as part of a name. *South* refers to the place, not the direction. *Vermont* and *New York* are states.
8. Dad studied **Russian** and **Spanish** when he worked for the **FBI.** *Russian* and *Spanish* are languages. *FBI* is an abbreviation of a proper noun (Federal Bureau of Investigation).
9. Many lakes, such as **Lake Champlain** and **Squam Lake,** attract tourists in the summer. When *lake* is part of a name, it is capitalized.
10. Did you know that **Grandma** liked **Nike's** commercials that aired during the **Super Bowl**? *Grandma* names a person. *Nike* is a company name. The *Super Bowl* is an event.

CHAPTER REVIEW

EXERCISE 1: *page 133.*

Every so often an author writes a book or a series that is really popular. Years[1] ago, young children loved *Little House on*[2] *the Prairie.* The authors, Laura Ingalls Wilder and Garth Williams, created a number of books that eventually became the basis of a successful television series. Many young children today enjoy books by Mary Pope Osborne. My son[3] read *The Knight at Dawn* and *Midnight on the Moon*[4] over and over again. Recently, many older readers have focused on *The Lightning Thief,* which began a successful series by Rick Riordan. Likewise, *Twilight* by Stephenie Meyer was a popular book that went on to become a hit movie with young teens.[5] Fortunately, authors continue to write books that all ages can enjoy.

1. Capitalize the first word in a sentence.
2. Do not capitalize articles, conjunctions, or prepositions unless they are the first word in a title.
3. *Son* is a common noun in this sentence. Do not capitalize common nouns.
4. Capitalize major words in titles.
5. *Teens* is a common noun. Do not capitalize common nouns.

EXERCISE 2: *page 133.*

Art, music, and literature touch our lives. A French[1] playwright said, "A[2] work of art is above all an adventure of the mind." Some people travel the world to see great works, such as *David* or the *Mona Lisa.*[3] Other people simply go to the library or turn on the radio to find great works. Books, such as *The Road Less Traveled,* make us think about our lives. Songs, such as "My Hometown," describe our feelings. We all can't travel to see art from the Renaissance[4] or hear great music, but we can enjoy the simple works that reach us every day.

1. Capitalize people and languages.
2. Capitalize the first word in a direct quotation.
3. Capitalize major words in titles.
4. Capitalize historic periods.

EXERCISE 3: *page 133.*

1. **1 replace <u>we</u> with <u>We</u>** The first word of every sentence should be capitalized.
2. **3 replace <u>Mother</u> with <u>mother</u>** *Mother* is a common noun in this sentence.
3. **2 replace <u>American idol</u> with <u>American Idol</u>** *American Idol* is a proper noun. It is the name of a TV show.
4. **3 replace <u>Junk</u> with <u>junk</u>** *Junk* is simply an adjective. It does not need to be capitalized.
5. **1 replace <u>Us</u> with <u>us</u>** *Us* is a common noun.

CHAPTER 8: WORD CHOICE

EXERCISE 1: *page 137.*

1. accept
2. already
3. affect
4. bored
5. lend
6. buy
7. dessert
8. hear
9. desert
10. except
11. whole
12. know

EXERCISE 2: *page 137.*

1. teach
2. meat
3. principle
4. quiet
5. there
6. too
7. two
8. they're
9. teach
10. quit
11. your
12. break
13. hour
14. new
15. past
16. write
17. their
18. weak
19. wear
20. You're

CHAPTER REVIEW

EXERCISE 1: *page 138.*

Buying a car takes time and effort. First, the buyer must ~~teach~~¹ about the different cars that are on the market and decide what type of car she wants. She may need to ~~lend~~² money and get insurance, ~~two~~.³ After the preparations, the buyer and salesperson ~~meat~~⁴ to agree upon a price. If the buyer ~~all ready~~⁵ ~~nos~~⁶ a lot about the car, she may get a better deal. After the sale, even more paperwork needs to be done. Many people are glad when the ~~hole~~⁷ process is finally over.

1. Use *learn* because the buyer is gaining information about the cars.
2. Use *borrow* because she will receive money that she must return.
3. *Too* means "also."
4. Use *meet* to show that the buyer and salesperson get together.
5. Use *already* because by now the buyer knows a lot.
6. Use *knows* because the buyer understands a lot about the car.
7. *Whole* means "complete."

EXERCISE 2: *page 138.*

Many boating accidents could be avoided if boaters learned important safety measures. Too often, motorboats dash ~~buy~~¹ shallow areas ~~wear~~² people are swimming. As a result, some states have ~~all ready~~³ restricted boat traffic on lakes and rivers to protect not only swimmers, but also wildlife and shorelines. Many states also require instruction courses that cover piloting techniques, proper boater behavior, and important safety information. Boaters who ~~no~~⁴ this material should be able ~~two~~⁵ pilot ~~there~~⁶ boats safely. Whether one is slowly navigating through a narrow strait or racing in the open seas, safety measures are important.

1. Use *by* because the boats are going past the shallow areas; they are not purchasing the shallow areas.
2. Use *where* to represent a place.
3. Use *already* because this sentence shows when the states restricted boat traffic. It happened before the paragraph was written.
4. Use *know* to show that boaters understand the material.
5. *To* is part of the infinitive form of the verb *to pilot.*
6. Use *their* to show ownership.

CHAPTER 9: WRITING CLEAR SENTENCES

EXERCISE 1: *page 143.*

Remember to include a comma before the conjunction.
1. Kira came to this country as an adult, **and** she learned English as quickly as she could. *And* adds two equal statements.
2. Lou wanted to buy a new car, **so** he saved his money. *So* shows why something happened. Why did Lou save his money?
3. Snakes are not cuddly pets, **yet** (or **but**) some people love them. *Yet* means however. *But* shows something is unexpected. Either conjunction would work in this sentence.
4. Many people order pizza for the Super Bowl, **or** they prepare food before the game. *Or* shows an option.
5. Yang is a great cook, **but** (or **yet**) she does not like to have friends over for dinner. *Yet* means however. *But* shows something is unexpected. Either conjunction would work in this sentence.

EXERCISE 2: *page 144.*

There may be more than one correct answer.
1. Junk food causes many problems; obesity is a major issue for children and adults.

   Obesity is a major issue for children and adults; junk food causes many problems.
2. I need to save more money; my grocery bills and car payments are high these days.

   My grocery bills and car payments are high these days; I need to save more money.
3. Food allergies are a big issue today; many fatal reactions occur every year.

   In this case, if you switch the order of the clauses, the new sentence doesn't make as much sense.
4. Gas prices have skyrocketed; many people are now walking or riding their bikes.

   Many people are now walking or riding their bikes; gas prices have skyrocketed.
5. Car seats help keep children safe; all states require them.

   In this case, if the clauses are reversed, the new sentence doesn't make much sense. *Car seats* appears twice in a row. Note the change of pronoun from *they* (subject) to *them* (object).

EXERCISE 3: *page 146.*

There may be more than one correct answer.
1. The detective searched the crime scene, traced phone calls, and questioned suspects; **nonetheless,** no arrests have been made. *Nonetheless* shows a contrast between the detectives' efforts and the results.
2. We were ready for a bad rush hour; **however,** the snow never came. *However* shows a contrast between what we were ready for and what actually happened.
3. We wanted to go to the beach; **instead,** we stayed home. *Instead* shows a contrast between what we wanted to do and what we actually did.
4. For years people thought that smoking was safe; **now,** we know that it causes cancer. *Now* shows a time relationship and a contrast. There is a difference between what we thought in the past and what we know now.
5. The game was delayed because of rain; **meanwhile,** the fans waited patiently. *Meanwhile* shows a time relationship.
6. Asthma is much more common these days; **in fact,** almost 6 million children in America have asthma. *In fact* shows that the second clause provides additional information.
7. Many schools have reduced recess time; **as a result,** children are often restless and distracted during class. *As a result* shows that reduced recess time causes restlessness and distraction.

EXERCISE 4: *page 148.*

There is more than one correct answer. Make sure you include a comma after a dependent clause that begins a sentence.
1. **After** I paid my debts, I felt a sense of relief. Instead of *after*, you could use *because* or a similar subordinate conjunction.
2. Juan will have to do more housework **because** Rose works two jobs.
3. **Even though** Kate is smart, she still needs to work hard. *Although* would also work in this sentence.

4. I will not get my driver's license **if** I don't pass this test.
5. Salma will plant her garden **wherever** the soil and sunlight are good.
6. **Before** the cold weather comes, the landlord needs to fix our heat.

EXERCISE 5: *page 149.*

There is more than one correct answer. Note that the correct sentences may have different meanings.

1. The housing crisis is hard on many families; foreclosures are difficult.
   Because foreclosures are difficult, the housing crisis is hard on many families.
2. Save your energy; it is a long walk.
   Save your energy because it is a long walk.
3. Colin's leg is broken; we need to get help immediately.
   If Colin's leg is broken, we need to get help immediately.
4. Put on bug spray; then, you go into the woods.
   Before you go into the woods, put on bug spray.
5. Make sure you are taking the medicine properly; some medicines must be taken with food.
   Make sure you are taking the medicine properly because some medicines must be taken with food.
6. Flu shots are recommended for many people; the flu can be quite serious.
   The flu can be quite serious; therefore, flu shots are recommended for many people.
7. Jacob struggles with reading; school is hard for him.
   Because Jacob struggles with reading, school is hard for him.
8. The candidates have different views on the issues; the debate should be interesting.
   The candidates have different views on the issues; as a result, the debate should be interesting.
9. Karim dropped the heavy box. It landed on his foot.
   Karim dropped the heavy box, and it landed on his foot.
10. Since gas prices have gone up, I can't pay my bills.
   Gas prices have gone up; therefore, I can't pay my bills.

EXERCISE 6: *page 151.*

1. Max dressed up because he wanted to charm his girlfriend, to impress his friends, and to please his parents.
2. Free food, great music, and good weather made the state fair a big hit.
3. People should save their money carefully, regularly, and wisely.
4. Tran needs to look hard for a quiet, bright, relaxing place to study.
5. When you go to the food store, drive through town, over the bridge, and past the town pool.
6. Before they admitted that nicotine is addictive, cigarette manufacturers ignored scientific research, testified before Congress, and fought lawsuits against them.
7. Many people in the community volunteer happily, repeatedly, and kindly.
8. Many students look for a college with a good reputation, athletic programs, and reasonable tuition.
9. Various books, online computers, and children's materials help the public libraries attract many different people.
10. Athletes who want a large, open, well-designed gym should go to the health club around the corner.

EXERCISE 7: *page 153.*

1. **watches** *Every Friday* shows that the action happens repeatedly. Therefore, both verbs, *orders* and *watches,* should be in the present tense.
2. **will cut** *Next week* signals that the action will happen in the future. Both verbs, *will clean* and *will cut,* should be in the future tense.
3. **moved** *Last month* signals that the action happened in the past. Both verbs, *bought* and *moved,* should be in the past tense.
4. **will pass** *Next year* signals that the action will happen in the future. Both verbs, *will pass* and *will sign,* should be in the future tense.
5. **acted** *On Monday* does not give enough information. The actions could have happened last Monday, or they may occur next Monday. However, *walked* is in the past tense, so *acted* should be in the past tense.
6. **ended** *Last week* signals the past tense. Both verbs, *signed* and *ended,* should be in the past tense.
7. **will invest** *In the next few years* signals the future tense. Both verbs, *will invest* and *will bring,* should be in the future tense.
8. **attracts** *Every year* signals that the actions occur regularly. Both verbs, *lures* and *attracts,* should be in the present tense.
9. **established** In this sentence, the only signal word is the verb *overturned,* which is in the past tense. Both verbs, *overturned* and *established,* should be in the past tense because they occur at the same time.
10. **taught** *Last year* signals the past tense. Both verbs, *took* and *taught,* should be in the past tense.

EXERCISE 8: *page 154.*

1. **Luke drove the car barely 1,000 miles before the transmission died.** In the original sentence, Luke barely drove the car. How do you barely drive a car?
2. **After school, children often watch TV until their parents come home.** *After school* describes when children watch TV.
3. **Homes with flood damage are being moved to higher ground.** *With flood damage* describes *homes.* Who would move <u>to</u> ground with flood damage?
4. **The working poor, struggling to pay the bills, often cannot afford good health care.** *Struggling to pay the bills* describes *working poor.* In the original sentence, *struggling to pay the bills* describes *health care.*
5. **Tired from the flu, I called in sick to work.** *Tired from the flu* describes *I,* which is the first noun after the comma. In the original sentence, *tired from the flu* describes *work.*
6. **Lim unintentionally found a good plumber to fix his sink.** *Unintentionally* is an adverb that shows how Lim found the plumber. The original sentence does not make sense; *unintentionally* describes how the plumber fixes the sink.
7. **Dr. Tim tells people with weight problems to eat a low-fat diet and exercise.** *With weight problems* describes *people.* In the original sentence, *with weight problems* describes *exercise.*
8. **Some people who want to choose their own doctors are frustrated with HMOs.** *Who want to choose their own doctors* describes *people.* In the original sentence, *who want to choose their own doctors* describes *HMOs.*
9. **Concerned about the risk of inflation, the Chair of the Federal Reserve will raise interest rates.** *Concerned about the risk of inflation* describes *Chair.* In the original sentence, the phrase describes *rates.*

10. **Some people use dogs that are trained to help the visually impaired.** *Trained to help the visually impaired* describes *dogs.* In the original sentence, the phrase describes *people,* which does not make sense.

EXERCISE 9: *page 156.*

There is more than one possible answer to each question.

1. **While I was climbing up the mountain face, my backpack slipped.** In the original sentence, my backpack climbed up the mountain face alone.
2. **While the police were searching for clues to the crime, the police car was stolen.** In the original sentence, the police car was searching for clues to the crime.
3. **When we were tired and hungry, our museum tour ended.** In the original sentence, the museum tour was tired and hungry.
4. **While I was checking my watch, the sun came out from behind the clouds.** In the original sentence, the sun was checking my watch.
5. **When the voters became frustrated with campaign funding, reform bills quickly passed through Congress.** In the original sentence, the reform bills were frustrated.
6. **Annoyed by Jamel's attitude, his boss stopped the raises.** In the original sentence, were the pay raises annoyed?
7. **Ty searched the want ads for a job with steady hours and good pay.** In the original sentence, Ty had steady hours and good pay.
8. **When I was running to catch the bus, my briefcase spilled all over the sidewalk.** In the original sentence, the briefcase was running to catch the bus.
9. **When we became angered by the slow response, the ambulance finally arrived at the scene.** In the original sentence, the ambulance was angered.
10. **The salesperson showed us the new cars, which were fresh off the delivery truck.** In the original sentence, the salesperson was fresh off the delivery truck.

EXERCISE 10: *page 158.*

There is more than one possible answer to each question.

1. **Many parents who are concerned about gangs have teamed up with the local police and schools to improve safety.** In the original sentence, it is unclear whether the parents or the gangs have teamed up with police and schools.
2. **Our food store caters to busy lives. It opens early, closes late, and carries prepared meals.** The pronoun *it* refers to *store.*
3. **When Katrina wore her new uniform to the soccer match, she knew the game would be exciting.** In the original sentence, is the match exciting or the new uniform?
4. **Before you interview for a job, you need to learn about the company.** In the original sentence the pronoun shifts from *one* to *you.*
5. **In 1846 James Smithson gave a fortune to help form the Smithsonian Institution. Today, it operates many museums in Washington, D.C.** In the original sentence, James Smithson and the Smithsonian Institution work together. James Smithson can't possibly operate museums today.

EXERCISE 11: *page 160.*

Each question has more than one correct answer.
1. Because ivory tusks are valuable, hunters slaughter elephants.
2. Although wildlife groups work hard to save the endangered species, some animals may not survive.
3. TV violence affects children.
4. Gas, maintenance, and insurance are expensive, so car owners must be prepared to spend a lot of money. OR Gas, maintenance, and insurance are expensive; therefore, car owners must be prepared to spend a lot of money.
5. Whenever one lifts something heavy, back support is important.
6. Rabid animals sometimes infect persons.
7. Because they do not pay their bills on time, some persons earn bad credit ratings.
8. People with bad debts are helped by financial planners.
9. The liver and other organs can be destroyed by alcoholism over time.
10. Because their child would go to college, Jim and Pat saved money each year.
11. Babies do not get the medical treatment that they need because many women do not receive appropriate prenatal care.
12. American officials tried to cooperate more effectively with other world leaders in an effort to track terrorists internationally.
13. Because childhood obesity is an epidemic in America, physicians across the nation are trying to address poor eating habits and sedentary lifestyles.
14. As a result of a severe nursing shortage, which is expected to worsen in the next few years, hospitals are struggling to recruit and retain nurses.
15. School, work, and family life demand a great amount of students' time and energy; therefore, many students work hard to balance different aspects of their lives.

EXERCISE 12: *page 164.*

These are suggestions. There is more than one correct answer to each question.
1. Kay was struggling to pay her **bills, so** she took an extra job on weekends. **or**
   Kay was struggling to pay her **bills; therefore, she** took an extra job on weekends.
   Kay was struggling to pay her bills shows why *she took an extra job on weekends.*
2. Han wants to let her daughter play **outside, but** there is too much violence in their neighborhood. **or**
   Han wants to let her daughter play **outside; however, there** is too much violence in their neighborhood.
   There is a difference between what Han wants to do and what she can do.
3. Tim drops Greg off at daycare in the **morning, and** Shavone picks Greg up after work. **or**
   Tim drops Greg off at daycare in the **morning; likewise, Shavone** picks Greg up after work.
   And and *likewise* show that two equal statements are added together.
4. Ray wants to star in the school **play, but** he has not learned his lines. **or**
   Ray wants to star in the school **play; however, he** has not learned his lines.
   But and *however* show that there is a difference between what Ray wants and what may happen.

5. Eve wants to learn a new software program by **Friday, yet** she needs to prepare for her presentation, which is tomorrow. **or**
Eve wants to learn a new software program by **Friday; instead, she** needs to prepare for her presentation, which is tomorrow.
Yet and *instead* show that there is a difference between what Eve wants to do and what she needs to do.

6. Credit card debt can destroy a family's **finances, so** it is better to buy only what one can afford to pay in cash. **or**
Credit card debt can destroy a family's **finances; thus, it** is better to buy only what one can afford to pay in cash.
So and *thus* show that the first statement explains why the second statement is true.

7. Most people know the dangers of **smoking, yet** teenage tobacco use continues to increase. **or**
Most people know the dangers of **smoking, nonetheless, teenage** tobacco use continues to increase.
Yet and *nonetheless* shows that there is a difference between what people know about smoking and what they do about it.

8. Politicians keep talking about cutting government **spending, but** few people want to give up the government services that they use. **or**
Politicians keep talking about cutting government **spending; however, few** people want to give up the government services that they use.
But and *however* show that there is a difference between what politicians talk about and what actually happens.

9. The tax code in America is **complex, so** many Americans must pay a professional to do their taxes. **or**
The tax code in America is **complex; consequently, many** Americans must pay a professional to do their taxes.
So and *consequently* show that the first statement explains why the second statement is true.

10. Faith needs more training for her **job, so** she is taking a computer class on weekends. **or**
Faith needs more training for her **job; therefore, she** is taking a computer class on weekends.
So and *therefore* show that the first statement explains why the second statement is true.

EXERCISE 13: *page 167.*

These are suggestions. There is more than one possible answer to each question.

1. **When Matt's mom came home from work, he was excited to see her.** The original sentences are related by time.

2. **We were sitting at the stoplight, and we could hear music blaring from another car, which was across the street.** In the original sentences, the second sentence gives additional information about the car in the first sentence.

3. **Because Salma had a bad cold, Salma's mother could not leave her at daycare.** The original sentences are related by cause and effect. The first sentence shows the cause, and the second sentence tells the effect.

4. **Although Anh finished his test in less than thirty minutes, he did not have many correct answers.** The original sentences show a contrast. One might expect that Anh would do well on the test because he finished so quickly.

5. **Whenever the lights on a school bus flash, cars must stop so that students can exit the bus safely.** The original sentences are related by time.

6. **Nathan paints landscapes as well as Kaila does.** The original sentences show a comparison between Nathan and Kaila.

7. **While the tornado whipped through the town, people huddled in their basements hoping they would be safe.** The original sentences are related by time.

8. **Very few people voted in the primary elections, which will determine the Republican candidates.** The original sentences are related by information. The second sentence provides additional information about the elections.

9. **Although Wolf wanted to swim to cool off from the hot weather, the water in the pool was too cold.** The original sentences show a contrast. There is a difference between what Wolf wanted to do and what he did.

10. **Many people in the Midwest desperately need flood relief, which politicians promised to give a month ago.** The original sentences are related by information. The second sentence gives additional information about flood relief.

11. **Jenna struggled to complete her assignments for school because she needed to work two jobs to help support her younger siblings.** The original sentences show cause and effect. Jenna's work caused her struggles in school.

12. **After Maharan traveled to India to visit his family for several weeks, he decided to live there permanently.** The two sentences are related by time.

13. **Before Colin filed the suit, he tried to settle his complaint with the store owner, who refused to give Colin a refund—even a partial one.** The second sentence provides additional information about the store owner.

14. **The stock market is down, and investors are getting nervous because Americans are concerned about terrorism, the economy, and the threat of war.** Americans' concerns explain why the stock market is down and investors are nervous.

15. **Even though life-threatening food allergies are much more prevalent today than they were twenty years ago, doctors still do not understand completely how food allergies develop or how to prevent them.** There is a contrast between the increased prevalence of food allergies and doctors' limited understanding.

EXERCISE 14: *page 171.*

1. **who** Use *who* for people.
2. **that** Use *that* for things or animals.
3. **which** *Which needs repair* is not important to identify which barn; we already know that it is Farmer Rick's barn. In addition, clauses starting with *which* are set off by commas.
4. **who** Who is used for people
5. **that** Khan does not want just any job. He wants a job *that will pay him more money.* The clause limits that noun and does not have commas.
6. **whom** *Whom* is used for people.
7. **which** *Which kills many people* is not restrictive. We already know that lung cancer kills.
8. **that** There are many jokes, but I told Dave a joke *that he had not heard before.* The clause limits the noun and does not have commas.
9. **who** *Who* is used for people.
10. **that** Joe will not buy just any dog. He wants a dog *that will be good with children.* The clause limits the noun and does not have commas.

CHAPTER REVIEW

EXERCISE 1: *page 172.*

1. **3 areas and creating** *Discovering* and *creating* form a compound verb. Both verbs should be in the same form.
2. **4 now** *Townhouses and strip malls now dominate the land where farms and orchards once stood.*
3. **1 but** *Although* and *but* show a contrast. There is a difference between how some people feel about the developments and how others feel. *These new developments delight some people, but they frustrate others.*
4. **5 burdens local services** *Changes, crowds,* and *are burdened* form a compound verb. All of the verbs should be in the same form.
5. **5 no correction necessary** Option (1) is wrong because a comma after *housing* is unnecessary. Option (2) is wrong because *are working* shows that the action is in the present tense. Option (3) is wrong because a comma after *leaders* is unnecessary. Option (4) is wrong because *with the need* does not modify *setting.*
6. **3 , which protects** The second sentence gives additional information about the project. *Which protects over 93,000 acres of land from development* is an adjective clause that modifies *project. In Montgomery County, Maryland, county leaders established a preservation project, which protects over 93,000 acres of land from development.*
7. **5 want** *Although* and *but* both show a contrast. There are different views of the project. *Although many people want the preservation project to continue, others want it to end.*
8. **1 move *that is preserved* after *land*** *That is preserved* is an adjective clause. In the original sentence, the clause modifies *money.* The clause should modify *land. Farmers, who own much of the land that is preserved, are losing money.*
9. **3 change *stores for retail* to *retail stores*** *New housing, office space, and stores for retail* form a series. Each item in the series should be in the same form (adjective + noun).
10. **5 no correction necessary** Option (1) is wrong because a comma after *jobs* is unnecessary. Option (2) is wrong because *they* is used for people, and *it* is used for things. Option (3) is wrong because the subject and verb should be plural. Option (4) is wrong because *to the county* works as an adverb clause that answers the question where.
11. **2 move *between developers and preservationists* after *debate*** *Between developers and preservationists* is a prepositional phrase that describes *debate.* In the original sentence, the phrase describes *years.*

EXERCISE 2: *page 174.*

1. **3 parties that are used** The second sentence gives additional information about *parties.* The adjective phrase *that are used to sell products* describes *parties. Home parties that are used to sell products are making a comeback.*
2. **2 move *with friends and neighbors* after *socializing*** *With friends and neighbors* is a prepositional phrase that describes *socializing.* In the original sentence, the phrase describes *goods.* The goods do not have friends and neighbors.
3. **4 , now many** *Although* and *but* show a contrast. There is a difference between home parties in the past and home parties today. *Although Tupperware has sold its products through home parties for years, now many different companies use home parties to market their goods.*

4. **5 no correction necessary** Option (1) is wrong because the comma sets off an introductory phrase. Option (2) is wrong because *parties* is the plural of party. It is not possessive. Option (3) is wrong because a comma after *baskets* is unnecessary. Option (4) is wrong because *today* signals that the sentence is in the present tense.

5. **1 trend, which started** The second sentence provides additional information. *Which started in the early nineties* is an adjective clause that describes *trend*. *This sales trend, which started in the early nineties, has developed for a number of reasons.*

6. **5 have become** *Have become* is in the present perfect tense so that it will agree with the rest of the paragraph. In this paragraph, the actions began in the past and continue into the present.

7. **3 shop** *Some people who have busy lifestyles shop in these social settings.* In the original sentence, *busy lifestyles* is the subject, and *have been encouraged* is the verb. In the new sentence, *some people* is the subject, and *shop* is the verb. *Who have busy lifestyles* describes *some people*.

8. **4 replace *have* with *has*** *Inventory*, the subject, is singular. (Do not be fooled by *of goods*, a prepositional phrase that should be ignored.) The verb should also be singular.

9. **5 no correction necessary** Option (1) is wrong because *whatever the reason* is an introductory phrase that should be set off by a comma. Option (2) is wrong because *this* is singular; therefore, the verb should be singular. Option (3) is wrong because *that will continue* is a restrictive clause; it tells which trend. Restrictive clauses use *that* and do not have commas. Option (4) is wrong because the sentence is about the future.

PRACTICE FOR CHAPTERS 1 THROUGH 9

1. **3 have neglected** *For the past few decades* signals that the action began in the past and continues today. *Have neglected* is in the present perfect tense, which shows actions that started in the past and continue into the present. *Had neglected* is in the past perfect tense, which shows actions that were completed before a specific time or event in the past.

2. **5 future, but** The conjunction *but* joins two independent clauses. A comma is needed before the conjunction. The clauses could be joined with a semicolon because the first clause is long. However, *but* should not be capitalized as it is in option (2).

3. **4 replace *peoples* with *people's*** Use the possessive form to show whose lives.

4. **2 replace *are* with *is*** The sentence refers to a job loss *or* a disability. When *or* is used, the verb must agree with the closest subject, which is *disability*.

5. **4 replace *his* with *their*** The pronoun should agree with *Americans*, which is plural.

6. **5 no correction necessary** The sentence is correct.

7. **4 fund that holds** When these sentences are joined, *that* introduces a clause that describes *fund*. The clause is restrictive, so *that* should be used instead of *which*. *First, they must create an emergency fund that holds enough money to cover expenses for three to six months.*

8. **3 debts, which** *Which* introduces a nonrestrictive clause. Nonrestrictive clauses are set off with commas.

9. **1 insert a comma after *future*** *Instead of saving for the future* is an introductory phrase. It should be set off with a comma.

10. **5 no change is necessary** The sentence is correct.
11. **4 insert a comma after <u>home</u>** *Home, college, and retirement* form a series. Commas separate items in a series.
12. **1 replace <u>learns</u> with <u>teaches</u>** *Learn* means "to gain understanding or information." *Teach* means "to give understanding or information." The planners give understanding.
13. **4 insert a comma after <u>care</u>** *Child care, work, and lifestyle changes* form a series. Commas separate items in a series.
14. **1 replace <u>parents'</u> with <u>parents</u>** *Parents* should not be possessive. It is simply the subject of the sentence.
15. **1 replace <u>there</u> with <u>their</u>** *Their* shows possession. Whose jobs do they enjoy?
16. **5 no correction necessary**
17. **2 money; some families** The second independent clause provides more information about the first clause. The other options are incorrect because they would change the meaning of the sentences. The new sentence would read as follows: *Likewise, many households simply need the money; some families depend on two incomes to pay the bills.*
18. **4 replace <u>are</u> with <u>is</u>** In this sentence, *finding good child care* is a phrase that works as a noun. It is also the subject of the sentence. Therefore, the verb must agree with *finding good child care.*
19. **3 insert a comma after <u>hours</u>** *Decrease their hours, work from home, or stop working altogether* form a series. Each action in the series needs to be separated by a comma.
20. **3 may outweigh** When the sentence is rewritten, *the cost of child care, commuting, and services* is still the subject and *may outweigh* is still the verb. The new sentence reads as follows: *The cost of child care, commuting, and services may outweigh the benefit of a second income in some families.*
21. **2 replace <u>too</u> with <u>to</u>** In this sentence, *to* is part of the verb *to be. Too* means "also" or "in excess."
22. **1 carefully and choose the best** The other options change the meaning of the two sentences. The new sentence reads as follows: *Parents need to evaluate their concerns carefully and choose the best options for themselves and their children.*
23. **3 emerge** *Every day* signals that the action happens repeatedly. In addition, the rest of the paragraph is in the present tense. Thus, the verb *emerge* should be in the present tense.
24. **4 replace <u>Departments</u> with <u>departments</u>** In this sentence, *departments* is a common noun, which should not be capitalized.
25. **2 replace <u>is</u> with <u>are</u>** The verb must agree with *traffic violations and crimes*. Therefore, it must be plural. *Such as disorderly conduct, panhandling, loitering, and prostitution* simply provides more information about the subject.
26. **2 new approach, but others are** There is a contrast between how some people feel about the approach and how others feel. Option (2) shows this contrast by using the conjunction *but*. The other options do not show the correct relationship between the two clauses.
27. **4 insert a comma after <u>upheld</u>** *When all laws are upheld* is an introductory clause. Insert a comma after an introductory clause.
28. **4 replace <u>has</u> with <u>have</u>** The verb must agree with the subject *businesses*, which is plural.
29. **2 insert a comma after <u>cities</u>** *But* is a conjunction that joins two independent clauses. A comma needs to be placed before the conjunction.
30. **1 replace <u>that</u> with <u>which</u>** *That works to protect people's rights* is a nonrestrictive clause that is set off by commas. Without the clause,

the reader still knows which group has noted the complaints against the police. Use *which*, instead of *that*, for nonrestrictive clauses.

31. **1 replace <u>they're</u> with <u>their</u>** In this sentence, *their* is correct because it shows whose neighborhoods are targeted. *They're* is a contraction for *they are*, which doesn't make sense in this sentence.

32. **2 replace <u>however</u> with <u>; however,</u>** *However* joins two independent clauses. To punctuate the sentence properly, place a semicolon before *however* and a comma after *however*.

33. **2 insert a comma after <u>activities</u>** In this sentence, use a comma to separate the dependent and independent clauses. *Their children excel* is an independent clause, and *when parents participate regularly in school activities* is a dependent clause.

34. **1 children: education** The second sentence provides additional information about the first sentence. It explains the message. The other options do not show the correct relationship between the sentences.

35. **3 replace <u>childrens</u> with <u>children's</u>** Whose classmates and friends? *Children* is plural. An apostrophe is needed after the *n* to show possession.

36. **2 replace <u>there</u> with <u>their</u>** Whose local schools? In this sentence, use the possessive form.

37. **3 replace <u>which</u> with <u>who</u>** *Educators* are people. *Who* should be used for people, and *which* should be used for animals or things.

38. **3 insert a comma after <u>classes</u>** *Attend classes, eat lunch, and go on field trips* forms a series of verbs. Use a comma to separate the verbs properly.

39. **3 replace <u>which</u> with <u>that</u>** *State exactly how parents should supervise homework, encourage good behavior, and support their child's teachers* provides necessary information about the contracts. *That* should be used in this sentence because the additional information is restrictive. In addition, if *which* were the correct word, a comma would be placed after *contracts*.

40. **1 replace <u>whomever</u> with <u>whoever</u>** The parents don't assist *whomever*. Instead, they assist *whoever needs help*. In this sentence, *whoever* is correct because it is the subject of the clause *whoever needs help*.

41. **5 no correction necessary** The sentence is correct as written.

42. **4 insert a comma after <u>styles</u>** *After reviewing many different brands and styles* is an opening phrase, which should be set apart with a comma. *I decided to buy the Blue Sky package from Summerset, which happened to be on sale* is the independent clause.

43. **1 replace <u>Salesperson</u> with <u>salesperson</u>** In this sentence, *salesperson* is a job description, which should not be capitalized.

44. **4 replace <u>too</u> with <u>two</u>** In this sentence, the number *two* is correct. *Too* means "also" or "in excess."

45. **2 replace <u>monday</u> with <u>Monday</u>** *Monday* is a proper noun, and it should be capitalized.

46. **4 replace <u>you're</u> with <u>your</u>** Whose customer service center? In this sentence, *your* is correct because it shows possession. *You're*, which is the contraction for *you are*, is not correct in this sentence.

47. **3 Obviously I don't want two different chairs because they will not match my patio set.** The second sentence explains why the writer does not want two different chairs. Option (3) shows the correct relationship between the sentences, and it is punctuated properly. Option (1) shows the correct relationship, but it is not punctuated properly.

48. **5 no correction necessary**

49. **1 insert a comma after <u>expense</u>** *At your expense* is an interruption. Place a comma before and after the interruption to keep the sentence clear. A comma is also needed after *expense* because *and* is a conjunction, which joins two independent clauses.

50. **3 years; thus, I am** *Thus* joins two independent clauses, and it needs to be punctuated properly.

CHAPTER 10: WRITING PARAGRAPHS

EXERCISE 1: *page 192.*

These topic sentences are suggestions. There is more than one correct answer for each question.

1. **Because Dan's habits have changed, he is not doing well in school** or **Dan's schoolwork has suffered from changes in his behavior.** The first four sentences give examples of Dan's poor performance. The fifth sentence shows what Dan needs to do about his poor performance.

2. **The townspeople's strong spirit will help them overcome this devastating flood** or **Even though this was the worst flood in years, our town will survive.** The first three sentences in the paragraph show how destructive the flood was. The last two sentences show why the town will survive.

3. **Parents need to evaluate their children's activities carefully** or **Although activities are important for children, they can become overwhelming.** The first two sentences show why children are involved in activities. The last three sentences tell what can happen if children have too many activities.

4. **Aggressive drivers have become a concern recently** or **Although keeping the roads safe has always been a challenge, the recent increase in aggressive driving has made the situation even more difficult.** The first two sentences show how aggressive driving has changed recently. The last two sentences show why aggressive driving is a concern.

5. **The labor laws in France hurt the nation's economy** or **The labor laws that are designed to protect workers in France actually create problems for the nation's economy.** The first sentence explains what the labor laws do. The other sentences show why the labor laws are bad for the economy of France.

6. **The snowstorm on April Fool's Day was frustrating** or **In April, a surprise snowstorm made life difficult for everyone.** Each sentence in the paragraph tells why the storm was frustrating.

7. **Understanding the symptoms of appendicitis can help one get medical help promptly** or **The symptoms of appendicitis are important to recognize.** The first three sentences describe the symptoms, and the last sentence tells what one should do about the symptoms.

8. **Walkers are dangerous** or **Walkers used to be commonplace in many households, but now most people recognize how dangerous they can be.** The first sentence explains how walkers have been used. The second sentence tells how doctors' views on walkers have changed because of the danger. The last four sentences explain why walkers are dangerous.

9. **Red meat is not as popular as it was years ago** or **In the past few years, Americans have changed their diets significantly.** The first and second sentences show that red meat was popular in the past. The last three sentences explain why red meat is not as popular as it used to be.

10. **Construction equipment thrills young children** or **Construction sites attract young children who are fascinated by the equipment.** The first and second sentences tell why children like construction equipment. The last sentence shows one effect of children's interest in construction equipment.

EXERCISE 2: *page 195.*

1. <u>Searching for a new job requires a lot of hard work and patience.</u> In some areas of the country, few jobs are available. As a result, one must be persistent. Job applicants have to write many letters and research companies. Likewise, completing applications and going on interviews takes time. ~~Congress recently increased the minimum wage~~. In addition, many people have to look for a new job while they are still working. Although a job search is demanding, the results can be quite rewarding. *Searching for a new job requires a lot of hard work and patience* ties all of the information together. *Congress recently increased the minimum wage* is related to work, but it has nothing to do with searching for a new job. *Although a job search is demanding, the results can be quite rewarding* may seem like a topic sentence; however, the other sentences in the paragraph do not mention results. This is a better transitional sentence, which helps the reader move from one paragraph to another.

2. <u>Soccer has become a popular sport in America</u>. Parents generally like soccer because every child has a chance to participate actively. As a result, recreational leagues and competitive teams abound in many regions. Some soccer leagues cannot keep up with the demand for new teams, equipment, and playing fields. Likewise, many college athletic directors have worked hard to develop their soccer programs for both men and women. ~~Because players run for long periods of time, leg injuries are common in soccer~~. It is too early to tell how long this enthusiasm for soccer will last.
Soccer has become a popular sport in America pulls the other sentences together. The rest of the paragraph focuses on the popularity of soccer. *Because players run for long periods of time, leg injuries are common in soccer* may be true, but this sentence does not relate to the popularity of soccer.

3. <u>Americans need to take food poisoning more seriously</u>. ~~Overeating and high-fat diets contribute to many health problems in the United States~~. Poorly processed or undercooked meats, as well as contaminated water supplies, often cause food poisoning, which affects thousands of people every year. Some cases of food poisoning are fatal. Everyone should take precautions to make sure that their food is safe to eat.
Americans need to take food poisoning more seriously focuses the paragraph on the severity of food poisoning. *Overeating and high-fat diets contribute to many health problems in the United States* is a true statement, but food poisoning is a different issue.

4. ~~It is hard for some individuals to save and invest money~~. Many people prefer mutual funds to stocks, which demand more research and attention. Baby boomers are using mutual funds to save for retirement. People in their twenties and thirties use mutual funds to save for a home or their children's education. <u>As a result, more Americans are investing in mutual funds now than ever before</u>.
As a result, more Americans are investing in mutual funds now than ever before ties the paragraph together. Topic sentences usually are not placed at the end of a paragraph, but in some situations they may be. *It is hard for some individuals to save and invest money* is a true statement, but it does not relate specifically to mutual funds.

5. Many people simply are not interested in caring for young children. Other jobs offer higher wages and better benefits. <u>As a result, a good babysitter is hard to find.</u> In an effort to improve child care, some local hospitals offer babysitting classes, which teach teenagers to care for young children. However, even teenagers often prefer other types of employment. ~~Likewise, parents are having fewer children these days~~. Instead of hiring a sitter, many parents simply choose to stay home.

As a result, a good babysitter is hard to find pulls the sentences together. *Likewise, parents are having fewer children these days* is a true statement. However, it is unlikely that parents are having fewer children because they can't find babysitters.

EXERCISE 3: *page 197.*

These answers are suggestions. Each question has more than one correct answer.

1. **Movie rentals are a major form of entertainment.**
   Personal Experience: On weekends and rainy days, my kids love to rent movies.
   Knowledge: Movie rental stores, vending machines, and on-demand video services all provide movie rentals.
   Observation: Watching a movie at home is more relaxing than going to a movie theater.
2. **Parenting is exciting, but it is hard work.**
   Personal Experience: I did not sleep well for months after my twins were born.
   Knowledge: Many adults enroll in parenting classes that help people deal with their children more effectively.
   Observation: Before becoming parents, adults must make sure that they are ready not only for the joy but also for the hard times.
3. **We often view life differently as we get older.**
   Personal Experience: Many of the ideas I had as a teenager seem crazy to me today.
   Knowledge: Maturity and personal experiences can change how an individual views the world.
   Observation: Perhaps there is some truth to the idea that wisdom comes with age.
4. **A great teacher can change your life.**
   Personal Experience: Last year my English teacher taught me to write well, so I can get a better paying job.
   Knowledge: Teach for America is a national effort to draw potentially great teachers into the profession.
   Observation: Teachers have the power and the responsibility to enrich their students' lives.
5. **Many Americans do not save enough money.**
   Personal Experience: When I graduated from school, my credit card debt was more than I could handle.
   Knowledge: Many families only pay the minimum each month on their credit cards.
   Observation: As a society, we need to spend less and save more.

EXERCISE 4: *page 198.*

The sentence in bold print moved to a new location. Explanations follow.

1. In addition to providing critical medical care, many pediatricians try to focus on safety and developmental issues. **Checkups include much more than a physical exam.** Now when children visit the doctor, they

are often encouraged to use seat belts in vehicles and helmets when riding a bike. Likewise, parents are often prompted to childproof their homes and monitor their children carefully. Many physicians also instruct parents to provide stimulating toys and read to their children daily. Doctors hope that this comprehensive approach will help children with their physical, emotional, and intellectual development. *Checkups include much more than a physical exam* describes changes in general. The three sentences that follow give specific examples of how checkups have changed.

2. **Paying taxes is a frustrating experience for many Americans.** Some people prepare their taxes on their own, using tax preparation software or materials from the Internal Revenue Service (IRS). However, many people, who find tax preparation too complicated or time consuming, hire accountants to prepare their taxes. Whatever method one uses, the result is often the same; taxpayers can expect either a tax bill or a refund sometime after April 15.

   Paying taxes is a frustrating experience for many Americans focuses on tax paying, overall. The following sentences describe how people deal with the frustration.

3. The computer, which I recently purchased, is not functioning properly. I have examined the cables and determined that it is set up correctly. However, I am still unable to run the printer. When I select "print" from the pull-down menu, an error message appears. **Usually the message says that the computer is having a communication problem with the printer, but I have had other error messages as well.** I contacted the printer manufacturer, and the technician assured me that the printer should be working properly. She insisted that the computer must be causing the problem. At this point, I am so frustrated that I am ready to return everything to the store.

   Usually the message says that the computer is having a communication problem with the printer, but I have had other error messages as well provides additional information about the error messages. It should be placed after the sentence that originally describes the messages.

4. The American space program has been so successful that most people take it for granted—until an accident occurs. After the *Challenger* explosion in 1986, seventeen years and more than eighty successful missions passed before Americans were awakened by another tragedy. **When the space shuttle *Columbia* was lost in 2003, some people questioned whether the NASA program should be continued.** However, most people recognized that space travel is now part of the American dream, a new frontier that we will explore. Certainly our nation needs time to mourn and examine what went wrong; nonetheless, we will learn from this experience and move on to even greater things.

   When the space shuttle Columbia *was lost in 2003, some people questioned whether the NASA program should be continued* describes "another tragedy" that happened after the *Challenger* explosion. The two events should be in the order in which they occurred.

5. Parents are a child's first teachers. **Many of us have heard that phrase before, but few people truly understand what it means.** Critical phases of a child's education begin long before kindergarten, or even preschool. Children learn a tremendous amount by watching their parents or caregivers and interacting with them. Parents help children develop not only academically, but also socially. Children who are nurtured, disciplined, and read to tend to make a much smoother transition to school than those who are not. Whether children are at home with a parent or in a child care situation, they are constantly

learning about themselves and the world around them.
Many of us have heard that phrase before, but few people truly understand what it means refers to *that phrase*, which means it should be placed immediately after the first sentence.

EXERCISE 5: *page 200.*

These answers are suggestions. Each question has more than one possible answer.

1. **It would take ten minutes to transmit one page, which would be hard for the recipient to read. Now, some fax machines are the size of a large book, and they can send multiple pages in minutes.** *Which would be hard for the recipient to read* is an adjective clause that describes *page*. The second sentence combines two equally important ideas. Both independent clauses in the second sentence focus on how fax machines will improve.

2. **Athletes often focus on improving their athletic ability and neglect their education. Very few athletes turn pro, and those who do often have short careers.** *Focus* and *neglect* form a compound verb. The second sentence combines two ideas that are equally important.

3. **Meanwhile, more schools are introducing science topics to elementary students. Second and third graders now learn about basic biology and physics.** *Basic biology and physics* is a compound object of the preposition.

4. **Often, many features that make computers helpful and easy to use expose private information. When people use computers for banking and investments, hackers enter their files and learn personal information.** The new sentences present the same information in a different way.

5. **Check the car carefully or hire a good mechanic to inspect the car for you. Get insurance, and, if necessary, arrange for a loan.** The original paragraph gives the reader advice. However, it repeats *you* far too often. The new sentences are commands, so the subject, *you*, is implied.

EXERCISE 6: *page 203.*

These answers are suggestions. Each question has more than one possible answer.

1. **whispered, shouted, announced**
2. **productive, relaxing, fun-filled**
3. **tremendous, huge, overweight**
4. **minor, insignificant, tiny**
5. **rainy, exhausting, boring**
6. **spicy, inexpensive, healthy**
7. **bumped, crushed, sideswiped**
8. **crashed, lingered, broke**
9. **daily, weekly, biweekly**
10. **noisy, never ending, not moving**

CHAPTER REVIEW

EXERCISE 1: *page 205.*

These are suggestions. Each question has more than one possible answer.

1. **Researchers are studying how daycare affects children.** Each sentence is related to the topic sentence. The first supporting detail describes a

particular study. The second and third supporting details focus on the positive and negative effects of day care. The fourth supporting detail states that research will continue because day care is popular.

2. **Roads and bridges in America need to be maintained more carefully.** Each sentence is related to the topic sentence. The first supporting detail shows that routes in America have not been well maintained. The second supporting detail explains that even though maintenance is costly, it must be done. The third and fourth supporting details show how poor maintenance affects us, and the fifth supporting detail emphasizes that road maintenance is a safety issue.

3. **Homeowners' associations are powerful in some neighborhoods.** Each sentence is related to the topic sentence. The first, second, and third supporting details show what types of power the associations have. The fourth supporting detail shows that some people like the power and others do not.

4. **Spring is a great time of year.** Each sentence is related to the topic sentence. The first, second, third, and fourth supporting details show why spring is great.

5. **People save money in many different ways.** Each sentence is related to the topic sentence. The first, second, and third supporting detail show how people save their money. The fourth supporting detail explains that one can use any technique to create a savings account.

6. **We need to teach our children to pursue their dreams.** The first and second supporting details show that children have many dreams when they are young. The third supporting detail notes that children often lose their dreams as they age, and the fourth supporting detail explains why it is important for children to follow their dreams.

7. **Babies are expensive.** Each sentence is related to the topic sentence. The first, second, third, and fourth supporting details show why babies are expensive. The fifth supporting detail emphasizes that parents need to prepare themselves for these costs.

8. **Today, many people depend on gadgets in their homes.** The first and second supporting details show what types of gadgets people have. The third and fourth sentences tell people's different reactions to these devices.

9. **School buses are not used effectively.** The first supporting detail explains why buses are needed. The second and third supporting details show why buses are underused. The fourth supporting detail tells that underused school buses are costly. The fifth supporting detail suggests that there must be a solution to the problem.

10. **Music is everywhere.** The first supporting detail tells where music is often found. The second, third, fourth, and fifth supporting details show where there is music in our daily lives. The sixth supporting detail suggests choosing one form of music over another.

EXERCISE 2: *page 207.*

These are suggestions. Each question has more than one possible answer.

1. **a. During the summer, the lawn needs to be mowed once a week.**
   b. Every few years, the house needs to be painted.
   Supporting details for this paragraph should include examples of work that needs to be done around the home.

2. **a. One can bike alone or with a friend.**
   b. In just a half hour, one can get a great workout.
   Supporting details for this paragraph should include reasons why biking is a good form of exercise.

3. **a. For a person who lives alone, a pet may be the only family member.**

   b. Many families travel with their pets.

   Supporting details for this paragraph should include ways that pets are members of the family.

4. **a. Love letters and greeting cards travel by mail.**

   b. Likewise, newsletters and magazines are delivered to some people's mailboxes.

   Supporting details for this paragraph should focus on items that travel through the mail.

5. **a. Many children like the ladders and hoses that firefighters use.**

   b. Other children are fascinated by all of the equipment that firefighters wear.

   Supporting details for this paragraph should include reasons why children like fire engines.

6. **a. Some people can work from home because of computers.**

   b. In schools, computers help students learn at their own pace.

   Supporting details for this paragraph should include specific ways that computers have changed our lives.

7. **a. More restaurants offer delivery services.**

   b. Many companies have in-house daycare centers so parents can be near their children.

   Supporting details for this paragraph should include new services that help people who are busy.

8. **a. Parents can volunteer in their child's classroom or coach an after-school sport.**

   b. In some schools, parents can eat lunch with their children in the school cafeteria.

   Supporting details for this paragraph should include ways that parents can be active in their children's education.

9. **a. Free trial offers encourage us to test a new product.**

   b. Sports figures, musicians, and other famous people help products become popular.

   Supporting details for this paragraph should include specific ways advertisers get people to buy a product.

10. **a. Walking or biking places, instead of driving, can help save gas.**

    b. Likewise, buying only what one needs and searching for sales can cut costs.

    Supporting details for this paragraph should include specific actions that can help save money.

EXERCISE 3: *page 209.*

Although anyone can lead, great leaders share certain characteristics. Strong leaders generally have good speaking skills, charisma, and a genuine interest in the people they serve. Perhaps most importantly, a great leader inspires others to make the world a better place. When many people think of great leaders, they focus on presidents or other political leaders. However, regular Americans can be great leaders, as well. Many people in my community work tirelessly to help the underprivileged, clean up the town, and create a healthy place for our children. Thus, great leaders remind all of us that we have the power to make a difference.

CHAPTER 11: PLANNING THE ESSAY

EXERCISE 1:   *page 216.*

These are suggestions. There are many correct answers to each question.
1. A hero sacrifices himself or herself in order to help other people.
2. As a nation, we must work harder to stop teenage drinking. **or** Older teenagers should be allowed to drink alcohol so they can learn to drink responsibly.
3. Televisions have helped Americans learn more about themselves and the world.
4. Drivers should experience many different driving situations before they get a license.
5. If I knew that I only had a few months to live, I would focus more on the important things in life, particularly my faith, family, and friends.

EXERCISE 2:   *page 218.*

These are sample ideas. There are many correct answers.
*   Good teachers show how the subject relates to our lives.
*   Teachers should understand basic psychology.
*   Teachers need a sense of humor.
*   A good teacher should have teacher training.
*   My math teacher makes the class interesting.
*   Good teachers believe everyone can learn.
*   When I was little, no one cared that I couldn't read.
*   My brother's history teacher just reads out of the textbook.
*   Teachers should have high expectations.
*   A good teacher knows the subject very well.
*   Good teachers treat the students fairly.
*   Good teachers give extra help.

EXERCISE 3:   *page 220.*

This is a suggestion. There is more than one possible answer.

Main Ideas	Details
A good teacher is well educated.	• a good teacher knows the subject very well • teachers should understand basic psychology • good teachers should have teacher training
Good teachers make the class interesting.	• my math teacher makes the class interesting • my brother's history teacher just reads out of the textbook • good teachers show how the subject relates to our lives • teachers need a sense of humor
A good teacher cares about his or her students.	• good teachers give extra help • teachers should have high expectations • good teachers treat the students fairly • good teachers believe everyone can learn • when I was little, no one cared that I couldn't read

EXERCISE 4: *page 221.*

This is a suggestion. There is more than one possible answer.

Details
- students can volunteer in programs that interest them
- teenagers become more interested in community issues
- my sister decided to become a nurse after helping in a clinic
- students help in nursing homes or daycare centers
- community service improves many students' self-esteem
- students learn to work with other adults
- teens work as tutors and hospital aides
- students learn how important it is to volunteer
- when people volunteer as teens, they are more likely to volunteer as adults
- I learned important job skills when I volunteered
- our high school students cleaned up the local playground and repaired the equipment
- high school community service programs have made students more active in college volunteer programs

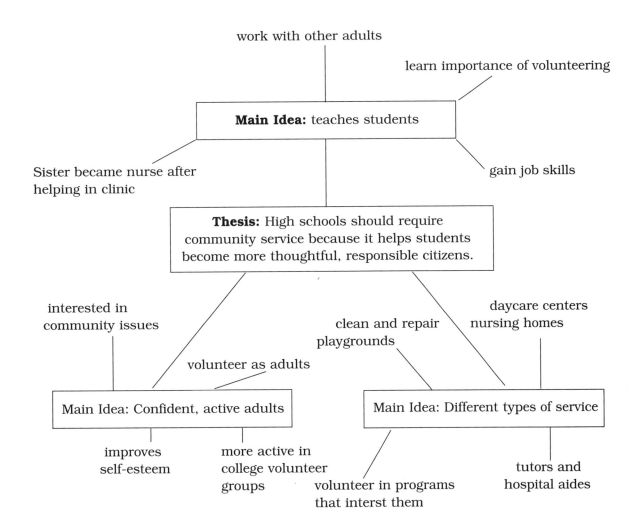

EXERCISE 5: *page 222.*

These answers are suggestions. Each question has more than one correct answer. Although these responses are in a T-list format, you can use whichever system works best for you.

1.

Main Ideas	Details
Heroes share certain characteristics.	• heroes sacrifice themselves to help others • heroes try things that others are afraid to try—like explorers or astronauts • heroes are caring, brave, thoughtful • many heroes don't even think what they do is heroic
There are many different types of heroes.	• police officers, firefighters, soldiers are heroes • on 9/11/01, many heroes died trying to save people • some doctors travel to dangerous places to help people • most athletes are not heroes, they don't sacrifice for others • some athletes are heroes because they use their fame to help people
Everyday people can be heroes.	• teachers who put in extra hours to help their students are heroes • my brother's special education teacher really works hard to help him • my friend organized a fundraiser to help a needy family

2.

Main Ideas	Details
Many teens don't understand the dangers of alcohol.	• the legal age doesn't really affect teenage drinking • teenagers need more education about alcohol • ad campaigns could teach teens about the dangers of alcohol • a lot of my friends started drinking in high school, some even drank in middle school • some advertisers target teens
Teens need to learn to be responsible with alcohol.	• teens should learn how to drink responsibly • teens drink alcohol, in part, because it is forbidden • teens should learn the difference between alcohol use and abuse before they go off to college or live on their own • in college, my cousin got into some dangerous situations when she drank
There are ways to prevent teen alcohol use and abuse.	• parents need to be more involved in their teenagers' lives • teens need stiffer penalties for underage drinking • teens need more programs for music, sports, and art to keep them busy and away from alcohol

3.

Main Ideas	Details
Television is a great form of entertainment.	• connects people to the outside world • inexpensive entertainment • creates a common culture because people all over America see the same shows • influences the way people dress and behave • families can watch shows together
Television shows can be educational.	• some good education programs for kids/adults • my mom likes to watch science programs on TV • easy to learn about the news • some immigrants use TV to learn English
Television has drawbacks.	• people watch too much TV • I eat a lot when I am watching TV with my friends • children are exposed to too much at a young age • when my little brother sees violent programs, he pretends to shoot people

4.

Main Ideas	Details
People who get licenses must be safe drivers.	• teenagers are involved in a lot of car accidents • some parents want their children to get a license so the kids can drive themselves places • everyone should learn to drive an automatic and standard car • watch videos on driving safety
Students should gradually earn their licenses.	• start with a daytime-only license • initially only drive to school or work • in New York City, my friend can't earn a driver's license until he is 18 • drivers should have a minimum of 40 hours behind the wheel with a permit first
Students need practical driving experience.	• require driving school • as kids, we drove our truck all over the farm • drivers must practice on highways, curvy roads, etc. • practice driving in rain and snow on a practice track • use machines that simulate driving conditions—like a flight simulator

5.

Main Ideas	Details
If I knew I didn't have much time to live, I would try new things and focus on my faith.	• I'd try things I was afraid to try—skydiving, singing on stage • worship more often • some people are afraid of dying • when my grandmother died, she seemed at peace with death
In my last days, I would focus on my family and plan for their future without me.	• spend more time with family and friends • tell people I love them • make a video of myself and keep a journal for my family • plan for my kids' future, like child care • make sure my family had the things they need • spend time with each child individually • go on a trip with family
Before dying, I would want to have fun with my friends and reconnect with some people.	• have a big party with friends • reflect on the good times we had together • apologize to the people I have hurt

CHAPTER REVIEW

EXERCISE 1: *page 225.*

These are suggestions. There are many possible answers.

Step 1: Thesis statement: If I could meet anyone, I would want to meet my grandfather, who died before I was born.

Step 2:
~~he was still alive when my brother was born~~
he lived through two world wars and the Great Depression
know more about my family
I feel like I only know part of our family history
learn about my mom from his perspective
~~grandpa died of heart disease~~
what was it like being a parent in his day
which family traits come from him?
Just get to know him
everyone says he was a good person
he was a friendly salesperson
it would be fun to be with him
learn about the past
hear his stories from the past
learn more about his generation and how things were different

Step 3:

Main Ideas	Details
If I could spend time with my grandpa, I would learn more about the past.	• hear his stories from the past • learn more about his generation and how things were different • he lived through two world wars and the Great Depression
My grandfather could teach me about my family.	• I feel like I only know part of my family history • learn about my mom from his perspective • what was it like being a parent in his day? • what family traits come from him?
I would just like to know my grandfather better.	• everyone says he was a good person • he was a friendly salesperson who liked to entertain people • it would be fun to be with him

EXERCISE 2: *page 226.*

This is a suggestion. There are many possible answers.

Step 1: Thesis statement: Educators, parents, and community members need to work together to improve public education.

Step 2:

higher expectations
~~my brother skips school all the time~~
companies can donate equipment
mentors for students
all students pass tests in major subjects to graduate
prepare students for college, job training, or both
~~Caitlyn's mom just got her diploma~~
Karim wants to be an electrician, but his school doesn't have a
    program
take at least 3 years of math, science, English, and social studies
demand discipline, keep schools safe
more afterschool programs for students
training programs
my friend Kashar graduated, but he still can't read or write well
    enough to get a job
keep school buildings well maintained
extra help for struggling kids
parents should attend conferences, check homework, volunteer
parents should read to children and educate themselves

Step 3:

Main Ideas	Details
Educators must raise standards and provide extra help.	• higher expectations • Kashar graduated but doesn't have skills to get a job • prepare students for college, job training, or both • Karim wants to be electrician, but he needs a program • at least 3 years of math, English, science, and social studies • all students pass major subjects to graduate • demand discipline, keep schools safe • extra help for struggling kids
Parents need to get involved and show that education is important.	• attend conferences, check homework, and volunteer • read to their children • educate themselves
The community should support the schools.	• Companies can donate equipment • provide mentors for students • more afterschool programs for students • keep schools well maintained • businesses can provide job training programs

CHAPTER 12: WRITING THE ESSAY

EXERCISE 1: *page 231.*

These are simply suggestions. There are many correct answers.

1.   In America, many people are described as heroes. Athletes, soldiers, and even politicians get labeled as heroes sometimes. However, a real hero is more than just a famous person. A true hero sacrifices himself or herself in order to help other people.

2.   Alcohol abuse is a national problem not only for adults but also for teenagers. Even though the drinking age is twenty-one, minors regularly drink alcohol. Teenage alcohol abuse leads to deadly car accidents, violence, and many health problems. As a nation, we must work harder to stop teenage drinking.

3.   Throughout history, different inventions have changed people's lives. However, few inventions have had as much influence as the television. Even though the television has had some negative effects, it has been a great invention overall. Televisions have helped Americans learn more about themselves and the world around them.

4.   Many Americans depend on their cars. As a result, getting a driver's license is very important for some people. Unfortunately, inexperienced drivers cause many accidents. Tougher standards for new drivers could save lives. Drivers should experience many different driving situations before they earn a license.

5.   Every day, someone learns that he or she has only a few years, months, or even days to live. Because I have not had this experience, it

is hard to predict exactly how I would respond. However, I am sure that I would reflect on my life and make some important changes. If I knew that I only had a few months to live, I would focus more on the important things in life—particularly my faith, family, and friends.

EXERCISE 2: *page 235.*

This is a suggestion. There are many correct answers.

Heroes share certain characteristics. Most importantly, heroes sacrifice themselves to help others. Generally, heroes are caring, brave, and thoughtful. Likewise, they are willing to try things that others are afraid to try. Explorers and astronauts, for example, go places other people can't imagine. Often heroes just do what comes naturally to them; they don't even think their actions are heroic.

There are many different types of heroes. Usually when we think of heroes, we think of police officers, firefighters, and soldiers. Every year on 9/11, Americans remember the many heroes who died trying to save others. Likewise, there are doctors who travel to dangerous places to help people in need. Although athletes are often called heroes, most are not. Athletes are only heroes if they use their fame and fortune to help others.

Some heroes are famous, but everyday people can be heroes, as well. Recently, my friend organized a fundraiser to help a needy family. To that family, my friend was a hero. Likewise, teachers who put in extra hours to help their students are heroes. My brother's special education teacher really works hard to help him in school and to prepare him for the outside world.

EXERCISE 3: *page 238.*

1. **however** *However* shows that there is a difference between the two statements. The first sentence focuses on positive features, and the second sentence notes a negative feature.
2. **For example** *For example* shows that the snail darter and the spotted owl are examples of protected species.
3. **Likewise** *Likewise* connects similar ideas. Both sentences focus on difficult transitions in school.
4. **First, Then** *First* and *then* show in what order the different actions take place.
5. **As a result** *As a result* shows a cause and effect relationship. Because many people cannot afford college, many students do not get the education that they need.
6. **Instead** *Instead* shows that there is a difference between where *we* wanted to go and where *we* actually went.
7. **Now** *Now* shows a change in time. The first sentence is about what happened in the past, and the second sentence is about what is happening in the present.
8. **for instance** *For instance* shows that the second sentence gives a specific example. The second sentence tells how immigrants work hard.
9. **Instead** *Instead* shows that there is a difference between what *we* thought *we* were buying and what *we* actually bought.
10. **However** *However* shows that there is a difference between what children need and what they are getting.

EXERCISE 4: *page 239.*

1. **For example** *For example* shows that the paragraph will focus on specific examples of positive effects.
2. **As a result** *As a result* shows a cause and effect relationship. People can telecommute because they can use computers to communicate.

3. **Likewise** *Likewise* shows that this sentence has a similar idea. Companies can hold meetings without getting people together because they can use computers to communicate.
4. **also** *Also* shows that this paragraph will explain more benefits.
5. **In addition** *In addition* shows that this sentence has a similar idea. It gives another way that computers help people learn more easily.
6. **On the other hand** *On the other hand* connects ideas that are different. The second paragraph focused on positive effects. This paragraph emphasizes negative effects.
7. **Likewise** *Likewise* shows that this sentence has a similar idea. This sentence also focuses on how computers isolate people.
8. **Nonetheless** *Nonetheless* shows a contrast. Even though computers have had positive and negative effects, they will continue to be an important invention.

EXERCISE 5: *page 241.*

These are suggestions. There are many correct answers.

1. More than most people, a hero sacrifices himself or herself to help others. A hero sees beyond his own world and tries to make a difference. Heroes can be famous, but they don't have to be. Some of the greatest heroes are just everyday people. Perhaps we all have the potential to be a hero in someone else's life.
2. Clearly teenage drinking must be stopped. We need not only to teach the dangers of alcohol but also to create positive activities for minors. As a nation, we must make sure that teenagers develop into healthy, responsible adults. Today's teenagers are tomorrow's leaders.
3. Televisions help Americans learn. Television programs focus on many different subjects, and they create a common culture. In addition, televisions connect people to the outside world. Although too much television has drawbacks, a small amount has many benefits. If you want to learn something new or just have a good laugh, turn on the TV.
4. People need a lot of driving experience before they earn a license. More practice driving, restricted licenses, and tougher driver tests could improve driver safety. If the states do not force new drivers to gain more experience, drivers should set higher standards for themselves. A license gives people a lot of freedom, but it also requires a lot of responsibility.
5. We will all die someday, we just don't know when. If I knew that I only had a few months to live, I would reflect on my life and focus on the things that really matter—my faith, family, and friends. Perhaps we shouldn't wait until we know that death is near. Instead, we should get our priorities in order now so that our lives will be complete.

CHAPTER REVIEW

EXERCISE 1: *page 246.*

This essay is a suggestion. Each essay has more than one correct answer.

When I hear stories about people whom I have never met, I often wonder what they are really like. Generally the stories focus on a few events or characteristics, so they don't give a complete picture. If someone is still alive, you might get a chance to meet that person and learn more about him or her. However, if the person has died, you have to depend on other people's thoughts and observations. Thus, if I could meet anyone, I would want to meet my grandfather, who died before I was born.

If I could spend time with my grandpa, I would learn more about the past. Many people talk about how difficult life is today. However, I know that my grandfather's generation truly lived through difficult times, two world wars and the Great Depression. If I met him, I would learn more about his generation and how things were different. I would also learn how he and others coped during those difficult times. Learning about the past from him would give me a better perspective on life today.

Likewise, my grandfather could teach me about my family. I feel like I only know part of my family history from stories that were passed down through my grandmother. My grandfather, however, might see things differently. I could learn about my mom from his perspective and what it was like being a parent in his day. In addition, I would see which family traits come from him. Perhaps his smile or friendly disposition has been passed down to my children.

Most importantly, I would just like to know my grandfather better. Everyone says he was a good person, a friendly salesperson who liked to entertain people. From what I have heard, it would be a lot of fun just to spend time with him.

There are a number of people whom I would like to meet and get to know better. Meeting my grandfather, however, would help me learn more about the past, my family, and even myself. I can't bring my grandfather back, but I can spend more time with the family members who are with me today. That way the family stories will live on.

EXERCISE 2: *page 249.*

This essay is a suggestion. Each essay has more than one correct answer.

Public education is an important part of American society. Through public education, every child in the United States has the opportunity to achieve his or her dreams. Unfortunately, many public schools in America do not educate children well. As a result, we have many students who do not have the skills that they need. Educators, parents, and community members need to work together to improve public education in America.

First, parents and educators need to set higher expectations for students. They must demand discipline and set high academic standards. Children learn more when they are challenged. High school students should take at least three years of English, math, science, social studies, and physical education. Students also should be required to pass tests in all major subjects in order to graduate from high school. In addition, courses for high school students should prepare them for college, job training, or both.

Likewise, parents need to get more involved in the schools and show their children that education matters. Parents must do more than check homework. Parents also should attend parent-teacher conferences and volunteer in the schools. In addition, parents must improve their own education to show their children that learning does not stop at the school door.

The community also needs to support the local schools. Community leaders can donate equipment to the schools and arrange more afterschool activities for students. Local businesses can work with job-training programs. Adults in the community can serve as mentors for students. In addition, the community as a whole can work together to make sure that school buildings are well maintained.

Clearly, educators, parents, and community members can improve public education in America. Higher standards, greater parental involvement, and more local support can make the public schools more successful. If we work together, public schools can help students develop their skills and achieve their dreams.

CHAPTER 13: REVISING THE ESSAY

EXERCISE 1: *page 255.*

There is more than one correct answer. However, note how the changes are explained because a number of changes are necessary.

Essay Topic 1:

   Public education is an important part of American society. Many public schools in America do not educate children well. As a result, too many students do not have the skills they need. **Parents, teachers, and community leaders must work together to improve our public schools.**

   First, parents and educators need to set higher expectations for students. Children learn more when they are challenged. High school students should take at least three years of English, math, science, social studies, and physical education. **Students should pass standardized tests to prove that they have learned the material. In addition,** courses for high school students should prepare them for college, job training, or both.

   Likewise, parents need to get more involved in the schools and show their children that education matters. Parents should attend parent-teacher conferences and volunteer in the schools. **Parents should get involved in afterschool activities that their children enjoy.** Parents **also** must improve their own education to show their children that learning does not stop at the school door.

   The community also needs to support the local schools. **Adults in the community can serve as mentors.** Community leaders can donate equipment to the schools and arrange for more afterschool activities for students. ~~Often teachers live in the community.~~ **In addition,** the community as a whole can work together to make sure that school buildings are well maintained.

   Parents, teachers, and community members can improve public education in America. Higher standards, greater parental involvement, and more local support can make the public schools more successful. If we work together, public schools can help students develop their skills and achieve their dreams.

Add a thesis statement to the first paragraph to give the essay direction. Insert at least one more supporting detail to both the second and third paragraphs. The last sentence in the second paragraph, Adults in the community can serve as mentors, should be moved to the fourth paragraph. In the fourth paragraph, cross out the sentence that is not related to the topic. For each body paragraph, add transitional words to make the information flow more smoothly. At the start of the concluding paragraph, insert a sentence that rewords the thesis statement.

Essay Topic 2, *page 256.*
There is more than one correct answer. However, note how the changes are explained because a number of changes are necessary.

   In America many people are described as heroes. Athletes, soldiers, and even politicians get labeled as heroes sometimes. A real hero is more than just a famous person. **A true hero sacrifices himself or herself in order to help other people.**

Heroes share certain characteristics. ~~Most importantly, heroes sacrifice themselves to help others.~~ Generally, heroes are caring, brave, and thoughtful. They are willing to try things that others are afraid to try. Explorers and astronauts, for example, go places other people can't imagine. Often heroes just do what comes naturally to them; they don't even think their actions are heroic.

There are many different types of heroes. Usually when we think of heroes, we think of police officers, firefighters, and soldiers. Every year on 9/11, Americans remember the many heroes who died trying to save others. Throughout history, soldiers have risked their lives to protect our country as well as others. **Likewise,** there are doctors who travel to dangerous places to help people in need. Although athletes are often called heroes, most are not. Athletes are only heroes if they use their fame and fortune to help others.

Some heroes are famous, but everyday people can be heroes, as well. Recently, my friend organized a fundraiser to help a needy family. To that family, my friend was a hero. Likewise, teachers who put in extra hours to help their students are heroes. **For example, my brother's special education teacher really works hard to help him in school and to prepare him for the outside world.**

More than most people, a hero sacrifices himself or herself to help others. **A hero sees beyond his or her own world and tries to make a difference. Heroes can be famous, but they don't have to be. Some of the greatest heroes are just everyday people. Perhaps we all have the potential to be a hero in someone else's life.**

The first paragraph needs a thesis statement that gives the essay direction. In the second paragraph, cross out the sentence that is repetitive. Add a transitional word to paragraph three. Move the sentence about the special education teacher to paragraph 4, which focuses on everyday heroes. Expand on the conclusion.

EXERCISE 2: *page 258.*

There is more than one correct answer. However, note how the changes are explained because a number of changes are necessary.

In every profession, you need certain skills to succeed. Teaching is no different. Teachers have the power and the responsibility to change **people's** lives. Therefore, it is important that **teachers** have certain attributes. A good teacher knows the subject and understands how to teach students effectively.

Perhaps most importantly, a good teacher is well educated. Teachers need to know **their** subject area well, and they should understand basic psychology. In addition, a teacher must have training so as to develop good classroom management skills.

Good teachers know how to make a class interesting. Unfortunately, a lot of teachers are like my brother's history teacher, who just reads out of the textbook. A good teacher, **on the other hand,** has a sense of humor and shows how the subject relates to the students' lives. When students have a great teacher, they **are** eager to work hard and learn as much as they can.

Students also know that a good teacher really cares about them. Strong teachers have high expectations for their students and treat everyone fairly. When I was younger, no one cared that I couldn't read. Eventually, I got a great teacher who knew I could learn and gave me extra help. By just reaching out, she made a difference in my life.

People choose to become teachers for many different reasons. However, great teachers stand out because **they have** the training, skills, and dedication. As **students**, sometimes we don't appreciate how hard these teachers work to help us learn. Therefore, when we have great teachers, it is important to thank them.

In the first paragraph, punctuate people's *properly and use* teachers, *instead of* they. *In the second paragraph, use* their *instead of* there. *For the third paragraph,* on the other hand *interrupts the sentence. It should be set apart with commas. In addition, use* are *instead of* is. *The verb must agree with* they. *In the fifth paragraph, use* they have *instead of* she has. *Both the pronoun and verb must agree with* teachers. *A comma after* students *isn't mandatory, but it will help the sentence flow more smoothly.*

EXERCISE 3: *page 259.*

There is more than one correct answer. However, note how the changes are explained because a number of changes are necessary.

Many people are active in volunteer activities. These projects not only get people involved in **their** communities but also help people in need. Some people want to make community service a high school graduation requirement; others think that schools should not force students to "volunteer." High schools should require community service because it helps students become more thoughtful, responsible adults.

Students learn from community service. Students discover different careers that might interest them, such as medicine or teaching. **For example, I decided to become a nurse after volunteering in my local hospital. In addition,** teens develop important job skills that will help them in the future. They learn to be on time, to follow directions, and to complete projects.

Students also get involved in many different types of community service. Teenagers can choose volunteer programs that interest them. **Students help in nursing homes and daycare centers. They work as tutors and hospital aides. Students also clean roadways and improve playgrounds.**

Likewise, when students are involved in community service, they develop into more **active, confident** adults. ~~Community service makes teens more self-assured.~~ **People who volunteer as teens are more likely to volunteer as adults. As a result**, high school community service programs have made students more active in college volunteer programs. In addition, teenagers who are involved in community programs are more interested in local issues.

Clearly community service can be an important part of one's high school education. Community service programs positively **affect** students not only when they are teens but also when they become adults.

In the first paragraph, use their *to show possession. Add a topic sentence and another supporting detail to the second paragraph. In addition, add transitional words to make the paragraph flow more smoothly. Add at least three supporting details to the third paragraph. For the fourth paragraph, add a comma between* active *and* confident, *two adjectives that describe adults. Cross out the second sentence, which is repetitive.* Confident *and* self-assured *mean the same thing. Add another sentence showing the benefits and add a transitional phrase. In the last paragraph, replace* effect *with* affect.

CHAPTER 14: EVALUATING THE ESSAY

SAMPLE ESSAY 1:

I think that art, music, and sports are important. Kids like them. They are a lot easier than other classes. They are more relaxing. You get to do things that you like to do and you can have fun. These classes teach students things that they can't learn in there other classes. Some students are really intrested in these classes. They may want to be artists, musicians or atheletes. When they get older. If these classes are cut some kids won't want to go to school. Schools should cut other things that aren't as important.

This essay probably would earn a 1 or 2. It consists of only one paragraph. The essay does have some supporting details; however, the information is poorly organized, and the writer's thoughts are not explained clearly.

SAMPLE ESSAY 2:

Art! everybody like art. Music to and sports. Long time ago people think that artrists are famous like monet and now they want to not spend money on art classes. Even music classes. Where will all the new artrists come from? Oh no! who will paint pictures and make music? We need sports to. Some kids, they liked sports. where will they play? what will they did if they don't play sports? who will played on pro teams? These classes keep kids off drugs. big problem. Theyll do more drugs. Keep art and music in school. Sports to! Kids want to go to school and go to these classes and learn lots about art and music. Some kids wont go. who will teach them? Art is great!

This essay probably would earn a 1. The writer has some ideas, but they are buried in an essay that has no organization, unclear writing, and numerous errors.

SAMPLE ESSAY 3:

Schools should work hard to keep their art, music, and athletic programs.

Art, music, and athletics are important for many students. Some enjoy the more relaxed atmosphere that these classes offer because it is different than their other classes. Other students want to learn more about these subjects so that they can study them in college or use them for jobs. For some students, these classes are the only reason they want to go to school. Schools that cut these classes may end up with a higher dropout rate.

These programs give students a better education. They learn to be creative, to appreciate other people's skills, to relax, to explore, and to take care of their health. They also learn to think better. For example, students who are involved in music often do well in math.

Some schools may want to cut these programs because they don't have enough money, but they should cut something else instead, like Spanish or something. Art, music, and athletics are important in the schools. They make education more interesting.

This essay probably would earn a 3. The writer states the purpose of the essay in the first sentence and tries to develop several ideas. Although the writing style generally is clear, some sentences are confusing or unrelated to the topic.

SAMPLE ESSAY 4:

Schools have many different programs. Some give extra help to students, and others make school more interesting. However, when money is tight, some programs have to be eliminated. The art, music, and athletics programs should not be cut.

Art, music, and athletics add variety to the school day. These classes are set up differently than other subjects. My art class, for example, is less structured than is math or science. Likewise, in physical education classes students are active. Some students need these subjects so that they can get through the rest of the day.

Art, music, and athletics also are an important part of an education. These classes help students learn more about different types of art and music. Otherwise the only music some students would hear would be on the radio. Athletics help students learn more about their bodies and how to keep themselves healthy.

In addition, these programs help students develop a variety of skills. Some people use these skills to pursue hobbies such as photography and drawing. Others play in bands or sell paintings to earn money. Through sports, students develop athletic skills that they can use there entire lives.

Art, music, and athletics are an important part of our schools. These educational programs add variety to the school day. They also help students develop useful skills.

This essay probably would earn a 3 or 4. The writer organizes the information well, and provides many good supporting details. There are only a few, minor errors, which do not affect the clarity of the essay.

SAMPLE ESSAY 5:

School leaders have to make difficult decisions. Some programs are easy to eliminate, but most are hard to cut. No one wants to lose a good program. The art, music, and athletic programs should not be reduced because they are too important.

Art, music, and athletics often attract students' attention. Many students struggle in their academic classes. For these children, special programs provide an opportunity to develop skills that they enjoy using. Some students would not even attend school if these special programs were eliminated.

When students learn about art, music, and athletics, they also have a more general education. Students learn to be more creative and innovative. They learn more about themselves and other people. Through sports, students learn to keep their bodies healthy. According to some studies, these classes actually help students do better in math, science, and English. Without these programs, one's education is limited.

The special programs help students interact better. In some schools, students are grouped in academic classes according to their abilities. They often spend most of the school day with the same students. In the special programs, however, students are more likely to be mixed together. Therefore, they learn to get along with a variety of people, and they learn that everybody has different talents.

Clearly, art, music, and athletics programs are necessary. These programs interest students and develop their general education. In addition, these programs help students interact better. Most budget decisions are hard, but this is one is easy.

This essay probably would earn a 4. The writer organizes the information quite well and provides many supporting details. The essay is clear and free of distracting errors.

PRACTICE ESSAYS

This is simply a suggestion. There are many different possible answers.

GUIDED SAMPLE ESSAY, *page 273.*

> **Essay topic:** If you could choose to live anywhere in America, where would you live and why? In an essay, explain your thoughts. Your response may include personal experiences, knowledge, and observations.

> **Thesis statement:** If I could live anywhere in America, I would live near Boston, Massachusetts.

Main Ideas	Details
Boston is an historic city.	• I love learning about American history. • the Revolutionary War began near Boston at Lexington and Concord • could visit historic sites such as Old North Church and Boston Harbor • celebrate the Fourth of July along the Charles River
Boston has a lot to do, and it has good public transportation.	• many museums such as the Museum of Science • many colleges and universities in the area • many cultural events • the city isn't too big, it's easy to get around
Boston is close to other tourist areas.	• can visit the Lakes region in NH • skiing in New Hampshire, Vermont, or Maine • close to beaches

America is a great nation. There are many areas to live, and they are all so different. Each location is attractive for many reasons. However, if I could live anywhere in America, I would live near Boston, Massachusetts.

First of all, Boston is an historic city, and I love to learn about American history. The Revolutionary War began near Boston at Lexington and Concord. If I lived in Boston, I could visit these sites, as well as the Old North Church, Boston Harbor, and other historic areas. In addition, I could celebrate the

Fourth of July along the Charles River. Celebrating Independence Day in Boston would be amazing.

Besides historic sites, Boston has many other activities. Boston is known not only for its museums but also for other cultural events. Boston has many professional sports teams, as well as many colleges and universities. Even though Boston has a lot to do, it isn't too large. Public transportation is great, so I wouldn't need to have a car.

Boston is also close to other tourist areas. During the summer, many people travel to the Lakes Region in New Hampshire or the beaches along the shore. In the wintertime, I could go skiing in New Hampshire, Vermont, or Maine. For a longer trip, I could even travel to New York City, which would be only about five hours away.

Clearly there are many reasons why I would like to live in Boston. The historic sites, cultural activities, and tourist attractions would keep me very busy. However, I would need to find a job, and moving isn't easy. So for now, I will stay right where I am.

SAMPLE TEST A, *page 276.*

Essay topic: What are the characteristics of a good role model? In an essay, explain your thoughts. Your response may include personal experiences, knowledge, and observations.

Thesis statement: A role model sets a positive example by doing what is right and reaching out to other people.

Main Ideas	Details
A good role model sets a positive example.	• show what is possible, blaze new paths • my older brother studies hard and works after school to help our family • my sister is first to go to college
A role model does what is right, even when no one is looking.	• sound moral values • it's easy to do what is right when we know people are watching • Tony Romo, the quarterback for the Dallas Cowboys, regularly helps other people, doesn't do it for the recognition
Role models reach out to other people.	• teachers, coaches, and religious leaders often are role models • basketball coach works with all of the players, not just the talented ones • at my church many volunteers tutor local high school students and help them with job placement or college entrance

Over the years, many people come in and out of our lives. However, only a few of them have a lasting impact and become role models. For some people, parents, grandparents, or teachers have the greatest influence. Regardless of who they are, role models can make a difference for all of us.

A good role model sets a positive example. They show us what is possible and blaze new paths that we can follow. My older brother, for example, studies hard and works after school to help support our family. Likewise, my older sister is the first person in my family to go to college. My brother and sister are role models because they have shown me that anything is possible.

A good role model does what is right, even when no one is looking. It is easy to do what is right when we know people are watching. However, a true role model does the right thing regardless. For example, Tony Romo, a professional football player, regularly helps other people, but he tries to avoid media attention. On one occasion, he invited a homeless man to go to the movies.

Role models reach out to other people in other ways, as well. My basketball coach, for example, works with all of the players, not just the more talented ones. She truly wants everyone to have a positive experience. Likewise, at my church many volunteers tutor high school students and help them with job placement or college. Working together, these role models really make a difference.

By setting a positive example, doing what is right, and reaching out to others, role models can have a lasting impact on many people. Someday, those who have had positive role models will grow up to be role models themselves. Thus, in their own way, role models make the world a better place.

SAMPLE TEST B, *page 276.*

> **Essay topic:** What can be done to prevent teen violence? In an essay, explain your thoughts. Your response may include personal experiences, knowledge, and observations.
>
> **Thesis statement:** As a nation, we must develop programs to prevent teen violence.

Main Ideas	Details
Teach teens how to settle their differences peacefully.	• peer mediation programs • model positive interactions • some kids have violent homes, so that's all that they know • mentor programs
Create positive programs for teenagers and younger children.	• get kids from different backgrounds involved in sports at an early age • even though I live in a diverse town, the community sports teams aren't diverse • create music, dance, and drama programs for teens
Develop volunteer opportunities and job training programs for teens.	• teens can put their energy into something positive • can clean up a playground or serve meals • job training helps teens see a future for themselves • Reshad helped on construction site, now he wants to be an architect.

To some degree, violence has been an issue for every generation. However, teenage violence has become worse in recent years. Violent teenagers often grow to be violent adults. As a nation, we must develop programs to prevent teen violence.

First, we must teach teens how to settle their differences peacefully. Unfortunately, some children come from violent homes, so violence is all that they know. As a result, schools must develop peer mediation and mentor programs that teach students how to interact in a positive way.

In addition, local communities need to create enrichment programs for teenagers and younger children. Music, dance, and drama programs are wonderful outlets for children, as well as teens. Likewise, children and teenagers should get involved in sports at an early age. Even though I live in a diverse town, the community programs are not diverse. These programs need to reach out to children from all different backgrounds.

Community leaders also need to develop volunteer opportunities and job training programs for teens. Volunteer programs help teenagers channel their energy into something positive. After helping in a soup kitchen, my cousin realized that he really could make a difference. Likewise, job training helps teenagers see a future for themselves. My friend Reshad helped on a construction site; now he wants to be an architect.

One program alone can't eliminate teen violence. However, different outreach programs can work together to make a difference. Preventing teen violence must be a priority for our nation.

POSTTEST 1

1. **1 replace will have increased with has increased** (See Chapter 3—Verb Usage and Chapter 9—Writing Clear Sentences) Both verbs should be in the same form because both actions are occurring at the same time.

2. **2 pressure; others insist** (See Chapter 6—Punctuation) The semicolon joins two independent clauses that are related. None of the other options punctuates the sentence correctly.

3. **3 replace are with is** (See Chapter 4—Subject-Verb Agreement: Special Situations) The verb, *is*, must agree with *nicotine*, which is the subject of the sentence. *Of cigarettes* is a prepositional phrase that describes *nicotine*. Option (1) is wrong because *unfortunately* is an introductory word, which should be set apart with a comma. Option (2) is wrong because *for many people* should be placed near *addictive*, the word that is modified. Option (4) is wrong because *have shown* is the correct verb tense.

4. **3 move sentence 7 to follow sentence 12** (See Chapter 10—Writing Paragraphs) Sentence 7 is a supporting detail for paragraph B. It is not related to the topic sentence in paragraph A. Sentence 7 focuses on people who sell to underage smokers. As a result, it should be placed after sentence 12, which describes efforts to identify underage smokers.

5. **4 replace which with who** (See Chapter 9—Writing Clear Sentences *Who, Which,* and *That*) *Who* is used for people. *Which* is used for animals and things. Option (1) is wrong because *their* is used to show possession. Option (2) is wrong because *thus* is an introductory word, which needs a comma to set it apart. Option (3) is wrong because *are* must agree with the subject, *teens.*

6. **1 replace is with are** (See Chapter 4—Subject-Verb Agreement: Guidelines and Special Situations) The verb, *are*, must agree with the subject of the sentence, which is *efforts. To stop teenage smoking* is an infinitive phrase that describes *efforts.* Option (2) is wrong because *across the nation and around the world* is an introductory phrase, which should be set apart with a comma. Option (3) is wrong because there is no reason to place a comma after *smoking.* Option (4) is wrong because *to stop* works as an adjective, not a verb, in this sentence.

7. **4 insert a comma after lawsuits** (See Chapter 6—Punctuation) *As a result of pressure from the federal government and various lawsuits* is an introductory phrase that needs to be set apart with a comma.

8. **4 photo identification, that proves** Sentence 12 provides more information about the photo identification in sentence 11. The other options do not show the correct relationship between the two sentences.

9. **3 smoking, but they** (See Chapter 6—Punctuation) In this sentence, *but* joins two independent clauses. A comma should be placed before the coordinating conjunction. Options (1) and (2) are punctuated improperly. Options (4) and (5) do not show the corrected relationship between the clauses.

10. **2 move for their children after safely** (See Chapter 9—Writing Clear Sentences) The original sentence is unclear. Parents are not struggling for the children. Instead, they are struggling to install car seats safely. Moving *for their children* after *safely* will make the sentence clear.

11. **3 replace is with are** (See Chapter 4—Subject-Verb Agreement: Special Situations) Don't be distracted by the word *there*. In this sentence, the verb must agree with *seats*.

12. **5 children's seats; they should** (See Chapter 9—Writing Clear Sentences) Sentence 5 provides additional information for sentence 4. The other options do not show the correct relationship between the sentences.

13. **4 replace there with they're** (See Chapter 8—Word Choice) In this sentence, the contraction *they're* is necessary because it refers to newborns and means *they are*.

14. **2 replace which with that** *Is designed for children between 20 and 40 pounds* provides necessary information about the seat. Restrictive clauses should start with the word *that*, and they should not be set apart with a comma.

15. **3 insert a comma after old** (See Chapter 6—Punctuation) In this sentence, *but* is a coordinating conjunction that combines two independent clauses. A comma is necessary.

16. **5 move sentence 11 to follow sentence 5** Sentence 11 and sentence 5 focus on the guidelines for car-seat safety. Sentence 5 introduces the topic, and sentence 11 provides additional information. Therefore, sentence 11 should follow sentence 5 at the end of paragraph A.

17. **3 replace they with car seats** (See Chapter 9—Writing Clear Sentences) The original sentence is unclear. The reader does not know if *they* refers to *parents* or *car seats*. It is important to eliminate confusing pronouns.

18. **3 to the car; the seat should** (See Chapter 6—Punctuation and Chapter 9—Writing Clear Sentences) This sentence has two independent clauses. The second clause provides additional information on how car seats should be installed. Options 1 and 4 are punctuated improperly. Options 2 and 5 do not show the correct relationship between the clauses.

19. **1 replace *whomever* with *whoever*** (See Chapter 5—Pronouns: *Who* and *Whom*) *Whoever needs help with car-seat installation* is a clause. Use *whoever* because it is the subject of the clause. Option (2) is wrong because *police* and *departments* are common nouns. Option (3) is wrong because there is no reason to place a comma after *help*. Option (4) is wrong because the verb should be in the present tense.

20. **5 no correction necessary** The sentence is punctuated correctly, and the verb tense is appropriate.

21. **4 replace *she* with *they*** (See Chapter 5—Pronouns: Pronoun Agreement) The pronoun refers to *women*, which is plural. Therefore, the pronoun must be plural. Option (1) is wrong because *even before*

women become pregnant is an introductory clause, which should be set apart with a comma. Option (2) is wrong because both verbs in the sentence, *become* and *consider*, should agree. Option (3) is wrong because there is no reason to place a comma after *prenatal.*

22. **3 insert a comma after <u>nutrition</u>** (See Chapter 6—Punctuation) The words *Proper nutrition exercise, and childbirth classes* form a series. The items in a series should be separated by commas.

23. **1 move sentence 5 to the beginning of paragraph A** Sentence 5 provides an overview for the entire passage. As a result, it should be placed in the beginning. Without sentence 5 as a topic sentence, paragraph A lacks direction.

24. **3 monitor the** (See Chapter 9—Writing Clear Sentences: Rewriting Sentences) In the original sentence, *the baby's health and the mother's condition* form a compound subject, and *are* is the verb. In the new sentence, *doctors* is the subject and *monitors* is the verb. *During checkups throughout the pregnancy, doctors monitor the developing baby's health and the mother's condition.*

25. **5 heartbeat, observe its growth, and perform tests** When the sentences are combined, the doctors do three things—listen, observe, and perform. Only option (5) combines these three actions effectively. The new sentence would be *Doctors listen to the baby's heartbeat, observe its growth, and perform tests that provide information about the baby's physical development.*

26. **5 mother's nutrition, exercise, and emotional well-being** (See Chapter 6—Punctuation) Items in a series should be separated by commas. Options (1), (2), (3), and (4) are wrong because they do not have commas separating the items. Option (2) also changed *mother's* to *mothers,* which is not possessive.

27. **1 move *who have good prenatal care* after *women*** (See Chapter 9—Writing Clear Sentences) In the original sentence, *who have good prenatal care* is a misplaced modifier. It describes *women.* Therefore, it should be placed next to *women.* Option (2) is wrong because *babies* should be plural, not possessive. Option (3) is wrong because *who* is used correctly. Option (4) is wrong because a comma after *healthier* is not necessary.

28. **1 replace womans with woman's** (See Chapter 6—Punctuation) *Woman's* should be possessive because it describes a person's pregnancy. Options (2) and (3) are wrong because the commas are placed correctly. Option (4) is wrong because *should be* is in the present tense, and it is consistent with the paragraph.

29. **3 insert a comma after <u>February 12</u>** (See Chapter 6—Punctuation) When a date is used in a sentence, commas should be placed after the day and year. *Your* is used correctly because it shows possession. *Hired* is also used properly because it shows the past tense.

30. **4 replace <u>was</u> with <u>were</u>** (See Chapter 4—Subject-Verb Agreement) In this sentence *were* agrees with the subject, *leaks.* Options (1) and (3) are incorrect because the commas are used properly. Option (2) is wrong because *which* should be used for nonrestrictive clauses.

31. **1 would cost $4,000, and that it would be completed** The complete sentence would read as follows: *The contract we both signed clearly stated that the project would cost $4,000, and that it would be completed by March 21, 2009.* But, therefore, because, and since, which are used in the other options, do not show the correct relationship between the two independent clauses. They would change the meaning of the sentences.

32. **4 replace <u>creates</u> with <u>have created</u>** The verb must agree with *workers*, and it must show the correct tense. In the sentence, *continues* suggests that the action began in the past and is still going on. *Have created* also shows an action that is continuing. Option (1) is incorrect because *workers* should not be possessive. Option (2) is incorrect because *and* joins two independent clauses. Option (3) is wrong because *continues* must agree with *roof.*

33. **2 move sentence 8 to the beginning of paragraph B** Sentence 8 shows the difference between what the contract stated and what has actually happened. It is the topic sentence for paragraph B because it makes a good transition, and it gives direction for the paragraph.

34. **4 replace *it was told to me* with *he told me*** *It was told to me* is confusing because it uses more words than necessary. Focus on the subject and verb to clarify the sentence. Options (1) and (3) are wrong because the commas are placed properly. Option (2) is incorrect because *was* should agree with *job*, which is singular.

35. **3 replace <u>you're</u> with <u>your</u>** (See Chapter 8—Word Choice) *You're* is the contraction for *you are.* In this sentence, *your* is correct because it shows possession. The writer is stating which company.

36. **5 no correction necessary** The sentence is correct as written. *Workers* should not be possessive. The commas are properly placed, and the company name is capitalized correctly.

37. **2 the damage, so you can pay me** The new sentence would read as follows: *I have enclosed a detailed estimate of $8,000 for the damage, so you can pay me for my losses.* Only *so* shows the correct relationship between the two clauses. *Although, or, likewise,* and *otherwise* would change the meaning of the sentence.

38. **3 move <u>for the damages</u> to follow <u>pay me</u>** The original sentence is unclear. *For the damages* should be placed closer to the word it modifies, *pay.* The new sentence reads as follows: *If you do not pay me for the damages by April 15, 2009, I will contact a lawyer as well.*

39. **3 replace <u>It is pleasing to us</u> with <u>we are pleased</u>** The original sentence is unclear because it has unnecessary words. The sentence should be in the basic subject-verb format. The other options are incorrect. *Cova University* should be capitalized because it is a proper noun. A comma after *us* is unnecessary, and the verb *are* agrees with *you.*

40. **1 insert a comma after <u>know</u>** (See Chapter 6—Punctuation) *As you know* is an introductory phrase that should be set apart with a comma. *With many opportunities* should remain next to the word it modifies, *field.* Likewise, the commas are placed properly in the original sentence.

41. **5 no correction necessary** The sentence is correct as written.

42. **3 replace <u>strait</u> with <u>straight</u>** A *strait* is a narrow passageway or waterway. On the other hand, *straight* means without bending, curving, or changing direction. *Their* is used correctly because it shows possession. A comma after *locally* is unnecessary, and *move* must agree with the subject, *nurses.*

43. **1 needs more highly trained nurses with your enthusiasm** The new sentence would read as follows: *The medical community needs more highly trained nurses with your enthusiasm.* The other options would change the meaning of the two sentences.

44. **2 insert a comma after <u>workforce</u>** (See Chapter 6—Punctuation) *As a result of changes in the workforce* is an introductory phrase, which should be set apart with a comma. Option (1) is wrong because *are*

expected should agree with *nurses*. Option (3) is wrong because *in the workforce* should be close to the word it modifies, *changes*. Likewise, option (4) is wrong because the infinitive, *to retire*, agrees with the words *in the future*.

45. **4 move sentence 9 to the beginning of paragraph C** Sentence 9, which focuses on the benefits of nursing, is a good topic sentence for paragraph C. The supporting details in paragraph C explain some of the benefits that nursing offers.

46. **2 replace <u>has</u> with <u>have</u>** (See Chapter 4—Subject-Verb Agreement) The verb must agree with *we*. The other options are incorrect because the commas are properly placed, and *which* is used correctly.

47. **4 replace <u>will have enter</u> with <u>will enter</u>** (See Chapter 3—Verb Usage) The sentence should be in the future tense because the person will become a nurse in the future. The other options are incorrect because the commas are placed properly, and *that* is used correctly.

48. **1 replace <u>is</u> with <u>are</u>** (See Chapter 4—Subject-Verb Agreement) The verb must agree with the compound subject, *flexible schedules, a variety of work environments, advanced job-training programs, and good pay*. Options (2) and (4) are wrong because the commas are placed correctly. Option (3) is wrong because the phrase *of the rewards* should be placed close to the word *few*.

49. **2 move <u>who continue their education</u> after <u>nurses</u>** The phrase *who continue their education* should be placed next to the word it modifies, *nurses*. The new sentence would read as follows: *Nurses who continue their education have even more employment options*.

50. **1 insert a comma after <u>application</u>** (See Chapter 6—Punctuation) The conjunction *and* joins two independent clauses; therefore, a comma should be placed after *application*. The first clause is a command, and the subject *you* is implied.

POSTTEST 2

1. **2 replace <u>her</u> with <u>them</u>** (See Chapter 5—Pronouns) *Them* agrees with the antecedent, *children*. Option (1) is wrong because *makes* is in the correct tense. Option (3) is wrong because there is no reason to place a comma after *prepared*. Option (4) is wrong because *for school* describes *prepared*, so it should be placed next to *prepared*.

2. **1 insert a comma after <u>skills</u>** (See Chapter 6—Punctuation) *Better language skills, longer attention spans, and a greater interest in learning* form a series of three items. The items need to be separated by commas. Option (2) is wrong because *helps* is in the correct tense. Option (3) is wrong because *stories* is not possessive. Option (4) is wrong because there is no reason to insert a comma after *interest*.

3. **4 insert a comma after <u>games</u>** (See Chapter 6—Punctuation) Option (1) is wrong because *to* is in the correct form. It is part of the infinitive *to compete*. Option (2) is wrong because *is* agrees with *reading*. Option (3) is wrong because *parents* is not possessive in this sentence.

4. **2 even before your child** (See Chapter 9—Writing Clear Sentences) The complete sentence would be *Discuss the sound each letter makes even before your child can identify all of the letters*. With the other options, one cannot create a clear sentence.

5. **4 move <u>in your child's life</u> after <u>experiences</u>** (See Chapter 9—Writing Clear Sentences) *In your child's life* describes *experiences*. Modifiers must be placed near the words that they describe. Option (1) is wrong

because *child's* should be possessive. Option (2) is wrong because the comma after *book* separates two independent clauses. Both clauses are commands, so the subject, you, is implied. Option (3) is wrong because *Ask* is in the correct tense.

6. **1 move sentence 10 to the start of paragraph B** (See Chapter 10—Writing Paragraphs) Sentence 10 is a good topic sentence for paragraph B, which describes various reading techniques. The other options simply don't make sense for this sentence.

7. **4 replace <u>there</u> with <u>their</u>** (See Chapter 8—Word Choice) Whose reading skills? *Their* is the correct form because it is possessive. Option (1) is wrong because *help* agrees with *techniques*. Option (2) is wrong because *skills* is not possessive. Option (3) is incorrect because there is no reason to insert a comma after *techniques*.

8. **2 insert a comma after <u>independently</u>** (See Chapter 6—Punctuation) A comma after *independently* separates the dependent clause from the independent clause. Option (1) is incorrect because *has* agrees with *child*. Option (3) is wrong because there is no reason to insert a comma after *more*. Option (4) is incorrect because *stories* is not possessive.

9. **3 replace <u>kept</u> with <u>keep</u>** (See Chapter 3—Verb Usage: Verb Tense) In this sentence, the verb must be in the present tense. Option (1) is incorrect because the comma after *importantly* separates an introductory phrase. Option (2) is wrong because *in reading* describes *child*. Modifiers should be placed near the words they describe. Option (4) is wrong because there is no reason to insert a comma after *interested*.

10. **2 insert a comma after <u>own</u>** (See Chapter 6—Punctuation and Chapter 9—Writing Clear Sentences) A comma after *own* separates the independent clause from the dependent clause. Option (1) is wrong because *their* shows possession. Option (3) is wrong because *they* agrees with *young adults*. Option (4) is incorrect because *on their own* describes *living*. Modifiers must be placed near the words they describe.

11. **3 insert a comma after <u>saving</u>** (See Chapter 6—Punctuation) *Budgeting, saving, and investing* form a series. Commas must separate items in a series. Option (1) is incorrect because *are* agrees with *budgeting, saving, and investing*. Option (2) is wrong because *do* agrees with *people*. Option (4) is wrong because there is no reason to insert a comma after *activities*. Commas are placed before *which*, not *that*.

12. **4 replace <u>needed</u> with <u>need</u>** (See Chapter 3—Verb Usage: Verb Tense) The sentence refers to *today's economy*, so the verb should be in the present tense. Option (1) is wrong because the comma after *economy* separates the introductory phrase. Option (2) is incorrect because there is no reason to place a comma after *know*. Option (3) is incorrect because *it* agrees with *money*.

13. **1 insert a comma after <u>small</u>** (See Chapter 6—Punctuation) *Small* and *unnecessary* are both adjectives that describe *purchases*. They should be separated with a comma. Option (2) is wrong because *add* agrees with *purchases*. Option (3) is incorrect because *to* is a preposition, not a number. Option (4) is wrong because *purchases* is not possessive.

14. **5 no correction necessary** Option (1) is wrong because the comma after *guideline* separates an introductory phrase. Option (2) is wrong because *will cost* agrees with *item* and it is in the correct tense. Option (3) is incorrect because *consider* is in the correct tense. Option (4) is wrong because there is no reason to insert a comma after *cost*.

15. **2 a car breaks down, a family member becomes ill,** (See Chapter 9—Writing Clear Sentences) The full sentence would read as follows:

When a car breaks down, a family member becomes ill, or an appliance needs replacing, these families are prepared. Option (1) doesn't keep the three unplanned events together. Option (3) loses the meaning of the sentence. Being financially prepared does not prevent a car from breaking down. Option (4) also loses the meaning of the sentence because being prepared and being ready are the same thing. What are they prepared for? Option (5) separates the three events in a strange way. One event doesn't necessarily happen instead of another.

16. **5 no correction necessary** Option (1) is wrong because there is no reason to place a comma after *expenses*. Option (2) is incorrect because *on expenses* describes what people are cutting down, not *month*. Option (3) is wrong because the comma after *month* separates the independent and dependent clauses. Option (4) is incorrect because *expenses* is not possessive.

17. **4 replace <u>which</u> with <u>that</u>** (See Chapter 9—Writing Clear Sentences) *That are appropriate* modifies *investments*. If one uses *which*, a comma must be placed before *which*. Option (1) is incorrect because *there* is not possessive. Option (2) is wrong because *are* agrees with *investments*. Option (3) is incorrect because there is no reason to insert a comma after *types*.

18. **2 after sentence 5** (See Chapter 10—Writing Paragraphs) Paragraph B is about controlling expenses, and sentence 21 is about unnecessary spending. With sentence 21 in place, paragraph B would focus on excess spending overall, unnecessary large purchases, and then unneeded small purchases. Both paragraph B and paragraph D would flow more smoothly.

19. **1 move <u>on money management and investing</u> after <u>tips</u>** (See Chapter 9—Writing Clear Sentences) Modifiers must be placed near the words they describe. *On money management and investing* describes *tips*. Option (2) is wrong because the comma separates items in a series. Option (3) is wrong because there is no reason to insert a comma after *web sites*. Option (4) is incorrect because *have* agrees with *books, magazines, and web sites*.

20. **4 important; however,** (See Chapter 9—Writing Clear Sentences) There is a contrast between sentence 27 and sentence 28. The first sentence focuses on the importance of learning to save and invest at a young age. The second sentence suggests that even if one doesn't begin at a young age, learning to save and invest is still important. The new, combined sentence also must show this contrast. Only Option (4) uses words and punctuation that show a contrast between the first clause and the second clause.

21. **2 insert a comma after <u>week</u>** (See Chapter 6—Punctuation) This sentence should have a comma after *week* to separate the dependent and independent clauses. Option (1) is incorrect because *spoke* agrees with *we*. Option (3) is wrong because *for additional information* does not relate to *spoke*. Option (4) is wrong because the sentence is in the past tense, so the verb must be in the past tense.

22. **3 a number of brochures and videos** (See Chapter 9—Writing Clear Sentences) The new sentence would be *We have a number of brochures and videos that focus on safety measures for adults and children.* The original sentence repeats *we have*, which is unnecessary. Options (2) and (4) are not punctuated properly. Option (5) says *brochures <u>or</u> videos*, which does not show the correct relationship between the items.

23. **4 matches and lighters; even a two-year-old** (See Chapter 9—Writing Clear Sentences) The second sentence simply provides more information about the first sentence. The other options do not show the correct relationship between the sentences. *However* and *but* imply a contrast. *As a result* implies cause and effect.

24. **2 replace should never have been with never should be** (See Chapter 3—Verb Usage) This sentence should be in the present tense because it is a general truth. Option (1) is wrong because the comma after *candle* separates the items in a series. Option (3) is incorrect because *stove that is being used* would upset the structure of the sentence. Option (4) is wrong because there is no reason to place a comma after *near.*

25. **1 routes, so they** (See Chapter 9—Writing Clear Sentences) The complete sentence would be *Children and adults should practice the routes, so they will be prepared if a fire occurs.* The second clause shows why children and adults should practice the routes. The other options do not show the correct relationship between the two clauses.

26. **4 replace he with they** (See Chapter 1—Parts of Speech) *They* agrees with *children.* Option (1) is wrong because the comma separates two clauses. Option (2) is wrong because *which* signals unnecessary information. Option (3) is incorrect because there is no reason to insert a comma after *taught.*

27. **2 replace buy with by** (See Chapter 8—Word Choice) *Buy* means to purchase something. *By* is a preposition. Option (1) is wrong because the comma separates introductory words. Even though the comma isn't necessary when there are only two words, it is not incorrect either. Option (3) is incorrect because there is no reason for a comma after *trucks*; there are only two items. Option (4) is wrong because *our* shows possession and *hour* shows time.

28. **4 replace whom with who** (See Chapter 5—Pronouns) *Who love to put on their gear* is a phrase that describes *firefighters. Who* is the subject of that phrase. Option (1) is wrong because *We* refers to the members of his station. Option (2) is incorrect because *their* shows possession. Option (3) is wrong because there is no reason to place a comma after *gear.*

29. **1 or concerns, please call** (See Chapter 9—Writing Clear Sentences) The full sentence would be *If you have any more questions or concerns, please call or stop by the station.* The other options do not produce clear sentences.

30. **4 remove the comma after schedules** (See Chapter 6—Punctuation) Do not place a comma after the last item in a series. Option (1) is wrong because *make* agrees with *school, sports, and work schedules.* Option (2) is incorrect because there is no reason to place a comma after *work.* Option (3) is wrong because *schedules* should not be possessive.

31. **1 important because they** (See Chapter 9—Writing Clear Sentences) The complete sentence would be *Nonetheless, family meals are important because they are a great way to reconnect and encourage healthy eating habits.* The second sentence explains why healthy meals are important. The other options do not show the correct relationship between the clauses.

32. **3 move compared to their peers before these children** (See Chapter 9—Writing Clear Sentences) Modifiers must be near the words they describe. In the original sentence, *compared to their peers* modifies *snacks.* Option (1) is wrong because *are* agrees with *children.* Option

(2) is wrong because there is no reason to place a comma after *food.* Option (4) is incorrect because *their* shows possession. *They're* is a contraction for *they are.*

33. **4 replace <u>there</u> with <u>their</u>** (See Chapter 8—Word Choice) Whose social skills? *Their* shows possession. Option (1) is wrong because the comma separates two clauses. Option (2) is wrong because *skills* should not be possessive. Option (3) is incorrect because there is no reason to insert a comma after *social.*

34. **3 replace <u>helps</u> with <u>help</u>** (See Chapter 4—Subject-Verb Agreement) *Help* agrees with *discussions,* which is the subject. *Around a family dinner table* is a prepositional phrase. When you are focusing on subject-verb agreement, ignore prepositional phrases between the subject and the verb. Option (1) is wrong because there is no reason to place a comma after *family.* Option (2) is wrong because *their* shows possession. Option (4) is incorrect because *with peers* describes with whom children become more outgoing.

35. **2 before sentence 6** (See Chapter 10—Writing Paragraphs) Sentence 11 is a good topic sentence for paragraph B, which focuses on how children benefit from family meals. Paragraph C focuses on how teenagers benefit, and paragraph D shows how children can be involved in meal preparation. Likewise, paragraph E is simply a quick summary.

36. **5 no correction necessary** Option (1) is wrong because *have* agrees with *teens.* Option (2) is incorrect because there is no reason to place a comma after *regular.* Both *regular* and *family* describe *meals,* but they are not interchangeable. Option (3) is wrong because *who have regular family meals* is a phrase that modifies *teens. Who* is the subject of that phrase. Option (4) is wrong because *in less risky behavior* modifies *engage.*

37. **2 habits, and they** (See Chapter 9—Writing Clear Sentences) The full sentence would be *They develop good eating habits, and they are less inclined to have eating disorders.* Both original sentences describe two benefits of family meals. The other options show a contrast between the two clauses, but there isn't a contrast.

38. **4 replace <u>teenagers</u> with <u>teenager's</u>** (See Chapter 6—Punctuation) Whose schedule? *Teenager's* is correct because it is in the possessive form. Option (1) is wrong because the comma after *plan* separates two clauses. Option (2) is wrong because *make* is in the present tense, as is the paragraph. Option (3) is wrong because there is no reason to insert a comma after *though.*

39. **1 store; however, trips** (See Chapter 9—Writing Clear Sentences) The full sentence would be *Many parents try to avoid bringing their children to the food store; however, trips to the store are an opportunity to teach a child about nutrition and making good choices.* The original sentences showed a contrast between what parents want to do and what is good for their children. The new combined sentence also must show that contrast. Only option (1) does.

40. **4 replace <u>they</u> with <u>he or she</u>** (See Chapter 5—Pronouns) *He or she* agrees with *child.* Option (1) is wrong because the comma after *meal* separates two clauses. Option (2) is incorrect because *helps* is in the present tense, as is the rest of the paragraph. Option (3) is incorrect because there is no reason to place a comma after *likely.*

41. **1 insert a comma after <u>children</u>** (See Chapter 6—Punctuation) A comma after *children* would separate two independent clauses. Option (2) is wrong because *to a number of people* modifies *recom-*

mended. Option (3) is wrong because *your* shows possession. Option (4) is wrong because there is no reason to place a comma after *speech.*

42. **2 replace <u>have been</u> with <u>has been</u>** (See Chapter 3—Verb Usage) The verb must agree with the subject, *situation*, which is singular. Option (1) is wrong because the comma sets off an introductory word. Although the comma is not necessary for one word, it is not wrong either. Option (3) is wrong because there is no reason to place a comma after *billing.* Option (4) is wrong because *will have been* focuses on the future. The billing has been a problem in the past.

43. **3 bill, but I want** (See Chapter 9—Writing Clear Sentences) The original two sentences show a contrast. Only Option (3) shows the correct relationship between the two clauses.

44. **2 insert a comma after <u>July 9</u>** (See Chapter 6—Punctuation) A comma should be placed between the date and the year. Option (1) is wrong because *is* agrees with *invoice.* Option (3) is wrong because *on July 9 2011* modifies *payment.* Option (4) is wrong because *to show* is in the correct tense.

45. **5 no correction necessary** Option (1) is wrong because the comma after *addition* sets off introductory words. Option (2) is wrong because *me* is the object of the verb. Option (3) is incorrect because a comma should not be placed between the month and the year. Option (4) is wrong because *charged* is in the past tense, and the sentence focuses on earlier invoices, which would have been received in the past.

46. **3 records; as a result, I know** (See Chapter 9—Writing Clear Sentences) The new sentence would be *Fortunately, I have kept accurate records; as a result, I know exactly what my payment should be.* The original sentences show cause and effect. *As a result* also shows cause and effect in the new combined sentence. The other options do not show the correct relationship between the clauses.

47. **1 replace <u>contact</u> with <u>contacted</u>** (See Chapter 3—Verb Usage) *Over the past few weeks* signals the past tense, so the verb should be in the past tense. Option (2) is wrong because *over the past few weeks* does not modify *situation.* Option (3) is wrong because *weeks* should not be possessive. Option (4) is wrong because *your* is possessive.

48. **4 replace <u>which</u> with <u>that</u>** (See Chapter 9—Writing Clear Sentences) *That* signals a restrictive clause. *Which* signals unnecessary information and requires a comma to set the information apart. Option (1) is wrong because the comma after *information* separates an introductory phrase. Option (2) is wrong because *got* is in the past tense and *will get* is in the future tense. Option (3) is wrong because the comma should be after the entire introductory phrase, not *instead.*

49. **3 replace <u>I</u> with <u>me</u>** (See Chapter 5—Pronouns) *Between you and me* is a prepositional phrase, and *me* is the object of the preposition. Option (1) is incorrect because the sentence should not have the possessive form. Option (2) is incorrect because there is no reason to place a comma after *you.* Option (4) is wrong because the verb should be in the present tense.

50. **3 insert a comma after <u>succeed</u>** (See Chapter 6—Punctuation) *For your business to succeed* is an introductory phrase, which must be set apart with a comma. Option (1) is wrong because *your* is the possessive form. Option (2) is incorrect because *provide* agrees with *you.* Option (4) is wrong because *business* should not be capitalized.

Glossary

ABBREVIATION   a shortened form of a word or phrase EXAMPLES: Dr. and FBI (Federal Bureau of Investigation)

ACTION VERBS   show the subject either performing an action or receiving an action EXAMPLES: She <u>swam</u> to shore. He <u>was hit</u> by the ball.

ADJECTIVE   a word that tells the size, shape, number, owner, or appearance of a noun or pronoun EXAMPLES: large, round, jagged

ADVERB   a word that gives information about verbs, adjectives, or other adverbs   EXAMPLES: carefully, soon, quickly

ANTECEDENT   a particular word, phrase, or clause to which a pronoun refers   EXAMPLES: The <u>dancers</u> shined <u>their</u> shoes before the show.

APPOSITIVE   a word or phrase that renames or explains a noun or pronoun EXAMPLE: Megan, <u>a lawyer</u>, works long hours.

ARTICLE   a word that is used to signal a noun EXAMPLES: a, an, the

CAPITALIZATION   the use of capital letters EXAMPLES: <u>W</u>e donated to the <u>R</u>ed <u>C</u>ross.

CASE   a form of a pronoun that is based on its role in the sentence—pronouns with related jobs are part of the same case. EXAMPLES: <u>He</u> drove. I drove <u>him</u>. Dave drove <u>his</u> car.

CLAUSE   a group of words with a subject and a predicate—the group works together to send a message (see independent clause and dependent clause)

COMMA (,)   a punctuation mark that is used to separate ideas, parts of a sentence, or items in a series EXAMPLE: Kay bought flowers, fertilizer, and a watering can.

COMMAND   a sentence that tells someone to do something EXAMPLE: Drive slowly.

COMMON NOUN   a noun that names a general group of people, places, or things EXAMPLES: brother, street, house

COMPOUND PART   one part of a sentence (subject, verb, etc.) that has two or more components EXAMPLES: Joe and Brie walked for miles (compound subject). Sean relaxed and read until noon (compound verb).

CONJUNCTION   a word that connects words, phrases, or clauses (and, but, yet, so, for, nor, or) EXAMPLE: Ruth and Russ looked at houses, <u>but</u> they did not see one that they liked.

CONJUNCTIVE ADVERB   a word that connects two independent clauses and shows the relationship between them EXAMPLE: They wanted to swim; <u>however</u>, the water was too cold.

CONSONANT a letter of the alphabet that is not *a, e, i, o, u,* or sometimes *y*

CONTRACTION a word that combines two words and leaves out one or more letters EXAMPLES: can't (can not), it's (it is)

DANGLING MODIFIER a descriptive word or phrase that has nothing to describe—a sentence with a dangling modifier must be rewritten EXAMPLE: *Wrong* <u>Swimming in the cold water</u>, the towel looked cozy. *Right* When I was swimming in the cold water, the towel looked cozy.

DEPENDENT CLAUSE a group of words with a subject and predicate that does not express a complete thought EXAMPLE: <u>When Ty was a boy</u>, his mother taught him to play soccer.

DIRECT OBJECT a noun or pronoun that receives the action in a sentence (see object of the verb) EXAMPLE: Rhea asked <u>him</u> to the dance.

DIRECT QUOTATION someone's exact words EXAMPLE: Mark Twain said, <u>"Wrinkles should merely indicate where smiles have been."</u>

END MARK a punctuation mark that appears at the end of a sentence EXAMPLES: Where have you been<u>?</u> That was the best joke I have ever heard<u>.</u> Watch out<u>!</u>

EXCLAMATION POINT (!) an end mark that shows emotion EXAMPLE: Ouch<u>!</u>

FRAGMENT an incomplete sentence—a fragment may lack a subject or a verb, or it may be a dependent clause that needs other words to have meaning EXAMPLES: Whenever we need help. Before noon.

FUTURE PERFECT TENSE a verb form that shows an action will be completed before a specific time in the future EXAMPLE: Before the curtain falls, we <u>will have sung</u> for hours.

FUTURE TENSE a verb form that shows that an action will take place in the future EXAMPLE: Vera <u>will take</u> the test tomorrow.

GERUND a verb that ends in *-ing* and acts like a noun EXAMPLE: <u>Running</u> is a great form of exercise.

INDEFINITE PRONOUN a word that does not refer to a specific person, place or thing EXAMPLE: <u>Everybody</u> needs to write well.

INDEPENDENT CLAUSE a group of words that expresses a complete thought and has a subject and a verb EXAMPLES: Vahid needs a date for the dance. After Kate changed her clothes, <u>she went to the store</u>.

INDIRECT OBJECT shows to or for whom or what an action was performed (see object of the verb) EXAMPLE: We bought <u>her</u> a birthday gift.

INDIRECT QUOTATION tells what someone said, but does not use that person's exact words EXAMPLE: Salma said that she will run for reelection.

INFINITIVE a verb form that usually begins with *to* EXAMPLE: He wanted <u>to see</u> the results.

INTERJECTION a word that bursts with emotion EXAMPLES: Wow! Ouch!

INTERRUPTER a word or group of words that breaks the flow of a sentence EXAMPLE: The car, <u>however</u>, would not start.

IRREGULAR VERB   a verb that does not follow the usual pattern to form the past or past participle EXAMPLE: swim (present), swam (past), swum (past participle)

LINKING VERB   a verb that connects the subject to words that rename or describe the subject EXAMPLES: was, are, were, look, become, appear

MISPLACED MODIFIER   a descriptive word or phrase that blurs the meaning of a sentence because it is misplaced EXAMPLE: Nadine with the cloudy water swam in the pool.

MODIFIER   a word or group of words that describes another word or phrase EXAMPLE: The child <u>who lost his truck</u> cried <u>endlessly</u>.

NONRESTRICTIVE CLAUSE   a clause that is not critical to the meaning of the sentence EXAMPLE: Joe's truck, which has over 100,000 miles, is in good shape.

NOUN   a word that names a person, place, thing, or idea EXAMPLES: George Jones, Maine, bus, fear

OBJECTIVE CASE   a group of pronouns (me, you, him, her, it, us, them, whom, whomever)—a pronoun in the objective case can work as an object of a verb or an object of a preposition EXAMPLES: Kim tripped <u>her</u>. Phil gave <u>her</u> a ticket. Tim knew about <u>her</u>.

OBJECT OF THE PREPOSITION   a noun or pronoun that is connected to a preposition EXAMPLE: Nate ran into <u>the wall</u>.

OBJECT OF THE VERB   a noun or pronoun that receives the action in a sentence, either directly or indirectly EXAMPLES: Megan mailed <u>the letters</u>. Megan mailed <u>Sean</u> the letters.

PARTICIPLE   a form of a verb that works as an adjective or creates certain tenses with a helping verb EXAMPLES: The <u>running</u> water is cold. I have <u>seen</u> that movie.

PAST PARTICIPLE   a form of a verb that works as an adjective or forms the perfect tenses—most past participles end in *-ed*. EXAMPLE: The <u>exhausted</u> workers have <u>labored</u> for days.

PAST PERFECT TENSE   a verb form that shows that an action was finished before a specific time in the past EXAMPLE: Bill <u>had wanted</u> to be a doctor before he went to college.

PAST TENSE   a verb form that shows an action took place in the past EXAMPLES: Yu Lin <u>worked</u> last weekend. Fran <u>was</u> at the game.

PERIOD (.)   a punctuation mark that is used at the end of a statement—it is also used for abbreviations EXAMPLE: <u>Dr</u>. Hawk said that all of the guests arrived<u>.</u>

PHRASE   a group of words that work together to perform one job EXAMPLE: <u>Wearing a seat belt</u> can save your life.

PLURAL   more than one EXAMPLES: we, they, cats

POSSESSIVE   a noun or pronoun that shows ownership EXAMPLES: <u>Tony's</u> basketball, <u>her</u> room

POSSESSIVE CASE   a group of pronouns (my, your, his, her, its, our, their, whose)—pronouns in the possessive case can be placed before a noun to show ownership or before an "ing" verb that is used as a noun—possessive pronouns also can substitute for nouns EXAMPLES: That is <u>his</u> book. <u>His</u> driving is awful. The bike is <u>his</u>.

PREDICATE   part of a sentence that describes the subject or shows the subject in action EXAMPLES: Jihye <u>is a great lawyer</u>. He <u>ran across the field</u>.

PREDICATE ADJECTIVE   an adjective that follows a linking verb and describes the subject of the sentence (see subject complement) EXAMPLES: This movie is <u>boring</u>. The milk smelled <u>sour</u>.

PREDICATE NOUN   a noun that follows a linking verb and renames the subject of the sentence (see subject complement) EXAMPLE: Jeff is a <u>pilot</u>.

PREFIX   letters that are placed in front of a word to change its meaning EXAMPLE: Gail <u>pre</u>viewed the show.

PREPOSITION   a word that links words or groups of words EXAMPLES: after, between, under, near

PREPOSITIONAL PHRASE   a group of words that includes a preposition, its object, and any modifiers EXAMPLE: Dave ran <u>after the wild horse</u>.

PRESENT PARTICIPLE   a form of a verb that works as an adjective or forms the continuing tenses—most present participles end in -*ing* EXAMPLE: The <u>running</u> water is <u>filling</u> the pool.

PRESENT PERFECT TENSE   a verb form that shows an action that began in the past and continues to the present—it also shows actions that have just finished EXAMPLE: We <u>have been working</u> on this project for months.

PRESENT TENSE   a verb form that shows that an action is taking place now EXAMPLES: People <u>ignore</u> the stop sign on Main Street. Joel <u>is</u> a lawyer.

PRONOUN   a word that substitutes for a noun and works like a noun EXAMPLE: I, you, she, they, everybody

PROPER NOUN   a noun that names a specific person, place, or thing EXAMPLES: Jesse Owens, Florida, Pepsi

QUESTION MARK (?)   a punctuation mark that ends a question EXAMPLE: What movie will you see<u>?</u>

QUOTATION MARKS ("")   punctuation marks that are used in pairs to set apart someone's exact words, the title of something that is part of a larger work, or words that are being defined EXAMPLES: Kim yelled, "Put on your coat!" "Expensive" is anything that I cannot afford.

REFLEXIVE PRONOUN   a pronoun that ends in -*self* or -*selves*—these pronouns show that someone did something to himself EXAMPLE: Fay hit <u>herself</u> with the car door.

REGULAR VERB   a verb that follows a common pattern to change form—add -*d* or -*ed* to the present tense to form the past tense or the past participle EXAMPLE: talk (present tense), talked (past tense), talked (past participle)

RESTRICTIVE CLAUSE   a clause that helps identify a noun in the sentence—without the clause, the sentence would not have the same meaning EXAMPLE: The doctor <u>who put in my stitches</u> was very careful.

SEMICOLON (;) a punctuation mark that joins independent clauses and separates items in a series—use a semicolon for a series when the items already have commas EXAMPLE: We were frustrated; the mayor would not give us a straight answer.

SENTENCE a group of words with a subject and a predicate that expresses a complete thought EXAMPLE: Lee quit his job on Friday.

SINGULAR one EXAMPLES: I, you, horse

SPLIT INFINITIVE an infinitive that has been divided into two parts EXAMPLE: *Wrong* They wanted <u>to really work</u> hard. *Right* They really wanted <u>to work</u> hard.

SUBJECT someone or something that a sentence is about EXAMPLE: <u>He</u> trained for the Olympics.

SUBJECT-VERB AGREEMENT the subject and verb in a sentence send the same message—they refer to the same number and gender

SUBJECTIVE CASE a group of pronouns (I, you, he, she, we, they, who)—pronouns in the subjective case can work as a subject or a subject complement EXAMPLES: Vera and <u>I</u> went to the mall. The top lawyers are Jake and <u>she</u>.

SUFFIX letters that are placed at the end of a word to change its meaning EXAMPLE: She was knowledg<u>able</u>.

VERB a word that connects related words or shows action EXAMPLES: run, show, are, were

VERB TENSE the form of a verb that tells when an action took place (past, present, future) EXAMPLE: Yesterday, Shantae <u>planted</u> the garden.

VOWEL the letters *a, e, i, o, u,* and sometimes *y*—all other letters are called consonants.

Index

Getting ready to take the GED?
Here's all the help you'll need!

ASPIRE HIGHER WITH THE POWER... OF WORDS!

504 ABSOLUTELY ESSENTIAL WORDS, 5th Edition
ISBN 978-0-7641-2815-8
Builds practical vocabulary skills through funny stories and cartoons plus practice exercises.

WORDFEST!
ISBN 978-0-7641-7932-7
Book and CD help improve students' word-power and verbal reasoning by offering word lists, a battery of short tests, vocabulary-building help, and recommended reading advice.

1100 WORDS YOU NEED TO KNOW, 5th Edition
ISBN 978-0-7641-3864-5
This book is the way to master more than 1100 useful words and idioms taken from the mass media.

WORDPLAY: 550+ WORDS YOU NEED TO KNOW, 2nd Edition
CD Package ISBN 978-0-7641-7750-7
Based on **1100 Words You Need to Know**; included are five CDs presented in comedy-drama form to add in the dimension of dialogue and the spoken word.

A DICTIONARY OF AMERICAN IDIOMS, 4th Edition
ISBN 978-0-7641-1982-8
Over 8,000 idiomatic words, expressions, regionalisms, and informal English expressions are defined and cross-referenced for easy access.

HANDBOOK OF COMMONLY USED AMERICAN IDIOMS, 4th Edition
ISBN 978-0-7641-2776-2
With 1500 popular idioms, this book will benefit both English-speaking people and those learning English as a second language.

BARRON'S EDUCATIONAL SERIES, INC.
250 Wireless Boulevard
Hauppauge, New York 11788
Canada: Georgetown Book Warehouse
34 Armstrong Avenue
Georgetown, Ont. L7G 4R9

Please visit **www.barronseduc.com** to view current prices and to order books

(#14) R 12/08